CW00779001

The People's Force

THE
PEOPLE'S FORCE

A history of the Victoria Police

ROBERT HALDANE

MELBOURNE UNIVERSITY PRESS

First published 1986
Paperback reprint 1991
Printed in Australia by
Globe Press Pty Ltd, Brunswick, Victoria 3056, for
Melbourne University Press, Carlton, Victoria 3053
U.S.A and Canada: International Specialized Book Services, Inc.,
5602 N.E. Hassalo Street, Portland, Oregon 97213-3640

National Library of Australia Cataloguing-in-Publication entry

Haldane, Robert K. (Robert Keith), 1951-
    The people's force.
    Bibliography.
    Includes index.
    ISBN 0 522 84306 9.
    1. Victoria Police Force — History. 2. Police —
    Victoria — History. I. Title.
363.2'09945

To those Police who created history without knowing it

Foreword

Some said that a serving member of a police force should not write a history of it. He would not be sufficiently detached. He would not even be allowed to expose those vested interests of politicians and policemen that cause and cover up inefficiency and corruption. If he attempted first to write it as an academic thesis, said others, his topic was so wide that it would have to be shallow. What's more, muttered a third group of critics, the Victoria Police should not have chosen a historian who was 'a yobbo from Reservoir'. So attempted insult was added to rigid dogmatism.

Yet a thesis was written, and professors from three universities passed it for the degree of Doctor of Philosophy. Melbourne University Press saw a good book in it, and accepted the manuscript for publication under its distinguished imprint. Researchers will be glad about that, as they find in the book a context and leads for their own work. And ordinary people will enjoy the book too: it is easy to read and full of interest, but will make them pause to think straight about police and the community. The book does expose vested interests, failures and cover-ups. Over and over again the Victoria Police is shown as being moulded, for good *or for ill*, by its political masters, its own members, and the general public—or sections of it. Some men and women in the police will think at first that their official history is too critical, but they—and everyone else—should soon realize that it is notably even-handed and unflinchingly honest, a good 'police book'.

Inspector R. K. Haldane—the yobbo and the historian—is also a 'real' policeman in his colleagues' terms. No mere theorist, he *would* know how to lock up a drunk. He was serving as a constable at Preston when he began a part-time course at La Trobe University, and later served as a detective at Broadmeadows and Bairnsdale. Over the years, while still a working policeman, he took an honours B.A. in legal studies, and then his Ph.D. in history, boldly and calmly trying to describe—not excuse—the police force as part of the people, to understand from within and assess from without. His degree of success was impressive.

The achievement is not Inspector Haldane's alone. Mr S. I. Miller, as Chief Commissioner, wanted a proper history, not public relations fluff, and he stuck to this determination through all the years, doubts and objections that followed. What he got was an official history that is both appreciative and critical—the best of all public relations.

You hold in your hands a book that two policemen willed, though others called it impossible and undesirable. Read it and judge for yourself. My bet is that you will decide for Miller and Haldane.

JOHN BARRETT
Reader in History
La Trobe University

Contents

Illustrations

Acknowledgements

This book is based upon a doctoral thesis presented to La Trobe University in 1985. Many people have rendered assistance, support and encouragement in connection with both the original thesis and the book. Although it is not possible to thank individually everyone who helped, I am sincerely grateful to them all and some need to be especially acknowledged.

The Chief Commissioner of Police, S. I. Miller, conceived the idea of a 'warts and all' police history, afforded me the opportunity to write it and gave me his full support at all times. Importantly for me, in a manner uncharacteristic of many policemen of his generation, he allowed me absolute freedom to write it as I found it.

In furtherance of Mr Miller's original 'warts and all' idea three accomplished historians influenced the course of my work. Professor A. G. L. Shaw of Monash University greeted Mr Miller's concept enthusiastically and steered it into an academic environment. He envisaged a work with a scholarly basis. The late Professor Roger Joyce agreed with this and warmly welcomed me into the History Department of La Trobe University. Finally, Dr John Barrett supervised my thesis. A tough, copybook supervisor, he always understood the policeman in me, while doing his best to make me a scholar.

I received willing assistance from the staffs of various universities, libraries, archives, and historical societies. Their advice and interest often meant the difference between a day of enjoyable historical discovery or a wasted day of dusty despondency. I am particularly grateful to the staffs of the Public Record Office (Laverton), the Borchardt Library (La Trobe University), the Central Correspondence Bureau (Victoria Police), the Royal Historical Society of Victoria, and to Christine Paterson of the Police College Library.

I received unstinting support from my police colleagues and especially thank Bob Stewart and Alan Tickell for their understanding and encouragement. I also offer my special thanks to the many retired policemen who patiently answered my questions and volunteered their reminiscences.

A fruitful source of inspiration, ideas and criticism have been the members of the History Department of La Trobe University, whose encouragement has been unfailing. I particularly thank Doug Morrissey who shared the fruits of his own scholarship with me.

I am especially grateful to Celia Thomas and Linda Barraclough who helped me unravel masses of archives, and Pam Vella, Tracey Davies, Loree Rochester and Kathy Murphy, who typed my often messy manuscript. Dennis Ball and Nancy Renfree willingly proof-read for me. Anne Mitchell assisted me with graphs and the Police Statistician, Dr Andrew Macneil, was a source of relevant statistics and valued constructive criticism.

My wife, Frances, I sincerely thank for her help and forbearance. She stoically shared the emotional moments of my academic and writing experience; and, her home brimming with police books and memorabilia, she was my severest critic and staunchest ally.

ABBREVIATIONS

(University degrees, military decorations and imperial honours
not included)

ADB	*Australian Dictionary of Biography*
ASIO	Australian Security Intelligence Organization
CIB	Criminal Investigation Branch
CCB	Central Correspondence Bureau (Victoria Police)
CEB	Counter Espionage Bureau
MLA	Member of the Legislative Assembly
MLC	Member of the Legislative Council
PAF	Police Auxiliary Force
PRO	Public Record Office of Victoria
RIC	Royal Irish Constabulary
SCF	Special Constabulary Force
VPA	Victoria Police Archives
VPD	*Victorian Parliamentary Debates*
VPRS	Victorian Public Record Series
VSSF	Victorian State Service Federation
WPAF	Women's Police Auxiliary Force

CONVERSIONS

Length
1 inch = 25.4 mm
1 foot = 30.5 cm
1 yard = 0.914 m
1 chain = 20.1 m
1 mile = 1.61 km

Mass
1 pound = 454 g
1 stone = 6.36 kg
1 ton = 1.01 t

Area
1 acre = 0.405 ha
1 square mil
= 2.59 km^2

Money
12 pence (d.) = 1 shilling (s)
20 shillings
= 1 pound (£)

When decimal currency was adopted in 1966 two dollars
were equivalent to one pound.

Introduction

Bushrangers and other bandits have a prominent place in Victorian history and have been immortalized in ballads, poems, films and books. So much has been written about the most famous of Victorian bushrangers—Ned Kelly—that a recent book about him was introduced with the reassurance, 'Yes! There was, after all, room for yet another book on Ned Kelly'. One bibliography of Kellyana lists over 350 items, and this number increased greatly after the centenary of his death in 1980. Substantial publications have been produced by Dr John McQuilton and Professor John Molony, and a spate of lesser works have looked at such things as Ned Kelly's school days and his sympathizers.[1]

Criminals and their activities do have a place in history and literature, and it is perhaps desirable that people know something about the life and influence of men such as Ned Kelly, John Wren and Squizzy Taylor. However, in Australia the focus on bushrangers and others of their ilk has contributed to a dearth of research and literature about the police. A Mitchell Library catalogue lists fewer than two hundred items in a section on Australasian police forces.[2] No comprehensive history of any of them has ever been published. The few publications available are generally either poor in quality, antiquarian or works dealing with public relations issues. During the past twenty-five years only three books have been written about police history in Victoria. Not one of them was by a historian and none contains full notes or a bibliography. Academics, postgraduate students and historians have almost universally avoided the subject. The main exception in Victoria was A. J. O'Meara, whose unpublished M.A. thesis, The Establishment and Development of the Role of Women Police in Victoria, was an important work, deserving of wider public attention. The only other university works have been three honours theses about aspects of the police strike.[3]

The paucity of historical material about the police restricts the opportunity for comparative study and compels those interested in the subject to avoid it or to use secondary sources that are unsatisfactory. Duncan Chappell and Paul Wilson, in their noted sociological text about police in Australia, lamented the lack of published historical material and observed that there were 'fruitful fields of study still open for Ph.D. and other students who wish to examine aspects of the historical development of Australasian police forces'.[4]

The field is certainly ripe for research and offers historians an exciting range of source material, including substantial collections of archives, extensive newspaper reports, and the personal reminiscences of thousands of police—men and women, serving and retired—some of whom can go back to the years before World War I.

The richness of these sources and their neglect by historians are the two main reasons for this book, and for taking the broad-based approach that has been used. It is a history that has been crying out to be written, demanding to be explored and told not in some narrow conceptual framework, focusing on one aspect or era, but in full-blooded style, so that it opens up a myriad of times and events, stimulating interest, ideas, debate and more research.

This book does not set out to supply details of famous crimes and criminals, catalogues of police uniforms, badges and firearms, or such antiquarian facts as the dimensions and location of the Donkey Hill police station in 1857.

Although it is general and spans more than a century, it is not an aimless narrative but a book whose purpose is to show which factors have most influenced the development of the force. The book traces the evolution of Victorian policing from the small beginnings of three drunken, untrained men in 1836, through to 1984, when it was a complex department of almost 8500, using 348 police stations and 1740 vehicles to cover a whole state, and having an annual budget of more than $300 million.

In many respects it is a study of 'firsts'—turning points and people, the development and introduction of a police uniform, fingerprint analysis, wireless patrols, forensic science and whatever markedly improved the standard and changed the face of policing in Victoria. However, once in general use these things became part of a working plateau and there is no definitive discussion of them here; such a treatment would soon become merely platitudinous. Similarly, events like the Kelly outbreak, the invention of the motor car, the police strike and both world wars are discussed at some length as events that significantly altered the course of the force's history, and it is as agents of change that they are here treated; no full narrative account is offered. The revolutionary effect of the motor car on policing is a particularly engaging topic, although in this work it is but a small part of the whole. It is a subject worthy of fuller attention and is signposted in the hope that more can be made of it.

Above all, this history is about people, but not about famous detectives or bandits. Relatively few individuals are mentioned or discussed, and no apology is made for that. The focus is on people in action collectively, and individuals figure only where they have key roles—such as the Chief Commissioners—or where there is special reason to set them apart and name them, such as Lionel Potter, who introduced fingerprint analysis, and Frederick Downie, who started the wireless patrol. More than 25 000 men and women have passed through the force. To mention them all might make their descendants happy, but might not make for good history.

Important to the work is the influence of those people outside the force who shaped it, as well as those who joined it. Variables such as recruiting, training, work conditions, duties, roles, status and management styles have been studied, and from them it is evident that the community gets the police it deserves. The single most important factor in shaping the force has been the influence of the mixed and changing groups that are the people of Victoria—Peter Lalor and the Ballarat miners, political parties, parliamentarians, lawyers, unionists, suffragettes, protest marchers, anti-corruption campaigners, criminals and hundreds of other groups, invariably interwoven and overlapping. Their influence has taken different forms—positive and negative, destructive and instructive, deliberate and accidental, violent and peaceful—but it has been vital. Few important changes or developments have come from within the force, generated by policemen. Basic innovations, such as the force's structure and organization, the preparation of a police manual, the use of photographs for criminal identification, training classes, promotion examinations, the use of cars, and promotion other than by seniority, were all ideas initiated by people outside the force, and often they had to be pressed upon policemen who resisted their introduction. An important element in all of this has been the recurrent public inquiries into the police; they were important forums where grievances were ventilated, ideas were aired and people were given a genuine opportunity to say what was wrong with the force and how it could be fixed. People outside the force have selected its leaders, set its recruiting and training standards, and determined its work conditions and pattern of duties. The Chief Commissioners have been key links in directing the force, and although they themselves sometimes did much to 'make or break' it, their performance has been closely tied to that of governments and dictated to a large extent by events of the day.

Throughout its existence the force has been a conservative, sometimes reactionary, institution, lagging behind the general community in almost everything. This has not in all ways been bad. The police are potentially a very powerful section of the community but they should be its servants not its masters. The conservative nature of the force has decreased the chances of its breaking the mould formed by government control, legal process and dependence on wide public support. The force has for the most part been made up of working men, usually strong six-footers able to fight, read and write, but not given to innovative ideas. These men have been recruited, trained, paid and treated according to public perceptions and expectations. Had the community wanted it otherwise it could have recruited other kinds of people, paid them more, or in various ways built the force differently. It did not. It has always been the people's force—ordinary Victorians working for a wage, according to the dictates of this or that section of fellow Victorians, and the desires or defiance of others, but essentially doing what they were told to do within the limits of public acceptability.

It is a story worth telling.

1

Redcoats, Bluebottles and Alligators

During the years 1836 to 1852 there was no Victoria Police Force. It was a period of growth and unco-ordinated experimentation, during which the Port Phillip District, later the Colony of Victoria, was policed by an assortment of autonomous police forces, including the Native, Border, Mounted, and Melbourne and County of Bourke police. It was a confusing situation, compounded because the generic title 'police' was applied to all these forces, even though they bore little relationship to each other and exhibited differences in their composition, status, duties and uniforms. Drunks, emancipists and men from the working class predominated in the police ranks, their status and pay were low, and there was a high turnover of personnel. Few people aspired to police work and it was just a transient occupation through which many men passed on their way to other, more desirable or higher-paying employment. It also served as a stopover for miners travelling to or from the goldfields. In an effort to provide a more reliable police service, colonial officials offered career opportunities to young men and tried a range of other options including a cadet system, the use of military pensioners, and the importation of police from London. No single alternative provided the level of security that was wanted and, faced with the dramatic social and economic changes of the gold era, concerned citizens prompted a consolidation of the disparate police forces. Using Irish and English policing models, an endeavour was made to upgrade the general standard of policemen and the service they provided. The result was the statutory formation of the Victoria Police Force in 1853 as the sole police authority in the Colony.

The Rattlesnake Arrives

Early in the first permanent white settlement in the Port Phillip District the cry was raised for police and protection, the two not necessarily being synonymous in nineteenth-century Australia. Permanent European settlement was established by the Hentys, at Portland Bay in November 1834, without the assistance of police or soldiers, but those who followed were quick to seek the services of police. John Batman and his fellow expeditioners of the Port Phillip Association settled near the present site of Melbourne in 1835. Batman was a trespasser yet it was only a matter of months before he and his colleagues wrote to Sir George Arthur seeking government protection, which was eventually provided in the form of three policemen.[1]

This action was significant in that it set the pattern of police development in Port Phillip for many years to come, and also began the often unhappy relations between community and police in nineteenth-century Australia. The provision and level of police service was rarely planned but was normally an *ad hoc* response to requests such as Batman's. As 'protection' the settlers usually gained inefficient men for whom they showed little or no respect and considerable enmity. Nevertheless, requests for police flowed unabated and, taken with the animosity shown toward the police, there evolved the curious anomaly of the community increasing its police services all the while being unfavourably disposed toward those who performed the task.

Police forces in Australia in the 1830s were abysmal, a source of worry to communities wherever they served. The police in Van Diemen's Land were no exception and, having come from there, Batman would have been aware of their poor reputation in that colony. Still he and others after him chose to request police protection rather than undertake co-operative efforts at self-protection and regulation, such as the hue and cry. Settlers, squatters and others engaged in commercial pursuits did not have time to devote to co-operative efforts of self-policing, but were more than willing to pay others to do the work for them. It might well have been the better way, for they were securing for the colony what contemporary English experience was convincingly demonstrating: community security through an organized preventative police.[2]

Batman's initial request for protection was turned down and it was almost a year before colonial officials again considered the policing of the Port Phillip District. Meanwhile reports had come of white settlers shooting Aborigines at Westernport and Portland. These incidents, together with the circumstances of Batman's occupation, prompted Governor Bourke to send a Police Magistrate and two Sydney policemen to Port Phillip to investigate and report on the situation. The magistrate was George Stewart, of Campbelltown, and he was accompanied by Sergeant John Sheils and Constable Timothy Callaghan.

Stewart arrived in Port Phillip on 25 May 1836 and found a European population of 142 males and 35 females occupying an area of about one hundred square miles. During his visit the residents held a public meeting and prepared a petition to the Governor, one section of which requested the permanent appointment of a police magistrate in the settlement. In his report Stewart wrote of the possibility of forming a 'Police Establishment' in the settlement and confirmed the general need for government protection.[3] As a result, on 14 September 1836, Captain William Lonsdale, of the 4th (or King's Own) Regiment, was appointed Police

Magistrate for Port Phillip, and Robert Day, James Dwyer and Joseph William Hooson appointed policemen. Lonsdale was then aged thirty-six and had previous experience as an assistant police magistrate and justice of the peace at Port Macquarie. Like many civil servants who followed in his wake as head of the Port Phillip Police, Lonsdale did not have previous experience in administering a civil police force. He, and a number of his successors, had a military background. Indeed, Lonsdale was issued with two sets of instructions, civil and military. The one made him virtually commandant of the settlement, whereas the civil instructions vested him with the authority to oversee land surveys and customs collections, and to administer law and order—and all persons, including Aborigines, were reminded that they were subject to the laws of England.[4]

Lonsdale was vested with the dual roles of head of the police and the magistracy, and thereby a precedent was set that endured until well after the Colony of Victoria separated from New South Wales in 1851. The same person directed the police in enforcing the law and making arrests, and sat as judge in those same cases. Such a system was not in keeping with the principles of British justice, yet was not seriously questioned in Victoria until 1852. The primitive state of public administration in the early days of the Port Phillip settlement, tempered by the need for economy, no doubt contributed to this anomaly. That the situation was not earlier and vehemently decried probably suggests that Lonsdale handled his dual roles creditably.

Lonsdale commanded civil police and also soldiers, the latter serving as both a military force and a military aid to the civil power, and this did provoke controversy. There were thirty-three soldiers and their policing of a civil population, though no problem for Lonsdale, soon started a long-running debate in the colony about civil versus military law-enforcement. What fulfilled the immediate needs of the settlement in 1836 proved in the long term to be a poor precedent, greatly at variance with contemporary principles of civil policing in England.[5]

A most salient point emerged at once in making the Aborigines subject to the laws of England. The Aborigines had not asked for police or government protection, and their view of the police was undoubtedly very different from that held by the likes of Batman, so there has never been a single community perspective on what the police symbolize. When Day, Dwyer and Hooson commenced duty in the settlement they represented many things to many people, not the least of whom were these Aborigines suddenly embroiled in a world of police, laws and courts they did not understand or want. The instructions to place Aborigines under English law thus highlight a fundamental aspect of police–community relations. In an abstract sense the police serve one public with one set of laws, but in reality 'the community' is a mosaic of interest groups in which the values and wishes of dominant groups have generally prevailed.

Of the three original policemen, Day was appointed District Constable for Port Phillip, and the other two his assistants, with the rank of constable. They were typical of that period. It has been claimed that all three were former members of the Sydney Police who were dismissed for drunkenness, but there is nothing about that in the available records. According to the only detailed study of the three men, Day was previously licensee of the 'Highlander' public house in Sydney and before that he was colour sergeant in the 57th (West Middlesex) Regiment of Foot. Hooson was a native-born New South Welshman of otherwise unknown background, and Dwyer was an Irishman who had served in the Sydney Police for several years—at one time as Assistant Chief Constable—and he was given special permission to bring his wife, a ticket-of-leave holder, with him from Sydney to Port Phillip. There is no evidence that any of them were ever convicts.[6]

At any rate 'law and order' came to Port Phillip when HMS *Rattlesnake* anchored in Hobsons Bay on 29 September 1836. In support of the three policemen was a bonded convict, Edward Steel, who was retained as the settlement scourger for a shilling a day. The state of gaol and watch-house accommodation in the settlement made Steel a handy expedient. If

Tullamarine and Jin Jin escaped from Melbourne's
first gaol after setting fire to the thatched roof

offenders were not flogged or fined, the only lock-up was a somewhat insecure slab hut with a thatched roof. During the early months of the colony, law-breakers were sentenced to up to fifty lashes for offences such as 'interfering with a constable in his duty', and twenty-five lashes for being drunk or behaving riotously, and Steel was kept fairly busy. Other offenders were confined on a bread-and-water diet, imprisoned in irons, detained or fined.[7]

Along with explorers, pioneers and surveyors, police were to the fore on the frontiers of European settlement in south-eastern Australia. The arrival of Day and his men may not of itself have amounted to much, but they and Lonsdale were the first of the police who, for many years, pierced the vague frontiers, either before or in the immediate wake of explorers and surveyors. The police were not always popular or efficient, but their services were in demand and their 'front-line' role added to the complexity of their being at once both friend and foe to the public.

Lonsdale soon added to the Civil Establishment by employing William Buckley as special constable and district interpreter. Buckley, the 'wild white man', was an escaped convict who had lived with the Aborigines for thirty-two years. More than any other European in the settlement at that time he understood the native culture and language and thus found himself performing the dual roles of interpreter and policeman for £60 a year. The police establishment then included a runaway convict and bonded scourger. It was not really a matter of setting a thief to catch a thief, for the quintet had little to do with pursuing thieves and were primarily occupied with arresting drunks and petty offenders, only occasionally dealing with more serious cases or runaway convicts from Van Diemen's Land. Indeed, of the first two arrests recorded in the settlement, one was the arrest by District Constable Day of Scourger Edward Steel for 'irregularity'. Steel, when supposedly on duty, was found in the tent of a female resident. He could not give a lawful explanation for his presence and was fined the sum of ten days pay. In this way the agents of law and order in the settlement were hardly likely to win public respect but did add to their own returns of work.[8]

Although the police dealt primarily with minor matters, this was not due merely to their ineptness or to the state of crime in the settlement. The fledgeling criminal justice system administered by Lonsdale did not have the capacity or authority to hear serious criminal cases. Any such offences prosecuted in Port Phillip were committed for trial to the superior courts in Sydney. When this occurred, the defendant and all witnesses were compelled to travel 600 miles by sea to Sydney to attend court. The cost in both time and money was inordinate, resulting in an almost unanimous reluctance on the part of Port Phillip residents to report any crime that might result in a Sydney court case. Consequently, Day and his men were not put to much test as sleuths, and restricted their activities to matters over which Lonsdale had jurisdiction in Port Phillip.[9] During their early period of service the police were not sworn as constables, and this was a source of concern to Lonsdale. Finally, in December 1836, the authorities were furnished with the form of oath to be administered.

> You shall well and truly serve our Sovereign Lord the King in the office of constable for the Colony of New South Wales so long as you shall hold that office, without fear or favour and to the best of your skill and knowledge. So help you God.[10]

Much the same oath has been sworn by Victorian policemen in the years since. While Lonsdale was finalizing arrangements for an oath, his police began to depart the service. Dwyer was suspended on 31 December 1836 for being repeatedly drunk. He had been a constable in the settlement for barely three months, and in the intervening period was the 'trusty person' engaged by Lonsdale, and paid additional money, to complete the first official census of the Port Phillip population. Dwyer set a precedent being the first constable to perform extraneous non-police duties in the settlement, work that escalated rapidly after Dwyer's small venture, and which proved troublesome and controversial well into the twentieth century.

On 11 January 1837, Dwyer was followed from the service by District Constable Day, also suspended for being repeatedly drunk. Hooson lingered in the police service for some months longer than the other two but was finally dismissed in even greater disrepute. In November 1837 he was found guilty of accepting a bribe from a prisoner to release him from gaol before his sentence was up. So all three original Port Phillip constables were dismissed from the force in disgrace and not again employed in that capacity in the settlement.[11]

The three men, and the reasons for their dismissal, were typical of the police in Port Phillip and Victoria for many years in the nineteenth century. Often drunkards, often former convicts, they were untrained, issued with no set of instructions, unequipped with staves or arms, and not in uniform. They indicate the thin line that divided members of the public from sworn police in those early days. They were drawn directly from a segment of the society they were intended to serve, and remained laymen rather than policemen. A 1980 newspaper item proclaimed, 'State's first police were drunken, corrupt', and so they were. Nor is it surprising. Police services, both in Australia and England, were at an embryonic stage. Peel's New Police in London had been in existence barely seven years and it was not an occupation to which people of money or ambition aspired. In Port Phillip the constables were provided with military rations and paid labourers' wages of 2s 3d a day, when clerks got five shillings a day, tide-waiters 5s 4d a day and customs officers eleven shillings a day.

Police pay was not the sort of remuneration to attract men of the Port Phillip Association, who were driven by visions of acquiring huge tracts of land and the creation of villages.[12]

A Discordant Evolution

The experience with Day, Dwyer and Hooson did not weaken the Port Phillip settlers' desire for police protection or Lonsdale's efforts to provide it. Soon after Dwyer's dismissal, another former convict, Constable Mathew Tomkin of the Sydney Police, was appointed to the Port Phillip constabulary. Tomkin has a special place in Victorian police history in that he was the first serving policeman to be killed on duty. He was murdered by musket fire in 1837 at the hands of George Comerford, a bushranger. The inglorious beginnings of the force did not lessen the dangers police faced for a labourer's pay.

The district constable who replaced Day was Henry Batman, brother of John Batman, and he was quickly elevated to a new rank of chief constable and paid a salary of £100 a year, but neither the rank nor the comparatively high pay was sufficient to place Batman above common temptations. Within a year he was suspended from duty for accepting a bribe from one of his subordinates to alter a rostered turn of duty.[13]

The likes of Day and Batman proliferated in the settlement and there was a long series of appointments, dismissals and resignations within the ranks of the police. Community patience must have been sorely tried, but Lonsdale persisted in his efforts to bring a modicum of efficiency to the police corps. He was a soldier, not a policeman, and policing was novel even in England and Ireland, so it was a difficult task of trial and error. A lack of fixed ideas as to the nature of policing may, in part, have assisted Lonsdale as he proved himself willing to try new approaches. An example was the appointment of Buckley, and it was followed later by the recruitment of two men in Van Diemen's Land to be constables for Port Phillip: John Allsworth, a former convict holding a conditional pardon, and James Rogers. Stationed at the principal places of disembarkation, Williamstown and Point Henry, Rogers and Allsworth were both well acquainted with the convicts in Van Diemen's Land, and their principal duty was the detection of runaway convicts arriving in the mainland settlement.[14]

Reports on the efficacy of this scheme are scant, but Rogers and Allsworth were replaced after resigning within a year of taking office. Indeed, one of the hallmarks of Port Phillip's early police establishment was the extremely short tenure of office of the men engaged. Whether they left of their own accord—as did Buckley—or whether they were dismissed, few men persisted in employment as police. It was a poorly paid, low-status occupation that, except in rare cases such as those of Rogers and Allsworth, was not seen to require any special knowledge or skills. It did, however, demand honesty, sobriety, able-bodiedness and a willingness to confront danger. The early history of the Port Phillip District shows clearly that few suitable men were willing to become police; even fewer were able to persist in the role.

No exception to this general trend were those Aborigines and Europeans involved in the next scheme implemented by Lonsdale. In 1837 he sought and gained approval to establish a Native Police Corps in the Port Phillip District. The Corps was intended to be a mobile force of Aborigines, equipped as police and led by European officers, to minimize confrontations between Aboriginal residents and European settlers, yet provide a ready force for admonishment should depredations occur. In October 1837 Christian L. J. De Villiers was appointed Superintendent of the Native Police on a salary of £200 per annum, with rations, and Constable Edward Freestun was appointed as his assistant. The men engaged the services of a number of Aborigines and a camp was established at Narre Narre, Warren about three miles from Dandenong. The Aboriginal police were provided with European-style clothing and food, but were not paid as police or included with De Villiers and Freestun in the government returns prepared in Melbourne. A series of administrative troubles beset the unit from its inception and, after a number of leadership wrangles, the Corps was finally abandoned early in 1839. The Corps under De Villiers is not credited with being effective as an arm of the district constabulary, apart from some success in tracking offenders. Yet the actual formation of the Corps was innovative. It was an ambitious scheme, never before tried in Australia, established by Lonsdale only twelve months after his arrival in Port Phillip, and set against a background of abysmal failure in the use of European settlers as police. Lonsdale's concept was developed more successfully when the Native Police Corps was re-established in 1842 by C. J. La Trobe. This enlarged corps, under the command of H. E. P. Dana, achieved considerable success before disbanding in 1852.[15]

Notwithstanding his relative lack of success in securing a permanent force of efficient police, Lonsdale persisted and a growing number of settlers added their voices to the call for an extended police service. Few people wanted to be police but many people wanted police protection. Lonsdale's force was not an unchanging group of skilled and trained men but an ever-changing parade of unskilled workers drawn from the lower classes and, in a bid to make them better known and more accountable to the public, Lonsdale took steps to minimize their anonymity. Dressed in civilian garb and unarmed, they were of little utility as a preventive force. In 1838 he equipped the police with staves, for which they paid two shillings each. He also introduced the first Port Phillip police uniform, a 'plain blue jacket with round metal buttons, red waistcoat and blue or white trousers according to the season'. Lonsdale wanted his men in uniform to let the constables 'be at once known as such, but also to ensure

Members of the Native Police Corps

some respectability in their appearance'. Staves and red waistcoats began the evolution of a uniformed preventive police in Victoria—a visible 'law and order' presence. A year later Lonsdale prepared a set of rules for the guidance of constables. While only at an embryonic stage, the establishment of police as a distinct group and vocation within the community was now headed along a clearer path.[16]

Even so, this development was *ad hoc* and discordant. Lonsdale, hard pressed to expand his force in Melbourne, was required to satisfy settlers in the Western, Ovens River and Goulburn River districts who petitioned for police protection. So keen were the Western District settlers for protection that their petition contained a pledge to defray the entire cost of maintaining a constabulary force in the area.[17] Like the earlier petition from Port Phillip settlers, this request was eventually met and a police office established at Geelong. The initial police strength there comprised District Constable Patrick McKeever, who was paid three shillings a day, and Constables Owen Finnegan and Joshua Clark, who were each paid 2s 9d a day. Some time later McKeever was given the extraneous appointment of Inspector of Slaughterhouses, a move, like that of appointing

'Tulip' Wright in front of the new gaol and watch-house

Constable Dwyer as census collector, that further set the police along the path of extraneous duties. A government inquiry held during the year of McKeever's appointment as slaughterhouse inspector recommended that police not be given non-police duties, as these impaired their efficiency and were not cost-effective, but this early and far-sighted recommendation went unheeded.[18]

The Geelong police appointments expanded the constabulary of Port Phillip, not including the Native Police Corps, to twelve men serving a European population of 1265 persons. The Melbourne police by this time were commanded by Chief Constable William Wright, who was appointed to succeed Henry Batman on 5 August 1838. Wright was a most colourful character, known as 'Tulip'. A former convict, transported to Van Diemen's Land for poaching, he had served as district constable in Hobart and came highly recommended, being seen by some as a mark of improvement in the standard of the police. He did not wear a uniform but dressed in a manner that has probably not been repeated. A contemporary account describes the appearance of Wright on patrol, and shows why the police chief was known to all as 'Tulip':

He was very corpulent, and had a large fat face, keen eyes and aquiline nose. He wore a furry white belltopper hat . . . Round his neck he wore a large white 'belcher' of fine woollen material, ornamented with

14

'birds-eye' dottings. His vest, somewhat long, was of red plush; coat, olive-green velveteen, cut away slopingly from the hips, with a tail that reached to the back of his knees; knee breeches, snuff-coloured, with four or five pearl buttons to fasten them; hunting boots, of the best leather, with mahogany or buff- coloured tops. His watch was carried in a fob pocket in his nether garments waistband and the guard was a broad watered silk ribbon, with a key and two massive, old-fashioned, gold seals depending therefrom. In his hand he bore a very stout oaken walking-stick.[19]

Apart from his resplendent garb, Wright was noted as the first person to hold the office of chief or district constable in Port Phillip and retire unimpeached. He was one of the longest-serving Chief Constables in pre-separation Victoria and acquired a reputation as an active thief-taker. His eccentric ways did not detract from his efficiency and appear to have been a valuable asset in distracting public attention from the shortcomings of his men.[20] Shortly before Wright's arrival two Aboriginal prisoners had fired the old thatched gaol and escaped. After Wright's appointment a new gaol and watch-house were erected, 'in the angle of the market reserve formed by William Street and the lane'. Also during Wright's term, on 5 November 1838, the Act for Regulating the Police in Towns (the Sydney Police Act), was extended by proclamation from Sydney to Melbourne. This legislation had been requested by Lonsdale to check annoyances such as discharging firearms, using indecent language and working on Sundays. He felt that the rapidly increasing size of Melbourne rendered the police impotent to control such occurrences, unless supported by the Sydney Police Act. With the settlement barely two years old there thus began the perennial clamour by law enforcement officials for increased powers, a clamour that has yet to be sated and which now, as in Lonsdale's time, is indicative of society's state of flux and the ever-changing community values and expectations. To Lonsdale's credit, his suggestion for increased police powers was accompanied by the recommendation that a manual of instructions be prepared for their guidance. In support of this recommendation he attested to the increasing complexity of the duties performed by untrained police, made harder by the frequent changes in personnel.[21]

In 1838 a detachment of mounted police was posted to Port Phillip. Their headquarters were in Sydney, under the command of Major Nunn, and they were in fact soldiers drawn from infantry regiments serving in the colony. Commanded by army officers, they were under military law and drew military pay and rations. Initially, the detachment posted to Melbourne was comprised of a sergeant and six troopers, but within a year mounted police in the District of Port Phillip numbered twenty-nine men, forming the Mounted Police Fifth Division. These troopers were pioneers who established themselves in five parties on the line of route from Port Phillip to the Hume River. Intended to secure the road from Melbourne to Sydney, their camps were located at Geelong, Melbourne, Goulburn River, Broken River and the Hume River. At locations such as Broken River the mounted police were the first semblance of permanent European settlement, and they were followed by surveyors and settlers who transformed the police camp and the country around it into towns such as Benalla (Broken River).

The mounted police provide an excellent example of the nature of police development in those early years. In contrast to Lonsdale's men, they were well equipped, disciplined, trained and, more importantly, they had the increased status and mobility of being horsemen. In many respects they were akin to the noted Irish Constabulary. Although amenable to military command and law, the mounted police administered the civil law and served the benches of civil magistrates. During a twelve-month period the mounted police in the colony of New South Wales (including Port Phillip) apprehended 322 bushrangers and runaway convicts. They also worked as prisoner escorts, served summonses, executed warrants and undertook routine mounted patrols.[22] Nevertheless, the existence of such a force was another example of the disorganized and uncertain state of policing. The Melbourne, Geelong, Native and Mounted police units each operated independently, without a central command or source of funding. They were a curious mixture of Aborigines, free settlers, former convicts and soldiers, and were characteristic of the early decades when civil and military resources were utilized to provide law and order in the settlement. Given Peel's aversion to any military associations with his New Police in London, that such a motley assortment of military and civil types were labelled collectively as police in Port Phillip shows the fluid state of the colonies and the *ad hoc* growth of their police services.

The arrival of the mounted police in Port Phillip was not the final phase in efforts to police the settlement. A less successful and less popular phase began in 1839 when Port Phillip was declared the ninth district for the purpose of restraining the unauthorized occupation of Crown Lands and to help meet the cost of yet another autonomous police force: the Border Police. Intended 'to prevent the aggressions, which in the absence of legal control, have invariably been found to occur between the Aboriginal inhabitants and the Settlers', the Border Police was a corps of mounted police made up entirely of well-conducted prisoners of the Crown. These men worked primarily in remote and outlying areas under the control of the District Commissioner for Crown Lands. The Commissioner responsible for Port Phillip was H. F. Gisborne, and his men— like all Border Police—were unpaid, working only for rations and clothing. Such a system was not designed to attract the most capable and honest of men. Reports of Border Police committing outrages against

Aborigines were frequent, and squatter Edward Curr described one case where Border Police shot and killed a fleeing Aborigine, who was not an offender but a reluctant police guide. In another instance, three Border Police troopers were tried for murdering two Aborigines. Such behaviour was yet another setback for the police reputation in the Port Phillip District, and the Border Police also added to the confusing array of police authorities and uniforms, so they did little to enhance any image of 'the police' as a readily identifiable and solid group.[23]

Back in Melbourne the metropolitan constabulary continued its halting development. In 1841 'Tulip' Wright resigned from the police, and the office of chief constable was occupied in succession by Edward Falkiner, Charles Brodie and William Sugden.[24] Falkiner and Brodie were not noteworthy, but Sugden heralded a new era. He took the ambitious step of appointing the first detectives in Port Phillip. Commanding a force of four sergeants and forty constables, Sugden directed five of this number—a sergeant and four constables—to work as detectives. The English, both at home and abroad, had shown a marked aversion toward any aspect of policing that hinted of spying, continental methods or provocateurs. So it was not until 1842 that a few detectives were appointed in England, amid public fears of police espionage. By contrast, the disorganized state of the colonies appears to have facilitated Sugden's moves to form a detective force in 1844. Social conditions within the settlement were very different from those in England, and the dispersed population and number of former convicts may well have justified, in many eyes, this early venture. The first detective sergeant was James Ashley, and he defended the appointment of detectives by indicating that their work was demanding, dangerous and produced results. Ashley's ideal type for detectives were 'honest, sober men, well acquainted with the town and the people who frequent it'. Sugden praised his detectives by highlighting the fact that although they comprised only 10 per cent of his total force, they were far more productive as thief-takers than the balance of his men combined. Statistical records have not survived to prove this claim, but the institution created by Sugden has, lending some credence to claims of greater efficiency.[25]

For many years detectives worked without the benefit of scientific aids or training; indeed often without previous experience as preventive police. Their craft was centred around the mysterious and deceitful world of the informer. It was this aspect of detective work that troubled many people and, notwithstanding all the talk of early successes by the detectives, they proved in subsequent years to be a constant source of controversy and intrigue. At a time when it was deemed desirable to discourage former convicts from becoming policemen, it was police policy to enlist emancipists as detectives, 'because they were better acquainted with the style and character of the arrivals from Van Diemen's Land', a contradiction in attitudes that placed emancipists in the position of working among and fraternizing with informers and criminals on a daily basis. Events in later years cast serious doubts on the wisdom of this practice.[26]

Nevertheless, Chief Constable Sugden formed a detective force and so added a note of interest to an otherwise prosaic period in the development of police services in Port Phillip. He resigned from the police in 1848 to become a publican, and was succeeded by Joseph Bloomfield, under whose command the constabulary remained static. Later convicted of assaulting a constable, Bloomfield is best remembered as landlord of the Merrijig Hotel.

For a long-suffering public and an ailing constabulary the year 1850 was a turning point. Bloomfield was reduced in status to assist E. P. S. Sturt, who was appointed to the newly created office of Superintendent of the Melbourne and County of Bourke police. Sturt, a graduate of the Sandhurst Military College, was then a police magistrate, who had worked as a grazier and commissioner of crown lands since migrating to New South Wales in 1837, and his new position was in fact the dual one of police administrator and police magistrate. Like Lonsdale, fourteen years earlier, Sturt was placed in the position of having command of the police and also presiding over the summary prosecutions that they placed before the courts. It was a far cry from the separation of judicial and police powers that emerged in later years.

Sturt only took command of the beleaguered Melbourne and Bourke Police (one force), and did not have control over the other autonomous police agencies in the colony. Shortly after assuming office, he wrote to La Trobe bemoaning the inefficient state of the constabulary as he found it. The scattered stations, a paucity of men and the lack of any mounted troopers meant that Sturt's police were travelling up to 150 miles on foot in pursuit of offenders. Those problems were mild, however, compared with events looming on the horizon.[27] The population in pre-gold rush Victoria was 77 345 and these were largely emancipists and free settlers pursuing a fairly orderly and slow expansion of the colony. It was not a lawless society and indeed, given the run-down state of the police, this was at once both fortuitous and fortunate. This all changed drastically in 1851. On 1 July Victoria separated from New South Wales and shortly after a declaration was made announcing the first official discovery of gold in Victoria. The rush to be rich was on and the police of the colony were inextricably caught up in it. One policeman later wrote, 'Crimes of violence abounded everywhere, from the Murray to the sea; the very scum of all these southern lands poured into Victoria'. It was an exaggeration but one that summarized the mood of many of his contemporaries.[28]

The Baton versus the Bayonet

> . . . the weapon for a gold-country is the baton not the bayonet. We shall try to have police protection; we shall NOT have martial law.

Such were the sentiments in the reeling young colony of Victoria trying to maintain equilibrium against the impact of the gold rushes. In the twelve months immediately following the official discovery of gold, the population of Victoria doubled to a figure above 160 000. The percentage of women in the colony was reduced as men flocked in for gold. Thousands of gold-seekers arrived from Victoria's traditional source of felonry, Van Diemen's Land. Although many of the new arrivals were steady, decent and hard-working men, many others were foot-loose adventurers. Egalitarianism prospered in the frontier conditions of the colony and generated ribaldry, revelry and chaos of a kind never before experienced by the colonial constabulary.

Sturt and his men, ill-equipped to cope with benign 1850, were virtually besieged in 1852. More correctly, Sturt was besieged, his men were off to the diggings! On one day in January 1852 a total of fifty-one men resigned from the City and District Police, an exodus that caused Sturt to lament that 'the rage for the Gold Fields continues unabated'. Of an authorized force of 139, Sturt managed to retain only seventy-eight, and of these he observed that 'only the clerks in the office appear in no way disaffected'.[29]

Even so, Sturt was hard-pressed to clothe and equip his men. He complained that 'There are no police stables, no barracks, no swords, no carbines, and though nearly three months since I ordered saddles, etc., only four are now complete, and those not of the best kind'. The uniform of the Melbourne police at this time was described as:

> a long-tailed blue-cloth coat, buttoned from the throat down to the waist with metal buttons. Blue cloth trousers were worn, and the bottoms of these were tucked into boots which were known as 'half-wellingtons'. The hat or helmet was of the usual glazed leather . . . For night duty, cloth caps with straight peaks of leather were worn. Overcoats of the 'long tom', or coachman, pattern were worn at night. With these overcoats a broad black leather belt was worn and upon that belt the constable suspended his baton, lamp and rattle.

In design the police uniform had changed considerably since first introduced by Lonsdale. The militaristic whites and reds had given way to blue as the police colour, and the stave had been replaced by the baton and the wooden rattle, which was used to sound alarms and summon assistance. Although the ideal Melbourne policeman was a well-accoutred rattler, the reality was that things had not changed much since Lonsdale's time. It was common for ill-equipped police to patrol in plain clothes, with a baton slung from the belt and a band upon the hat bearing the words 'Melbourne Police'.[30]

The police commanded by Sturt were still from the lower classes and their status was little elevated above what it was in convict days. Serle has suggested that the police ranks in 1852 contained 'perhaps a majority' of ex-convicts, but such a proposition is purely speculative as quantifiable evidence does not exist to support or rebut it. In 1852 constables were paid 5s 9d a day, which was less than labourers on the roads earned. Indeed, in assessing the relative worth of constables, Sturt in his correspondence to the Colonial Secretary equated them with day labourers. No minimum educational or physical standards governed entry into the constabulary, no special training was given upon enlistment, and no comprehensive body of regulations or code of ethics existed to govern police conduct. The community was remarkably tolerant of errant police behaviour, perhaps not so much because it condoned misconduct but because people willing to work as police were scarce. In any event, the day labourers in blue serge were drawn directly from the community they were employed to serve.[31]

Police drunkenness was a perennial problem, partly because habitual drunkards within the force were not dismissed but briefly gaoled. Drunken police were charged publicly in open court and their prior convictions were read to the court before sentence. Initially, convicted police went into the general prison, but later a special lock-up was maintained at the rear of the police station for police prisoners. Upon serving their sentences and drying out, the besotted constables returned to normal police duties. It was a sorry spectacle but one not restricted to Victoria. Drunkenness among nineteenth-century police was commonplace in the Australian colonies and overseas. Although apparently willing to retain drunkards in the police force, community tolerance did not extend to more serious aberrations such as robbery and perjury, which were not altogether uncommon. In one case, two newly recruited constables, on duty, loitered outside a theatre and robbed a pedestrian of his money. In their defence they protested that since joining the police they had not been paid.

If the community was loath to pay its police for some duties, there were other activities that were encouraged and which paid well. One was dog killing. To the ever-expanding range of extraneous responsibilities vested in the police was added the task of killing unwanted dogs about the towns. To encourage constables in the pursuit of this duty, city aldermen offered rewards of up to £3 3s to the constable 'who shall during the next three months, kill the greatest number of unregistered dogs, and £2 2s to the destroyer of the second greatest number'. With this bounty scheme in operation, a zealous dog-killing constable could earn—in three months—more than one week's full wages by slaughtering the dogs of the town. One can only speculate as to how the criminals fared while police were occupied in the work of hunting unregistered dogs.[32]

Incentive payments were a dangerous practice. The underlying philosophy was simple: pay incentives and thereby ensure a greater level of zeal in enforcing the law. It led, however, to police malfeasance of all kinds, and it provides an example of how society can shape the behaviour of its paid police. Sturt's despatches during the gold rush provide clear evidence that insufficient suitable men from the community were willing to join and remain with the constabulary. He also attests to the low status and low pay of the police, and evidence exists of the drunken state of many of the constables and the fact that often they were destitute because of arrears in pay. It is an unsavoury picture, only made worse by the fact that those same police were paid a half-share of the fines for many of the cases they prosecuted, such as obscene language, selling liquor without a licence (sly-grogging), and mining without a licence.[33] At a time when police were paid only 6s 9d a day, they could earn four times that amount by securing the conviction of one person for using obscene language. The incentive system really encouraged the suppression of 'victimless crimes' and revenue offences, for which the penalties tended to be fines, rather than more serious offences against persons and property, which were usually punished by much more than a fine. Consequently, there were rarely complainants, civilian witnesses or physical evidence to corroborate police who laid such charges, the evidence being merely the word of a constable who stood to make money if he secured a conviction. In one published case, two constables were sentenced to a term of imprisonment for conspiring together to secure the conviction of a woman on a charge of obscene language, in order to obtain a share of the fine. Sturt spoke ill of the fine-sharing scheme, the *Argus* criticized it regularly, and La Trobe in correspondence with Sir John Pakington hinted at the monstrous system they had created, observing in relation to illicit liquor sales:

> I regret to say that the very inducement held out to the Constable by our recent Act of Council to exert himself in the suppression of this particular offence, necessary and judicious as it might appear to be, would seem to carry with it the disadvantage of inducing the Police to neglect, in the diligent prosecution of this branch of their duty, other functions equally important but less remunerative.

One contemporary but uncorroborated account suggests that some police on the goldfields, pursuing offences for which they received a half-share of the fines, could amass £1000 in just six months. Although that figure would seem exaggerated, there is little doubt that some police did profiteer from the incentive system. Sturt experienced difficulty getting police to work in localities or at duties where the opportunity for shares of fines was limited, and the Mounted Police Corps had trouble retaining men on gold escort duty because they mostly wanted to patrol the gold-fields, where they could share in the proceeds from 'seizures of sly grog shops, and the fines for working [mining] without a license'. Mounted troopers on the goldfields were known to earn up to £30 a week from their share of fines, at a time when gold itself was bringing only £3 5s an ounce. In addition to the potential for perjury and corruption that the incentive system spawned, it caused jealousy among police and further unsettled the harried constabulary.[34]

Another scheme used to disburse incentive payments was the Police Reward Fund, established in 1849 by statute as a central account to which a half-share of certain fines could be paid for later distribution to police. Under this scheme there was no direct payment of fines to individual policemen, but lump sums of money were paid from the fund at the discretion of senior officers. During 1851 thirty policemen received payments ranging from £2 to £10 each, but the total amount disbursed for the second half-year was only £125 and fell well below the incentives offering under the other fine-sharing scheme. Because the reward fund was not lucrative it did not receive full police support, but it did serve as a forerunner to police superannuation and workers compensation schemes, in that money was paid to constables not only as an incentive but also as compensation for injuries received on duty and excessive hours worked.

Much has been written about the conflicts between police and miners. It is unfortunate that little has been said about conditions of police service and the incentive system that prevailed at the time. Police drawn from the labouring classes, untrained, poorly paid and including many former convicts and drunks, were presented by the authorities with an opportunity to zealously and substantially increase their incomes by collecting half-shares of fines. No better example of a community getting the police it deserves could be found than the incentive system that operated in nineteenth-century Victoria.[35]

Notwithstanding speculation that half-shares of fines could earn policemen £1000 in six months, colonial officials were hard-pressed to recruit and retain men in the constabulary. Sturt complained of the young men who joined his force: 'They enter the force as a temporary convenience, the inducements of the Goldfields unsettle their minds, they take no interest in learning their duties, are impatient of any control, having the diggings to fall back on'. The vast majority of able-bodied men preferred to try their luck as diggers rather than as bluebottles, and one of the major drawbacks for the police was that 'really active, energetic characters' shunned the police service, often leaving only the most indolent and dissolute to join it. Such reluctance served to further depress the standard of the depleted ranks and fuelled the perennial debate over civil versus military law enforcement. The *Argus* was a vociferous opponent of the use of soldiers to preserve law and order. However, it and others were forced to succumb in the face of increasing lawlessness and a shortage of police. From all quarters of the colony could be heard cries for assistance from a public beset by crime, cries accompanied by talk of Lynch Law, or the formation of a National Guard, a Yeomanry corps, a Special Constabulary, a Committee of Safety or other vigilante groups like the Mutual Protection Association.[36] In a desperate bid to bolster the ailing constabulary and as a means of forestalling widespread vigilante action, colonial officials in Melbourne commissioned Samuel Barrow to recruit military pensioners from Van Diemen's Land. On 19 February

Pensioners on guard at Forest Creek

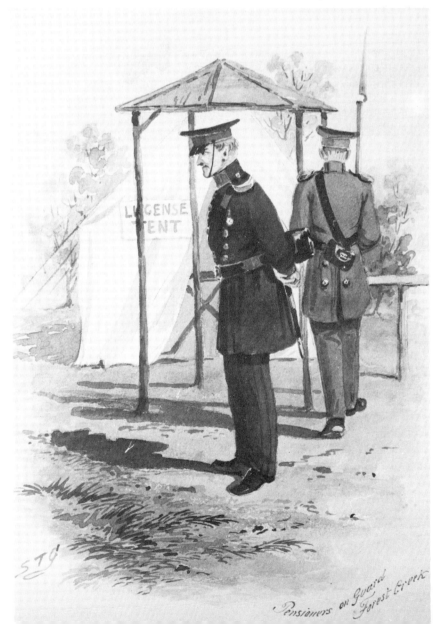

1852 there arrived in Melbourne 130 pensioners 'to maintain good order and enforce respect to the laws'. These men were mostly aged or invalids and were unsuited to almost any kind of responsible work. Attired in a gaudy, red-striped, military-style uniform, they added further to the inefficiency and denigration of the police force, and to its reputation for insobriety. An *Argus* editorial described them as being 'half-horse half-alligator', while Sturt more precisely called them 'the most drunken set of men I have ever met with; and totally unfit to be put to any useful purposes of Police'. After a year the military pensioners were returned to Van Diemen's Land.[37]

Colonial officials had also requested that a substantial military force and one or two ships of war be sent to Victoria, and in 1852 there arrived the first large military force in the colony, 560 soldiers under the command of Lieutenant-Colonel T. J. Valiant. Reviled throughout the gold districts as 'lobsters' and 'redcoats', the soldiers were paid only one shilling a day and were generally regarded as being less efficient and more repressive than the regular constabulary. Few men could countenance odious laws administered at the point of a bayonet or the barrel of a gun. The *Argus* propounded its theme that 'we want thief-catchers not soldiers', and made some prophetic predictions about the practice of using soldiers to police civilians. The large body of soldiers served as a bulwark not only against rebellion but also reform. It undoubtedly hindered the development of a proper police force. For some colonial officials the military was a ready, armed and inexpensive alternative to civil police.[38]

Sturt was not content to see the civil police role usurped by military authorities, and other community groups, including the public press and the Committee of Victorian Colonists, agreed with him. Certain thieves gave a sudden impetus to efforts to improve the thief-catching abilities of the police. During the night of 1 April 1852 a gang of more than twenty armed men pirated the barque *Nelson*, which was anchored in Hobsons Bay, and stole 8183 ounces of gold stored in the lazarette. It was the most daring robbery committed in the colony up to that point, and it yielded the robbers tens of thousands of pounds when £6 was the price of a prestigious suburban building allotment. The scale of this crime alarmed an already reeling community and realized everyone's worst fears as to the extent of crime. Reports of the robbery filled the Melbourne press, and public apprehension increased during the many weeks before arrests were made. The police acquitted themselves well in apprehending twelve of the robbers and recovering an amount of gold, but this was not enough. The magnitude and daring of such piracy within view of Melbourne had disturbed the public imagination. Support was raised for the Australasian League—a group pledged to work for the abolition of transportation to Van Diemen's Land—and even the most sceptical of critics felt the need for an efficient, preventive civil police.[39]

Aided by the *Nelson* affair, Sturt could be more venturesome, and came up with the novel scheme of recruiting educated young men—not boys—from the upper classes into the constabulary as cadets. His idea was not totally dissimilar to the Irish cadet system, but it was a radical departure from the previous recruiting policies of colonial officials and stands as a landmark in the development of policing as a vocation in Australia. In September 1852 Sturt's first batch of twelve cadets were selected on the basis of their general standing and education, and were intended to provide the nucleus of a corps from which future officers could be selected. According to John Sadleir, who was one of them, the cadets were made up of men from a wide range of callings, including military officers, lawyers, bankers and students. They were equipped as mounted police and drilled at the police camp on the corner of Punt Road and Wellington Parade. The cadets initially performed mounted duty in teams of seven and patrolled throughout the city and suburbs between seven o'clock in the evening and midnight. As their numbers increased they were gradually spread throughout the colony and worked as both foot and mounted police. The scheme operated for only three years, 1852–1854, by which time 244 young men had joined. Many of them served only brief periods, but 46 were ultimately promoted to officers. The cadet corps was, in fact, quite a popular choice of vocation, and it was this that eventually led to its disbandment. Intended to be a small, select group, the corps was too popular; so many young men were allowed to join that promotion opportunities were curtailed, and many of them became disillusioned. By this time, however, in many respects the scheme had served its purpose and W. H. F. Mitchell wrote:

> the Cadet Corps was found beneficial as a Constabulary Force from the higher tone of the young men, and their being above the temptation to accept bribes, to commit breaches of duty. They have been highly advantageous both for duty and as setting an example of discipline and good order to the ordinary police.

They numbered in their ranks such later luminaries as Hussey Malone Chomley and Edmund Walcott Fosbery. Chomley served with the Victoria Police for fifty years, from 1852 to 1902, and rose through every rank to become Chief Commissioner, the first career policeman to be appointed to that position. Edmund Fosbery became Inspector General of Police in New South Wales, and headed that force longer than any other person in its history. As a tribute to Sturt's recruiting, the two largest police forces in Australasia entered the twentieth century under the command of men who began their careers over four decades earlier as Victorian police cadets.

Nevertheless, Sturt's cadet scheme had inherent limitations. The promotion wrangles and accompanying disillusionment marred the scheme and its immediate impact was limited. It was, however, an important phase in the evolution of police services and partly answered the plea of an *Argus* editorial:

> We want thief-catchers, not soldiers ... Brains, brains, brains, we repeat, are what we want, and not mere firearms and muscle.[40]

A Troubled Community

Leading members of the Victorian community, alarmed at the rise in crime and the sorry state of the police, moved to recruit trained police from the United Kingdom and to establish a government inquiry to suggest ways of improving the local police. Both moves now stand as milestones in the development of police services in Victoria.

The importation of trained police from the United Kingdom was a popular idea during the gold rushes, and was seen as a means of bolstering the depleted local ranks with professional policemen from a respected overseas constabulary. Much misinformation has gathered about the circumstances surrounding the proposal, and the credit for it is often attributed to the wrong quarter. Those most often credited with suggesting the scheme are E. P. S. Sturt, W. H. F. Mitchell and the Snodgrass Committee. Although all three wholeheartedly supported the concept, none can lay claim to its conception. A committee of colonists from Victoria, acting independently, initiated the idea early in 1852. Four men, led by Captain Stanley Carr, approached the Secretary of State for the Colonies, Sir John Pakington, in London during May 1852, and told him about the condition of the colony and their desire for a better police force. Shortly afterwards, the committee petitioned Pakington in writing to send fifty men from the Irish Constabulary to serve in Melbourne, for three years, at the rate of ten shillings a day. Considerable correspondence passed between the colonists and Whitehall before it was agreed that fifty volunteers from the London Metropolitan Police, instead, would be sent to Melbourne. They were a very different type of policeman from those in the Irish Constabulary. The latter, formed by Robert Peel in 1814, was a paramilitary force of mounted and foot police, dressed in rifle-green uniforms, armed with flint-lock carbines and stationed in barracks commanded by inspector generals. It was a repressive force, used to suppress internal disorders and dissent, the very antithesis of his later creation, the New Police of Metropolitan London, who were unarmed and at great pains to shun militarism. The contrast between the two forces was striking and suggests that someone at Whitehall envisaged the problems that might have ensued from unleashing a body of armed and mounted Irish police among the goldfields population of Victoria, which included a large number of Irish expatriates. The official reason given for not providing Irish police was that no such men could be spared and no evidence exists to cast doubt on this explanation. However, large numbers of former Irish policemen later came to Victoria as migrants and joined the force, giving it a strong Irish identity.

The 'London Fifty', as the English foot police came to be known, were a valuable acquisition and over time significantly altered the style of policing in Victoria. The London men—who actually numbered fifty-four—consisted of three sergeants and fifty constables, led by Inspector Samuel Freeman, a 46-year-old career policeman who had served with the Metropolitan Police for fourteen years. John Sadleir wrote of Freeman's contribution to policing in Australasia:

> Freeman . . . furnished an object lesson in police methods, and in high ideals of duty unthought of before . . . The reputation of the service soon spread far and wide, so that the authorities in New South Wales, New Zealand and Queensland were glad to get from Victoria officers and men qualified for the work of building up the police service in the several States.[41]

Although arrangements to recruit police in the United Kingdom were begun in May 1852, officials in Victoria were not advised of these until after 30 October 1852. The London Fifty did not arrive in Victoria until May 1853.

During the intervening period other colonists, particularly members of the Legislative Council, were taking steps to improve the efficiency of the police. On 7 July 1852 Peter Snodgrass, MLC, successfully moved a motion 'That a Select Committee of this House be formed, to consist of six Members together with the proposer, to take into consideration and report' upon the state of the police in Victoria. A Committee of seven, chaired by Snodgrass and including the Attorney-General, commenced sitting on 9 July 1852. It was the first inquiry touching upon police in the colony since the 1839 New South Wales Report on Police and Gaols, and it produced substantial changes to police organization. It also created a precedent for the regular public inquiries, judicial and otherwise, that have served ever since as a valuable medium for the community to participate in shaping and directing the development of the force—even though at times they have been painfully searching and vitriolic.

The Snodgrass Committee received evidence in nineteen sittings from sixteen witnesses including policemen, aldermen, court officials and settlers. The main witness was E. P. S. Sturt, whose basic suggestions and sentiments were supported by the others. The *Argus* carried daily reports of serious violent crime and police ineptitude. Read in isolation, these accounts appear sensational and exaggerated but they accorded with those given by witnesses to the Snodgrass Committee. At the time of the hearings no fewer than seven autonomous bodies of police had jurisdiction in Victoria, including the City Police (headed by Sturt), Geelong

Police, Gold Fields Police, Water Police, Rural Bench Constabulary, Mounted Police and Gold Escort. These forces were funded and operated separately, without co-operation or even regular communication with each other. Such a system was not unusual. It also operated in New South Wales, Western Australia, Queensland and England, so parochialism and duplication of police functions was the rule of the day. This splintered organization might have endured in Victoria, as it did in many other localities, but for the gold rushes. Victoria was a distant colony, many times the size of England, with a rapidly increasing population that included a disproportionate number of males and a significant proportion of emancipists, who were scattered throughout the colony and who shifted population centres as new fields were opened. Against the background provided by these social conditions the Snodgrass Committee heard evidence about the high incidence of crime and the insufficiency and inefficiency of police. Evidence was also given about police filling the dual roles of 'thief-catcher and judge', the evils of the Police Reward Fund and the incentive system of sharing fines, the need for a police superannuation scheme, and the desirability of obtaining police from the United Kingdom.[42]

One of the most important themes to wend its way through the Committee hearings related to police conditions of service—until then they had never been an issue. Wage rates had dominated recruiting efforts, but little regard had been given to work and living conditions, uniform standards, occupational status or benefits such as superannuation. With the Snodgrass hearings much of this changed, when the committee heard of the unattractive and often deplorable conditions under which police lived and worked. Many people outside the police service also worked under sub-standard conditions, but the Snodgrass Committee had the task of devising new initiatives to induce suitable men to join and remain with the constabulary, and there was a general consensus that the immediate need was for a locally recruited and properly constituted civil police—'redcoats', 'alligators' and United Kingdom imports were interim measures, not long-term panaceas. Consequently, ideas emerged about such things as proper police barracks, a superannuation fund, the issue of adequate rations and clothing (including the suggestion of 'a showy uniform'), and improved promotional opportunities. The majority of police forces in England and Wales did not have pension schemes and it was not until 1875 that a select committee was established in England to investigate police superannuation, so on issues like that the Snodgrass Committee was acting in advance of its time; but on others it lagged behind. Recruiting and training standards were not investigated but, given the reluctance of men to join the police, it is not surprising that the committee avoided those subjects. Its task was to bolster and maintain the police numbers, which were objectives not readily met if men were to be lost because they failed to meet arbitrary standards.[43]

The Snodgrass Committee Report was tabled in September 1852 and the opening paragraphs criticized the state of policing in Victoria, concluding with the observation that the existing forces were 'insufficient in numerical strength, deficient in organization and arrangement—and utterly inadequate to meet the present requirements of the country'. The committee recommended the formation of a single force of no fewer than 800 men, the organization, superintendence and control of which was to be entrusted to one man to be called the Inspector General of Police. The substance of this recommendation was implemented and the amalgamation of small, autonomous forces into a single unit was a first for Australia, and came before many similar moves in Europe and North America. Victoria preceded its parent colony, New South Wales, by a decade in the consolidation of its police groups. The status of the Victoria Police as a vanguard force in the immediate post-Separation era highlights the role of the gold rushes in forcing social change through this period. The low status of the police, and events such as Eureka, have served to cloud achievements in police reform at that time. Development and reforms were at an early stage but, when compared with events in neighbouring colonies and overseas, they placed the Victorian constabulary to the fore as a progressive force. Critics of the police can indicate many facts to the contrary, and in some respects they are right. Viewed in isolation the Victoria Police Force of the 1850s does not appear outstanding; instances of corruption, brutality, inefficiency and maladministration abound. Yet, when seen comparatively and in its own times, it appears as a leading force, guided toward increasing efficiency by the likes of Carr, Sturt, Freeman and Snodgrass.

In addition to the recommendation that the colony's police be organized as a unified force, the Snodgrass Committee suggested changes to wages, rank structures, uniforms and rations, and recommended that policemen be provided with comfortable, free barrack accommodation and a superannuation scheme as 'an inducement not merely to enter, but to continue in the service'. The committee hoped its work would 'lead to the speedy formation of a force, sufficient in number and effective in organization and discipline, to carry the laws into execution and afford protection and security to Life and Property', a somewhat optimistic hope, but not an impossibility.[44]

Within a matter of weeks a Police Regulation Bill was the subject of legislative debate and public speculation. Modelled on the London Metropolitan Police Act, it avoided the quasi-military Irish model and provided for a civil force, using civil ranks and terminology. This contrasted with some other forces, notably the Royal Canadian Mounted Police, which was later founded upon the Irish model and adopted many military procedures and titles. In practice, however, there was some confusion of these models in Victoria, and considerable paramilitary behaviour was evident at times, particularly when the police were used as agents of social repression (or the rule of law?) during goldfields uprisings and outbreaks of bushranging. This was partly because the Irish model served more readily when repression was thought to be necessary, and also because its mounted aspect was better adapted to rural policing away from the towns. The essence of the London model was foot patrols in an urban environment and although this worked well in Melbourne and the larger towns, it did not work in the wide and sparsely settled Victorian countryside.[45]

The Police Regulation Act was assented to on 8 January 1853. It repealed earlier New South Wales legislation and provided for a Chief Commissioner of Police to take charge of all police in Victoria and combine them into one force. The title of Chief Commissioner was unique to the Victoria Police and, although the reasons for adopting it were not publicly stated, it coincided with the titles accorded other civil officials of the period, such as goldfield and crown land commissioners. In keeping with the tone of the Victorian Act, it was less militaristic than the proposed title of Inspector General, which was used in the Irish Constabulary and later adopted in New South Wales.

The new Police Act established six ranks, inspector, sub-inspector, chief constable, sergeant, cadet and constable. No provision was made for a structured promotional system, whereby men could expect to rise through the ranks according to a pattern based on seniority or experience. Instead, the patronage system operated and it was open to the Lieutenant-Governor to make all personnel changes and promotions for ranks above constable 'as he shall think fit'. The Chief Commissioner was empowered to appoint or dismiss any constable. The Lieutenant-Governor and the Chief Commissioner were somewhat restricted in the exercise of their discretion to make appointments by laws which, for the first time in Victoria, specified the qualifications required by men joining the force. However, surviving records show the appointment of men who were beyond the maximum age, and, as men already serving were retained, the nucleus of the Victoria Police Force was comprised of men who in many cases were not what they were supposed to be:

> of a sound constitution, able-bodied, and under the age of forty-five years, of a good character for honesty, fidelity, and activity, and unless circumstances shall render it necessary to dispense with this qualification in any case, he shall be required to read and write, and no person shall be appointed to be such Constable, who shall have been convicted of any felony or who shall be a Bailiff, Sheriff's Bailiff, or Parish Clerk, or who shall be a hired servant in the employment of any person whomsoever, or who shall keep a house for the sale of beer, wine or spirituous liquors by retail.

In comparison with present standards such qualifications were low, but they were a substantial advance on the unregulated recruitment of illiterates, alcoholics and transported felons, and were not markedly different from those laid down for Peel's New Police. The most notable differences being that Peel's standards specified that applicants were to be under thirty-five years of age, at least 5 feet 7 inches in height, and men who 'had not the rank, habits or station of gentlemen'. An urgent need to recruit police, and the values of a gold society, might have accounted for the disinclination of Victorian officials to turn away 36-year-old 'gentlemen', 5 feet 6 inches tall, who wanted to join the force.

The 1853 legislation also laid down some police duties and created a number of statutory offences to cover police misconduct, such as accepting a bribe, conniving at the escape of a prisoner, desertion, and assaulting a superior officer. It was made an offence for any member of the public to impersonate a policeman or possess police equipment, and for any person to induce a policeman to forgo his duty or offer him a bribe. These provisions contributed further to the establishment of policing as a distinct occupation within the community, and the penalties attaching to them indicated a relative increase in the level of public expectation and occupational responsibility attaching to the office of constable. The maximum penalty for a member of the public trying to bribe a policeman was a fine of £50. The maximum penalty for any policeman accepting a bribe was set at twelve months imprisonment with hard labour. The rationale, apparently, was not as much to discourage members of the public offering bribes as it was to discourage policemen from accepting them.

The underlying principle of occupational responsibility served to secure for the police some compensatory benefits. A feature of the 1852 Act was that it established a pension fund expressly for police. Known as the Police Superannuation Fund, it was financed by deducting 4 per cent from the salary of each policeman, which was then credited to a central, interest-bearing fund, that paid benefits to police who retired on account of age, ill health or injury. Benefits were also payable to widows of policemen. The sums of superannuation provided for were quite liberal, and ranged up to the annual payment to a superanuee of the amount equivalent to the whole of his salary as it was at the time of his retirement, provided he had served in the constabulary for more than twenty-five years and had reached the age of fifty-five. Provisions such as these were innovative and indicative of the generous inducements deemed necessary to recruit and retain suitable men. The scheme was so novel, however, that some recruits objected to the 4 per cent deduction as something not experienced in other lines of work, and those complaints, together with administrative complications, eventually caused it to be abandoned.

1852 was an important year for police in Victoria. Crime was increasing, immigrant ships arrived almost daily and the search for gold and land

Chief Commissioner
W. H. F. Mitchell

dictated the rate and spread of development. The sense of urgency created by these conditions proved conducive to reform. Sturt established his cadet corps, Freeman and his men were despatched from London, and the Snodgrass inquiry provided a valuable forum for debate on the police and brought about the enactment of vanguard legislation to organize a unified police force.[46]

Police for Victoria

The reforms of 1852 and the passing of the Police Regulation Act were mere formalities compared with the task that confronted William Mitchell upon his appointment as Chief Commissioner of the Victoria Police Force. Provisionally appointed to the post on 3 January 1853, the 42-year-old Mitchell was the first person to hold the office. An Englishman, he had lived at Barford station near Kyneton since 1842 and before that had held a number of administrative positions in Van Diemen's Land, including that of writer in the Office of the Executive Council. Mitchell's appointment set a precedent that lasted for forty-six years, during which no career policeman was appointed to head the police in Victoria. Instead the practice was to appoint prominent public figures who had not served in the ranks, and was in many respects justified by a lack of suitable men within the force.

Mitchell did not seek the position and before accepting it he insisted that it be offered to E. P. S. Sturt, because he believed Sturt was better qualified. Sturt, however, declined the offer and accepted the lesser post of chief inspector, which he left after a short time to resume his career as a magistrate. Mitchell successfully argued for autonomy from the Police Magistrates and the Colonial Secretary, and was allowed direct access to the Lieutenant-Governor on police matters. In doing so he elevated the administrative status of the police and saved them from subserviency to the magistracy.[47]

In support of Mitchell the government appointed twenty-six officers, many of whom were permitted to operate private businesses outside the force in recognition of their 'gentleman' status and as a condition of their entering the service. In addition to Sturt, they comprised one paymaster, one stud master, four inspectors, four acting inspectors and fifteen sub-inspectors. Two of the 'new' men, paymaster William Mair and acting inspector William Dana, were experienced police with a good knowledge of the colony. Mair was a colonial identity, who as a career soldier had first arrived in Australia during 1842 as part of a military detachment escorting convicts to Van Diemen's Land. He remained in the colonies, serving as adjutant with a mounted police force in New South Wales, and gained prominence when he commanded a detachment of mounted troopers sent to quell sectarian riots in Melbourne. After the riots Mair held a number of positions, including that of police magistrate, before joining the Victoria Police Force. As paymaster Mair was third in command, behind Mitchell and Sturt. Dana arrived in the colony in 1843 and joined the Native Police Corps, serving as Third Officer under the command of his older brother until the corps was disbanded. He was then employed hiring men and purchasing horses and equipment for the mounted police. Due to his expertise in this field he was a key witness before the Snodgrass Committee and that led to his commission as an officer with the Victoria Police.

Not all Mitchell's officers had previous colonial experience. New arrivals too had their place in the young force and one of these was Captain Charles MacMahon, late of the Dublin Militia. MacMahon, who eventually succeeded Mitchell as Chief Commissioner, arrived in Victoria during October 1852 with the intention of establishing his own mining company. He was, however, a former riding-master and veterinary surgeon in the British Army and instead of mining he applied for the sinecure of police stud master. Mitchell thought him better qualified for other work and persuaded him to take the position of Inspector of Police for Melbourne, which was the most demanding officer position in the colony.[48]

On 1 January 1853 the force, including the twenty-six officers, numbered 875 men, who were classified by Mitchell as: 26 officers, 106 non-commissioned officers, 471 foot constables, 223 mounted constables and 49 cadets. The population was marginally above 168 000 and, based on these figures, Victoria had an estimated police to population ratio of 1:198—a figure Mitchell described as still being 'inadequate to the wants of the Colony'. Within six months of taking office he had increased the force by 82 per cent, giving him a total of 1589 men and an estimated police to population ratio of 1:100. This ratio was far better than those of later years and the force in 1853 was larger than it was early in the twentieth century, when it served more than a million people. The high number of men commanded by Mitchell might indicate an effort to use numbers to compensate for police inefficiency. It might indicate that the unusual conditions of the gold rushes— particularly gold escorts and mining licence checks—demanded more police than has since been the case, or it might have been that the police growth was an unplanned, unwarranted deployment of excessive numbers of men. It was Mitchell's opinion that too many policemen were deployed on guard duty, a task he felt 'would be far better performed, and at much less expense by soldiers'. Mitchell also had under his command a detachment of fifty soldiers 'trained at very considerable expense to act as mounted troopers'.[49]

The strength of the force exceeded the figure authorized in the estimates by 520 and Mitchell advised the Lieutenant-Governor that even this figure was not enough and that for the year 1854 he would need 2000 men. The Lieutenant-Governor had agreed to Mitchell's initial expansion of the force, and when asking for the further increase Mitchell advised him that more men were needed because 'A large portion of the country is still very inadequately protected, and as new diggings break out, they must at once be provided with ample police whilst it is impracticable to diminish the numbers now employed at any one station'. Mitchell's constant recruiting was accompanied by the complaint that he could not properly clothe and equip the force, nor could he provide sufficient barrack accommodation or horses. He never made the complaint of earlier chief constables that he could not recruit enough men and, aided by peak migration levels and a downturn in gold production, he adopted a policy of recruiting at all costs. He did not, however, match his recruiting efforts with provisioning for his force. While the well-dressed Chief bemoaned a lack of equipment, the *Argus* described his men:

with 'shocking bad' hats, seedy and threadbare clothes, some with caps, and most of them with trousers of various hues, and in various states of dilapidation. A stranger looking at them, would suppose them to be a part of Falstaff's troop, or the unfortunate creditors of an insolvent Government.[50]

The *Argus* at this time was a regular critic of the administration of the police force but also a champion of the cause to improve police working conditions, and it published many letters of complaint from disenchanted policemen. In an era when police unions were unthought of and police discipline was often rough justice, the more literate of the constabulary vented their frustrations in letters to the editors of newspapers. These letters generally corroborated journalists' descriptions of life in the force and usually accorded with Mitchell's official accounts. At the same time as Mitchell complained about a lack of equipment, a number of constables wrote to the *Argus* about undue delays in receiving their pay, both problems being due in part to the recruitment of more than five hundred men too many. The pay delays troubled many people because of the risk that they might prompt some policemen to earn ready cash by arresting people for offences for which they were paid a half-share of the fines.[51]

A small part of the increase in the size of the force was due to the arrival of the London Fifty on 9 May 1853, and almost at once they created problems. The Londoners were brought to Victoria on the understanding that they would contract themselves to serve for a minimum of three years, with the penalty for any breach of contract being set at £50. When the day came for them to be sworn in they all initially refused and only relented under threat of being fined. Their action annoyed Mitchell, who wrote:

> it is my conviction that any similar importation from the London Constabulary, if at the expense of the Colony, would be undesirable. It is to be regretted that the detachment of a certain number of the Irish Constabulary for service in the Colony could not have been carried into effect.

The force included a number of other former English policemen and Mitchell thought that they were 'more valuable' than the London Fifty because they had 'emigrated at their own expense', and had experienced colonial life, most of them having 'tried the diggings and failed'. He did not explain his preference for Irish policemen but he did mention that they were 'mounted', whereas the Londoners were foot police, and he was then using soldiers as mounted troopers due to a shortage of trained mounted men. While Mitchell expressed disappointment with the London men and longed for Irish police, they were discontented with his force and wanted to return home. Within weeks of arriving in Melbourne, men of the London Fifty wrote to the *Argus*, protesting at the conditions under which police were expected to work in Victoria, the vehemence of their letters serving as an indication of the low standards in the colonial force. The London Fifty had the benefit of service in the Metropolitan Police, whereas Mitchell and many of his contemporaries had never served as policemen and were ignorant of comparative standards. One of Freeman's men wrote to the *Argus* in disgust because he, like many police in Melbourne, had one shilling a day deducted from his salary of ten shillings, to pay for barrack accommodation. The police administration viewed the barracks as 'comfortable lodgings', but the writer expressed concern that there was often no fuel, no hot water, no breakfast and no provision for dinner. He described how men who completed night duty at six in the morning slept in the beds of men who rose to commence day duty, and one room was reportedly occupied by twenty-one constables who each paid the same rate of a shilling a day, regardless of whether or not they had a bed of their own. With some justification he concluded, 'Should this continue, there can be but little hope of the police ever being but of little service in this town and quite unlikely to remain in the force'. The disaffection of the new arrivals came to a head about six weeks after this when two of them were charged in the City Police Court with insubordination and refusing to do duty. The two had refused to cut firewood and procure water for the use of the cook at the police barracks and were each fined fifty shillings, in default of payment to serve seven days in gaol. Their defence was that they were policemen, not soldiers, and that menial work such as cutting wood was not done by police in London and should not be the work of policemen in Melbourne. In raising such a defence the two constables struck a sensitive chord. Although the Police Act in Victoria was modelled on the English version there was an obvious preference among some officials in the colony for the Irish military model. Local authorities had not asked for English police, and even after their arrival in Victoria, Mitchell expressed a preference for men from the quasi-military Irish Constabulary. The Irishman, Inspector MacMahon, agreed; he prosecuted the two London men, while Chief Inspector Sturt chided them that soldiers were not degraded by doing fatigue duty. The two reluctant wood-choppers were embroiled not so much in an individual dispute as they were the unwitting parties in a larger debate about the appropriate policing model for Victoria.[52]

One unit formed within the force during 1853 typified the militaristic tendencies of some police officials and also highlighted the embryonic state of policing as a public service. MacMahon formed a mounted city patrol in Melbourne and equipped it in a manner similar to the Irish Constabulary. Numbering twenty-five men, this unit was housed in comfortable barracks, separate from the foot police, and was provided with a farrier, messman and servant. The men were mounted and wore the uniform of police cadets and each was armed with two pistols, a sabre and a repeating carbine rifle. A far cry from their foot colleagues of 'Falstaff's troop', they worked in groups of not less than four and patrolled the city day and night. As part of a novel scheme they were issued with a second uniform and detailed to work as firemen should an alarm of fire be raised in the city. Decked in black leather helmets and red shirts bound in black, those troopers not on police patrol responded to fires with their own horse-drawn fire engine and fire-fighting equipment. It was an age of adventure when a young man could at once be a soldier, policeman and fireman, but it did not last. Although the formation and early work of the mounted city patrol drew praise from the *Argus*, little else is known about it and it appears that the unit ceased to exist as an élite police-fire service, about the time that the police cadet scheme was abandoned. Mounted policemen continued to patrol Melbourne streets for many decades but it is not known when they stopped doubling as firemen.

Another source of adventure for police recruits, and of pride for Mitchell, was the Detective Branch, twenty-seven detectives dressed in mufti, performing arduous and often dangerous work throughout the colony. They were commanded by James Ashley, who had headed the first detective force in 1844, and Mitchell wrote of them that they had 'proved an admirable auxiliary in the suppression of crime . . . it is a matter of congratulation that Bushranging is of rare occurrence and that apprehension almost invariably follows immediately the commission of crime'. During a five-month period in 1853 the twelve detectives stationed in Melbourne made 197 arrests, including 88 arrests for felonies such as bank robbery. They were days of success and favourable comment, and few of those involved could have anticipated what lay ahead for their successors. Large outbreaks of bushranging had not yet occurred in Victoria but, when they did, the successes of Ashley and his men were forgotten and the detective branch was properly disgraced as a degenerated shambles. In the meantime, however, Mitchell's detectives enjoyed support from a ruling class and respectable citizens eager for life and property to be protected. That their protectors came dressed in mufti was of little concern; fears of police 'spying' seem to have abated.[53]

Whether the sight of smartly attired young police-firemen or reports of efficient detectives in mufti induced others to join the force is not recorded. More than likely they joined for such reasons as an inability to find gold and the need for work. Whatever their motives, Mitchell was able to report that police recruits were in plentiful supply at last. Few personnel records from the period have survived, but the oath sheets of 168 men who joined during the second half of 1853 give a hint of what was happening. Each of them—perhaps anticipating a return to the goldfields or to Europe—signed up only for a minimum period of twelve months. None of them was born in Australia—they were predominantly Irish labourers. The youngest was nineteen and the oldest fifty-two, seven years above the specified maximum age. Six per cent did not sign their names but instead put their mark, and because no minimum height was stipulated, as it was in London, men of 5 feet 5 inches were enlisted. So few records from a force of more than fifteen hundred men do not enable generalizations to be made, but they do indicate some diversity in the age and literacy. The previous occupations of recruits also varied, although almost all were from the lower trades and callings. Apart from one German, all were from the United Kingdom.[54]

Constables wanting to resign from the force were required by law to give three months notice in writing and the penalty for not doing so was a fine or imprisonment for up to four months. After signing up, many constables became so eager to leave the force that they disregarded the prospect of gaol and deserted. Public advertisements offering a £5 reward for information leading to the apprehension of absconding constables were common, and those deserters who were arrested suffered a similar fate to Constable Walter Wright who was sentenced to two months gaol with hard labour. Late in 1853 the force commenced publication of the *Victoria Police Gazette* and the first edition included a list of twenty-seven men wanted for absconding from the force. So strong was the lure of gold that the same gazette also listed forty-nine soldiers and seamen wanted for desertion, and advertised rewards of up to £10 a man for their apprehension.

The publication of the *Police Gazette* was of itself an important advance for the force. First published on 30 December 1853, it has chronicled police matters in Victoria on a weekly basis ever since. The need for such a publication had long been urged in the colony, and its absence was said by some to be due to illiteracy in the constabulary. The gazette published in Victoria closely followed the style of the original police gazette produced in England on a weekly basis since 1828. The first gazettes contained reports of crimes, lists of stolen property, details of escapees, deserters and missing persons, notifications of rewards, and general matters relevant to the administration of the police. The publication of this information, for distribution to all police on a weekly basis, was an important attempt at co-ordinating police efforts and reducing the parochial tendencies of police removed from the centre of police activity in Melbourne. Nor was it only the police who received these gazettes; copies were also sent to newspaper offices and other government departments as a means of encouraging community co-operation.[55]

The close of 1853 saw the departure of Mitchell as Chief Commissioner; he was suffering from poor health and travelled overseas to recuperate. Some months before his departure he issued a notice in the *Government Gazette* proclaiming that 'the Constabulary Force of the said Colony is fully organised according to the provisions of the said Act', and indeed Mitchell had largely fulfilled the promise of his appointment. He was doubtless glad to have achieved so much. Did he foresee that turbulent days loomed on the horizon? His sojourn overseas was brief, and when he returned to Victoria he declined to take up his place in the force but instead embarked upon a long and successful political career. MacMahon was left to lead the police into 1854, while the *Argus* paid a tribute to Mitchell:

The police of Victoria is not perfection—very far from it; but under Mr Mitchell's hands it has improved in a manner which stamps that gentleman as one of our masterminds. Nothing could be worse than its condition when he took the reins ... Corruption, perjury, ruffianism of every description were rife throughout the force, till it had become a public nuisance, not a safe-guard. In a few short months, with the aid of a strong will, a sense of duty, and a competent intelligence, all this has been so far reformed, that to calm observers like ourselves, it appears little short of miraculous.[56]

The *Argus* had often criticized the police, more in frustration than anger, but at the end of 1853 it felt that the reorganized force was getting on top of its problems. The newspaper was fair-minded, but too optimistic.

2

Drunks, Soldiers or Policemen?

Charles MacMahon assumed command of the Victoria Police Force in 1854 and was succeeded as Chief Commissioner in 1858 by Frederick Standish. Both were 'gentlemen' and former soldiers, and between them they headed the police force for twenty-six years. Their combined period of commissionership began with the the hopes of Mitchell's reformed police and concluded with the capture of Ned Kelly. Yet during that time the force's ability to cope was strained to the limit and the force was buffeted from within and without by a seemingly endless series of problems. Major events such as the Eureka rebellion and the Clunes riot were testing times, while widespread drunkenness, excessive militarism, political interference and a host of other factors regularly plagued Victoria's police.

They were tough times for the young force, but behind a large element of remaining ineptitude there *was* emerging the promise of a sober, efficient and truly civil police force, although it remained unfulfilled under MacMahon and Standish. Police wages declined, work conditions improved only marginally, no training was conducted and no real effort was made to define the police role or the nature of police power. Hundreds of police were deployed on a wide range of tasks that included duty as sailors and soldiers.

Joe! Joe!

The *Argus* did not greet with enthusiasm the promotion of Inspector MacMahon to Acting Chief Commissioner in 1854. As a career soldier, MacMahon served with the 71st Regiment in Canada, the 10th Hussars in India, and later the Dublin Militia. He had already, under Mitchell, applied militaristic methods to the imported English police and to his formation of the mounted city patrol. When given command of the entire force, grossly overmanned and still wanting in efficiency, MacMahon was in a position to practise his ideology on a grander scale, prompting public condemnation of excessive military discipline in the police force, and rebuke from a Government Commission of Inquiry:

the attention of the officers had been too exclusively directed to imparting to the force the features of a military body, rather than those of a preventive force.

It must be obvious that, although a preventive police may occasionally be called upon to act as a disciplined or quasi-military body, their useful action is much more frequently called for in their individual capacity as police constables.

Their individual training and instruction as a preventive police is much more important than as a military force, and although the Board by no means undervalues their discipline as a body, they submit that it should not have almost an exclusive attention, to the comparative neglect of the training of the force for preventive and detective purposes.[1]

MacMahon was also inclined to use army ranks, such as lieutenant, not provided for in the police legislation and criticized by the Police Commission as having 'no meaning' yet giving 'a military character to the force'. MacMahon himself clung to the title of captain, his rank in the Dublin Militia, although—after being invalided from the army with sunstroke—he was reduced to lieutenant. Of greater concern than the use of military titles was the use of weapons. For a civil constabulary, the Victoria Police Force was a heavily armed body with more weapons than there were men to use them: 2207 firearms, 932 swords and bayonets, and

The Government Camp at Ballarat in 1854

41

almost 1000 batons among 1639 men. Such militarism within the ranks of a civil police force is hardly desirable in any democratic society; in the 'gold' society of colonial Victoria it was a precursor to disaster.[2]

MacMahon, and seemingly Mitchell before him, were parties to the practice of administering the police force with two sets of tenets: one for the goldfields and another for the remainder of the colony. It was an approach not unique to the police, as the Government also seemed to view the miners with a jaundiced eye. The outcome was the deployment of excessive numbers of armed police on the goldfields, who operated largely as a repressive tax-gathering force rather than as a civil preventive police to protect the lives and property of taxpayers. By mid-1854 the population of Victoria had increased to 236 798 and the strength of the Victoria Police Force was 1639 men, giving a police to population ratio of 1:144 in the colony. But there was a significant variation in the police to population ratios in different areas, particularly between the goldfields and other districts.

TABLE 1

Distribution of police and population in six major population centres during April–May 1854

	Population	Police	Ratio
Melbourne (incl. County of Bourke)	101 086	410	1:247
Geelong	20 324	132	1:154
Ballarat	16 684	164	1:102
Bendigo	15 480	173	1:89
Castlemaine	12 129	217	1:56
Beechworth	3 339	105	1:32

Ballarat, Bendigo, Castlemaine, Beechworth } Goldfields

Population data obtained from census conducted 26 April 1854. Census of Victoria—1854, Melbourne, Government Printer, 1855. Police District data from police count of 12 May 1854. VPRS 1189, unit 150, file E54/5132.

The figures in Table 1 show quite clearly that high numbers of police were deployed on the goldfields, resulting in police to population ratios of repressive dimensions. Admittedly, many of the goldfields police were used for escort duty—approved by miners—and it took them away from their camps, but they and their weapons were based on the goldfields and added to the overall police presence. In fact 40 per cent of the total police manpower was used to police just 17 per cent of the colony's population, residing on four goldfields. At these fields police were issued with 1021 firearms or 46 per cent of the police armoury. To sustain this firepower, large reserves of ammunition were held, including more than 10 000 rounds at Beechworth alone.[3]

It might be suggested that additional police and arms were required at the goldfields to curb lawlessness and crime, but such a suggestion would be wrong. Contemporary sources, including the Chief Commissioner of Police, show that the goldfields were treated as a special case and that police numbers were not calculated to protect but to defeat. There were far fewer committals for serious crime from goldfields districts, such as Ballarat, than from other areas, such as Geelong. Colonel Valiant, commander of the military at Bendigo, described the miners as 'the most orderly and well-disposed body that I have ever seen in any part of the world'; the Surveyor-General, Andrew Clarke, considered the goldfields to be peaceful, with 'a remarkable absence of serious crime'; while the *Argus* commented on the few and trifling cases that appeared and described Ballarat as one of 'the quietest and unlitigious places in the world'. Acting Chief Commissioner MacMahon admitted that the police at Ballarat were used as tax-gatherers and were inefficient as police. It is no wonder that the Gold Fields Commission of Enquiry found that twice as many police as necessary were deployed on the goldfields, and their 'annoying duties' antagonized the miners, who in turn upset the police, whose 'proper duty of protecting the people' was not well carried out. Nor would it be, so long as the police collected those resented licence fees in tactless ways.[4]

The breakdown of civil policing principles was worsened by confusing administration. Police on the Victorian goldfields were commanded by both their local district Inspector and the local Resident Gold Fields Commissioner. This divided the allegiance of constables and weakened the control of inspectors. In the words of MacMahon, it was 'rather a mixed up responsibility'. The Resident Commissioners made the decisions regarding the numbers of police required and the manner of their deployment on the goldfields; the Chief Commissioner of Police in Melbourne simply provided men at the behest of these civil officials. So the numbers of police on the goldfields escalated and preventive police duties were rendered subservient to tax gathering. By contrast, MacMahon deployed the police in all other areas.[5]

That unique establishment, the Camp, showed the alienation of police from the public on the goldfields. Commissioners, police and soldiers clustered together in camps, sallying forth from them to conduct licence hunts. The Gold Fields Commission found the concept of the Camp odious, and decried the notion of police 'banded together . . . as if in hostility to the people'. There were good relations between the police and law-abiding citizens 'everywhere but on the Goldfields', and the camp system did not help. An *Argus* correspondent said the same of police and officials at the Ballarat Camp, who behaved as if they 'were in a real enemy's country'. So extreme was this alienation that inhabitants of the Ballarat Camp maintained a standing 'Plan of Camp Defences', for immediate implementation 'in case of attack'.

For the soldiers present on the goldfields this sort of environment may not have been unusual. The Resident Gold Fields Commissioners and their clerical staffs were properly tax collectors, and the insulating shroud of the Camp was not a real hindrance in their work. For the police, however, Camp life was the very antithesis of what effective policing and good community relations were all about. Even at that time, police policy was that constables should have a local interest in the areas where they worked, and it was considered 'highly desirable that many of the police should reside among and identify themselves with the citizens'. Away from the goldfields, particularly around Melbourne, this had become the policy and the practice. Certainly most of the goldfield settlements were tent towns, but this of itself should have been no barrier. In Melbourne many married police constables lived with their families in tents pitched on the banks of the Yarra River, amid the poor and the transient.

Away from the goldfields, police were also detailed for duty differently. In Melbourne, constables usually worked alone and on foot, pounding regular beats near where they lived and where they could identify with the community. On the goldfields the police usually only left the Camp cocoon in groups and mainly to conduct licence hunts. Upon leaving the Camp, police were met with the derisive catchcry, 'Joe! Joe!', as miners yelled across the diggings to each other, warning of the predatory presence of the 'Traps'. Of this unfortunate situation the Gold Fields Commission observed, 'Scenes between the police and the miners were of daily occurrence, where mutual irritation, abuse, and gross violence would ensue'. The Victorian goldfields in 1854 thus presented a sorry picture of the Victoria Police Force: excessive numbers of heavily armed and militaristic police, isolated from the mining community, and engaged almost solely in the collection of universally unpopular licence fees. It was a scene limited to the goldfields and not evident in the other towns and rural areas.[6]

Yet one practice that was widespread throughout the colony festered on the goldfields and irritated an already seething community. The incentive system of distributing fines—a half-share going to the police—was obnoxious enough in a normal context, but bred hatred on the goldfields. The nuances of the system as it operated on the goldfields are particularly pertinent, for the odious manner of policing the goldfields was exacerbated by the relentless zeal with which the police pursued unlicensed miners.

In September 1854 Lieutenant-Governor Sir Charles Hotham ordered that licence hunts be conducted at least twice a week. For each unlicensed miner the police arrested they received a half-share of the fine and with some small parties of police averaging twenty arrests a day it was a lucrative duty. Miners were hunted like kangaroos and treated like felons; contemporary accounts describe how men not engaged in digging for gold were arrested for being without a licence, while others were ordered to produce their licence for inspection several times in one day, often having to climb over 100 feet from the bottom of a shaft. Francis Hare, one of the most famous policemen in Victorian history, began his colonial life as a digger. Hardly one to be prejudiced against the police, he wrote of his days as a digger and attested to 'many instances of the iniquitous law of arresting diggers'. It was an iniquitous system, aggravated by the failure of many police to display prudence and good temper.[7]

Given the militarism, the camps and the general animosity that prevailed on the goldfields, the moiety system—with money its essential ingredient—stands as one of the most unfortunate blights on the development in Victoria of good relations between police and the general community. The Board that reported on the Ballarat Riots provides a succinct account of the evils of the moiety system:

> Your Board are of opinion the police are much crippled in the performance of their more legitimate duty, viz, the protection of life and property and the preservation of peace and order, by having their energies expended in hunting sly grog sellers and taking up unlicensed miners. The police in both of these duties have made themselves very obnoxious to the diggers, and it has had a most pernicious effect on the morals of the police force—on one hand holding out inducements to the police, by giving them shares of fines, to pay an undue amount of attention to this lucrative branch of their duty, and in some cases to commit perjury for the gain in prospect; on the other hand exposing them to bribery by the sly grog sellers, for winking at the practices of such delinquents.[8]

The many months of government maladministration and police persecution culminated in the events at Ballarat during the last months of 1854. On 7 October a miner named James Scobie was murdered near the Eureka Hotel by a group including James Francis Bentley, the hotel owner. A subsequent magisterial inquiry discharged Bentley, and this erroneous decision so outraged hundreds of the miners that they rioted and burnt Bentley's Eureka Hotel to the ground. The burning of the hotel once again placed the police in hostile conflict with the miners, but the behaviour of the miners was largely vindicated when their actions resulted in the re-arrest and conviction of Bentley for manslaughter and the dismissal of Police Magistrate Dewes and Police Sergeant-Major Milne for corruption. The Scobie murder and subsequent events confirmed in public and spectacular fashion the popular suspicion that those who administered the goldfields were corrupt.

The Eureka Hotel Riot further fomented miner dissent and cast the die for later clashes between miners and camp officials. That the police were preparing for a showdown well before it occurred is shown in a despatch from Acting Chief Commissioner MacMahon to the Colonial

Secretary, dated 9 November 1854, in which MacMahon asked permission to requisition a number of wagons for the specific purpose of rapidly conveying large numbers of men to Ballarat. The Chief Commissioner did not get his wagons, but on 28 November troop reinforcements arrived in Ballarat, heralded by skirmishes between camp officials and miners. The following day witnessed the monster Bakery Hill meeting of miners, accompanied by mass licence burning and the first appearance of the Southern Cross flag, the standard of the Ballarat Reform League. Camp officials countered this act of defiance on 30 November with the final digger hunt, an officious and violent check of mining licences accompanied by a reading of the Riot Act. Events then moved quickly. The miners encamped at Eureka and, amid much arming and drilling, completed their stockade on 2 December. Before daybreak on 3 December a combined force of 276 soldiers and police attacked and over-ran the stockade; 114 miners were taken prisoner and many more were wounded, including up to thirty believed killed. Sixteen soldiers were wounded, four fatally. The police escaped relatively unscathed with none of their number being killed and only one constable wounded.

The saga of Eureka did not end with the capturing of the insurgents at the stockade. Martial law was briefly proclaimed and thirteen men were eventually tried for high treason. All were acquitted, and soon afterwards the universally unpopular licence fee was abolished and replaced by a Miner's Right that conferred electoral rights on the holder. These legal reforms enabled MacMahon to reduce police establishments on the goldfields to conventional preventive policing levels, which at Ballarat meant a halving of police numbers. For many, a genuine oppression had been lifted, and there even arose the view that 'Australian democracy was born at Eureka'.[9]

More certainly, some of the hopes the Victoria Police had of throwing off the yoke of public enmity died at Eureka. Just as the police were gradually improving in organization and efficiency and gaining limited public recognition for their work, they became embroiled in the events at Ballarat. Against the barbarism of many police at the Eureka Stockade even the depredations of the digger hunts paled into insignificance. Although there were far more soldiers than police involved in the storming of the stockade, it was the mounted police whose behaviour will always be remembered:

> The foot police appear, as a body, to have conducted themselves with creditable temper; but assuredly on the part of the mounted division of that force there seems to have been a needless as well as ruthless sacrifice of human life, indiscriminate of innocent or guilty, and after all resistance had disappeared with the dispersed and flying rioters.

Another contemporary account contains references to miners' bodies being bayoneted repeatedly after death, and it goes on:

the military did their duty with steadiness and courage, and under excellent discipline; the police, exasperated by their long standing feud with the diggers, got quite out of hand, committing many acts of brutality and wanton cruelty in the hour of their triumph.

Any triumph was lost. Acting Chief Commissioner MacMahon, barely one year in office and the inheritor of a force whose tradition embodied convictism, felonry, alcoholism and corruption, was additionally burdened with the brutal legacy of Eureka. The police and their licence hunts were far from being the sole cause of events at Ballarat, but the police were numerous, uniformed and armed, thereby constituting a highly visible foe. The land-hunger, lack of franchise and bureaucratic behaviour of other camp officials were relatively intangible compared with the more obvious presence and behaviour of the police. At Eureka the mounted police fulfilled the miners' worst fears.[10]

MacMahon's task of salvaging some public esteem for his force was an unenviable one, not assisted by the annual pilgrimages of many to the site of the rebellion and the inevitable mythologizing of the event. There were, however, some lessons for the police in the events of 1854, and they did not go unheeded. For a while, efforts were made to avoid militarism within the police force, greater emphasis was placed on the preparation of police for preventive work, and the police hierarchy displayed a marked aversion to the deployment of police on non-police duties, such as tax gathering.

The lessons of Eureka, although costly, were for a time well learned. The most indeterminate aspects concern how much long-term damage it did to the image of police in Victoria, and to what extent it retarded the development of police service as a vocation. It did not, in fact, seem to impede police recruiting efforts, or reduce public requests for extended police protection, and certainly it added impetus to the movement for police reform. In these functional areas it is arguable that the negative impact of Eureka was minimal. Where Eureka has left its most telling stamp upon the police is in ideological and philosophical terms. In literature, poetry, art, pageantry and politics the spirit of Eureka is immortalized. The actions of the police are caught up in symbolism and, as suggested by Hume Dow, the most violent disagreement between Eureka writers is in depicting the police. An incident starkly highlighting this symbolic dichotomy is that involving the Eureka flag. When the stockade was stormed, Trooper John King hauled down the Eureka flag, whereupon it was bayoneted, trampled on, dragged in the dust and tied to the tail of a trooper's horse.[11] The symbolism manifested in these actions for both sides is perpetuated today in Victor Daley's ballad:

> The bitter Fight was ended,
>   And, with cruel coward-lust,
> They dragged our sacred Banner,
>   Through the Stockade's bloody dust.

> But, patient as the gods are,
>> Justice counts the years and waits—
> That Banner now waves proudly,
>> Over six Australian States.

It is this symbolism that has confronted police in Victoria since 1854. Public support of the police in a functional sense has never really been denied. Instead, like the perennial debate over the true political ramifications of Eureka, there remains the unsettled and unsettling question of the true impact of Eureka upon the police image in partly subconscious folk memory.

At the Shrine of Bacchus

Although the events surrounding the Eureka Stockade overshadow the Victorian police scene in the mid-1850s, there was much else happening that is equally worthy of attention. Some events, such as the 1854–55 Police Commission of Inquiry, constitute important stages in the development of police organization in Victoria, and some 'routine' changes are also notable.

The year 1854 began not only with the elevation of MacMahon, but also with a shuffle of other positions. The experienced Samuel Freeman was appointed to MacMahon's old post in the key position of Inspector of Police and Police Magistrate for Melbourne. Robert O'Hara Burke, who later gained fame in the ill-fated Burke and Wills expedition, was appointed Inspector in Charge of the Ovens Police District,[12] but it was the less-known Freeman who had the greatest impact on policing in Victoria. Freeman reorganized the method of working beats, and imparted to many Melbourne police the principles and practices of policing in London. One novel but practical innovation made by Freeman was the equipping of watch-houses with special hand trucks, so that foot constables could wheel drunks in a semi-conscious state to the lock-up, instead of dragging and lugging the dead weight of drunks to the cells. Beat duty in the mid-1850s was an unusual arrangement whereby constables spent only six hours out of every twenty-four on patrol, and this was divided into two separate shifts of three hours duration. The interim period was spent at a police station on reserve duty. A Government Commission was critical 'of the lightness of the labour of a policeman, compared with that of an industrious man of the same class in any walk of life'. The principal outcome of the observation was that the Chief Commissioner was pressed into altering the beat duty for foot constables. By 1856 they were working a twelve-hour day comprising two four-hour lots of beat duty, broken by one four-hour segment of reserve duty.

In the earlier part of the 1850s police were not formally trained for preventive police work nor issued with a set of written instructions as to what was expected of them. Instead, new constables were assigned for the first week, as unpaid supernumeraries, to work with older constables who were supposed to show them the course of their beats and the locations of brothels and hotels. Men engaged as supernumeraries were drawn from the 'labouring classes' and were thought of as being 'in close contact with the unemployed'. It was the regular paid, unskilled nature of police work, coupled with the socio-economic status of police, that accounted in large part for the criticisms of the lightness of police duties. Because it did not entail the physical exertion required for other jobs open to the 'labouring classes', such as roadbuilding and mining, police work was seen by some people as a sinecure for uneducated, unskilled workers.[13]

Although men of the upper classes viewed police work with disdain, and its 'lightness' as a problem to be reckoned with, Inspector Freeman and his fellow officers were beset by more pragmatic problems, such as widespread drunkenness within the police ranks. Perhaps the 'idleness' of police work facilitated excessive hotel patronage, or perhaps the backgrounds of those who joined the police inclined them to heavy drinking. Whatever the cause, alcoholism and its associated evils were a constant worry to the police hierarchy. Constables were found drunk in brothels, drunk on their beats, drunk in the witness box, drunk in watch-houses, and in drunken sleep when supposedly on patrol. During 1854 more than one-quarter of the Melbourne City police appeared in court charged with alcohol-related offences committed while on duty. One constable charged with being a habitual drunkard had fourteen prior convictions for being drunk on duty. Consequently, the Government made it a criminal offence for publicans to 'permit any constable to become intoxicated on his premises or to be supplied with fermented or spirituous liquors whilst intoxicated or whilst on duty'. As with many such enactments, this provision was a precursor to further problems, as drunken constables were later known to make trouble for publicans who tried to abide by the new law.

To accommodate police who persisted in paying homage to the Shrine of Bacchus, the Government also established a special Police Prison at the Richmond Police Depot. Erected during 1854, the Police Prison comprised ten separate cells and was formally proclaimed a gaol, with its own Visiting Justice. It played host to a multitude of constables convicted of drunkenness, desertion, accepting and soliciting bribes, and assault.

Special instructions were issued to supervising officers to help them avoid being assaulted by drunken constables. Firmer discipline was instituted. Gaol sentences were made mandatory for all offences connected with drunkenness on duty, and a third conviction for any such offence brought automatic discharge from the police force. To divert attention from the Shrine of Bacchus to the Church of God, Sunday church parades were made compulsory for all constables, and it was the duty of sub-officers to march their men to church in a group, to avoid absenteeism.

Although the picture of drunkenness within the police force was a bleak one, it was yet another example of the community getting the police it deserved and of the police ranks in many respects reflecting the society from which they were drawn. The daily parade of drunken policemen before the courts, and the erection of a special Police Prison, caused barely a ripple in the young colony. There is no record of a public outcry in the newspapers, little continuing concern in the Legislative Council debates, and no mention of it by the public committees that inquired into the police from the 1830s to the 1860s. Newspapers like the *Argus* did report some cases of police 'misconduct', such as that of a constable eating an oyster when on duty, but these reports occupied small paragraphs lost in stories of public crime, misbehaviour and drunkenness. Public drunkenness was a perennial problem among the working classes, and its high incidence might account for a seeming community tolerance of it amongst the police. It would have been strange if the community had expected newly recruited and untrained police to exhibit traits very different from those they took with them to the police service.[14]

Notwithstanding the rate of police drunkenness and the view of some people that police work was light, it was an occupation that had inherent hardships. There was a lot of sickness among policemen, diseases like dysentery and typhoid fever being common. The all-weather, all-hours, foot-slogging nature of police duties predisposed constables to pulmonary tuberculosis and varicose veins, and the need to traverse all terrains in all weathers exposed many constables to the elements and often put them in danger of drowning, while attempting rescues and fording swollen rivers. The danger of physical violence was ever present. Assaults were common and police, then as now, were maimed, shot and murdered in the line of duty. One notable case of the 1850s, the murder of Constable Edward Barnett at Havelock, was followed by a riot of about 1500 miners who wanted to lynch the policeman's killer. After the experience of Eureka and the strained relations between miners and police, the Havelock diggings riot was a welcome change: enraged miners seeking to avenge the death of one of their local police.

Constables were liable to be transferred at a moment's notice to any part of the colony, and were invariably housed in tents or other rudimentary structures. It was a common lament that police lived in conditions that were the same as or worse than their quarry's. Police were expected to perform fatigue duty such as woodchopping and cleaning, and in some cases vacancies were limited to married men whose wives were willing to cook and wash for other men at police stations. Off-duty hours were also subject to regulation, and off-duty constables were compelled to attend regular drill parades and church parades. One order forbade police from appearing in public at any time unless in uniform.[15] In 1854 an amendment to the Police Regulation Act banned all police from voting at parliamentary elections. Police in Victoria were thus disenfranchised at a time when most other groups, especially miners, were clamouring for and getting the right to vote. The denial of the vote remained for many decades, and is a sharp example of the isolated position into which police in Victoria were placed. As an added touch of irony, Acting Chief Commissioner MacMahon, a gentleman by birth and background, pressed for the disenfranchisement of the police but was appointed a member of the Legislative Council when still head of the force. While constables from the working class were disenfranchised, their Chief was joining the ex-Eureka rebel, Peter Lalor, as a member of parliament.[16]

It was this parliament that appointed the Police Commission of 1854 that, over twelve months, investigated the police in Melbourne. The commission touched upon many matters, but its most important decision was to press MacMahon to issue a comprehensive code of instructions for the guidance of the police. Since the founding of the settlement in 1836 no code had been published, even though it was a feature of police forces in other Australian colonies and in England. MacMahon and a police clerk, Henry Moors, prepared the first *Manual of Police Regulations for the Guidance of the Constabulary of Victoria*, published in 1856. Bound in a form suitable for carrying in saddle bags, the manual was of 109 pages and became the 'policeman's bible', an indispensable guide containing instructions on everything, from what time to rise in the morning to the speed limit to be observed (5 miles an hour) when riding police troop horses. Such a code of instructions has been an integral part of police training and duties since 1856 and, when it first appeared, it was a watershed like the coming of the *Police Gazette*. Although the appearance of the manual was not accompanied by a periodical examination system, as recommended by the Police Commission, it was the first tentative step in training men for preventive police work and in imparting to them skills that would distinguish the 'lightness' of their labour from that of day labourers on the roads. The manual itself encouraged this step toward occupational status by advising police thus:

> The position in which members of the Force are placed is totally different from that which they occupied as private individuals. They become peace officers, and are in an entirely new situation; they are by law entrusted with certain powers, which they must exercise with great caution and prudence, and it is most essential that they keep under complete control their private feelings . . .
>
> Every member of the Force should bear constantly in mind, how essential it is to cultivate a proper regard for its honor and respectability, and should be governed by the principle, that the more they can raise those either above or below them in public estimation, the more they elevate their own official position, and with it, the general character of the Force.

51

Chief Commissioner
C. MacMahon

The sentiments expressed in the manual were admirable and as the decades elapsed they moved closer and closer to fruition. It was, however, an awfully slow process.[17]

Around the time of the manual's publication the appointment of MacMahon as Chief Commissioner was confirmed, enabling him to drop the title 'Acting', which he had carried for almost two years. Unfortunately for him, and for the aspirations espoused in his manual, he soon became embroiled in the worst scandal of his career and was labelled in parliament as a murderer. In 1857 a drunk imprisoned in the iron cells of the police lock-up at Sandhurst died from exposure. The coroner held that 'the place was perfectly unfit for the use of a lock-up', and it was publicly alleged that MacMahon, as a private investor, had profiteered from the erection of iron police buildings. A select committee, including Peter Lalor, was appointed to inquire into MacMahon's case, specifically the allegations of profiteering, the cell death at Sandhurst, and the method of contracting works in the police force. The committee, in guarded terms, exonerated MacMahon of the charges, and included in their report a carefully worded rider that 'irregularities were, in some measure, rendered necessary by the peculiar state of the times'.

The Sandhurst cell-death inquiry cast the force generally into a bad light because of matters that emerged during the inquiry. It became a matter of public record that MacMahon only accepted office with the

52

police on the express condition that he could have the right to pursue private business. He and his fellow officers acted as paid police administrators while also being engaged as investors, contractors and entrepreneurs. Ex-Chief Commissioner W. H. F. Mitchell was called before the Committee and made the point that 'everybody did something or other; if a man did not dabble in timber he dabbled in land'. MacMahon was one who, among other things, dabbled in timber and iron buildings. The practice of permitting high-ranking policemen to do so was defended on the grounds that it was only by such indulgences that educated and qualified men could be lured into a police career. The argument was not totally sound, as is proved by the quality of recruits attracted to the force by Sturt's cadet scheme, and the disturbing fact remained the pervasive class distinctions that led to double standards within the police force. Gentlemen like MacMahon were allowed to 'dabble' while constables drawn from the working classes were required to 'devote their whole time to the police service', were forbidden to marry without permission, or live where they liked, or eat an oyster while on duty, or smoke in public even when off duty. The police constable's loss of voting rights denied him equality with an increasing number of working men, and within the police service itself he was denied reasonable rights while others enjoyed unreasonable advantages. Policing was still a long way from being a career that men of different socio-economic backgrounds could hope to share on fair terms.[18]

One who ultimately found how unequal life could be was MacMahon himself. When cleared of any wrongdoing by the Select Committee he reported that he was relieved from a 'very painful odium'. His relief was shortlived. He promptly became embroiled in a vitriolic administrative conflict with Superintendent W. A. P. Dana, who was supported in his action by the Chief Secretary, John O'Shanassy. Dana, one of the longest-serving policemen in the colony, wanted a transfer from the rural districts, where he had spent the bulk of his service, to a position in close proximity to Melbourne. MacMahon opposed this request and also objected to the Chief Secretary's support of Dana, but O'Shanassy and Dana had their way, and MacMahon resigned as Chief Commissioner. In tendering his resignation, MacMahon touched upon a key principle of police administration, one that has often been raised in public debate since. MacMahon wrote:

I would respectfully point out that the control and management of the police department is, both by law and the regulations of the service, vested in the head of it, and that heretobefore it has so remained; and that, however advisable it may be for the Government to interfere in any important matter affecting the peace and well-being of the community, such necessity cannot exist in a question pertaining merely to an internal arrangement.[19]

The points made by MacMahon (even if he was unfair to Dana) revealed how great a change had been developing in the years up to 1858. In the time of Lonsdale and La Trobe, government officials and politicians were key figures in the daily running of the force. Under Sturt and Mitchell this practice had given way gradually to the point where MacMahon expected politicians to confine themselves to matters of policy only, leaving the internal management of the force to him. Even so, upon leaving the police service MacMahon, like Mitchell before him, embarked on a long and successful political career and at times found himself sitting in judgement on those police whose autonomy to act he had so strongly defended.[20]

Given the nature of things in 1858, MacMahon's response to political interference might also be regarded as an over-reaction. Class distinctions prevailed within the police force, drunkenness was rife, police were still basically untrained, recruiting standards were nominal, and people were far from agreeing on the occupational status and role of the police in Victoria. Since 1836 there had undoubtedly been an enormous improvement but in the 1850s, as in the 1830s, the drive for changes and improved police performance came not so much from the police themselves as from the public and the Government. Fundamental innovations, such as the publication of a *Police Manual* and the more efficient rostering and deployment of police manpower, resulted from suggestions by bodies such as the 1854–1855 Police Commission. Given the dependence of the police upon public direction and impetus, it is not surprising that the Chief Secretary felt the need to intervene in internal police arrangements.

Although the period of MacMahon's commissionership was at times troubled by political 'interference', unwanted militarism and happenings like the Eureka rebellion and Sandhurst cell death, he did steer the nascent force creditably through the difficult gold-rush years into calmer times. By 1858 socio-economic conditions in the colony were stabilizing and this stability flowed to the force. Large numbers of miners leaving the goldfields had the twofold effect of reducing the demand for police in dispersed rural areas and providing a plentiful supply of candidates for the police force—particularly since, by a gradual process of attrition, MacMahon reduced the size of his force by 23 per cent. Police wages were also reduced from the artificially high levels of the golden years as ample numbers of men were willing to leave behind the uncertain livelihood of the diggings for the relative security of the police force. They were years that witnessed an increase in the tenure of police service and a relative stabilization of manpower. Although the occupational status of constables remained low, police work offered men from the labouring classes secure employment and reasonable pay, and the opportunity of promotion and upward social mobility. Class distinctions still permeated the force, and officer positions were generally prestigious and well paid, with liberal allowances and the services of a batman. Under MacMahon, promotion up to the rank of superintendent was opened to all men in the force, subject to seniority, length of service, good conduct and 'a zealous attendance to their duties'. After an existence of almost twenty-five years, policing in Victoria was moving hesitatingly toward recognition as a community service and a vocation for young men. The police ranks, however, were not deemed to contain men possessed of the qualities necessary for Chief Commissioner. When MacMahon tendered his resignation the search began for a replacement and, as in the past, the ranks of gentlemen were scoured for a police leader. The stately Melbourne Club held the answer and Captain Frederick Charles Standish, gentleman, soldier and inveterate gambler, was appointed as the third Chief Commissioner of the Victoria Police Force.[21]

Not on the Square

> August 20 1858. Heard about 4.30 that I had just been appointed by the Executive to the C.C. of Police.

It was with these words that 34-year-old Frederick Standish entered in his private diary his appointment as Chief Commissioner of the Victoria Police. Standish confided many things to his diary over many years and it now stands as testament to his indolent and pleasure-seeking way of life. He was the bachelor son of Charles Standish of Standish Hall, Wigan, Lancashire, and had been educated at the Roman Catholic Prior Park College and the Royal Military Academy, Woolwich, subsequently serving for nine years in the Royal Artillery. His army service included a period on the staff of the lord lieutenant of Ireland and he retired with the rank of captain.

To escape heavy gambling debts, Standish fled England for Victoria in 1852. He worked for a time on the diggings before securing appointment as Assistant Gold Fields Commissioner at Sandhurst in 1854. He was later appointed Chinese Protector and held this position until transferring to the post of Chief Commissioner of Police. He had no previous police experience; his qualifications for the post, like those of his predecessors, were a military career and some experience in the civil service. A note of sour irony attaches to Standish's appointment as Chief Commissioner in that in 1853 he had used an assumed identity in trying to join the police force as a constable. Chief Commissioner MacMahon denied Standish, alias Selwyn, admission to the force on the grounds 'of his having held a position in society which would render him unfit for such a comparatively humble office'. Standish himself defended his use of a false identity on the grounds that lowly occupations, like that of a constable, were entirely foreign to his education and former occupations.

Chief Commissioner
F. C. Standish

In later years when questioned about his unsuccessful attempt to become a constable he retorted, 'I have been more than punished by the annoyance which that action has occasioned me'. The poor regard in which two Chief Commissioners held the 'humble office' of constable is stark evidence of the class division within the police force. Standish, however, brought with him to the Chief Commissionership some different values from those of his predecessor. If MacMahon's period of office was marked by militarism, Standish's peculiar stamp was one of hedonism. Standish became an official of the Melbourne Club and was universally identified with that élitist institution, which later became his home. He was also a prominent Freemason and in 1861 was installed as provincial grand master for Victoria. His pursuit of pleasure led him to mix with the wealthy élite of Melbourne, and his gambling pursuits were legendary. All-night gambling sessions were common, and on one occasion he lost £650 at a card game when his annual salary was only £1200. The private life of this Chief Commissioner became so notorious that the public image and internal morale of the force suffered. It is arguable that the pervasive maladministration that derived from Standish's indulgences contributed substantially to the inefficient hunt for the Kelly Gang.[22]

A common criticism levelled at Standish was of the open favouritism he displayed toward officers who shared his hedonistic lifestyle. In the words of John Sadleir:

> He was too much a man of pleasure to devote himself seriously to the work of his office, and his love of pleasure led him to form intimacies with some officers of like mind, and to think less of others who were much more worthy of regard. From the first, this mistake led to trouble, and lowered the tone and character of the service.

Sadleir was not a favourite, but Standish certainly had them. His own diary records the select few from among the officers with whom he dined and gambled regularly. Included were Frederick Winch and Thomas Lyttleton, two men who shared the limelight with their Chief. Under Standish's tutelage, Winch committed a number of serious offences but survived them all relatively unscathed. Only when Standish left the office of Chief Commissioner did a Royal Commission rid the police force of Winch. During the formative years of the friendship between the two men, Winch became involved in the use of public funds to illegally erect a police officers' boatshed on the Yarra River. Similarly, he used police staff and materials to maintain his private house and garden, and permitted his cronies to use police horses for their riding recreation. He came closest to dismissal when he used the police funds under his control for private spending and then borrowed money from his subordinates to balance the books. Under the generous patronage of Standish, he was charged not with stealing the funds in the first place, but with borrowing from his subordinates to repay them, an offence that carried the light penalty of a reprimand and a transfer.

Lyttleton, too, figures in all this. He was a renowned breeder of fighting cocks and, contrary to regulations, some police stations in his district housed a chicken coop and a few of his fighting birds. A serious incident of another kind occurred when Standish made Lyttleton Superintendent in Charge of the Melbourne police district, so the two men could be closer. To achieve this aim, Standish transferred the ageing Superintendent Samuel Freeman away from his home and family in Melbourne and sent him to Geelong. Freeman's entire police service in Victoria had been spent in Melbourne, and the move to Geelong so upset him that he committed suicide by slashing his throat with a razor.

The Police Hospital operated as a sly-grog shop under Standish, at the very time he was urging the Government to purge the colony of the flagrant evil of sly-grog selling 'carried on to an extent almost incredible'. The best known of all sly-grog shops was that within the walls of the Police Depot. Patients, visitors, police and public, men and women alike, could all buy good liquor from the obliging Sergeant Waugh of the Police Hospital. That such an operation could so blatantly be conducted by the police is perhaps an indication of Standish's influence on the force. After all, the Chief's personal delights allegedly included the giving of private dinner parties where nude women sat about the table, 'the whiteness of their forms contrasting with the black velvet of the chairs'.

Such antics were not just isolated instances of individual misconduct, but were symptomatic of deep-seated problems besetting the force, attributable in large measure to Standish's leadership. From 1860 to 1863, three separate Government Select Committees investigated the administration of the Victoria Police and ultimately recommended that Standish be replaced by a board of three commissioners.[23]

Yet the troubles in the force were not simply attributable to Standish. He was actually a man with considerable administrative acumen, and when he applied himself wholly to the task he proved a capable leader. He was, as one of his officers described him, 'a strange mixture of weakness and of strength'. When Standish assumed command of the force in 1858 it numbered 1260 man located at 194 stations. Government cutbacks required Standish to spread fewer men over a wider area, often without the capital to provide support facilities. Reductions in manpower were forced on Standish even while public requests for police service poured into his office unremittingly. To meet these conflicting demands, Standish adopted a policy of decentralization, opening sixty new police stations for what he saw as 'the greater protection of the country districts'. These stations were invariably small, often remote, and usually staffed by only one or two mounted constables. It was a scheme designed to placate a demanding public by the provision of a visible police presence in even the remotest corners of the colony, and it has endured to the present day, proving a boon to police–community relations in that the solitary constables have been readily accepted by small local communities.

In addition, Standish reorganized the Melbourne police district and in 1859 oversaw the erection of the first police station and barracks in Russell Street, enabling many unmarried policemen to move from small and inconvenient wooden houses into proper police barracks. A feature of the new Russell Street complex was the inclusion of a police library, in the hope that the promotion of harmless and constructive recreation, such as reading, would improve the behaviour and literacy of the man. In an effort to ease the financial burden of constables, and to properly assimilate the Melbourne police with those in country districts, Standish changed the police uniform. He introduced an open-necked tunic, discontinued the use of the military stock, and generally altered the uniform to render it more suited to the Victorian climate and conditions than was the previous 'inconvenient dress, copied. . . from that of the Metropolitan police in England'. The standardized appearance of police made them readily identifiable wherever they served. The constables, too, were appreciative of the new Chief Commissioner's efforts because they purchased uniforms with their own money and the standardization of dress meant that they were not required to buy new uniforms when transferring to and from Melbourne.

Standish was also quick to use new technology in the form of the electric telegraph and the railway, both of which greatly assisted the police. Messages could be sent without the despatch of route riders, and escorts of prisoners and valuables could be made by rail rather than by the more vulnerable mounted escort parties. Efficiency increased and police numbers could be reduced—although the technological advances did lessen police visibility, which was not necessarily a good thing. However, in his second annual report, Standish wrote:

> It would be wrong in me to pass over the subject of crime without expressing how much I appreciate not only the importance to the police of the lines of electric telegraph throughout the colony, but also the promptness and courtesy which the authorities of that department have uniformly shown in circulation of information respecting criminals.[24]

After the frenetic confusion of the gold-rush heyday that had confronted Sturt, Mitchell and MacMahon, Standish was operating in calmer times when things were acquiring an air of permanency. Decentralization of police to settled communities, new police barracks, railways, telegraphs and a new police uniform more suited to the Australian climate, all suggest that the force was at last developing a sense of stability and direction. The innovations made by Standish endured well into the twentieth century and, although they might now be regarded as unexceptional, they were considerable advances at the time.

Standish did more. He chided the Government over the futility of designating geographical areas as 'Police Districts', when those areas bore no relevance whatsoever to the police force or police duties, and he advocated that references to police districts be restricted to areas of relevance to police. He also called for a separation of police and judicial functions. In the days of Lonsdale and Sturt, the meshing of the judicial and law-enforcement arms of government had perhaps been necessary, but by the 1860s they had begun to run their separate courses, and Standish's efforts aided a desirable separation of powers.

Standish was very outspoken against extraneous duties. The precedent set by Lonsdale in appointing police to undertake non-police duties had been steadily built on throughout the 1840s and 1850s. By the time Standish took command of the force there were no fewer than two hundred police engaged as clerks of petty sessions, goldfields bailiffs, treasury guards, inspectors of distilleries, crown land rangers, inspectors of slaughteryards, searchers of customs, inspectors of weights and measures, registrars of births, deaths and marriages, curators of intestate estates, and court-house cleaners. Almost the entire force of mounted constables was employed at different times of the year in circulating agricultural statistics forms. Standish argued that the use of police in this way was a waste of time and money, and—as a sign of the improved status of constables—argued that the cleaning of courtrooms was demeaning work for police. Worse still, it diverted substantial numbers of police away from their primary duties, and the community suffered from a lack of proper police protection. The police were there; they were just not doing police work.

> There is a remarkable diversity of opinion on the part of officers of other departments as to the duties the police can be legitimately called upon to perform. Many officers of the civil service appear to regard the police in much the same capacity as a servant-of-all-work in a household . . . It is far from my intention to object to the police being made as useful as possible to the Government, provided their being so turned to account be not allowed to interfere with their efficiency as police constables, or to affect the discipline of the Force.

Standish also argued strongly that police in other countries were not bur-

HMCSS Victoria

dened with extraneous duties as they were in Victoria.[25] On that point Standish (and his successors) did not receive the support of other public service departments or a succession of governments. The 'servant-of-all-work' concept proved popular. A few of the more menial duties, such as court cleaning, were given up, but Standish's men remained saddled with most of the other non-police tasks for the duration of his commissionership.

One particular battle that Standish did win, however, was freeing the police force from the responsibility of commanding, funding and manning Victoria's 'navy', the steam sloop HMCSS *Victoria*. The ship's commander held the rank of superintendent, and all the crew, including cabin boys, were sworn and paid as constables after the original crew, comprised of merchant seamen, refused to put to sea in an emergency after 6.00 p.m. Standish, however, felt that an armed, seagoing vessel had no place in police work, and he described the position as 'singularly anomalous', 'altogether unconnected with police duties' and 'almost useless to the department'. His protests on the subject of the *Victoria* were so frequent and strong that the Government did in fact remove it from the control of the police and placed it with the defence forces. That government officials even considered placing a warship under nominal police command shows how uncertain they were about the role of police in the colony. Indeed, during the first decade of its existence, the Victoria Police Force had probably been unique in that constables had worked as policemen, firemen, sailors and soldiers.[26]

It was over this last role that Standish had his next parry with officialdom. He informed the Government that it was far from his wish to have the force engaged in unnecessary military parades, after a government defence commission suggested that 'the whole of the Metropolitan Police Force [should] be held in readiness to perform military service'. The concept was the antithesis of civil policing, and Standish was further aggravated by the claim that 'the police force are not generally so proficient in the use of the arms with which they are entrusted as they might be, and . . . are also deficient in their knowledge of drill'. Standish, himself once a professional soldier, reluctantly acquiesced in having his men drill for possible defence contingencies, but stressed before a Select Committee that displays of militarism should not be allowed to isolate the police from the community. He viewed the military character of the force as 'more in semblance than in reality', adding, 'I see no necessity, nor do I think it advisable, to drill them so much as soldiers'.

In arguing against using police for military purposes, Standish was only partly successful. After the 'lessons' of Ireland and Eureka there were still people who permitted, indeed desired, the police to assume a military character. It may have derived from xenophobia and fears of a foreign invasion, or it might have been due to a desire of the propertied classes to have an armed body ready for the suppression of rebellion, but colonial defence was the reason most often cited for attaching a military character to the police, even though an armed and drilled militia outnumbered them and was always available. In any event the defence mania of the 1860s held sway over Standish's desire for a proper civil police force, and he was compelled to despatch drill instructors throughout the colony to prepare his men to act as soldiers.[27]

So Standish displayed considerable insight and administrative skill, yet his reform efforts were only partly accomplished, and even his successes were obscured by his far more public hedonistic pursuits, his favouritism and abuse of power. He was the first Chief Commissioner to publish annual reports and criminal statistics, but it was his other antics that captured the public imagination and limelight. He was also faced with trouble from some of his own men and politicians who sought to undermine him. During the early 1860s things were not going altogether well for Standish or his force, and, in the parlance of the beat constables of the period, all was 'not on the square'.

A Union of Sentiment

> ... during heat and cold, summer and winter, day or night, week day or Sunday, without intermission or holiday, the police constable has to discharge his long and wearisome duties of twelve hours, with judgement, integrity and perfect command of temper.
>
> —'A Melbourne Constable'[28]

On a number of issues Standish's men were restless and increasingly making their grievances public. Their most general complaint was about their pay and ancillary benefits. It was an issue on which Standish supported his men in principle but found himself locked into difficulties. On one side was a government, with little respect for the police, proposing to cut the money spent on the force; on the other side was a body of men becoming increasingly aware of the essential role they played in society.

Bureaucracy, too, was stabilizing in Victoria, and the urgency attaching to decisions in the gold era was giving way to ponderous change. It showed up in the police force, but was generally evident in all areas of the government and civil service. The Government, seeking to reduce expenditure, felt that in calmer times this could be partly effected by a reduction in the numbers of police and in police wages. Fewer but more efficient police, aided by the electric telegraph and railway, were able to serve a gradually settling population, and Standish did reduce police strength through annual wastage. MacMahon had at times commanded a force of more than 1700 men, and worked with a police to population ratio in the region of 1:150. By 1861 Standish headed a force closer to 1200 men, and a police to population ratio of 1:450. Although there was

Officers of the Victoria Police Force in 1861

some concern that the force was 'not numerically equal to the demands made upon it', there was a wide agreement among the general public and even the police themselves that reductions in the police numbers were desirable.[29]

It was police wage-cuts that aroused police ire. A Civil Service Commission recommended to the Government that increased reductions in the annual vote for police could be made by 'adopting the amended scale of pay both for officers and men on the occurrence of any vacancy, either in promotion or a fresh entry to the force'. The amended scale of pay had been devised by the Commission, and was based upon the belief that the police force bore 'a great resemblance' to a military regiment. Consequently the commissioners proposed prospective reductions in police pay, for all ranks, based upon army pay. Standish described the parallel as incomplete and anomalous, informing the Government that he considered it 'unadvisable' to reduce salaries. His warning went unheeded. Not only were prospective salary reductions made, but in 1861 the Government reduced the existing pay of all constables by 20 per cent, from ten to eight shillings a day. This was soon followed by a further reduction to 7s 6d. The reductions included the abandonment of the system instituted in 1855 whereby police were paid sixpence a day from the Police Reward Fund as good conduct pay. Standish objected that the pay of constables was only enough to live on, and that an amount less than eight shillings was 'just sufficient to enable them to live from hand to mouth'. Even so, Standish miscalculated the response of his men to wage cuts when he reported that he did not anticipate much trouble.[30]

Upon the implementation of the cuts in 1862, however, he was confronted with the first general and organized industrial action taken by police in Victoria's history. In an action variously described as a combination, a strike, an action wanting in principle, and a union of sentiment, the men of the force rallied together to oppose the pay cuts. A petition was circulated throughout the force and submitted through the Chief Commissioner to the Government. This was then followed by the refusal of more than a quarter of the men to accept their reduced pay. In a concerted drive for solidarity, funds were collected to pay for telegrams sent about the colony urging men 'to remain firm'. These efforts did not go astray and, at country centres as well as in Melbourne, the public witnessed the spectacle of police at their monthly pay parades refusing to accept their money. Although all police continued to work, some without being paid for three months, the *Age* described their actions as a strike 'emulous of the doings of trades unions'. Other sections of the public press were more tolerant, and the *Ovens and Murray Advertiser* lamented the plight of the 'Blues', describing them as being poverty-stricken and thrown entirely on their own resources.[31]

The public debate over the police pay reductions and the resultant industrial action taken by the police devolved to a large extent upon the status and role of police constables in Victorian society. No one, least of all the constables themselves, was quite sure where police constables fitted into the salary and social scales. Their socio-economic status was uncertain, and was to remain so for many years. Consequently, the public debate over their worth and status was generally couched in clichés or emotive language. Some people, such as Standish and 'A Melbourne

Constable', endeavoured to explain in more rational terms that policing was a unique essential service that could no longer be equated with day labouring on the roads. Standish spoke of the dangers and violence facing police, together with the constant exposure to the elements, night work and disease. Others argued that constables worked twelve hours a day, seven days a week, and were granted only three days paid leave of absence. If they worked overtime—for example, when attending court for arrests made on night shift—they were not paid extra money or granted time off, conditions that contrasted sharply with most other occupations, where money was paid for extra work and some time off was granted on Sunday.

The 7s 6d a day paid to police was precisely the wage of railway labourers and, notwithstanding such inequities, even this amount was regarded by some politicians as too much. The Catholic spokesman, John O'Shanassy, was of the view that if constables could refuse 7s 6d a day 'they were not in want of money', John Woods, MLA for Crowlands and former digger, who had 'first "mounted the stump" at the Goulburn diggings to lead passive resistance to the licence fee', expressed the opinion that one ordinary labourer or ploughman, paid six shillings a day, was 'of more value to society than two policemen'. Fortunately for the police, people like Woods expressed a minority view and it was generally agreed that constables should be paid more than a private in the army, and more than ordinary labourers.[32]

But how much more than an ordinary labourer was a constable worth? O'Shanassy fuelled the debate when he insisted that police could never be placed on an equal footing with other civil servants. Relatively junior clerks in the civil service were paid more than police constables, and O'Shanassy approved of that because civil servants were 'working in an office and devoting their lives to a higher pursuit'. When the dangers of police work were put to O'Shanassy as being worthy of special consideration, he rejected the suggestion on the grounds that police were no more liable to accidents in the discharge of their duties than other civil servants. Yet a chart, prepared by the Police Medical Officer before O'Shanassy made his statements, listed 356 admissions to the police hospital in two years, including more than sixty men suffering from gun-shot wounds, broken bones, lacerations and contusions. Eventually it was agreed that a constable's pay 'should be set at between that of a labourer and a mechanic'. After almost thirty years, Victorian police constables had marginally improved their socio-economic status to an indeterminate level between unskilled labourers and tradesmen.[33]

The principal factor detracting from any immediate elevation in the status of police was a lack of special skills. Almost any literate, able-bodied, adult male could gain admission to the force and commence police duties with only the most rudimentary training. The unique conditions of police service placed it above ordinary labouring, but the lack of special training

left it below skilled trades, and this was the most obvious retardant of increased status during the nineteenth century. As head of the force for over two decades, Standish must bear a great share of the responsibility. It was his emphatic belief that formal training for police was a waste of time. Classes, lectures and instruction in criminal detection were of no value: 'It is good in theory, but in theory only'. Although pressed to institute training for police and to correlate police patrols with crime patterns, Standish held steadfastly to the dictum that 'no lectures on police duty could give him half the experience which he will obtain by having to perform the duty himself'. So his policemen went on being initiated by on-the-job trial and error, with little hope of attaining artisan status.[34]

The industrial dispute over police wages ended without the police achieving restoration of the original pay scales. All was not lost, however, as none of the police who took part in the dispute were disciplined, and in the police climate of the 1860s this of itself was a milestone. Standish, too, survived the pay reduction controversy with his credibility largely intact, but he was confronted soon afterwards by two further disputes spawned by the preparation of petitions. Quick to see the value of publicity gained by the pay action, forty constables combined to demand the right to wear beards. This was not successful, but was an important indicator of the growing 'union of sentiment' within the force. Constables were not frightened to take collective action in the expression of grievances. The beard matter had barely been dealt with when a third petition, signed by 117 men, was forwarded direct to the Chief Secretary. This action, mooted by Sergeants William Kelly and James Unsworth Browne, was an open attack upon Standish's administration of the force. Because of the document's nature it was not sent through Standish, and the Chief Secretary, when acknowledging its receipt, refused to reveal its contents. In a minute dated 13 March 1863 O'Shanassy wrote:

> their first duty, if they have complaints to make, is to send them through the Chief Commissioner of Police, who will thus have an opportunity of stating his views upon them before I receive them . . . but the course of action adopted is not to be repeated.

O'Shanassy was the man who had forced MacMahon from the police force and appointed Standish in his stead. In refusing to accept the complaint against Standish he again proved a friend to him; the petition was never returned to its signatories, the allegations contained in it were never investigated by O'Shanassy, and Sergeants Kelly and Browne were dismissed from the Force for 'exciting a conspiracy against their Chief

Mounted Police in Bush Dress in 1861

Commissioner'. It is difficult to see how two signatories of a document containing 117 signatures and published in the daily press could be held solely liable, but that was the way of things; for the police force, justice was rough. Although 440 residents of Richmond appealed to the Government to reinstate Browne and Kelly, their dismissals were not reversed.

But all was not in vain. A Select Committee investigated the Kelly and Browne case and the allegations against Standish, and after considerable deliberation reported:

> that the dismissal of these men, accompanied as it was, with every possible ignominy, was, under the circumstances, a harsh expedient . . . [and the action of the Chief Commissioner] was highly injudicious, and calculated to create well-founded suspicion and discontent.

Additionally, the Committee found that the members of the police force would be better satisfied if Standish were replaced by a Board of three commissioners. These were strong words from a government board about the colony's leading policeman, yet they were ignored by the Chief Secretary. Standish kept his position, and Browne and Kelly were not reinstated or compensated.[35]

The bland indifference was perhaps not surprising, in view of the way the Chief Secretary had involved himself with Standish in running the police force. Whereas MacMahon had resigned over ministerial interference with the internal arrangements of the force, Standish became a reluctant but active party to similar meddling. Collusion between Standish and O'Shanassy as Catholics involved the compilation of a special list of candidates for the police force. By using it, O'Shanassy and Standish circumvented the normal recruiting procedures and were able to give favoured candidates almost instant entry into the force. Standish did not particularly like the special list, but lacked sufficient principle to resign or take a stand over it. So he maintained two lists of applicants, a general list containing the names of more than seven hundred men who waited, on average, fifteen months for a place in the force, and a special list of men who received almost immediate appointment, most of them being Catholics who had served with the Irish Constabulary. Some men on the general list never gained a place with the police, and for a time its use was suspended because O'Shanassy's private selections filled all vacancies occurring within the force. In 1862 almost half the candidates who enlisted were special appointments. When the special list was instituted by O'Shanassy, he dismissed Standish's remonstrances on the grounds that the Constitution Act gave him the right to personally appoint constables. This was notwithstanding that the Constitution Act

The general uniform of the Victoria Police in 1861

had been in existence for six years but the 'power' to appoint constables had never previously been exercised by O'Shanassy or his predecessors in the office of Chief Secretary. The 1863 Select Committee recommended that the special list appointments cease, and it further observed that:

> a mode of appointment, inconsistent with that previously adopted and generally known, is improper and inexpedient, calculated to affect injuriously the management and efficiency of the Force, and to inflict injustice on those persons whose names were on the general list.[36]

The scandal over the politically-dictated special list of police candidates was yet another sorry example of politicians improperly intervening in the internal management of the police force. Mitchell had wrested himself away from it, MacMahon resigned over it and Standish succumbed to it. An unfortunate side-effect of O'Shanassy's action was that it further lowered the tone of the force and injected an element of sectarianism into the controversy. Worse still, he gave his personal recommendation and patronage to some candidates who could not read or write, or who for other reasons were entirely unsuited to the police force. It could never be said that special list candidates were chosen for the betterment of the force. Indeed, Superintendent Power Le Poer Bookey, who was responsible for examining candidates wanting to join the force, expressed the opinion that the ex-members of the Irish Constabulary were 'not nearly so sharp as they ought to be'. Bookey preferred to recruit raw hands who had not previously served as police because it was possible to enlist more intelligent men. He found that, contrary to popular belief, the Irishmen so favoured by O'Shanassy were not overly adept or experienced at police work, and were not entirely suited to Victorian conditions due to 'the quiet life they live in the small towns in Ireland'.

Notwithstanding Bookey's sentiments, the force under Standish did comprise a very large majority of men who had served with the Irish Constabulary. This Irish dominance in the lower ranks dated from the 1850s and under MacMahon's commissionership an effort was made to 'mix the nationalities of the men' by occasionally favouring former 'members of the English and Scotch police'. During debates over the land question it was proposed to make grants of land to police who had served the colony well over a number of years. The motion was defeated, and among the many reasons given in parliament for rejecting the scheme was one bold claim that 'ninety-nine per cent of the police are Irish'.[37]

So, along with all his other problems, Standish was confronted with criticism—partly justified, partly prejudiced—because of his force's high proportion of Irishmen. Yet Standish withstood the storm. He resisted all efforts to have him replaced by a Board of three commissioners, and gradually the criticisms and controversies surrounding his administration faded. At the same time, the stalwarts who had been with the force since the early days passed from the scene. Not all these men had been admirers of Standish, but their breadth of experience served to keep some things 'on the square', and now Standish lost them. Evelyn Sturt became a full-time magistrate, Robert O'Hara Burke died at Cooper's Creek, Samuel Freeman committed suicide, William Dana died in 1866, Inspecting-Superintendent P. H. Smith died in 1868 and William Mair went on half-pay. The cadre of pioneer police, some of whom had been in the colony since the 1840s, was no longer there. For all the vagaries in their behaviour, they were in the vanguard of police reform in Australia, and had experienced colonization, separation, police amalgamation, the gold rushes, Eureka and much else beside. They had a different spirit from that exhibited by a generation of police who took industrial action, and without them Standish found in the turbulent times that lay ahead his greatest test and ultimate downfall.[38]

Power and Ambivalence

> The Chief Commissioner would here impress upon all members of the police force, that they belong, not to a military, but to a civil Force, and that he altogether discountenances all unnecessary military parade and show . . .
>
> (1856 *Police Regulations*, p. 25)

The turbulence that engulfed Standish in the 1870s was far from all his own doing. It began in 1870 when the English government withdrew the Imperial troops stationed in Victoria who, since the foundation of the colony, had provided the bulk of its defences. This ended on 21 August 1870, when troops of the Second Battalion (Royal Irish) departed, leaving the colony's defences to a volunteer force and the Victoria Police.[39] Although the history of the police force to that time had been marked by periods of militarism and the perennial military versus civil policing debate, the Police Regulations of 1856 strictly distinguished police from soldiers, but that meant nothing to a government faced with the problem of mounting its own defences. Within a short time, civil policing precepts were forgotten and aspiring police recruits manned muzzle-loading cannons and wore busbies.

The principal architect of this scheme was former Chief Commissioner of Police, Captain Charles MacMahon, MLA for West Melbourne. MacMahon's administration of the police force had been criticized for excessive militarism, and he had resigned after political interference with his force, but, as a politician himself, he persisted with his tendency to militarize the police, subjecting Standish to the sort of political meddling he had resented. Before the withdrawal of Imperial troops, Colonel W. A. D. Anderson, commandant of naval and military forces in the colony, proposed that, in the event of the withdrawal of the Imperial garrison, the Government raise a regular force of 120 soldiers and that a Militia Act be passed empowering the Governor-in-Council to form a militia of ten thousand volunteers and balloted men. Anderson's plan, which did not involve the police at all in the colony's proposed defences, was not adopted, but an alternative plan, with the police force as its corner-stone, was keenly touted by Captain MacMahon and implemented in September 1870. A permanent artillery corps, commanded by Captain James A. Stubbs, was formed as the nucleus of Victoria's defence force. This corps of paid soldiers—Stubbs's Bulldogs—was comprised of two categories of men: Class A—a company of 'picked men', selected on account of their efficiency and good conduct, who had been trained as artillerymen or engineers in the British army or navy; and Class B—a subsidiary body of about eighty men intended to be single, aged under thirty, of good character and qualified to be members of the police force.[40] Recruitment into the police force was made conditional upon previous service with this artillery corps, and the police force itself was envisaged as a standing army for deployment in case of invasion or war. With these changes, MacMahon succeeded in giving the police force a military character and role unprecedented in its history.[41]

Before September 1870 entry into the police force was open to married and single men, aged up to 45 years, and of any previous occupation. Provided such men furnished suitable references and passed basic literacy and medical tests, they were listed for a place in the force when vacancies occurred. Upon joining the force these men were paid a minimum wage of 6s 6d a day and set to work as uniformed police. A number of single men were required to live in police barracks, but most men lived in the community with their families. With the formation of 'Stubbs's Bulldogs' much was changed, and only single men aged under thirty who were serving in the artillery corps were eligible to fill vacancies in the police force. The artillerymen were paid only two shillings a day and required to live in military barracks for up to three years. During their time with the military they wore a blue army uniform with scarlet facings and busby, and underwent infantry and artillery drill, overhauled and cleaned stores and magazines and performed general garrison duties.[42]

The artillery corps was described as 'a nursery for the police', but was nothing of the sort. The promise of a place with the police or penal department was used as a lure to induce men to endure colonial military life for two shillings a day. It was readily conceded that the MacMahon scheme benefited the artillery corps, but no such advantages followed for police recruiting. When first formed, Stubbs's Bulldogs absorbed all those men on the police waiting list who were prepared to join. The prospect of army life did not, however, appeal to a large number of them and thirty-three qualified police candidates did not join the artillery corps—and how

The Victorian Permanent Artillery —
'gateway to the police force for a decade'

many other good men were lost to the police force because of the artillery scheme? On the face of it, a type of man similar to those who joined before 1870 continued to enter the force via the artillery corps, but many of them 'contracted objectionable habits' in the corps due to 'association with low characters and women of abandoned morals', or perhaps because of inherently weak characters. Barrack life may itself have ruined many a potentially good police recruit, or perhaps it only attracted men of lower moral tone. It was not good for the police image, and Standish must have smarted when parliamentarians decried the corps as a 'fresh refuge for the destitute—for vagrants and able-bodied spongers' and as 'a band of mercenaries'. These were savage criticisms of the gateway to the police force for a decade.[43]

Although Standish warned that it was a bad mistake, politicians and officials ploughed ahead with the MacMahon scheme that planned a police force in which all constables had served in the artillery corps and were regularly drilled for army duties, so that 'the police should be withdrawn in case of invasion or war, and their places supplied by special constables, selected from the ratepayers'. No invasion or war came, so the police force was not mobilized as an army, and extensive military drill and manoeuvres were not practised, which helped to limit the military aspect of the force, but did not entirely remove it. Initially the colony's newspapers embraced the idea, but qualms emerged as the decade wore on. This was particularly evident during the Kelly era when it appeared that the 'standing army'—that despatched an artillery cannon for use at the Glenrowan siege—could not capture four bushrangers, and policemen-soldiers were found deficient in bushcraft and the use of firearms, and ill-trained to act as a disciplined body in the field.[44]

Well before the Kelly outbreak, however, the parliament itself displayed a measure of ambivalence toward the police force generally and its military role in particular. During 1873 two spirited debates took place in the Legislative Assembly about the quality of the colony's police and the benefits that should be granted to them for their service. The principal issues debated were a proposal to extend manhood suffrage to the police, and the restoration of a comprehensive police superannuation scheme.

During the Superannuation debates plaudits for the force flowed freely:

> a body almost unrivalled in efficiency—a body of which the country had reason to be proud . . .

> the police form the most important item of the civil service of the colony . . .

> We ought, as colony, to be proud of our police . . .

> The police force is generally acknowledged to be of very creditable character . . .

> If we want to compare the Victorian police with the English police, I do not think the former will shrink from the test . . .

Such parliamentary rhetoric was good for force morale and actually put money in the pockets of policemen. The 1873 Police Regulation Statute established a generous police superannuation scheme to replace the one abandoned in 1854. Members of the force were provided for in case of age retirement, infirmity, death or bodily injury. The police gained added occupational security in the form of both money and esteem, clearly having travelled a fair way along the road to public acceptance. When the original pension scheme had been abandoned, citizens were clamouring to import police from the United Kingdom, while sections of the local force were denounced and ridiculed as being inefficient, drunken and corrupt. They were seen to have improved from that time, but the situation was far from ideal.[45]

Parliamentary trust in the police was not as universal and steadfast as the glowing praise and superannuation scheme suggest. Ambivalence marked the debates whenever the subject of suffrage for the police was raised. In the end the vote was 29 to 17 against granting policemen this right. Discussion on the subject credited the police with considerable power—to persuade, dissuade, coerce and overthrow governments. Perhaps more than anything else, the acknowledgement by parliament of the potential political power of the police denoted that the force was no longer seen as a motley parody of Falstaff's troop, but as a centrally-controlled and armed body of men, with the means to usurp the Government. It was all highly improbable, yet some in power feared the outcome if police were given the vote and thereby encouraged to become actively involved in partisan politics. The Government opposed enfranchising the police, so the electoral issue debates were steeped in distrust of the police and their potential power:

> it was desirable not only for a military force but also for a police force to be restrained from any participation, or any active exhibition of sympathy, in the proceedings of an election . . .

> if it should unfortunately happen, at a time when party feeling ran high, that these men, by having the power to vote, had become partisans, what would be the consequence?

> imagine honorable members having to touch their hats to policemen for their votes . . .

> In France also, the effect of the military and the gendarmerie having votes was to overthrow the late Government and produce most disastrous results.

This attitude was obviously due in part to the force's link with the army.[46]

Opposition to extending manhood suffrage to the police was based on a perceived potential abuse of power rather than evidence of a propensity on the part of Victorian police to engage in insurrection. It is undeniable that the police were involved in politics, and they were known to canvass votes, participate in political meetings, petition members of parliament and organize as a lobby group. Their activity in such areas was confined to legal and democratic means, and those with more direct political ambitions resigned to pursue them; the President of the Legislative Council and the Speaker in the Legislative Assembly were both former Chief Commissioners. For serving police the absence of the right to vote did not diminish their level of political interest but channelled it into activities that were not dependent upon the ballot box. Indeed, the Civil Service Royal Commission conducted from 1870 to 1873 provided ample evidence of the way in which police, denied a vote at elections, were willing and able to utilize alternative public forums. Members of the police force and penal service submitted half of the eight hundred submissions accepted by the Commission and, in addition, the police elected delegates to give oral evidence on behalf of different ranks and police districts. It was one time when relatively junior policemen were given an opportunity to suggest changes and a number of their ideas, combined with those of other officials and politicians, were adopted by governments during the next twenty years: a police superannuation scheme, a new manual of police regulations, a non-monetary merit award, promotion examinations and changes to police procedures and uniforms.[47] So it cannot be denied that many of the police were possessed of political acumen and interest, and the obvious concern felt by a number of politicians seems partly justified in the light of police immunity from dismissal during the drastic civil service cutbacks of Black Wednesday.[48] It is arguable, however, that the withholding of the vote to police heightened their interest in politics and improved their organizational skills. Denied a vote and access to local members of parliament, the police became skilled in exploiting alternative political avenues and, compared with the enfranchised sections of the civil service, were an organized and politically active unit.

The ambivalence that marked the police suffrage and superannuation debates reflected certain realities, and soon after the passing of the Police Regulation Statute the police acted in a manner that heightened parliamentary fears. In December 1873 armed police, acting without precedent or specific government approval, intervened in an industrial dispute to assist in strike breaking. In September, miners at the Lothair Mine, Clunes, had gone on strike for improved wages and working conditions. All work at the mine stopped for fourteen weeks and the mine directors took action to break the strike by introducing Chinese labour. On 9 December 1873 five coaches laden with Chinese miners travelled from Ballarat to Clunes with an escort of sixteen armed police. Strike sympathizers warned Clunes workers of the approaching convoy, which was met outside Clunes by two thousand protesters who had erected barricades and armed themselves with brickbats. The police, under Sergeant J. N. Larner, were not to be denied their mission and, with guns drawn, tried to breach the blockade. It was a brave but questionable action. The police did not fire their guns nor did they break through the mob. Instead, many of the Chinese strike-breakers and a number of policemen were assaulted and the convoy returned to Ballarat bloodied and beaten. No lives were lost in the affray but the violent spectacle caused the Lothair Mine directors to relent. Once the Chinese strike-breakers had left the town, the miners did not object to the presence of police. A police guard was mounted over the mine to prevent vandalism and the mine directors were given police protection. An uneasy calm settled over Clunes, but the Chinese did not return and the dispute was eventually resolved. Those men regarded by the police as the ringleaders of the riot were summoned to Clunes Court and four of them were fined £5 each. It was the first time in the history of Victoria that armed police intervened in an industrial dispute. In a scathing editorial, the *Age* declared that 'the standing army of the colony, were wrongfully employed in furnishing aid to the one set of disputants against the other'.

The Chief Secretary, J. G. Francis, was a merchant and a reformist, yet opposed to radical causes and agitation. Even so, he raised his voice against the police action, describing it as an inexpedient course that went against government policy. He wrote to the Chief Commissioner that he knew 'no precedent for this course, whereby a lot of foreigners are escorted by the police into a place of excitement, occasioned by a dispute between employer and employed as to rate of wages . . .' The decision to deploy police in breaking a strike was made by Standish personally, after consultation with the mine directors, and he later described Francis as a 'cowardly low-bred cur'. Standish was not a newcomer to industrial disputes over wages and conditions, as his own men had first organized and taken their grievances into the public arena in 1860, but the Lothair Mine case posed special problems for him in that he was bound to consider the rights of the mine directors and Chinese as well as the strikers. It was generally agreed that, had the police not supported the employers, there would have been no attempt to break the strike by using Chinese labour. Police involvement in the dispute contributed to the overnight transformation of a fourteen-week passive protest into a riot. Standish's decision was not so much indefensible as imprudent, and he defended his actions on the grounds that his object 'was not to support one sector of the community against another but simply to preserve the peace'. His remonstrations had a hollow ring when it was disclosed that the police originally intended to smuggle the strike-breakers into Clunes at 3.00 a.m., under cover of darkness, and that after the initial confrontation Standish wanted to disarm members of the volunteer military force in Clunes and move one hundred police into the town. Amid shades of Eureka, the Chief Secretary urged conciliation, and the dispute ended without further serious violence. The police had by then been exposed as willing to intervene in an industrial dispute, and the *Age* reminded the public that Standish's men were not just police but also the colony's standing army.[49]

The furore over the Clunes Riot, like the artillery corps inquiry and franchise debates, became a questioning of the police role and police power. The force had improved considerably from the time of MacMahon and the troubles of the gold years, but its role was still unclear, and neither the Government nor the Chief Commissioner knew how to properly harness the force's potential. The armed force of 1100 men showed a great deal of promise, but parliamentary ambivalence highlighted the fact that it was a promise unfulfilled.

3

Erinmen, Wren and O'Callaghan's Men

Late in the nineteenth century and early in the twentieth there was a marked influence of Irishmen and their descendants on the Victoria Police Force. The police were very often Irish, and so were those opposed to the police, including Ned Kelly and John Wren, whose illegal activities resulted in Royal Commissions that exposed the force and its operations to searching public scrutiny, and ultimately produced important changes in police procedures, personnel and conditions of service.

One milestone passed in this era was the appointment of serving members to the top police post, and the image of the force was also enhanced by an unusual public interest in the activities of police personalities, such as David O'Donnell, John Christie and Thomas Waldron, who became household names. However, the police were at times subjected to searing criticism and were troubled by internal industrial disputes and confrontations between policemen, trade unionists and unemployed people. Under Chomley and O'Callaghan, police administration was generally conservative—often reactionary—and the force failed to keep pace with Victorians' changing values, attitudes, expectations and technology.

The Irish Influence

Ned Kelly had an emotional but uncompromising view of those who hunted him. The police were:

> a parcel of big ugly fat-necked wombat headed big bellied magpie legged narrow hipped splay-footed sons of Irish Bailiffs or English landlords which is better known as officers of Justice or Victorian Police . . .[1]

Kelly was born in Australia and never set foot in Ireland but his ancestry produced in him a sense of Irish heritage and prompted his vilification of Irish police in Australia as men who betrayed their ancestors and religion. Kelly criticized the police often and contrasted 'cowardly' Irishmen, who became police, with the 'bold and blooming' Irishmen, who died bravely in chains. Although Kelly was one of the few people to acknowledge publicly the role of Irish police in Victoria, his general view of the Irish was romanticized and biased. Even he probably underestimated the extent to which Irishmen dominated the police force, and certainly he overstated the degree to which the Irish were heroic rebels fighting for social justice.

Long after Kelly, writers have persisted with the romanticized depiction of Irishmen in Australia as underdogs championing the cause of the underdog. Works such as *The Irish in Australia, Australia's Debt to Irish Nation-Builders,* and *The Irish at Eureka* revere Irish-Australians and perpetuate the image of them as poor, honest and brave men, moved to action by a sense of justice and social inequality. References to Irish police are few, and are often anecdotes about the likes of the genial Sergeant Dalton, 'a kindly, good natured giant' from Kilkenny, whom some credit with coining the word 'larrikin'. The importance of Irish police throughout the nineteenth century sits poorly with any narrow view of the Irish as natural rebels, yet it has not found much place in Irish-Australian literature or mythology.[2] That pro-Irish publications and the writings of Ned Kelly have taken this course is understandable, if inaccurate. However, at least one contemporary researcher with pretensions to greater accuracy promotes this Irish-Australian mythology. Neil Coughlan claims that the 'generally high crime rate' of the Irish-born in Victoria

> bespoke a group alienated from the colony's social structure (by lower income, education and social standing, if nothing else) and perhaps from its British system of law, and concepts of rights and property . . . young, unsettled, poorly educated and employed, and in general, comparatively untouched by any prevailing ethic of social responsibility and propriety.

Places mentioned in Chapter 3

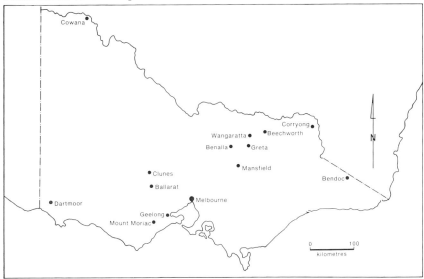

VICTORIA POLICE.

Register No. *1114.*

Candidate *(name in full)* *Michael Kennedy*

place of birth *Ireland, Parish of Moyne* , date of birth *10th June 1847* ,

height *5* feet *9¼* inches, eyes *blue* , hair *brown* , complexion *fresh* , trade *none* , religion *Roman Catholic* ,

general appearance *smart* , appointed on the *nineteenth* day of *August* 1874.

The rate of pay of a Constable is _____ per day, exclusive of allowances, as per Appropriation Act. Three months' notice of resignation will be required.

EXAMINATION OF A CANDIDATE FOR THE SITUATION OF POLICE CONSTABLE.

Questions. **Answers.**

Have you ever served in the Victorian Police Force? ....

Have you ever been in any Police or Public Service? If so, in what? ....

For what time? ....

When discharged, and why? ....

By whom last employed, and where? ....

By whom recommended? ....

Are you married or single? .... *single*

Do you belong to any Secret Society? If so, what? .... *No*

Are you fully aware of the provisions of the Police Act? .... *Yes*

Signature *(at length)* *Michael Kennedy*

OATH.

I, *Michael Kennedy* , do swear that I will well and truly serve our Sovereign Lady the Queen, as a member of the Police Force of Victoria, in such capacity as I may be hereafter appointed, promoted, or reduced to, without favor or affection, malice or illwill, for the period of *twelve calendar months* from this date, and until I am legally discharged; that I will see and cause Her Majesty's peace to be kept and preserved, and that I will prevent to the best of my power all offences against the same; and that while I shall continue to be a member of the Police Force of Victoria I will to the best of my skill and knowledge discharge all the duties legally imposed upon me faithfully and according to law. SO HELP ME GOD.

Signature *(ordinary)* *Michael Kennedy*

Sworn before me at *Beechworth* on this *tenth* day of *January* 1874.

Alfred Wyatt J.P.

While this view undoubtedly contains elements of truth, it panders to the myth-makers and ignores the facts that, during the period studied, a former Chief Commissioner of Police, Charles MacMahon, was Irish, as were the vast majority of officers and sub-officers in the police force, and three out of every four Victorian attorneys-general and solicitors-general were Irish-born. Recent literature perpetuates one-sided views such as Coughlan's, without qualification and balance. Niall Brennan is one who propounds the Coughlan hypothesis of Irish-Australian outlawry and cites as 'evidence' the fact that a disproportionate number of Irish-born were gaoled in Victoria in 1870. In fact, the proportion of Irishmen taken into custody during 1870 was much less than their proportion of the police force. Irish males taken into custody numbered 6352 (33 per cent) of a total 19 525 males. Irish police numbered 867 (82 per cent) of a total police force of 1060.[3]

Few—if any—authors, whether writing of the Irish- Australian tradition, bushranging or the police, seem to have been aware of the *pervasive* influence of Irishmen in the Victoria Police Force. It is misleading to go only as far as Garry Disher, who wrote that 'The police were a mixture of native-born and immigrant men, many of them Irish'. The police were overwhelmingly Irish, although even accomplished historians like John McQuilton seem not to have realized the full extent of the Irish domination. He wrote: 'The officers had been drawn from outside the colony, some having served with the notorious Irish Constabulary. None were native-born. But the rank and file did include the native-born and hostility developed between the native and the immigrant'. Certainly, much of this inaccuracy is due to the fact that precise figures have not previously been collated. However, the public statements of senior police and John Woods, MLA, early in the 1860s, that the force was being over-run with Irishmen, might have alerted people to the fact that the Irish police presence was more than fairly common. The real situation was closer to being an Irish invasion. Nor was Victoria unique. The prominence of Irish policemen in Western Australia prompted the *T'othersider* to offer this definition: 'A Policeman: A man with a uniform, a brogue and a big free thirst'. Statistically, the thirst is unproven, but there are figures to demonstrate how commonly a police uniform and a brogue were combined. In December 1873 a new Police Regulation Act became law in Victoria, necessitating the re-swearing of all the police. The ceremonies were held during January 1874 and all 1060 police were required to state their place of birth (as well as previous occupation, and religion, and to declare membership of any secret society).[4]

The Oath Sheet of Senior Constable Michael Kennedy,
who was later murdered by Ned Kelly at Stringybark Creek

81

Table 2 shows clearly that the force was not a representative mixture of Australians and immigrants, but was overwhelmingly dominated by Irishmen, whose numbers in the police were at a level significantly—and quite astonishingly—disproportionate to their percentage of the Victorian population. Of all male ethnic groups, Irishmen formed the only group statistically over-represented in the police. By contrast, Australian-born males in the colony numbered more than 170 000—or almost half all the males—and yet only thirty of them were in the police force. Although a high percentage of Irishmen has been found in other police forces, none has approximated the level of Irish domination evident in Victoria in the 1870s. Researchers looking at the New South Wales and Western Australian police have discovered significantly high levels of Irish membership, but the respective percentages of approximately 60 and 30 per cent are well short of the Victorian figure of 82 per cent.[5]

TABLE 2

The ethnic composition of Victoria Police Force in January 1874, compared with estimated percentage of male ethnic groups in total Victoria population

Birthplace	Absolute Frequency	Percentage	% Male* Population
Ireland	867	82	12
England	106	10	24
Scotland	38	3.5	8
Australia	30	3	45
Other†	19	1.5	11
	1060	100	100

* The percentage of males in the population is an estimation based upon figures published in the 1871 Census of Victoria.

† Other includes 'At Sea', Canada, Cape of Good Hope, China, East and West Indies, France, Guernsey, Holstein and Mauritius.

Irish police also figured in a large number of overseas forces in Canada, England, Scotland and the United States, and enlisted in the British Colonial Police Forces in Africa, Asia, Palestine and the Caribbean. In most of these forces the Irish presence was representative rather than dominant. Although it was sometimes the latter, rarely was the enlistment rate anything like 82 per cent. The proportion of Irishmen in the Victoria Police Force put it into a class with police forces in New York city and New England, where their domination by Irishmen is legendary.

Irish police historian Seamus Breathnach has considered the role of Irishmen in foreign police forces (not including Australia) and suggests that the Irish have had a particular interest in 'policemanship' and that, like Irish militarists, *émigré* Irish police extend over time and territory from eighteenth-century France to twentieth-century America. Although the work of Breathnach and others shows that Irish domination

*The Royal Irish Constabulary: a model and a source
of recruits for the Victoria Police Force*

TABLE 3

Religion and previous occupation of Irish-born members of the Victoria Police Force, January 1874

	Former Member RIC	Labourer	Other Police	Military	Trade	Mining/ Fishing	Farming	Sales/ Service	Other	Not Given	Total
Catholic	267	56	22	14	19	9	42	23	5	99	556
Protestant	130	25	18	10	12	4	31	18	6	57	311
Cum. Freq.	397	81	40	24	31	13	73	41	11	156	867
%	(46%)	(9%)	(5%)	(3%)	(4%)	(1%)	(8%)	(5%)	(1%)	(18%)	(100%)

Source: Victoria Police Archives. Oath Sheets: 1874 Re-sworn Series

of a police force was not unique to Victoria, no study so far has successfully explained what attracted Irishmen to police work, or shown what influence they had upon the forces they joined.[6]

In the case of Victoria a partial explanation is found in an analysis of the occupational backgrounds of the Irishmen who joined the force. Table 3 shows that more than half of the Irish members of the Victoria Police in 1874 had previously worked in other police forces, and that 46 per cent of all Irishmen in the force were former members of the Royal Irish Constabulary (RIC). By any standards, these figures are significant, although it still remains difficult to say precisely what attracted such large numbers to Victoria. Although Irish-born men were prominent in Victorian politics, Chief Commissioner Standish was a leading member of the Freemasons and an Englishman. In the 1850s efforts were made by a committee of colonists from Victoria to recruit police from Ireland, but the attempt failed, and although O'Shanassy later displayed favouritism in recruiting Irish-Catholics, that was stopped in 1863 after a Select Committee criticized the practice. Apart from these incidents there is no evidence of a deliberate campaign to recruit Irishmen, whether policemen or not, into the force. Indeed, the reverse applied, and MacMahon at times favoured Scotsmen and Englishmen. The explanation for the heavy presence in Victoria of former members of the RIC seems to rest with events in Ireland.

Throughout the latter half of the nineteenth century the RIC was a large force, usually over ten thousand men, but subject to substantial fluctuations in manpower levels according to the rise and fall of political unrest. During the later 1850s and early 1860s more than six thousand men resigned from the Irish Constabulary, and by the mid-1860s resignations outpaced recruiting. Apart from retrenchments whenever the country went quiet, RIC numbers were reduced by a high resignation rate due to low wages and poor working conditions. During those lean years a large number of young policemen resigned, with the express intention of emigrating to Australia or America where policemen 'were earning heaps of money'.[7] There is obviously some correlation between mass resignations of police in Ireland and their recruitment in Victoria. The 'heaps of money' might also account for many of the Irishmen who were not former members of the RIC but joined the force in Victoria. One student of Irish police history has suggested that an important factor attracting Irishmen to places like Victoria was the opportunity of marriage. Irish police regulations forbade policemen to marry unless they had served for at least seven years and could produce 'evidence of solvency considered appropriate to a married state'. In addition, only one-quarter of the men in the force were allowed to be married and there was a long list of bachelors waiting their turn. Strict moral standards were enforced and there was a disciplinary offence of 'criminal intercourse': extramarital sexual relations and marriage without permission were punishable by dismissal from the force. Although policemen in Victoria needed permission to marry, it was almost always given and none of the other Irish Constabulary restrictions applied. Irishmen, and others, in the Victoria Police Force were free to get married, raise children, and live away from police barracks. This prospect, when combined with the attraction of generally better work conditions and higher wages, was perhaps a lure to Irishmen who wanted to be policemen but also wanted a wife and children. Such a theory is speculative, but given the importance of marriage and children to Irish life it is one of the better explanations of what attracted hundreds of Irishmen to the Victoria Police.[8]

Other theories merit investigation. Apart from Breathnach's theory of 'Irish policemanship'—the idea that Irishmen are natural policemen—there is also Hobsbawm's theory that policemen are often recruited from the same material as social bandits. He claims that: 'The tough man, who is unwilling to bear the traditional burdens of the common man in a class society, poverty and meekness, may escape from them by joining or serving the oppressors as well as by revolting against them'. Almost a century before Hobsbawm developed this theory of peasant bandits and state bandits, Ned Kelly suggested a similar idea in his letter from Jerilderie. Kelly argued that the Irish police were rogues at heart who were 'too cowardly to follow it up without having the force to disguise it'. Hobsbawm and Kelly were both suggesting that the oppressors and those who opposed them were often drawn from the same basic stock. It is a notion given some weight by figures showing that Irish-born males in Victoria dominated both the prison population and the police force—yet such a theory needs more investigation and testing.[9]

An equally likely explanation for the dominant role of Irish police in Victoria is to be found in the work of MacDonagh, Coughlan and Fitzpatrick on Irish emigration to Victoria. Although the specific question of Irish police was not raised by them, their work does suggest some answers: Irish emigration to Victoria was largely state-aided, Irish immigrants filled the lowest places on the Victorian social ladder, the majority of Irishmen were fitted only for unskilled manual work, and many of them exhibited a craving for security. Fitzpatrick found that Irishmen were:

> unusually adept at securing the best of the worst jobs displaying ubiquity as dogsbodies to the rich and as ruthless rivals of the 'established' poor ... any employment, however degrading or ill-paid, marked an improvement on home opportunities.

Although this poverty-striken aspect can be pushed much too far, it remains at least part of the picture.[10]

Given all these factors, police work might have been attractive to Irishmen arriving on Victorian shores. It was unskilled manual work requiring no special training, just a sound body and minimum literacy levels. Police work paid moderately well and carried with it the promise of long-term job security and improving social status. It also offered fringe benefits in the form of a uniform, housing, a reward system and a police hospital. From the early 1850s onwards, the number of Irish-born men in the force increased steadily, giving it that strong Irish identity which undoubtedly attracted even more arrivals from Ireland. Whereas Australian-born men shunned police work, and English and Scotsmen often had the skills, resources or status to avoid it, it was open and acceptable to many Irishmen who arrived as poor state-aided migrants and who belonged to a race that displayed a world-wide interest in 'policemanship'.

It is quite obscure why Australian men shunned police service, but—with only thirty native-born constables in a force of 1060—they obviously did so. Two historians have raised the general subject of Australian antipathy towards the police, and have concluded that native-born men did not join the forces because of the 'Currency ethos' and 'the ill-repute of the force among colonials'. These theories are not supported by suffcient evidence and, until some comprehensive research into this subject is done, they are destined to remain unproven. One sidelight on this whole question is that police recruitment in the late 1880s showed a marked downturn in applications from Irishmen and a corresponding increase in applications from Australian-born men. In the absence of complete records it is very hard to know if the native-born applicants were the sons of Irishmen, but by the early 1920s the Irish-born element was fast disappearing and the force was dominated by men born in Australia. Using the 636 police strikers as a sample, 93 per cent of them were native-born.[11]

An important question prompted by Irish domination of the force in the 1870s is the extent to which their presence influenced the development and public image of the police. The Irishmen came from a country where the police system was political, repressive and unpopular. Members of the RIC were drilled and equipped as infantrymen and had all the attributes of a standing army. During the 1850s and 1860s the Irish Constabulary came under severe criticism from both the public and the magistrates. It was thought by some that the constabulary was too centralized, militarist, and inefficient in the prevention and detection of crime. One observer of the Irish Constabulary wrote that it was 'an Imperial political force, having none of the qualities of a police body . . . its extra-political duty and *raison d'être* is to form a bodyguard for the system of Irish landlordism'. The force was generally regarded as efficient in the suppression of civil disorder, and the tactics it used in dealing with secret societies and agrarian outrages made the Irish style of policing a popular choice with the ruling classes in other commonwealth countries. Sir Charles Jeffries, author and deputy Under-Secretary of State for the Colonies, was an advocate of the 'paramilitary' Irish Constabulary because men from it and forces modelled on it worked well as agents of central governments, in countries 'where the population was predominantly rural, communications were poor, social conditions were largely primitive, and the recourse to violence by members of the public who were "agin the government" was not infrequent'. The Irish policing style was one that also utilized the gathering of political intelligence data, secret surveillance and the extensive use of informers. The activities of the Irish Tenant League, agricultural crop returns, and the 1850s elections were but three areas where the Irish police monitored public activity.[12]

Although the political climate of Ireland was different from that of Victoria, it is reasonable to expect that many of the Irish police in Victoria were inured to the ways of the RIC, accepting such duties and methods as normal. Indeed, given that no police training was conducted in Victoria, it is fair to expect that the ethics and skills of many Irish police in Victoria were unaltered from those taught in Ireland. Apart from the incidental participatory influence of former Irish police in Victoria, the force was largely modelled on the Irish Constabulary in its operational aspects, although the authorities chose to use the London model for administrative and discipline procedures. Thus the public face of the Victoria Police was Irish in appearance and design. It was a centrally controlled force of armed police, mounted and foot, not representative of the community it served, and reviled in some parts of the colony no less than were the police in Ireland.[13]

Some evidence of the result of Irish policing in Victoria was displayed in rural areas during the 1860s and 1870s. With the passing of the Land Acts, police were empowered to report on selections and could recommend the abolition of licences and leases. They were also used to remove selectors' fences interfering with squatters' runs, pursue alleged selector-duffers on behalf of the squatters' Stock Protection Association, and deal with shearers engaged by squatters under the Masters and Servants Act. One officer described the presence of his men in parts of northeastern Victoria as 'an army of occupation'. Although the performance of such duties was not of itself 'Irish', the work was analogous to that performed by the RIC on behalf of landlords in Ireland. Victorian police were known to resort to perjury, brutality and the use of extensive 'spy' networks in order to control the selectors, to whom the police were synonymous with authority and the squatters. In Victoria the squatters had much for which to thank the Irish landlords' policing precedent.[14]

Did the actions of the police result from the ethnic composition of the force, or from the deliberate policy of the government to use the Irish policing model? More than likely the police behaviour resulted from a compatible combination of men and policies. It is evident that trained Irish police using Irish police methods predominated in Victoria before

Mounted Police in 1875

the Kelly outbreak and rode roughshod over many small selectors. Their pursuit of the Kelly gang thrust the shortcomings of the police and their methods into the limelight. Two decades before the Kelly outbreak Superintendent Power Le Poer Bookey described former members of the Irish Constabulary as 'not nearly so sharp as they ought to be', and the same sentiments echoed through the Warby Ranges when many of these men pursued Ned Kelly, a police killer and bushranger sometimes thought of as 'an extraordinary man . . . superhuman . . . invulnerable, you can do nothing with him'. At least he was one sharp Irishman against others not so sharp, and he had the added advantage of not being a squatters' man.[15]

The Pursuit of Ned Kelly

Never in the history of the force has a clash between police and criminals had such public and dramatic consequences as did the Kelly hunt. Lives were lost, careers ruined and the innermost workings of the force made the subject of public scrutiny, debate and ridicule. In the final analysis it was found that many of the police—Irishmen and others—were not as efficient as they ought to have been and that Kelly although not invulnerable was certainly extraordinary.

Before 1878 Ned Kelly was known to few people outside north-eastern Victoria. The native-born son of an Irish Catholic ex-convict, he was a self-confessed horse thief with a criminal history that was not uncommon for one of the larrikin class: horse stealing, assault, assaulting police, drunk and disorderly, and sending an indecent letter. Although his brushes with the law spanned a decade, his criminal background was hardly noteworthy and its adolescent character is typified by his conviction for having a pair of calf's testicles delivered to a childless married woman, with a note suggesting that they might be of some use to her. Contrary to popular mythology Ned Kelly and his family were not typical selectors and Ned was not a true representative of the selector class, championing their cause against the squatters. His family were indifferent farmers, and his mother's small selection of eighty-eight acres at Lurg was cultivated only twice. Ned did not take up his own selection when he had the opportunity, nor did any of the money that he boasted he made from horse stealing appear to find its way back into the family farm. Whereas other selectors and their sons were known to go shearing in New South Wales, using their earnings to improve their selections, Ned and his close associates did not. A recent study by Doug Morrissey has shown that the majority of selectors in north-eastern Victoria were honest and hard-working farmers, who kept up the payments on their selections. A Royal Commission described Ned as one who 'led a wild and reckless life, and was always associated with the dangerous characters'. He was a bush larrikin whose real friends were drawn from an extensive network of families tied to one another by blood, marriage and criminal activity. Members of this network, including Ned and his immediate relatives, often came under police notice—sometimes unfairly and roughly—but there is little evidence that this police activity amounted to victimization, or that it justified the acts of killing and robbery that later made the Kelly gang infamous. A Royal Commission found no evidence that Ned Kelly or his friends 'were subjected to persecution or unnecessary annoyance at the hands of the police'.

The Kelly saga began in earnest on 15 April 1878 when Constable

Alexander Fitzpatrick, of Benalla, visited the Kelly home at Eleven Mile Creek. Fitzpatrick, later described by Acting Chief Commissioner Chomley as 'a liar and a larrikin' and by himself 'as not fit to be in the police force', was not typical of the policemen of that region and had more in common with the likes of Ned Kelly than his police colleagues. Fitzpatrick claimed that he visited the home with the idea of arresting Ned's brother Dan, who was wanted on warrant for horse stealing. He made no arrest, but he precipitated what is generally known as the Fitzpatrick Affair. The constable disobeyed instructions in imprudently going to the Kelly selection alone and without the warrant. Accounts of what then happened differ greatly, but two basic versions emerged. Fitzpatrick claimed that while trying to arrest Dan he was confronted and assaulted by a number of the Kelly clan, then shot in the wrist by Ned. The Kelly version is that Ned was not present at the time of Fitzpatrick's visit and that Fitzpatrick was ushered from the premises without the use of arms. Whatever the true facts—and Fitzpatrick is even harder to believe than the Kellys—the incident became a turning point. Fitzpatrick's allegation that Ned Kelly tried to murder him was used to issue arrest warrants against Ned, Dan and Ellen Kelly, Bill Skillion and Brickey Williamson. The latter three were quickly arrested, but Ned and Dan evaded capture.

The Kelly brothers, joined by two friends, remained at large for some months and, in October 1878, the police decided to mount a pincer movement, police parties of four men being sent from both Mansfield and Greta to hunt the gang. Disguised as diggers, they were armed with revolvers, Spencer rifles and double-barrel shotguns. The Mansfield party was led by Sergeant Michael Kennedy, an Irish-Catholic, married with children. After fourteen years service, he was selected for the Kelly pursuit because he knew the country well. With him were Constables Thomas Lonigan of Violet Town, Michael Scanlon of Mooroopna and Thomas McIntyre. These three were hand-picked for the patrol, Lonigan because he knew the Kellys, Scanlon because of his local knowledge, and McIntyre because he was a good camp cook. Only the cook returned alive.

On 25 October 1878 the Mansfield patrol camped overnight in a remote bush clearing on Stringybark Creek. The following day Kennedy and Scanlon went in search of the Kellys, leaving the other two at the camp. McIntyre, like many policemen at that time, was not a good bushman and in the absence of the patrol leader he shot at some parrots and lit a large fire. Unbeknown to any of the Kennedy party, they were based only a mile from the Kelly camp and the actions of McIntyre were a beacon to Ned and his companions, who knew the bush well. Later that day the outlaws raided the police camp, killing Lonigan and detaining McIntyre at gunpoint. Having gained initial ascendancy over their would-be captors, Kelly and company then lay in wait for the return of

Kennedy and Scanlon. Some hours later the unsuspecting pair returned and were greeted by McIntyre who called on them to surrender. At first Kennedy thought it was a joke, but he was quickly put right and he and Scanlon engaged the outlaws in gunfire. McIntyre, survival uppermost in his mind, fled on foot and hid in a wombat hole. The Kelly gang was superior in number and had the added advantage of surprise. Kennedy and Scanlon were both shot down and, as Kennedy lay dying, Ned Kelly—in an act later described by a Royal Commission as 'cruel, wanton and inhuman'—placed a gun against his chest and shot him dead. Then the bodies of the three fallen policemen were robbed.

In the clearing at Stringybark Creek the Kelly gang passed the point of no return. For a few brief hours they had reversed the roles of hunter and hunted, but the violence that marked the end of the Kennedy patrol was the beginning of the gang as outlaws. Ned Kelly, Steve Hart, Dan Kelly and Joe Byrne embarked together on the path to infamy, for most of their remaining short lives leading the police a humiliating dance. During a period of twenty months they were pursued through a labyrinth of rural sympathizers in a saga that included spectacular bank robberies at Euroa and Jerilderie and reached its climax in the siege at Jones's Hotel, Glenrowan, on 26 June 1880. Hart, Byrne and Dan Kelly died there, but Ned was spared for one last performance and on 28 October he stood trial for the murder of Lonigan. Found guilty, Kelly was hanged at the Melbourne Gaol on 11 November 1880.[16]

The Kelly outbreak lasted almost two years and in the end Ned Kelly met a violent and controversial death. During his time as an outlaw he and his companions tested the capabilities of the police to the limit—and beyond. It was both a tragic and humiliating time for the police; they were pilloried in the newspapers, criticized in parliament and made antagonistic to each other in the field. The destruction of the gang did not, however, bring respite for the beleaguered force, for the spectre of Kelly caused them as much anguish in death as he did in life. When sentenced by Redmond Barry, Kelly warned the Judge, 'I will see you there where I go'. It proved an apt epitaph for Barry, who died twelve days after Kelly's execution. It also served as an appropriate parting curse for the police force as Kelly knew it.[17]

Only weeks after the Glenrowan siege Chief Commissioner Standish was forced to retire by the newly elected liberal government of Graham Berry. After twenty-two years as the colony's leading policeman, Standish was dumped unceremoniously and replaced by Charles Nicolson, who was temporarily promoted from Assistant Commissioner to Acting Chief Commissioner. Berry and his liberal colleagues, both in government and in opposition, had long been critical of the police and Standish, even though he had so astutely survived Berry's Black Wednesday in 1878. Standish's personal failings during his last years in office had, however, contributed substantially to the farcical hunt for the Kellys and destined him to relative obscurity. He accepted his sacking unquestioningly, but his last official despatch, pathetic and lonely, was to Berry, asking for permission to retain his official despatch box 'in remembrance of my 22 years connection with the Police Department'. For the fallen Chief there were no testimonials or accolades. With his despatch box and a pension, Standish retired on 30 September 1880. He died in Melbourne before the Longmore Royal Commission, inquiring into 'his' force, had produced its final report.[18]

Standish's sacking and the execution of Kelly were followed by a public inquiry that lasted another two years. Almost as if it were the reincarnation of Ned, the inquiry brought alive the Kelly years. The sympathizers and the newspapers had a field day as the police force was again lambasted and lampooned. Ironically, some of the police had themselves requested an inquiry but they had obviously not counted on its vituperative and searching nature. Instead of the anticipated exoneration and acclaim, several of them received rebuke, embarrassment and retirement.

The Royal Commission was appointed to inquire into the force on 7 March 1881 and, with Francis Longmore, MLA, as chairman, its terms of reference were to inquire into:

1. the circumstances preceding and attending the Kelly outbreak;
2. the efficiency of the Police to deal with such possible occurrences;
3. the action of the Police authorities during the period the Kelly gang were at large;
4. the efficiency of the means employed for their capture; and
5. generally to report upon the present state and organization of the Police Force.[19]

The Commission was faced with difficulties from the outset. A number of prominent men, including Alfred Deakin, were asked to sit on the inquiry but for undisclosed reasons they declined to do so. Others accepted the role initially but resigned either just before the inquiry sat or while it was in progress. Eventually eight commissioners, including Longmore, began hearing evidence on 23 March 1881. Longmore was a staunch temperance man and loyal Irish Protestant, described by Deakin as 'little above the average of the ordinary man in the street', vituperous and having 'all a selector's distrust and all an Irishman's hate of great landlords'.[20]

Suitably equipped or not, the Commissioners faced an arduous task that not only involved investigating the very divisive Kelly outbreak, but also entailed penetrating the quasi-secret world of detectives and informers. The Commissioners, for the most part, manfully took up their work, and Longmore proved assiduous as chairman. During the first series of hearings, when the Board inquired into terms of reference 1-4,

Longmore was present at 65 of the 66 meetings convened. The Royal Commission spanned more than two years, taking evidence from 183 witnesses, and publishing five reports. It stands as the most extensive inquiry ever undertaken of the workings of the Victoria Police. During the life of that Commission, the government in Victoria changed three times, a new Chief Commissioner was appointed, and over three hundred men left or joined the police force.[21]

As soon as the inquiry began, Acting Chief Commissioner Nicolson and Superintendents F. A. Hare and J. Sadleir were relieved from duty and forced to take leave of absence. Nicolson and Hare, who along with Standish had at different times led the hunt for the Kellys, never returned to duty and were retired from the force as police magistrates. It was a hard decision that not only deprived the community and force of two of their most experienced policemen, but also deprived Nicolson of almost certain appointment as Chief Commissioner. Nicolson and Hare had been with the force since 1853 and 1854 respectively, and their careers had been exemplary before the Kelly outbreak. Both men had figured in the capture of the infamous bushranger Harry Power in 1870, and Nicolson in particular had built up an excellent reputation in the colony as a thief-taker. Yet the testing nature of the Kelly hunt found them wanting, and also exposed the intensity of their personal rivalry—the Commission deciding that the community suffered greatly because of the 'want of unanimity existing between these officers'. Sadleir, who did not figure in the Kelly hunt to the same extent as Standish, Nicolson and Hare, escaped the full wrath of the inquiry but was found 'guilty of several errors of judgement', and he was placed at the bottom of the list of superintendents.

In addition to criticism levelled at the senior superintendents, the Commission strongly rebuked several other policemen for their actions during the Kelly hunt. Inspector Brook Smith was accused of 'indolence and incompetence', and was forced to retire on a pension; Detective Michael Ward was censured and reduced one grade for 'misleading his superior officers'; Sergeant A. L. M. Steele was censured for 'impromptitude and poor judgement'; and Constables H. Armstrong, W. Duross, T. Dowling and R. Alexander were found guilty of 'arrant cowardice'. Armstrong resigned and the other three were dismissed.[22]

The presentation of the Commissioners' report on the Kelly outbreak concluded the first part of their inquiry into what they termed 'a disgraceful and humiliating episode in the history of the colony'. The report on the Kelly saga as the Commissioners saw it sent shock-waves through the police force. Their frank and hard-hitting account had policemen disagreeing with each other, and it prompted impassioned and comprehensive responses from a number of them, including Nicolson, Hare, Sadleir, Ward and Alexander.

Sadleir later accused the Commission of using methods that 'were repugnant to all ideas of justice and fair play', and he described Longmore as a man who 'went relentlessly for scalps' a judgement with which Deakin might have agreed. Yet, for the most part, the plaintive protests of Sadleir and other police were not well-founded. Sadleir in particular bleated about the character of some of the witnesses who appeared before the Commission, and the fact that he and his brother officers were not allowed to cross-examine them personally. He appeared to forget that it was a public Royal Commission, held in an age when even accused persons on trial could not give sworn evidence in their own defence. Indeed, the tenor of his grumblings suggests that, had Ned Kelly been alive, Sadleir would have objected to Kelly's appearance before the Commission on the grounds that he was a 'disaffected witness'.[23]

Sadleir's argument that Longmore 'went for scalps' does, however, find support in the Commission's Report and it highlights the main weakness in Longmore's inquiry to that point. Notwithstanding their very broad first term of reference, the Commissioners focused almost exclusively on the actions and personal failings of individual policemen and ignored more general social, economic and political considerations. It was an approach that constrasted sharply with the inquiries held at the time of Eureka, when investigators not only criticized individual police but also considered in detail the broader social questions of mining licences, electoral rights and the land question. The Longmore Commission, without even canvassing serious social questions like rural unemployment, land selection and rural class conflict, determined that the Kelly outbreak was rooted in police actions that 'weakened that effective and complete surveillance without which the criminal classes in all countries become more and more restive and defiant of the authorities'. The almost exclusive attention given by the Police Commission to individual police failings undoubtedly heightened the sense of victimization felt by police like Sadleir, and contributed to the Commission's lack of credibility with sections of the press.

Not even Sadleir doubted that a number of individual policemen were culpable, but the general police view was that they alone were not responsible for the Kelly outbreak. It was a view shared by others, including the Kelly Reward Board, which made individual payments of up to £800 to police involved in the Kelly hunt, and the Government, which refused to fully act upon some of the Longmore recommendations against individual policemen and later cut across the Royal Commission's final terms of reference. Since the Longmore Inquiry a number of researchers have identified socio-economic, racial, political and geographic factors as being relevant to the cause and nature of the Kelly outbreak. It is perhaps unfortunate that Longmore—former Minister for Lands and selectors' advocate—and his colleagues, did not consider these aspects at all in their

Second Progress Report. Their failure to do so alienated many honest policemen, and the loss of credibility undoubtedly hindered their work during the second part of the inquiry—generally to inquire into and report upon the state and organization of the police force.[24]

The hearings to finalize this last term of reference began in December 1881 and by that time the liberal Berry Government had been replaced by that of the Irish-Catholic lawyer Sir Bryan O'Loghlen. O'Loghlen, who had gained office on 9 July as premier, attorney-general and treasurer, headed a 'scratch team' comprised of prominent conservatives and discontented liberals. The political turmoil that saw O'Loghlen rise to power did not leave the Longmore Commission or the police unaffected. O'Loghlen appointed Hussey Malone Chomley as Chief Commissioner of Police and instructed him 'to draw up a special report embodying his views upon the re-organisation of the force'. Longmore and his team initially regarded Chomley's appointment as an action 'designed to supersede the Commission, or at least to render further investigation superfluous', and the inquiry was suspended until they received an assurance from the Government that such was not the case.

Chomley's record as a police administrator was not outstanding and did not warrant his sudden and inexpedient appointment as Chief Commissioner and special adviser during a crucial stage of the Longmore Inquiry. He was an Irish Protestant from Dublin, whose police career began in 1852 when he joined Sturt's Melbourne and County of Bourke Police as a cadet, and he had risen through all ranks of the force, although his time was spent mostly in rural areas. At the time of the Kelly outbreak he was superintendent in charge of the South-Western District, with headquarters at Geelong, and at the time of Ned Kelly's capture Chomley was in Brisbane on police business, which was fortunate for him in that he did not become involved in the hunt for Ned Kelly or the Police Commission's 'scalp hunting'. When Graham Berry removed Standish and left the Chief Commissioner's position vacant, Chomley was third in line for the post, after C. H. Nicolson and F. A. Winch, and was hotly pressed by younger and more accomplished men like Hare and Sadleir. The chances of the other four being ended, Chomley was left as the most senior man in the force. He was not, however, insensitive to the circumstances that placed him in such a fortunate position and he felt obliged to make public a copy of a personal letter from Standish, in which Standish had written, 'I beg to say that you never at any time showed the slightest disinclination to proceed to the North-Eastern district in connection with the pursuit of the outlaws'. At the age of forty-nine H. M. Chomley became the fourth Chief Commissioner of the Victoria Police Force and the first career policeman in the colony's history to fill the senior police post.[25]

In one sense Chomley's appointment marked the stage the force had

Chief Commissioner
H. M. Chomley

reached. During the years when Mitchell, MacMahon and Standish were appointed it was unthinkable to choose as Chief Comissioner a man who had joined and served in the ranks. On the other hand it might have reflected the slogan of O'Loghlen's conservative government—'peace, prosperity, progress'—in that Chomley was loyal, honest, disciplined, conservative and a man ready 'to sacrifice a good deal as long as things went smoothly'. So police organizational development and political conservatism came together in fortuitous circumstances after the turmoil of the Kelly outbreak. From the outset, however, it was evident that the head of the force lacked the intellect and administrative ability of his three predecessors. His 'easy-going disposition', 'genius of commonsense' and 'long apprenticeship to police work' were no doubt handy attributes and a stabilizing influence on the force, but his brief, simplistic report to the O'Loghlen ministry on the state of the force highlighted his prosaic nature. The Longmore Commission rightly dismissed Chomley's modest suggestions for reform as 'sanguine anticipation', and it forged ahead with its own undertaking.[26]

The final three Police Commission reports were concerned with the Inquiry's fifth term of reference that did not directly touch upon the Kelly outbreak. All the reports, however, owed their existence to the Kelly gang. In these later sessions the Commissioners displayed a greater sense of balance than they had in their Kelly Report; broader social issues, such as larrikinism, prostitution, liquor control and gambling were investigated during the hearings. Individual policemen still figured prominently, and a number were censured in unmitigated language. Superintendent F. A. Winch and Sub-Inspector J. N. Larner were both found guilty of corrupt practices and retired from the force on a pension. Winch, who held the key position of superintendent in charge of the Melbourne Police District, had a history of corrupt behaviour over twenty years but all that time he had been shielded from public exposure, criminal charges and dismissal by his good friend, Chief Commissioner Standish. With the retirement of Standish, Longmore used the full power of the Royal Commission to rid the force of Winch, who even then escaped criminal charges and was allowed to retire with a pension. For personal gain Winch had allowed prostitution and gambling to flourish in Melbourne and ensured that zealous and honest police did not 'grapple with the evil'. Larner, who some years earlier had figured so prominently in the Clunes riot, was not as crooked as Winch; the basis of his offences was the regular borrowing of money from hotelkeepers. In an unusual twist for the Longmore Commission, Larner admitted his guilt but 'urged in extenuation the great expense to which he was subjected in consequence of his promotion'.[27]

A number of other policemen were individually censured by the Royal Commission for general acts of inefficiency and misconduct, but these cases were minor compared with the damning condemnation levelled at the Detective Branch as a whole. This section of the force was described as 'a standing menace to the community', 'a nursery of crime' and a department 'inimical to the public interest'. Commanded by Inspector Secretan—'one of the most useless men in the service'—the detective force numbered twenty-six men. The Longmore Commission recommended that Secretan be retired and the detective force disbanded, and a new Criminal Investigation Branch formed as part of the general police force under the command of the Chief Commissioner. This was in some ways a curious development as only six years earlier the Metropolitan Police in London had abandoned this form of organization and replaced it with the more autonomous model then in use in Victoria. Nevertheless, a century later, in the 1970s, the London CID was again made part of the general force, in a bid to reduce corruption and inefficiency among detectives. So the Longmore Commission might have recommended wisely.[28]

The basic fault with the detective force was that its mode of operation had changed little from the convict years. The methods that had produced successes for detectives during the 1840s and 1850s, when the population was much smaller and unsettled, were not nearly so effective in later years. Originally a small, select group, the detectives were judged efficient as thief-takers because they infiltrated the criminal classes and by fraternizing with criminals they were privy to information that was not readily available to other policemen. The detectives initially made many arrests but, as the population increased and settled over a wider area of the colony, they only increased in number and failed to adapt to the changing economic and social conditions. They did not develop any special investigation skills but continued to rely simply on the use of informers and 'fiz-gigs'. Under this system, criminals and others were employed by detectives and paid 'secret service money' for details about crimes and the whereabouts of offenders. It placed the detectives in close contact with men and women of the criminal class and gradually rendered the detectives 'comparatively helpless' and by themselves 'almost powerless to trace offenders'. The informer system worked well amongst the Vandemonian population in the seedier parts of Melbourne during the early years but was found wanting during the hunt for the Kelly gang, when police could not effectively induce enough people in the North-East to inform on the outlaws. The essential ingredients of the system were infiltration and betrayal, and a mixture of rural sympathy for the Kellys and fear of them rendered the detective system virtually impotent. Fear of the gang was not without foundation, and stark evidence of the precarious world of the police informer was provided when Joe Byrne executed one of the few police spies, Aaron Sherritt, as a prelude to events at Glenrowan.

The extensive use of informer networks was strongly discouraged by police authorities in England and Ireland, but their unbridled usage in Victoria pushed the system to an extreme, where criminal agents were used as decoys and detectives more or less connived at the agents' own crime. The Royal Commission provided a succinct account of that system:

> A 'fiz-gig' is paid to start the prey which the expectant detective captures without trouble or inconvenience. He is supposed to receive not only a subsidy from the detective who employs him, but a share in the reward, and a certain immunity from arrest for offences with which he may be chargeable. He may plan robberies and induce incipient criminals to co-operate, but provided he lures the latter successfully into the detectives' hands, his whereabouts and antecedents are not supposed to be known to the police.[29]

It was the basic informer system, with various modifications, that Superintendent C. H. Nicolson and Detective Michael Ward tried constantly to use against the Kelly gang. Nicolson in particular had great faith in

99

the system of spies and informers, and his network included 'Diseased Stock', arch-spy of the Kelly years. Such activities were still common outside Victoria; although overseas scholars, including Hans Gross and Alphonse Bertillon, were pioneering scientific investigation methods, detective work around the world was dependent upon 'native skill and cunning'. Indeed, even the much-vaunted sleuths of Scotland Yard were denounced by the British prime minister as being 'especially deficient as a detective force', and labelled in *Punch* as the Defective Department. Longmore's devastating criticism of the Victorian detective force was aimed not so much at the inadequacy it shared with most of its counterparts elsewhere, but at the sinister lengths to which the 'fiz-gig' networks had developed.[30]

In its assessment of the police force generally, the Longmore Royal Commission touched upon such matters as recruiting, training, promotions and transfers, and concluded with a list of thirty-six recommendations for the reform of the force. Certain of the recommendations related only to routine matters, such as the abolition of white gloves for men on patrol. Other proposed reforms were more important and included instructional classes and promotional examinations for police, the compilation of a police code and new recruiting procedures. Also contained in the list were the perennial issues of police enfranchisement and a proposal to vest the management of the force in a board of three men.[31]

The final Longmore Report highlighted yet again the characteristic inability of most senior police willingly to undertake reform and adapt to changed circumstances. Since 1852 important changes had been forced on the police by outside inquiries, and in 1883 the effort was repeated by Longmore. Sturt, Mitchell, MacMahon and Standish had all displayed remarkable adaptability and a desire to introduce reform when first appointed from outside the police sphere. The impetus given to the force by these administrators was not sustained, but languished, particularly during much of the Standish era. It is also evident that the older and more senior career police generally lacked the intellect and administrative ability of leaders appointed from outside the force, and did not engender the supportive climate so necessary for innovation and reform. Their world was largely insular and reactionary, and was illustrated by Sadleir's vehement criticism of basing police promotion on a system of written examinations.

The Kelly gang exposed serious police weaknesses in the field, including a general lack of bushcraft, horsemanship and firearms training, together with lax discipline, low morale, and an inability to relate to sections of the rural community and maintain their confidence and respect. These shortcomings were ultimately attributable to mismanagement at a senior level, and the Longmore Commission exposed serious deficiencies in the force's administration: a lack of provision for police training, poor planning, injudicious manpower deployment, insufficient attention to ordnance requirements, sub-standard officering and the generally debilitating leadership of Standish, which 'was not characterized either by good judgement, or by that zeal for the interests of the public service which should have distinguished an officer in his position'. Ironically, many of the changes mooted by Longmore were originally suggested by police from the lower ranks but had never been acted upon by Standish or his senior officers. Internally and externally the senior police were seemingly committed to maintaining the status quo.[32]

The history of public inquiries into the Victoria Police Force before the Kelly outbreak proved them to be valuable community forums where important reforms were germinated and cancerous sections of the force were exposed and excised. The Longmore Commission had this effect, and if the enormous expense and tragedy of the Kelly outbreak was ever at least partly redeemed, this was one way it occurred. The Longmore Commission was far from perfect and did not provide a panacea for all ills. Nonetheless, the force was cleansed of some of its more openly corrupt influences, aged and ineffective senior police were retired and many important administrative changes were introduced. Most importantly, however, the force was once again exposed to searching public scrutiny, and sections of the community and many policemen were moved to take more than passing interest in the state of the force and the doings of its senior officers. The long term of Standish's commissionership had lulled many people into thinking that all was as well as possible with the colony's police, quite a few of whom had been basking comfortably in a widespread belief that Victoria's police were the finest in Australia. It was a debatable notion; even if it had been well-founded, it would not have warranted any resting on laurels. In 1878 it was certainly not a view shared by Ned Kelly, and by 1883 there were many others who agreed with his assessment.[33]

The Policeman's Lot

> Many persons think that a policemen's lot is an easy one. It is really nothing of the sort . . .
>
> (John Sadleir, *Recollections* . . .)[34]

John Sadleir's lament no doubt found its inspiration in Gilbert and Sullivan's *The Pirates of Penzance*, which parodied rustic police and criminals. Although first performed in New York (1879) and London (1880), its sentiments were equally felt by many policemen then working in Victoria.

The Kelly outbreak and Longmore Royal Commission diverted attention away from the 'ordinary copper' and focused it firmly upon the dramatic and sometimes scandalous lot of senior policemen like Standish,

*An arduous life: a constable and his makeshift
police station in Gippsland, about 1900*

Winch, Nicolson and Hare. The tendency to focus on those in the
limelight was natural, but it cast into shadow many hundreds of urban
and rural policemen, who were not directly involved in the Kelly hunt,
whose footsteps never ceased in towns across Victoria. They were the bulk
and backbone of the police force, and to bring the everyday world of the
constable into sharper focus gives a necessary balance to the Kelly-
Longmore years.

The 1880s saw the disbandment of Stubbs's Bulldogs and the separation of police recruiting from that of the defence forces, which suited
the police very well. Entry into the foot police became open to men 'under
30 years of age, at least 5 ft 9 in. tall, who were smart, active and could
read and write well'. Mounted recruits had to be under 25 years of age, at
least 5 ft 7 in. tall and weigh under 11 st. 7 lb. In the 1880s, as in the 1860s,
the emphasis was on physical attributes, as long and wearisome periods

102

of beat duty and mounted patrol were the staple of a constable's working life. The requirement that they 'read and write well' was very elastically applied, for the force included 'lots of men' who could barely write, and the only educational test for recruits was a basic dictation and spelling exercise. There were no university graduates in the force but a spirometer test did ensure that policemen had the lung capacity for strenuous outdoor work. Upon joining the force men were not given any classroom instruction in their duties; once outfitted, they were sent to police stations for beat and patrol duty. In the case of mounted recruits that often meant the testing and solitary life of a one-man station in a remote mountain district or the Mallee-Wimmera. The policy of sending new police into the fray without any training or preparation was a legacy of Standish's administration and reflected his philosophy 'that a constable is born, not made'. It was this policy that saw some young constables, 'raw, and knowing no more about the police duty than a man from North Africa', pitted against the likes of Ned Kelly. Through no fault of their own, policemen were at times embarrassed and admonished because they lacked bush skills or knew little about laws, firearms, horsemanship, tracking and police patrol. Many of them did well just to survive; only a minority were natural policemen, like Constable Robert Graham who had charge of the Greta police station *after* the execution of Ned Kelly. Graham, a native of Victoria and an accomplished bushman and horseman, displayed considerable courage and intelligence in hostile Kelly country. He not only survived but effectively policed the district and won the support of many local people. A sign of his competence and fairness was the mutual respect that developed between him and Ellen Kelly—Ned's mother. When Graham had trouble with some of Ned's former cronies it was Mrs Kelly who helped him and kept the peace. Graham was officially commended for his work at Greta and later promoted. Graham's skills and reputation were, however, unusual and could never justify the overworked excuse that policemen were born, not made.[35]

The basic starting wage of a constable was 6s 6d a day and out of this money the new recruit was expected to pay £12 for his police uniform of tunic, trousers, shirt, jumper, white gloves and boots. His shiny black helmet, worth nine shillings, and other accoutrements, were issued free by the force. Unless a constable had some money saved, the first weeks of his new job placed him under considerable financial strain and many men took at least a year to clear their uniform debts. Dress standards, including the changing of underpants, were governed by regulations and constables were paraded regularly and instructed to replace worn or damaged clothing at their own expense. Apart from the cost of uniform items, constables complained about such things as a lack of proper wet-weather gear, the oppressiveness of tunics and helmets in summer and the useless, ornamental nature of white gloves and swords. In a style befitting the *Pirates*

of Penzance, hapless Constable McEvoy described the lot of a white-gloved constable:

> I have often felt ashamed on the wharf; having to take a drunken man, I took my gloves off. I met an old drunken woman in the street, and had my gloves on; I had not time to take them off. I was trying to take off my glove, and had my hand round her, and had to put my hand up to my mouth to take the glove off, and they had a great laugh at me, as if I was going to kiss the old woman. They are an ornamental and useless thing.[36]

Yet other aspects of their work caused policemen even greater concern. They were the lowest-paid of any force in the Australian colonies and their basic wage of 6s 6d a day was below the 'rate of pay ruling the country'. In addition, there were inequities in the different allowances paid to officers and other ranks, and also in the different benefits allowed to married and single constables.

The constables' basic wage fell between the rates paid to tradesmen and labourers and was generally less than the pay of other civil servants, transport workers and even shop assistants. Married constables in particular found it difficult to support a family on such low pay, when living expenses included rent of fifty shillings a month, bread at 6d a loaf, milk at 6d a quart, mutton at 4d a pound and firewood at 1s 3d a cwt. Due to such costs it was suggested that young police recruits be prohibited from marrying for five years so that they could pay for their uniforms and then save money to provide for a family. In 1881 constables petitioned the Chief Secretary for a pay rise and in support of their claim sought to highlight the unique and arduous nature of their duties. They worked a seven-day week, with no rest days or public holidays, and were granted only twelve days leave a year. This was in contrast to all other civil servants, including charwomen, who were paid annual wage increments, and received at least one rest day each week, ten public holidays a year and twenty-one days paid annual leave.[37]

The *Police Regulations* required constables to rise no later than 5.30 a.m. every day (6.30 a.m. in winter) and after dressing and cleaning their rooms, they were to be at stable parade by 6.00 a.m. For those men not working night shift, curfew was 10.00 p.m. Beatmen in Melbourne and the larger towns rose about 4.30 a.m. and worked a constant round of shifts that commenced daily at 5.00 a.m. Day duty of eight hours was divided into two four-hour reliefs, broken by four hours of reserve duty, which meant that a constable who started work at 5.00 a.m. did not go off duty until 5.00 p.m. Night duty was a fixed shift from 9.00 p.m. to 5.00 a.m.,

Constable James Thyer, with the white gloves and sword
that were so unpopular with many of his colleagues

and constables worked this continuously for fourteen days before rotating back to day shift. Such hours of work were themselves tiresome but in the 1880s they were not unique to the police. Bakers, butchers, transport workers and shop assistants were just a few of the other occupations where employees regularly worked up to ninety hours a week. Where the police differed was that they were paid less for their labour and worked every day; no Sunday rest day, no Christmas Day holiday and no public holidays. Even the toughest of other occupations usually granted some time off on Sunday, and most workers in sales and commerce worked a five-and-a-half-day week. Leave of absence was granted to constables only if they could be spared, and even then they were 'to consider themselves subject to every order, rule, and regulation of the force' and needed special permission to visit Melbourne.[38]

The relative lack of rest days and leave for constables constrasted sharply with those available to other civil servants who, in addition to normal rest days, could qualify by length of service for paid holidays abroad. The policeman's lot lacked both the extra benefits of the civil service and the full provisioning of the army. There were some similarities between the control and discipline exercised over policemen and soldiers, but whereas soldiers were paid, clothed, housed, equipped and fed, the 777 married policemen in Victoria were expected to form part of the general community and to clothe, house and feed themselves and their families. Indeed, it was the married policemen who formed the bulk of the force and who felt most disadvantaged by inequities in the distribution of allowances. Single constables lived in police barracks and were provided with free accommodation, light, water and fuel—quite a saving when housing rentals in Melbourne averaged fifty shillings a month and light, water and fuel cost one shilling a day. During the Kelly years the married constables and sub-officers petitioned the government for an allowance in lieu of quarters, and argued that they were being compensated at a lower rate than single men for doing the same work. The single men might have retorted (although they did not) that any monetary savings made by living in barracks did not compensate for the personal inconvenience of constant station life and discipline, and the ease with which they could be mustered in emergencies.

The inequities in benefits and allowances were not limited to differences between married and single men but were also evident in the payments to officers, who received much larger allowances for fuel and travelling and were paid transfer expenses. All policemen were entitled to a wood allowance and in winter married constables received 6 cubic feet a week, which they protested was 'not sufficient to boil a kettle'. They pointed to officers who, regardless of their home or family situation, were allowed 20 cubic feet of firewood a week. By protesting in such terms the constables were out of order for Victorian times and met with little success.[39] Privileges of rank were common in the force and the constables, not really expecting full parity with officers, might have used the 'kettle boiling' issue as a device to lead into another issue that they saw as the real grievance.

This was the hardship involved in transfers and transfer expenses. Over a period of years, constables pushed for changes to the system. There were more than 330 police stations scattered throughout Victoria, some in locations as remote and distant as Bendoc, Corryong, Dartmoor and Cowana. The *Police Regulations* stated that police were distributed 'as the requirements of the country demanded', and policemen were liable to be transferred to any station, at any time, for any reason. There was no right of appeal. What worried the men even more was that a transfer involving a move to another town or suburb had to be paid for by the policeman being transferred. Officers were paid a transit allowance for 2 cwt of luggage, but other ranks received nothing. Chomley agreed that such a system caused great hardships and, depending on the distance of removal and the amount of luggage, it was not uncommon for constables to incur large debts for removal expenses. Efficient men suffered most, as they were moved about very often, at their own expense, 'for the good of the country'. Misjudged men also suffered because forced transfers were declared in the regulations to be a legitimate 'punishment' and, without trial or appeal, constables could be capriciously shunted about the colony, dragging their families behind them.

Another example of this mean type of administration was the decision by Standish, during the Kelly hunt, to cancel the travelling allowances of all those Melbourne constables engaged on the hunt in the north-east. He transferred them indefinitely to the strength of the local police district to save paying the five shillings a day travelling money for being away from home. Married men either had to leave their families behind or themselves pay to move them to the north-east. Standish argued that his decision saved the government money, but he did not cut the travelling allowance of twelve shillings a day paid to officers in the north-east. Later, he admitted that many of the men worst affected 'were married men separated from their wives and families'.[40]

The regulations controlling transfers and allowances were part of a much larger code of rules that governed the daily lives of policemen. It was not a code restricted to official matters but one that sought to control their personal conduct and private lives at all times. Policemen could not vote at elections and were to 'observe strict neutrality in all matters connected with politics'. No constable could marry without permission and then only after his intended wife and her family were judged unlikely 'to bring discredit on the force'. They were not allowed any outside employment and, 'unless by special permission of his Officer', no constable was to allow his wife 'to practise any profession, trade or business'. Except on necessary duty, policemen were prohibited from frequenting places of amusement or public houses. They were not allowed to incur debts or obligations that might 'shackle their exertions' and were expected to 'at all times and in all ways maintain a character for unimpeachable integrity'. Married constables were directed to live as near as possible to their station and all members, whether on duty or not, were to 'at once turn out when called upon in cases of emergency ... or whenever required'. Policemen were not paid overtime; extra duty was regarded as being part of the job. A particular source of frustration to married men was the requirement that, no matter where they were stationed or what their family situation was, if they were injured or fell ill they had to go to the police hospital in Melbourne. This often meant leaving their families behind and hundreds of miles of travel. It was intended to reduce malingering, but was regarded as being unduly harsh, particularly as patients in the police hospital had half their wages stopped to pay for meals and medical expenses. One constable described the police hospital as 'a good place for loafers' and those young fellows 'suffering from venereal disease', but 'a great hardship' for a married man, with his own house, his own doctor and his 'own comfortable bed'.

When not ill or called upon after hours, married constables presumably sought some sanctuary from the *Police Regulations* at home. For single men in barracks there was no respite. They were not allowed to smoke or gamble in barracks, their rooms, beds and clothing were subject to inspection, and regulations governed cleaning and bed-making procedures. As the barracks usually formed part of police stations, constables were also directed that at all times they 'will stand at attention, or, if sitting down, will rise when officers or persons entitled to a salute are passing'. In the age of social distinctions and sweated labour, police conditions of work were not unusually severe. They were, however, indicative of a regimented and all-consuming lifestyle, where the line between on and off duty was barely perceptible. Policing was not just a job but a way of life, and the men in blue serge whose duty it was to superintend the lives of others were themselves closely supervised and controlled.[41]

A principal legacy of the Kelly outbreak is the popular notion that police work was haphazard and the police themselves generally inefficient. It is an exaggerated notion, given some credence in police behaviour during the Kelly hunt, but not generally applicable to policemen and police work of the period. The Kelly saga was an extraordinary series of events that highlighted particular police inadequacies and belied the fact that most police work was routine and completed satisfactorily according to set procedures. Policemen, particularly during the early years of their service, had their shortcomings but, once they overcame their initial lack of training, average constables completed many demanding tasks. The majority of constables spent their working day either on beat duty or mounted patrol, while a minority of them worked as clerks and watch-house keepers or performed extraneous duties, including guard duty at Government House, Parliament House, the Royal Mint, Public Library, General Post Office and University Gardens. Beat duty was confined to Melbourne and the larger towns, and the beat constables themselves were as much a part of the city streetscape as were veranda posts and street lamps. Constables patrolled set beats alone and on foot and, in rotating shifts, they were there twenty-four hours of every day. These men were not detectives; although crime prevention was an element of their presence, their primary role was a service one. They were 'the proper class to be applied to for assistance' and, to this end, beat constables were instructed to acquire local knowledge of all kinds and to 'in fact be a walking directory'. The need for civility and politeness was stressed. They checked the security of doors and windows, and were alerted to watch for leaking waterpipes, overflowing closets and dead animals lying about. They were also responsible for obliterating obscene words and drawings in public places and to 'in every way diminish as far as possible, the risk of accident to the public'. In the interests of public safety no task was too menial, and beatmen were specifically directed to watch for and remove pieces of orange peel from the pavement.[42]

Beat duty regulations were enforced by sub-officers and officers, using a system of reports and monetary fines. It was a system which showed that the regulations only outlined the beat duty ideal and could not guarantee universal compliance or commensurate performance. It was also a system that struck hard at the earnings of policemen, who were liable to fines of a week's pay for being drunk on duty, and a day's pay if found sheltering under a veranda or dawdling on their beats. There were still a number of constables who were alcoholic, lazy or just plain unlucky, and discipline charges were not uncommon. These covered a wide range of conduct, from simply being late for duty to the serious offence of assaulting a prisoner. Some of the more common breaches were: absent from beat, improperly working the beat, asleep on beat, sitting down on beat, in a hotel on beat, found gossiping, drunk on duty and loitering under a veranda. Many constables were never charged and led exemplary careers that included awards, rewards and high public praise. Others, like Constable M. Carroll, 'a drunken, useless man', amassed seventeen convictions for offences committed while on duty.[43]

In rural districts the local equivalent of the beat constable was generally the mounted trooper. These men were often responsible for patrolling large tracts of country and it was expected that they be competent horsemen, with a knowledge of the bush and an ability to go it alone. The Kelly outbreak left many people with the impression that policemen were bumble-footed urbanites. However, the daily routine of many mounted policemen necessitated patrols to outlying farms that sometimes took days

FIGURE 1

Diary of Duty and Occurrences at the Mount Moriac Police Station, week ending 11 November 1871

	5th (Sunday)	6th	7th	8th	9th	10th	11th	Special Occurrences
HAGGER,* Newman Const. 1979 Mtd. Const.	Stables 2 hours Foot patrol 10 a.m. to 1 p.m. Attending Divine Service 2.30 p.m. to 4.30 p.m.	Stables 2 hours Mounted patrol to Winchelsea with pay and abstracts 2 p.m. to 7 p.m. Foot patrol 9 p.m. to 11 p.m.	Stables 2 hours Attending police court 11 a.m. to 3 p.m. Foot patrol 7 p.m. to 10 p.m.	Stables 2 hours Mounted duty to Lake Modewarre and vicinity warning parents of non-vaccinated children. 9 a.m. to 2.30 p.m. Foot patrol 8 p.m. to 10 p.m.	Stables 2 hours Foot patrol 9 a.m. to 11 a.m. Mounted patrol about Duneed and Paraparap warning parents of non-vaccinated children 4 p.m. to 7.30 p.m.	Stables 2 hours Foot patrol 9 a.m. to 11 a.m. 2 p.m. to 4 p.m. and 7 p.m. to 10 p.m.	Stables 2 hours Mounted patrol to Shank Hill, Pollocksford and Barrabool Hills 9.30 a.m. to 2.30 p.m. Foot patrol 8 p.m. to 10 p.m.	7/11/71 Martha Hunter* was this day committed for trial by the Bench at Mt. Moriac to the next circuit criminal court at Geelong and released on bail.
Horse Brand K14	Resting	Ridden to Winchelsea and back 24 miles	Resting	Ridden round Lake Modewarre 22 miles	Ridden about Duneed and Paraparap 25 miles	Resting	Ridden to Shank Hill, Pollocksford and Barrabool Hills 20 miles	

* Author's notes — Martha Hunter, mentioned in the Special Occurrences column, was a local servant girl charged by Hagger with 'concealment of birth' for allegedly killing her baby son shortly after she gave birth.

Hagger was a married Englishman then aged 36. A former member of the Mauritius Police and Bombay Horse Artillery he joined the Victoria Police Force on 3 March 1864 and his record includes a commendation for his part in the Kelly hunt. He was certified insane and discharged from the force in 1882 but during his time at Mount Moriac he was rated by his superiors as 'careful and efficient'.

on bush tracks and over unsettled country. In one celebrated case, Mounted Constable Fane completed a month-long patrol of over 600 miles. A country trooper was not only expected to be a 'walking directory' but 'to make himself as thoroughly acquainted as possible with all the peculiarities and characteristics of the part of the country over which his duties range', including the natural features of the country, all the roads and bush tracks, the nature of the soil and other topographical features. Some of the mounted men never came up to standard, but the acquisition of local knowledge and bush skills was regarded as an ongoing activity, and troopers were encouraged to use different routes and to 'proceed through the bush, and call at the houses of settlers to learn what is going on'. The early police historian, A. L. Haydon, felt that there was 'an appealing picturesque touch' about the solitary trooper, 'a highly important personage' and 'ruler of a good many square miles, doing several men's work in one'. He perhaps romanticized, but he had a true sense of the individuality and authority of the mounted trooper. Rural mounted men were key official figures who did more than police work in the generally accepted sense. In small rural communities they served as a general government representative and their wide-ranging duties included the collection of agricultural statistics, enforcement of compulsory vaccination programmes, truancy prosecutions, handling mental health cases and bushfire prevention.[44]

Each country trooper was required to maintain a weekly 'Diary of Duty and Occurrences' in which he not only recorded his own activities but also the work performed by police horses. A typical one-man police station was located in the quiet and settled farming district of Mount Moriac near Geelong. This station was manned in 1871 by Constable N. Hagger, who was the local policeman to 3300 people living in the Shire of Barrabool. Figure 1 is a copy of entries from Hagger's duty book. His records also show that in the weeks before and after those entries, his working day of up to twenty-four hours was occupied cleaning the police station, serving summonses, and attending to reported cases of larceny, an insane woman, a missing person, the death of a boy, cruelty to cattle and the concealment of a birth. He also made regular mounted patrols of up to thirty-five miles a day, and was visited by his inspector. His work routine was typical of that experienced by most rural mounted troopers in the last decades of the nineteenth century.[45]

Hagger had an unblemished career that lasted eighteen years, until in 1882 he was declared a lunatic and discharged from the force as medically unfit for police duty. Premature retirements from the force on medical grounds were not uncommon and long-term police work was recognized by authorities both in and outside the force as taking a heavy toll on the physical and mental health of policemen. The daily, all-weather, outdoors regimen of beat constables and mounted troopers was often lonely, tiring and uncomfortable. The pattern of police work usually comprised extended periods of routine duty, often boring, interspersed with stressful events when lone constables needed to think and act quickly in response to acts of violence, crimes and other crises. Chief Commissioner Chomley expressed the view that 'after twenty years police service a man is generally done for', and this was a view shared by the police medical officer, who felt that 'the continual wear and tear of a policeman's life tells very much on their constitutions'. Medical witnesses before the Shops Commission gave evidence about the effects of long hours, shift work and continual leg-work on the health of workers. It was not an inquiry concerned with the health aspects of police work but the evidence given was equally as relevant to policemen as to other workers, in an age when the common work-related ailments of policemen were consumption, rheumatism, catarrh, sciatica, bronchitis and varicose veins. The Longmore Royal Commission accepted the proposition that constables at 55 years of age were 'unserviceable' owing to the 'debilitating effects of their

Proud of their lot

duties', and recommended that all policemen who attained that age be allowed to retire on a pension.[46]

From the diaries and record books of men like Hagger it is possible to capture a faint impression of the ordinary working lives of constables in colonial Victoria. Their lot was not one of high social status, public display or spectacular crimes. For the most part they served in a regimented occupation and worked at routine tasks for average pay and benefits. Apart from marginal salary differences, general work conditions and benefits for policemen in Victoria were comparable to those enjoyed by police in other Australian colonies, England and Canada. The police pay scale placed them beneath tradesmen, but so too did their educational backgrounds and lack of apprenticeship or formal job training. Essentially, they were uniformed unskilled workers and for them, like many others of their class, life was not always easy or happy. It was not, however, abnormally harsh, and Sadleir reminisced about policemen who loved their work and knew 'something of what the term Duty means': men who revelled in the occasional bursts of exciting work and enjoyed the physical challenge, freedom of the bush and spirit of camaraderie. For the less competent, Carroll's sorry record of seventeen convictions showed that the police force offered fairly secure employment for even the most unworthy. For one reason or another, during the 1880s hundreds more men applied to join the force than there were vacancies.[47]

A. L. Haydon perhaps summed up the policeman's lot best when he wrote, 'The duties may be prosaic' and not 'all gas and gaiters' but 'taken all round, the lot of mounted policemen of Victoria is not the unhappy one sung of in Sir William Gilbert's ballad. He is a picked man, and worth his price'.[48] He was worth, indeed, more than his price.

The Darling of the State

Haydon's description of police work as prosaic could also have been applied to the commissionership of H. M. Chomley, who headed the force from the Kelly years into the twentieth century. Chomley's style of leadership was lack-lustre and marked by resistance to change. It was a style that saw him labelled in parliament as 'a very amiable, simple, weak man' but it also prompted successive governments to extend his appointment beyond the normal retiring age. Described by a critic as the 'darling of the State', he was a malleable and loyal senior public servant of high integrity, who did his best to maintain the status quo. Although in office for twenty years, he did not update the Police Regulations because 'it was a big undertaking', and he refused to prepare annual reports on the grounds that they involved expense and trouble. When pressed on the subject by a Royal Commission, he defended the lack of published statistical data about the force with the retort, 'Who cares how many resign?'

He was one of the staunchest opponents of moves to enfranchise the police, arguing that it was in 'their own interests' for them not to be allowed to vote. His stand was criticized by parliamentary liberals who compared him with plantation owners in the southern states of America, 'always quite sure that the best thing for the "darned nigger" was that the white man should be allowed to legislate for him'. The analogy was harsh as Chomley was generally popular with his men and not prone to treating them like 'darned niggers'. Still, police around the world, including those in South Australia and Tasmania, had been granted the right to vote and Chomley's opposition highlighted his reactionary approach to police administration.[49]

A number of changes were actually made during Chomley's time, but the impetus for them came from outside the force, and in some cases public pressure rendered them unavoidable. Several of the Longmore Commission recommendations fell into this latter category, but for the most part Chomley was slow to act upon suggestions for reform; even the much-publicized Longmore recommendations were only partly adopted, and then in piecemeal fashion over a period of many years.

Shortly after assuming office Chomley, who had never been a detective himself, was uncharacteristically quick to act in merging the autonomous detective force with the general police. It was the beginning of a new era in crime detection and was the genesis of the criminal investigation branch. The new plain clothes section was far more accountable than the old detective force and was open to all policemen, not just a favoured few. Men in the new section were required to keep a diary of their duties, to account for all their dealings with informers and to co-operate fully with general uniformed police. The criminal investigation capabilities of the force were improved and the Commissioner dealt with corruption and inefficiency. Yet Chomley could not really claim credit for these initiatives. In publicly condemning the detective force as 'a nursery of crime' the Longmore Commission had virtually forced such changes.[50]

One other area where Chomley readily responded to pressures for change was in the introduction of a promotional examination system. It had long been requested by policemen in the ranks, and was one of the first recommendations of the Longmore Commissioners, who observed that in no other area had 'the Victoria Police system so signally failed'. Examinations had formed part of the promotion system in English police forces since the early 1860s, but neither Chomley nor his examining officers drew on that experience when establishing the Victorian system. No instructional classes were held, no study materials were issued, and no effort was made to update or codify the Police Regulations. The Longmore Commission had recommended 'the compilation of a handy book for the use of members', as was issued in London, and also suggested that instructional classes be held, similar to those conducted in England

and Ireland. They were not introduced by Chomley before he established an examination system. Instead, policemen were given six months notice that it had been resolved to conduct examinations for promotion, and were advised that they would be tested in reading, dictation, report writing, mathematics and the provisions of the Police Regulation and Offences Acts. Men wanting to study for the examinations did so in their own way, in their own time, and only those who passed were paid travelling expenses for attending regional examination centres.

The first examination for promotion to the rank of sergeant was held on 10 January 1884 and sixty-four men passed, eleven with credit. Details of those who failed were not released, but the Board of Examiners did report that 'in by far the greater number of cases, the answers have been derived not so much from a study of the acts, as from experience acquired in the performance of general police duty'. Given the manner in which the examinations were organized this observation is not surprising. Still, the first dux eventually rose to become Inspecting-Superintendent and second in command of the force, and one of the most junior constables to sit the examinations passed with credit, in eighth place overall, and some years later became Chief Commissioner.[51]

It took a number of years for the police education system to develop to the stage where it embodied teaching as well as testing. Comprehensive police training was still many decades away, but in 1888 Senior Constable John Barry, of Sandhurst, made a substantial personal contribution to police education when he published the *Victorian Police Guide*. Barry was an Irish-Catholic and former farmer, with twenty-four years experience in the force. A senior constable since 1877, his record was unblemished and he was regarded as 'intelligent' by his superiors. Although the idea of a police guide was not new, Barry's actual production of a comprehensive book of 226 pages was very enterprising. It was the first work of its kind published in Australia and was produced privately by Barry to give 'a little advice on matters' that experience had taught him 'frequently perplex members of the force'.

Although positive in his advice, Barry did dare to criticize some police practices and ventured to offer advice to senior officers. For a nineteenth-century country policeman so junior in rank, his effort was a bold one and indirectly indicted his timorous Commissioner, shying away from such big undertakings. Barry's *Guide* was well received by other policemen, and was even discussed in parliament. The force eventually ordered four hundred copies, and one was kept at each police station. No mention of Barry's contribution was ever made on his police record sheet, nor did it assist him with promotion; he retired from the force in 1893, still a senior constable at rural Sandhurst. His legacy was, however, a generous one and, long after he retired, his *Guide* remained in use.[52]

The publication of Barry's *Guide* coincided with an even more important change for all policemen. On 26 November 1888 they were given the right to vote in parliamentary elections. They had been denied a vote for almost half a century and all that time their continued dis-enfranchisement was urged by Commissioners MacMahon, Standish and Chomley, solidly supported by members of the Legislative Council. The amendment of 1888 was largely brought about because 'the mother country had lately set the example of letting the police vote', and 'even Chinamen' could vote in Victoria. During the debate Victoria's police-men were described as 'a well-educated and highly intelligent set of men', but there was still a measure of reserve about their potential political influence. The new law allowed policemen only to vote; it stipulated that policemen could not 'take any part in any election', or 'in any manner influence or seek to influence' any other elector in giving his vote. With a police force dominated for so many years by Irishmen, the spectre of Tammany-style politics apparently worried some of the more conserva-tive elements in the community. Despite the reservations of Chomley and other conservatives, there was no open display of political activism by large numbers of policemen until twentieth-century police unionization made it necessary and acceptable.[53]

Although Chomley's disposition made him in some ways weak, it had its conciliatory side and was well tested during the Maritime Strike and economic depression of the 1890s. The strike was an intercolonial union dispute that began in 1890 with striking seamen and quickly spread from the waterfront to involve shearers, miners and gas stokers. The strike in Victoria was not as large or general as it was in New South Wales and Queensland, but was nevertheless the first major strike in the colony and the first since the Lothair Mine riot to involve police in a dispute between employers and employees.

The Victorian troubles began in August when the Mercantile Marine Officers' Association decided to affiliate with the Trades Hall Council in Melbourne. The move was strenuously opposed by ship owners, who were members of the Employers' Union of Australasia, and their oppo-sition sparked a strike by the 150 MMOA members. Other seamen, wharf labourers and gas stokers were quick to rally to the cause and soon some fifteen hundred men were on strike, leaving ships, wharves and gasworks idle. It was not a dispute that would have involved the police, except that strikers picketed wharves and gasworks, directing abuse and some viol-ence at workers who refused to strike or who filled the jobs of striking men. These actions, particularly in the vicinity of gasworks, alarmed many people including members of the Government and city traders. City gas supplies during the strike were intermittent and of low fuel value. Had the gasworks been effectively picketed and shut down there might have been a general black-out and escalating violence.

The extent and nature of the strike 'caused a flutter in police circles', but there were few serious incidents, either between unions and non-unionists or between pickets and police. Chomley was keen to avoid any open conflict between police and the feuding parties, and there was no garish confrontation of the sort precipitated by Standish at Clunes. Plain clothes police did maintain security at gaswork gates, and non-striking workers were escorted to and from work, but the police were loath to become involved in open conflict with strikers or to be seen as siding with capital against labour. Some radical politicians and unionists did criticize the police for even their limited role in the strike, but a measure of Chomley's success at holding middle ground was that he was also criticized by employers. His conciliatory approach drew protests from capitalists and the anti-union press, urging tougher treatment of strikers. The *Argus* described police efforts as 'wholly inadequate', while the *Age* reported cases of 'police apathy' in dealing with unionists and echoed employers' complaints about the low-key police approach.

Although Sadleir described the police situation as one where their hands 'were strangely tied', the non-confrontationist policy of Chomley worked well until the Government, alarmed by untrue reports of mob violence, issued a formal proclamation banning unlawful assemblies of people on wharves and other public places. Signed by the Premier, the conservative Duncan Gillies, reserved and unsympathetic although a 'one-time working man', the ban raised the ire of more than strikers. It was followed two days later by a monster meeting of forty thousand people in Flinders Park. The proclamation was not simply defied but defied *en masse*. Police in Victoria had never before been confronted by a 'People's Forum' as large and potentially hostile as the Flinders Park gathering. The police remained unobtrusive at the park, and in small groups remained on the perimeter of the crowd with instructions to 'exercise prudence' and not be too officious in their interference.

On the day, the principal worry for the police was not the peaceable crowd of forty thousand but the reserve of military men at Victoria Barracks. As a precautionary measure the Government had not only called in over two hundred country police, recalled police pensioners, sworn in 630 special constables—'chiefly merchants and their clerks, property holders and residents', but had also mustered the colony's volunteer military force. The soldiers were not needed, and the monster meeting passed without serious incident, but throughout the day Colonel Tom Price continually despatched messages from his military post to the police commanders asking where he should 'draw up his men'. The police begged him to keep his soldiers out of sight altogether, and he did, but even a reserve presence of military men agitated some parliamentary liberals, who objected to the use of 'imitation soldiers' in a police role. The indignation of many people was later heightened when it was disclosed that Price allegedly ordered his men:

You will each be supplied with forty rounds of ammunition and leaden bullets, and if the order is given to fire don't let me see one rifle pointed up in the air. Fire low and lay them out—lay the disturbers of law and order out, so that the duty will not again have to be performed.

There has been considerable debate as to whether Price actually gave this order, but oral tradition credits him with it firmly. Confused oral tradition also credits the police with giving and receiving this order, but there is neither evidence nor likelihood of that. Indeed, the picture of restraint that was Chomley's men at Flinders Park might well have provided him with his finest hour. Amid their haranguing of the capitalist classes, speakers on the rostrum complimented the police on their 'non-interference with the right of free speech', and this was followed in parliament with the statement that 'all the working men who assembled at the great meeting on Sunday regarded the police not as enemies but as brothers'. These sentiments might have caused some employers and capitalists to smart, but not the police themselves. The strike ended peacefully in October 1890 when the ship owners capitulated, and the police closed their file on the dispute with the report that 'at no other period of its history has the police service given better proof of its loyalty and zeal, and of the moderation and discretion of its members'.[54]

Victoria's police did not fare so well in their dealings with the unemployed during the depression years. Policemen had responsibility for enforcing the vagrancy laws and this meant arresting people who had no visible, or insufficient lawful means, of support. To enforce the payment of rent and civil debts policemen also executed warrants of ejectment and distress. They monitored the activities of unemployed 'agitators', and police 'intelligence men' checked the backgrounds of unemployed people who registered at the Labour Bureau. During buoyant economic times these duties were not uncommon but they did not place the police in widespread conflict with the poor. During hard times many more people were involved and the police, as agents of landlords and the propertied classes, came into contact with many respectable but unemployed people. Policing the unemployed became a 'growth industry' and poverty itself a 'crime'. Arrests for vagrancy ranked second in number only to drunkenness, and the previously routine task of warrant execution became a common public spectacle as crowds of unemployed people gathered to jeer police distraining goods or evicting tenants. In one noted case a hostile mob thronged a Carlton street while an agitator warned police that 'there would be blood spilt' and 'some of the detectives and constables would have holes put through them'.

Policemen were insensitive neither to the plight of the unemployed nor to their own role of policing the poor. During the Longmore Commission, policemen protested about being used to execute ejectment and distress warrants, and one police delegate urged that the task be given to civil bailiffs because 'it places the police very low in the estimation of a great many of the public'. John Barry, in his *Police Guide*, also warned of the problems inherent in using policemen as debt collectors, declaring that 'there is no portion of a constable's duty that requires more care, is surrounded with greater difficulties and about which he receives less instruction'.

Such comments largely went unheeded, and almost another century passed before policemen received some relief from the odium of civil debt collecting. During the 1890s depression there was open hostility between policemen and the poor which Chomley's conciliatory vagueness could not dissipate. Whether they liked it or not, policemen were regarded by many people as agents of the monied ruling classes. No positive steps were taken to ease the strain existing between the two groups, and only a gradual improvement in economic conditions alleviated both financial hardship and threats of blood-letting aimed at the police.[55]

While the Maritime Strike and economic depression dominated the public duties of policemen, other developments of an administrative kind were taking place within police circles. In June 1891 policemen from Russell Street sought permission to form a Police Brass Band and were allowed to do so, as long as it did 'not interfere with police duty'. It was not an encouraging response from Chomley, who obviously failed to foresee the public relations potential of such a venture. The intending band members were not deterred by their Chief's muted reply and staged a football match at the Melbourne Cricket Ground to raise funds for band equipment. It was an enthusiastic move on their part, and a successful one. The newly formed band was soon able to give its first public performance, a charity concert in the Fitzroy Gardens. The band proved very popular with the public, and the force was quick to utilize the services of bandsmen, who continued to perform in their own time and at their own expense, enhancing but not interfering with police duty. Although brass bands were common in Melbourne during the 1890s, the Police Brass Band was one of the first police bands formed anywhere in the world, and has since had a continuous existence spanning over ninety years.[56]

Although Chomley was indifferent to its initial formation, the police band did not cause him the anguish of another event of that year: the Government's move to fix a new retirement age for policemen. From 1873 policemen had been able to retire on a pension when they reached 55 years of age, but no maximum compulsory retirement age was set, and many men chose to work beyond the age of 55 to reap the benefits of a higher pension. In 1883 the Longmore Commission recommended that all policemen, irrespective of rank, be forced to retire at 55 years of age. The suggestion was ignored, and nothing was done about the retirement age until 31 August 1889, when Chomley issued a memo to all policemen advising them that 'the age of compulsory retirement has by Ministerial

*The Jubilee Parade, 1897: H. M. Chomley is the officer
in uniform in the foreground; the police band is at the rear*

authority been fixed at 65'. Chomley held the personal view that it was
'absurd' to allow men to retire at 55 and, although past 65 himself, preferred that all policemen be forced to retire at 60 years of age. His rationale
was that, when past 60, 'a man is beginning to feel he is not as active as
he was' and he 'could not go into a row'. Sir Bryan O'Loghlen was one
who opposed the compulsory retirement of sexagenarian police; he cited
his 'old country' experience where 'five judges on the bench' were over
80 years of age. Due to the physical nature of many police duties, the
retirement age was a contentious issue and, in the 1890s, discussion was
spurred on by the lack of employment and promotional opportunities,
caused by sexagenarians delaying their retirement. In 1891 there were
no vacancies in the force, but 1040 men applied to join. In order to ease
the recruiting bottleneck the Government proposed reducing the compulsory retirement age to 60 years thus forcing sixty men, including
Chomley, to retire immediately. The scheme met with vocal opposition
and political lobbying by senior police and sections of the press, who
argued that it would instantly rob the force of its most experienced and
senior officers and was unfair to those who had planned their retirement

and finances around the age fixed in 1889. The debate caused some bitterness among the different vested interest groups within the force, and the *Argus* denounced ambitious young policemen wanting promotion, sarcastically describing them as men knowing 'that they are qualified for the very highest offices' because 'they can tell how many revolutions a coach wheel will make between Melbourne and Bacchus Marsh'. The *Argus* commentaries were critical of youth, ambition and the police examination system, but C. F. Taylor, MLA, a barrister and a captain in the militia, reminded people of the need to provide young policemen with the incentive to work themselves up in the force, adding that 'Napoleon used to say that every private carried a marshal's baton in his knapsack'. Eventually a compromise was reached whereby the compulsory retirement age was fixed at 60, but sexagenarians within the force at that time were allowed to retire over a period of four years. Phasing retirements appeased the older officers while creating vacancies and promotional opportunities for younger men.[57]

As the twentieth century drew closer, so too did the retirement of the most senior of police sexagenarians, H. M. Chomley. Before leaving he

121

finally acted upon a long-standing suggestion made by policemen to the Longmore Commission, and introduced a non-monetary award for merit. Introduced in August 1899, the award for 'pre-eminent valour and bravery displayed in the performance of police duty' was approved by the Chief Secretary and was in the form of 'a similar stripe to the sub-officers', worn reversed on the left arm, above the elbow. The idea of a stripe did not last long and recipients were soon awarded a badge, but in both forms the award was popular with policemen. Until the introduction of such an award for bravery, policemen were rewarded with gifts of money or other presentations, or by an award by the Royal Humane Society of Australasia. Policemen in Victoria frequently received RHS awards, but they wanted an award of their own. Now they had one, made retrospective and eventually awarded to policemen for events that had occurred up to twenty-five years before its inception. Considerable confusion surrounded the initial introduction of the award and its retrospective application, and this has produced debates about who was first to receive it. The first actual recipients were Sergeant W. Rogerson and Constables M. A. Pigott and A. Nicholson, who each received a badge for actions done before August 1899. The award introduced by Chomley has undergone some name and design changes, but a valour award has been a feature of police life in Victoria since his time.[58]

The introduction of a police bravery award was the last noteworthy action taken by Chomley before he retired on 30 June 1902. Under his command the force entered the twentieth century in a sedate manner, befitting a Chief Commissioner with fifty years police service and nearing his seventieth birthday. In many respects he left the force in better shape than he found it, but much of the credit for that was due to the government and the Longmore Royal Commission, pressing for changes in spite of Chomley's resistance. By 1900, policemen had the right to vote, were tested by an examination system, paid removal expenses when transferred, granted seventeen days annual leave, did not have to wear white gloves on patrol and were using telephones for communication. Their lot was such that each time Chomley advertised for recruits between six and seven hundred men applied for the sixty vacancies.[59] Policemen of Chomley's vintage were not, however, quite ready for the twentieth century and the technological and social change it heralded. Police administration in Victoria was still set very much in an 1850s mould, and many years were to elapse before police generally gathered and maintained the momentum necessary for the new century.

'O'Cally-ghin'

Thomas Callinan walked up the Bourke Street hill. He was a big man, six feet tall and inclined to be fat. He was fashionably dressed; a top hat covered his white, thinning hair, and he flourished a walking cane . . .

Thomas O'Callaghan —
or Callinan?

'How old are you Callinan?'
'Mind your own business.'
'You're over sixty, aren't you? And there's been an outcry against you raising the retiring age to sixty-five, so's you can keep your job, isn't there? There are a lot of ambitious men who want your job, aren't there? I think it's wrong to extend the retiring age to sixty-five; so I think I'll bring my influence to bear to have it lowered again, so's the Chief of Police and his doddery old pals will be put out of the force!'
Callinan straightened, 'You're a ruthless, vicious, man West.'

That fictional passage from Frank Hardy's book, *Power Without Glory*, bears an uncanny likeness to Chief Commissioner Thomas O'Callaghan and his old pals. Hardy has said that John West, the hero-villain of *Power Without Glory*, was based on John Wren, and that the policeman featured in the book, Detective Sergeant Dave O'Flaherty, was in reality the famous Detective Sergeant David O'Donnell. Hardy did not link Callinan to O'Callaghan, but there is little doubt about it. Thomas O'Callaghan was just such a man.

O'Callaghan was Inspecting-Superintendent of Police when on 1 July 1902 he succeeded H. M. Chomley as Chief Commissioner. A Catholic and native of New South Wales, he was then 57 years of age and gained the highest post as a result of seniority. He was the second career police-man to make it to the top, and the first one born in Australia. The latter was important to O'Callaghan, and he had been the first Chief President of the Australian Natives Association, having been an active member of the ANA during its formative years. In conjunction with George Turner, later the Premier of Victoria, he framed the first set of rules for the ANA, and in 1885 he was editor of the first edition of its journal, the *National Australian*. The ANA undoubtedly helped O'Callaghan form contacts with influential Australians, including Alfred Deakin, Edmund Barton, Hartley Williams and Isaac Isaacs. In 1902, when O'Callaghan was first appointed Acting Chief Commissioner, the Premier was Sir Alexander Peacock, a member of the ANA Board of Directors and a former Chief President.[60]

Dubbed 'O'Cally-ghin' by the *Melbourne Punch*, O'Callaghan was an enigmatic figure. He headed the force during much of the campaign against John Wren and his totalizator empire, and he embroiled the force in public controversy of a sort not seen since the days of Standish. Like Hardy's Callinan, he was a conceited man who seemingly enjoyed 'the prospect of power and social status which the position promised him'. He was described in parliament as a bombastic individual of peculiar tem-perament, with an infirmity of temper and 'want of capacity to deal with the men of the force'. Later a Royal Commission reported on his 'most unsympathetic character and his brusqueness', and the 'antagonistic spirit' he provoked in the force, leading to the 'gravest' incidents.

O'Callaghan joined the force as a detective in 1867 and quickly proved to be an astute thief-catcher. He was rewarded and commended numer-ous times, his record sheet was filled with adjectives like zealous, active, persevering, efficient and intelligent, and he was nominated for individ-ual praise by the Marquis of Normanby for work performed during a Royal visit. Yet there was another side to O'Callaghan. In 1871 he was charged and reduced in rank for supplying liquor to a prisoner, and on four other occasions he was formally charged and reprimanded for breaches of discipline. In 1882 he was reprimanded and suspended from duty for 'disrespectful demeanour towards the Royal Commission on Police'. In 1883, only three years before being promoted to officer, he was a member of the Detective Branch when the Longmore Royal Com-mission described it as 'a standing menace to the community', and labelled him personally as 'not trustworthy', and his retention in the force 'not likely to be attended with credit or advantage to the public service'. The Longmore Commission—and its judgements were usually sound—also described some of O'Callaghan's actions as being 'enshrouded in an atmosphere of suspicion reflecting discredit upon the department'. Nevertheless, O'Callaghan was not dismissed but promoted, so that by

1905 when another Royal Commission inquired into the force he was again a key figure, this time as Chief Commissioner. This Royal Commission, chaired by James Cameron, MLA for Gippsland East, found that O'Callaghan's administration had 'many blemishes' and that, among other things, he fomented dissent by refusing to retire at age 60 and that, contrary to the Police Regulation Act, he had an improper interest in licensed premises in Carlton. First appointed to office by Peacock in 1902, O'Callaghan received generous political patronage from later conservative governments headed by William H. Irvine, Sir Thomas Bent and John Murray. He survived the Cameron hearings and benefited from retirement age extensions that kept him in office until he resigned in 1913 aged sixty-seven.[61]

Back in 1902 O'Callaghan was not long in office before the relative calm and conciliatory style of Chomley's command was but a faint memory. On 25 November 1902 drastic changes were made to the Police Regulation Act; two days later a notice in the *Police Gazette* extended the retiring age for officers to 65 years. The two changes were unrelated, except in as much as they saved the government money, but together they sent shock-waves through the force. They were government decisions, not administrative actions on the part of the Chief Commissioner, but O'Callaghan was generally regarded as a collaborator on both changes and the principal advocate of the retiring age extension. He personally did not stand to lose from either change.

The Police Regulation Act amendment abolished pensions for future members of the police force. Instead, any men who joined on or after 1 January 1903 were required to 'lodge in the Office of the Chief Commissioner of Police a policy or policies on his life'. The object of the amendment was to save money and 'to place the police force in exactly the same position as the rest of the public service', which had largely lost state pension rights by legislative enactment in 1883. The new police scheme created two categories of men within the force, the 'old hands' (pre-1903 recruits) who were fully covered by a state superannuation fund, and the 'new hands' who were simply covered by an insurance policy paid for by themselves. When the subject was debated in parliament one member argued that constables deserved special consideration because they served the State 'in a hazardous occupation'. Such calls went unheeded and the Bill passed speedily with little debate. This shrewd political exercise did not alter the pension benefits due to O'Callaghan or other serving policemen. Consequently, the Bill did not meet with much opposition in 1902, but unrest spread like a cancer later as the number of policemen without pensions steadily increased. In 1903 only sixty-four men of a force of 1500 did not have pension rights, and it was many years before those men not entitled to a pension were numerically superior. In 1923 they and the pension issue rose to the fore as central features of the police strike. The retired H. M. Chomley foresaw trouble in 1905, when he warned the Bent government and the O'Callaghan administration that 'if there were a strike in the police, or the police were disaffected, we would be in a queer state. A pension always keeps a man safe'. Of the 636 policemen who went on strike in 1923, only two had the contingent right to a pension.[62]

The talk of police strikes and disaffection in 1905 was not without foundation. The Order-in-Council of 1902, which raised the officers' retirement age to 65 years, prompted police agitation of a kind unprecedented in Australia. In direct terms the extended retiring age applied only to the thirty-eight officers, but in reality it affected policemen of all ranks with aspirations to promotion. The Government claimed that the change was made to save £4000 in pension payments, but it was revealed in parliament that O'Callaghan had pushed the plan to keep him and his senior officers in power for an extra five years. During the 1890s O'Callaghan was a ringleader of the successful movement to have the police retiring age fixed at sixty. This accelerated his own promotion, and because of his stand many policemen supported his appointment as Chief Commissioner. Upon attaining that post the ageing O'Callaghan had the retiring age for officers raised to 65, and successfully resisted all efforts to force him to retire until he was 67 years old.

Many younger policemen felt betrayed by O'Callaghan's 'right-about-face movement'. It would block promotion opportunities for at least five years and cost junior police dearly in terms of wages, allowances and positions. Constables then took twenty years to get promoted to sergeant, and many men felt that the extended retiring age gave them 'no earthly chance of ever getting promotion'. There was much rhetoric bandied about regarding Napoleon's batons in knapsacks, and concern was expressed that the police force was 'a mass of seething discontent'. The Government added more fuel to the discontent when the Chief Secretary, John Murray, said, 'Economy had guided the Government . . . the Government had not to consider only what the men might like or desire. They had no statutory rights with regard to this at all'.

A number of policemen took a bold stand and banded together to oppose the new Order-in-Council. They collected subscriptions, engaged the services of a solicitor and held a protest meeting in the Friendly Societies Dispensary, Bowen Street, Melbourne, on 19 March 1903. Not since the police pay disputes of the 1860s had policemen in Victoria combined to oppose so forcefully a government decision. Indeed, so assertive were the men in 1903 that their solicitor wrote to O'Callaghan advising him that they were meeting 'as a matter of right' to debate the Order. O'Callaghan replied that he did not object to their meeting, but asked that the press be excluded and gave the hollow order 'that no discussion as to the action of the Governor-in-Council will be permitted'.

The meeting went ahead without representatives of the press being present, but a full account of it did appear in newspapers such as the *Argus*, which supported the agitating policemen and made reference to the need for 'some epidemic, particularly fatal to the higher ranks' to break out in Victoria. The combined force of organized policemen, a sympathetic press and concerned politicians was eventually successful in cancelling the 'obnoxious Order-in-Council'. The men won their battle over all the officers except O'Callaghan, whose political patrons kept him in office.[63]

The success of this campaign was regarded as the first step rather than the end of agitation by some policemen, and a committee was formed to formally establish a Victoria Police Association. Nowhere else in Australia had policemen so openly dared to form a combination of the sort constituted by trade unions, and police associations were rare even in Europe and North America. Not surprisingly, many Victorian policemen were reluctant to openly support or identify themselves with the fledgeling Police Association, but two key figures in the 'retirement-at-sixty campaign' put their names to public documents urging the formation of such a unit. Sergeant W. J. Costelloe, of Royal Park, and Constable A. E. Strickland, of Russell Street, signed themselves as 'proposed Honorary Treasurer' and 'proposed Honorary Secretary' respectively, when on 29 November 1904 they wrote to O'Callaghan asking him to approve the 'Rules of the Victorian Police Association'. O'Callaghan and the pro-O'Callaghan government of Thomas Bent did not approve of any such association and the move lapsed until World War I. Most policemen were not prepared to push the matter and were content with the success gained in the retiring-age campaign. Costelloe and Strickland were part of a notable minority in the force. Even by world standards, they were in the vanguard of moves to improve the lot of policemen and were making open efforts to force change in a highly disciplined occupation controlled virtually by an oligarchy. The stated objects of the proposed association had been: 'To guard the interests of its members individually and collectively. To instil in them the need of mutual improvement, and for the interchange of opinions in respect to police matters generally'. Neither O'Callaghan nor his senior officers were ready for an interchange of opinions and the proposed association was denounced as being 'designed with a view to not only exercise political control but also to support its members in any conflict with constituted authority'. Fortunately for Costelloe and Strickland, the end of their movement was all that O'Callaghan desired. They accepted his decision, and no disciplinary or other action was taken against them. Strickland, however, regretted his part in the retirement-at-sixty agitation and the moves to form an association because his prominent role as secretary to both groups saw him 'classed as an agitator', and that was not a stigma easily carried in the conservative world of policemen.[64]

Costelloe and Strickland were not the only agitators in the force, and O'Callaghan was confronted in ensuing months by a barrage of accusations from serving and former policemen. In April 1905 O'Callaghan's authority was challenged when a delegation of constables from Russell Street, accompanied by their parliamentary representative, personally approached the Chief Secretary and asked him to annul an order with which they disagreed. The order, which confined a number of constables to barracks as a reserve force in case of emergency, was cancelled after a few weeks. In the interim, however, the men involved by-passed their senior officers, including O'Callaghan, and ignored the chain of command and *Police Regulations* to take their case directly to the Chief Secretary. It was further evidence of the unrest in the force, and also evidence of the gains to be made by policemen who took organized and direct action.[65]

Shortly after the controversy over the barracks deputation, complaints about the force reached such a pitch that the Bent government appointed a Royal Commission on 15 August 1905 to inquire into the police. It was the first such inquiry since the Longmore Royal Commission of 1881–83 and was beset from the outset 'by members of the Force coming forward with grievances which they imagined were serious enough for a Royal Commission to deal with . . . charges and complaints of the most trumpery character'. The Royal Commission held fifty-six public sittings and heard evidence from 134 witnesses, including Chomley and O'Callaghan. Many of the allegations and much of the evidence were of a trifling nature but a number of important areas were studied by the Commission, including police administration, methods, training and pay. The Commissioners also devoted considerable attention to lotteries and gaming, gambling clubs, and the inability of the police to permanently close the Collingwood totalizator, or Wren's Tote. Given the attention focused on Wren's Tote by the Commission, the non-appearance of John Wren as a witness was undoubtedly one of the Inquiry's principal shortcomings. No reason was given for his failure to testify, but he was alive and well.

Wren and his totalizator empire had flourished since 1893 and Wren had thwarted all attempts by policemen to permanently shut down his illegal operations. The Royal Commission found that policemen were 'powerless to suppress' Wren, due to 'the inefficacy of existing legislation', and it advocated sweeping legal reforms. After lengthy and heated parliamentary debates, reforms were given effect on 28 December 1906, with the passing of the Lotteries Gaming and Betting Act. It gave the police the power they needed to control illegal gambling effectively, and Wren's Tote was closed for good in 1907, ending a unique phase in the development of policing in Victoria and signalling the dawn of a new era. Policemen had been confronted by organized criminals who treated illegal activity as commercial enterprise and used the combined skills of lawyers, politicians, petty gangsters and corrupt officials. Wren's team flagrantly exploited and flouted inadequate legislation to make illegal gambling a profitable business, doing so on a scale that individual poicemen could scarcely comprehend, let alone counter. Wren's operations fit the classic organized crime mould common in the 1980s but, until the time of Wren, policemen had principally dealt with crime and criminals on an individual level: the idea of the solitary and local beat constable being a 'Jack-of-all-trades' was entrenched. Wren's activities, however, forced policemen to plan special operations, using large numbers of policemen, and produced police personalities who matched the public profile of Wren and his henchmen. Early identities like Senior Constable Tom Waldron and Detective Inspector J. M. Christie were public figures not just because they were policemen, but because of their physical strength and sporting prowess. The twentieth century, however, heralded a 'cops and robbers' cult, and saw many policemen become identities solely because of their work. Detective Sergeant David O'Donnell, a mammoth of a man who stood 6 feet 2 inches tall and weighed 22 stone, was the main police protagonist in the war on Wren, and he subsequently became a household name throughout the State. During the police campaign against illegal gambling, O'Donnell was daily followed home by criminals, his house was bombed and young policemen who worked on his team were assaulted, threatened and offered bribes. O'Donnell had at times used up to seventy-five policemen, equipped with guns and battering rams, in his operations against Wren's Tote. Not since the Kelly days had the police been forced to combine, plan and operate on such a scale.[66]

Although the Cameron Royal Commission and subsequent legal changes helped to suppress illegal gambling for a time, the influence of the Commission was limited. It did provide a forum for policemen and others to ventilate their grievances, and thereby facilitated public insight into, and control of, the police force, but overall the inquiry fell far short of the Longmore Royal Commission. This was due in part to a premature closing of the hearings by the Premier, Thomas Bent, who refused additional funds to sustain the inquiry. The Commission did, however, expose O'Callaghan's shortcomings and offered constructive suggestions for some police reforms, including proper police training, an improved method of working the beat system, and the general introduction of photographs and record sheets for use by policemen in identifying criminals. In some respects, Wren's activities, like those of Ned Kelly, precipitated important reforms for the police who pursued him.

O'Callaghan, like Standish, weathered the accusations and innuendo directed at him before the appointment of an inquiry and survived the subsequent probing to continue as Chief Commissioner. He impressed the Royal Commission 'with his intimate knowledge of every phase of the Police Service', and won praise for his new *Police Code*. Published in 1906 to replace the 1877 *Police Regulations*, O'Callaghan's code was described as 'an excellent work', and was the most comprehensive of its kind published in Victoria to that time, in many respects demonstrating O'Callaghan's enigmatic nature. Unlike Chomley, O'Callaghan was prepared to tackle big tasks and he wrote the code himself. Notwithstanding his brusque manner and history of misconduct, O'Callaghan was clearly willing to experiment with tasks that his predecessor shied away from. O'Callaghan also experimented with formal training classes to prepare policemen for examinations, and was responsible for introducing fingerprint classification and identification into the force.

Detective Lionel Frank Potter commenced in 1904 to compile a fingerprint collection at the Russell Street Detective Office. The science of fingerprint analysis was then new to police forces around the world. Potter's main duty was to compile the weekly *Police Gazette*, but he was above average in intelligence and performance and was quick to learn fingerprint identification from Edward Henry's classic 1900 study, *Classification and Uses of Fingerprints*. Within two years, Potter was commended for the character and class of his work in compiling a fingerprint system, and in 1906 he was commended for his knowledge of fingerprint analysis and good work in securing the conviction of a man who stole a cash box containing £90. This case appears to be the first in Victoria where fingerprint evidence was used to secure the conviction of an offender. The climax for Potter came some years later, when in 1912 the High Court of Australia handed down a landmark decision in the case of *R. v. Parker*, ruling that 'where it is proved that a crime has been committed, resemblance of fingerprints may of itself in connection with other circumstances be sufficient evidence of the identity of an accused person with the person who committed the crime charged'. Potter gave expert evidence in this case, and the decision—applying to all Australian States and Territories—still stands. From small beginnings in the *Police Gazette* room, the collection begun by Potter was, over eighty years, increased to more than 500 000 sets of fingerprints that form an essential part of modern police investigation.[67]

O'Callaghan had encouraged fingerprint analysis, and he also experimented with anthrometrics—a system of criminal identification using body measurements. He undoubtedly made a genuine effort to nudge his force into the twentieth century. Although he resisted changes of the kind sought by progressives like Strickland and Costelloe, he at least resisted the temptation to victimize them. And, although O'Callaghan was gradually throwing off the vestiges of nineteenth-century policing, there was one other advance he was not ready for: the onslaught of the horseless carriage. The automobile was about to revolutionize life in Victoria and overwhelm men like W. H. Colechin, MLA for Geelong, who ridiculed the 'desire on the part of a number of persons to encourage motor cars and traction engines in preference to horses'. Few people had any real notion of how dramatically and permanently motor cars would change their lives, and not the least among them were 'O'Cally-ghin' and his men.[68]

4

Fighting with the Gloves Off

The opening decades of the twentieth century produced some of the most far-reaching changes to police organization ever. It was a time of social, economic, technological and industrial upheaval, and was marked and marred by conflict. The key event was World War I, which involved policemen to an extent and in ways that have long gone unnoticed. Just as the war touched the lives of many other Australians, so also it touched the police force and influenced attitudes, ideas, recruiting, duties, workload, and ultimately the direction of policing. The appointment of women police came about partly because of the war, while the advent of the motor car and the formation of a police union were other important innovations. Indeed, the motor car irreversibly altered the nature of police work and police community relations. While these broader events were taking place, the force had four Chief Commissioners, men whose leadership ranged from exceptional to mediocre. The pressures of war, command changes, unionization, social conditions and political climate combined to create an environment in which a police strike was possible—and finally came in 1923. Conflict and change were the essence of this age, when policemen fought battles on many fronts, against foes that at times included motorists and motorization, Germans, politicians and each other.

The Horseless Carriage

In 1912 a new mounted police depot was built at the corner of Grant and Dodds streets, South Melbourne. Costing £14 064, the complex was reputed to be the best in the southern hemisphere and included a riding school, horse-breaking yards and stables for seventy-five horses. The men of the force had a long and proud association with horses dating back to the 1830s, but the new stable complex was bigger and better than anything they had known in that time. Mistakenly, it was built in the twilight years of mounted policing, in an age when the automobile was about to take over from the horse. Instead of building stables the police should have been building garages. Motor cars were soon changing streetscapes across Victoria, revolutionizing personal transport, and altering the nature of policing and community relations.

The first motor car in Melbourne was built locally in 1897 by the Australasian Horseless Carriage Syndicate and was described as having the appearance of 'a stylish double-seated dog cart'. It was a time of swift invention and, by 1903, there were sufficient motoring enthusiasts in Victoria to form the Automobile Club of Victoria. In 1904 these motorists held their first rally and boasted that their 'chariots race without horses'. In 1905 Dunlop held the first motor car reliability trial in Australia and, also, the first Victorian motoring fatality occurred when a car collided with a cyclist. New expressions crept into common usage as cyclists and pedestrians spoke of 'road hogs' in motor cars, and motorists spoke of 'police traps'. In only eight years the horseless carriage eclipsed the bicycle as the ideal mechanical hack and sped along the road of public acceptance to challenge the horse.[1]

Motor cars were generally faster, noisier and often smellier than any horse-drawn vehicle and, at an early stage in their development, displayed a potential in the hands of mere mortals to kill and maim their occupants, pedestrians, cyclists and animals. They also frightened children, horses and others not yet initiated into the new world. It was the motor car's awesome combination of speed and noise that prompted moves to control its use. The need for controls loomed large in the minds of many people and, in 1905, Sir Samuel Gillott introduced the Motor Car Bill 'to regulate the use of motor cars'. Gillott's Bill was modelled on the English Motor Car Act of 1903 and proposed that all motor cars be registered, all drivers licensed, and a maximum speed limit of 20 miles an hour apply to motor cars on public roads throughout the state. Gillott intended that municipal councils would undertake the registration and licensing functions and that council officers would join with police to enforce the speed limits and other regulations. This was the case in England, where county and borough councils had traditionally controlled the use of locomotives, traction engines and motor cars. The ACV argued strongly against the controls proposed by Gillott, and parliamentarians divided for and against the motor car. During debates on the Bill the notion of police checking drivers' licences was compared to 'the old digger hunting days at Ballarat that led to Eureka', and concern was expressed about the possible 'over-officiousness' of policemen enforcing speed and licence regulations: 'Honorable members desired to be assured that the power of restriction in these matters would not be placed wholly in the hands of policemen'. The Gillott Bill did not become law, but it did promote considerable lobbying and debate, thus heightening public awareness about the potential of motor cars.

Opposition to the Motor Car Bill and the proposed police role served as a valuable indicator of things to come. The police in Victoria had always had a part to play in the regulation of horse riders and horse-drawn vehicles and it was a role where their involvement and authority were

*A changing streetscape: Elizabeth and Collins Streets,
Melbourne, in the 1920s*

rarely ever questioned. Constables kept a watchful eye over cabmen, lorry
drivers and bullockies, and under the provisions of the Police Offences
Act could prosecute larrikin horsemen and others who rode or drove 'furi-
ously or negligently' through any public place. Cabmen, traction engine
operators and other paid transport drivers were licensed by municipal
authorities, but policemen were not involved there and confined their
role to preservation of the public safety. Individuals who rode or drove
horses or bicycles for private pleasure or transport did not need a licence,
and there were no fixed speed limits. The motor car, however, introduced
elements of danger, arbitrariness and class into this scene and from the
outset hardened the attitudes of those involved.

The new standards, embodied in the 1903 English Motor Car Act and
proposed in Victoria by Gillott, were not unduly restrictive but they were
in some respects arbitrary, and they did impose general legal obligations
upon motorists that had never been applied to horsemen. Laws intended

to protect all road users might have stood a good chance of early acceptance but for the fact that they struck first and hardest at wealthy and influential people. Although the popularity of motor vehicles was spreading
quickly they were an expensive luxury item, costing up to £2000 each,
when workers' wages were only several pounds a week. The people who
then owned motor cars were not the types usually checked or arrested by
the police, and the thought of this occurring because they were motorists
was anathema to them. Debates on Gillott's Bill were punctuated by talk
of wealth and class, with proponents of the new laws arguing that 'the
people who drive motor cars are usually well-to-do, and there ought certainly not to be one law for the rich and another for the poor'. Opponents
to the Bill objected that 'no constable should be at liberty to arrest a gentleman straight off the reel' and that arrest 'depended, of course, on the position the man occupied'. An indication of the exclusive state of motoring
was the time devoted during debates to the question of chauffeurs and
their wages, and whether chauffeurs or car owners would be liable for
civil action or criminal prosecution under the proposed laws. It was a time
when chauffeurs had their own club, and when Tarrant's Garage in Melbourne provided a waiting room and a billiard table for chauffeurs, waiting at the works while their employers' cars were being repaired. Had the
majority of motorists in 1905 been poor workers, rather than well-to-do
gentlemen, there is little doubt that the Motor Car Bill would have had a
speedy passage through parliament. However, the spectre of policemen
stopping gentlemen and their chauffeurs for licence and registration
checks was enough to stall the Bill in its infancy. The prolonged period
of estrangement between motorists and policemen had begun even before
laws regulating motor traffic were enacted.[2]

The ACV and other influential motorists managed to defer motor
traffic regulations until 1908, when another Motor Car Bill was brought
before parliament, this time by Sir Alexander Peacock, with the introduction 'that motors are being generally utilised now, not only for pleasure,
but also for business . . . it is essential that there should be some legislation
to deal with this new and increasing traffic which takes place throughout
the metropolitan area'. In the few years since Gillott's Bill was shelved,
the cost of motor cars had steadily dropped, the number of cars and motor
cycles in use had steadily increased and, almost as Peacock spoke, cars
were being used in military exercises in Victoria and by the publishers of
the *Herald* to deliver newspapers around Melbourne. The 1908 Motor
Car Bill differed markedly from Gillott's proposals in that it vested
responsibility for registration, licensing, and enforcement with the police
and in its final form did not stipulate a set speed limit, but instead prohibited any person from driving a motor car 'on a public highway reck-
lessly or negligently or at a speed or in a manner which is dangerous to
the public'.

Parliamentary and public discussions on the new Bill were couched in similar terms to those of 1905, but experience had removed some of the obstacles to enactment that had blocked the first Bill. There was still a great deal of debate about wealth, class, police power, speed and danger but all parties appear to have drawn upon the comprehensive finding of a 1906 English Royal Commission that had studied most aspects of motor car regulation, including speed limits and police methods. The English experience was that fixed maximum speed limits were not feasible and that their regulation placed the police in open conflict with motorists, diverting valuable police manpower from other duties to traffic work. The English Commission recommended that the 'general speed limit of 20 miles an hour' be abolished and, principally because of that recommendation, no general speed limit was included in the first Victorian Motor Act. When the legislation was being debated, the policing of speed limits was seemingly uppermost in the minds of many people. The practice of timing speeding motorists was described as 'un-English' and 'rather humiliating'; indeed, as something that 'detracted from the proper and dignified duties of the police'. The manner of enforcing speed limits overseas worried Norman Bayles, MLA for Toorak, motorist and member of the ACV, and he described them in the hope that they would not be adopted in Victoria:

> They have a policeman stationed behind a hedge with a signal wire along a measured furlong. The policeman has a stop watch and he signals to a man at the other end of the wire when a car passes, and if a person drives only half-a-mile over the 20-mile limit he is a law breaker.

Some members of the House could see 'nothing trappy' in the police behaviour described by Bayles, and complimented the police for their 'ingenuity in bringing to justice people who infringe the laws'. However, Bayles and the ACV won the day and, in place of a general speed limit, there was substituted the notion of driving to the common danger, whereby motorists could drive as fast as they liked unless it was proved to be dangerous to the public. This provision was analogous to that of 'furious riding', which was the principal and traditional legal control over horsemen who endangered public safety.

Although discussion about general speed limits was an important feature of the 1908–9 Motor Car Bill debates, considerable attention was also devoted to general police powers over motorists and the question of socioeconomic class. Concern was expressed about the move to give policemen full control of all registration, licensing and enforcement duties relevant to motor cars, and a number of people urged that municipal councils should undertake some of the work, as in England. Peacock, however, successfully pushed his proposals through parliament, arguing that a centralized system for recording licence and registration details was the most viable and that the police force was the logical government department to do the work. He also stressed that the police, unlike municipal councils, were 'under the control of Parliament' and that 'administration will cost nothing'. The last facile statement was in reality a euphemism meaning that the cost of administration would be absorbed within the police budget. Sixty years later Colonel Sir Eric St Johnston inspected the force and reported that nowhere else in the world were policemen 'responsible for the registration of motor vehicles. It is clearly not a police function and should be carried out by a different organization', but in 1908 the force was a cheap expedient. Two members of parliament sought to raise the question of police manpower and suggested that 'the proper control of the motor car traffic will require a great addition to the police force', but the subject lapsed without further debate. It was not a topic that Peacock or his government were prepared to take up, particularly as they were going to administer the Motor Car Act at no cost.

Once the legislators had satisfied themselves about the questions of licensing, registration and speed control, the principal subject of contention was class: how would policemen deal with wealthy motorists? This big obstacle of 1905 was more readily overcome in 1908. John Murray, MLA for Warrnambool, and a man with some sympathy for Labor, argued without being contradicted that 'far and above the luxuries of the rich man, far above the privileges of caste, is the safety of the general public', and that 'no duty is more properly the duty of the police than to protect the lives of the public'. Murray's line might have met the fate of similar arguments propounded in 1905 except that even the wealthy could now see a need for regulation: 'motor cars have come to stay' and 'cars will come within the reach of the man with moderate means'. There was even talk of cars coming 'within the means of humbler individuals', and of a time when 'every poor person' could drive a car. The motor car was confusing the class barriers. Rich motorists would need as much police protection from poor motorists as pedestrians would need from chauffeur-driven limousines. The Motor Car Act and Regulations came into operation on 1 March 1910, and the Victoria Police Force became the single statewide authority for licensing drivers, registering motor vehicles and enforcing all the provisions of both the Act and Regulations.[3]

The new motor car laws added to police work and altered relations between policemen and the steadily increasing motoring section of the community. During the first four months of the Act's operation the force registered 2645 motor vehicles and licensed 3204 drivers. By the end of 1911 these figures had grown to 4844 vehicles and 5935 drivers; within a decade they had raced to 29 354 and 34 236 respectively. The annual renewal and maintenance of records, and the collection of revenue related to that work, in 1912 prompted the formation of a special group, the Motor Police, who operated a central office in Melbourne and were the genesis of the vast Motor Registration Branch. The Motor Police, however, performed only a small amount of the total registration and licensing work, most of which fell to policemen across the state. During the 1920s attempts were made to transfer responsibility for motor vehicle registration and record keeping from the force to the Treasury and Country Roads Board, because it was 'a fruitful source of revenue'. However, these moves were successfully resisted by police administrators on the ground that 'the closest contact between the police and the registration system' was essential 'to ensure as effective a control as possible over traffic offences, burglaries, thefts of cars [and] movements of organised criminal gangs'. The full import of the awesome rise in vehicle and driver registrations is best shown in relation to other factors. The first ten years operation of the Motor Car Act included the duration of World War I, and in the years from 1910 to 1919 the number of policemen per 10 000 population fell from 12.28 to 11.49. The number of horses actually rose in this time from 442 829 to 523 788, but, while the death rate in horse-drawn vehicle, tram, bicycle, and railway accidents remained relatively static, together amounting to less than two a week, fatal motor vehicle accidents rose to an average of one a week, and from 1913 warranted specific mention in the *Victorian Year Book*. Traffic control, of both horses and motor vehicles, was just one facet of police work and a declining number of policemen still had to cope with special wartime duties and increases in general patrol and crime work.[4]

Motor traffic control also altered the relationship between police and large numbers of citizens. Horsemen and policemen had long experienced cordial relations. Although fruit vendors and drivers of hansom cabs were at times prosecuted, policemen regulating street traffic were expected to have 'a knowledge of horses', to 'display intelligence, steadiness and discretion' and to 'assist the public', by zeal and attention avoiding prosecutions rather than increasing them. This philosophy was epitomized by pointsmen at the intersection of Swanston and Flinders streets, Melbourne, who were directed to facilitate at all times the unimpeded progress of horse-drawn lorries and who were issued with a shovel and a box of sand, to be used if lumbering Clydesdales' hooves were slipping on the road. The shovelling of sand was a service happily rendered by policemen, and one gladly received by drivers of struggling horse teams. At the other end of the spectrum, policemen also played a vital role in the stopping of bolting and runaway horses. It was dangerous work, requiring a special brand of strength, skill and courage, but was nevertheless a common feature of police life at the turn of the century. Many policemen were commended for such deeds and eleven of them received Valour Badges for 'stopping bolting horses at great personal risk'.

The advent of the motor car gradually altered this picture, and the policeman with sand and shovel was replaced by one with a stopwatch and notebook. Soon after the passing of the Motor Car Act, police methods for regulating motor traffic were described as 'the veriest moonshine', and Chief Commissioner O'Callaghan was forced to publicly defend the traffic work of his men, claiming that they were 'not after scalps'. Although the Motor Car Act did not contain a general speed limit, much of the traffic duty done by policemen centred on the detection of motorists driving at a speed that was considered dangerous to the public, which thrust the force and motorists headlong into conflict. The ACV started a legal defence fund to fight police cases, and there were constant suggestions that police methods were defective, their stopwatches inaccurate and their attitude to motorists jaundiced. Police in Victoria adopted the English system of using stopwatches to check the speed of motor cars over a measured distance, but—as with their later use of speedometers, amphometers, breathalysers and digitectors—they were continually accused of making inaccurate readings or using inaccurate chronographs, and policemen found themselves locked into vitriolic legal arguments with motorists and their solicitors. Heated and difficult court cases were not new to policemen but, whereas they had traditionally been contests between policemen and criminals, they were increasingly becoming disputes between policemen and ordinary motorists. The class element still played a part, and the Prahran Court was the venue of the most public and hard-fought cases, when the bench heard charges against wealthy speedsters, booked while travelling along the road to Toorak. The press found that reports of motor accidents and traffic cases were popular with readers, so they became regular features. So frequent were such reports that indexes to the *Argus* included special entries on motor prosecutions and accidents. It had not happened in the day of the horse.

The estrangement between motorists and policemen, first coming to light in 1905, increased in scope and intensity as motor cars became more common. It was a seemingly irreversible trend and one succinctly described by T. A. Critchley when writing of similar events in England:

> to a growing number of citizens for whom any dealings with the police would have been exceptional, the policeman of every village and town became a man to be reckoned with . . . a figure of authority . . . the town policeman was showing more interest in catching speeding motorists than in his traditional weaknesses for rabbit pie, plump cooks in basement kitchens, and pretty parlourmaids.[5]

There were other consequences. Thefts of and from motor cars constituted a new and lucrative form of criminal activity and, soon after numbers of motor vehicles appeared on Melbourne streets, advertisements appeared for steering-gear and ignition locks to prevent misuse and loss by theft. Motor vehicles also offered the criminal classes greater mobility, the speed and adaptability of motor vehicles having many advantages over horses, trains and boats—although plans could still be upset. In 1916 William Haines was found shot dead in a hire car at Doncaster, allegedly murdered by Squizzy Taylor in a quarrel after they had rented a Unic open tourer in the city and driven toward Templestowe with the intention of robbing a bank agency.

The same features that attracted criminals to cars also caught the eye of others. Before the outbreak of World War I motor cars were being used in Victoria for commercial and military purposes, and as mail vans and ambulances, but the men who administered the Motor Car Act were slow to utilize motor cars in their own work. In 1904 it was suggested that policemen swap some of their horses for motor cars to 'lend wings to the feet of the law', but the proposals were filed without comment. So policemen were motorless in an increasingly motorized society; by bicycle and tram they pursued motor cars. It was a source of derision, and it heightened friction between motorists and policemen, sections of the motoring community regarding non-use of the car as clear evidence of police prejudice against motor vehicles and their drivers. This contrasted sharply with the situation in some overseas police forces, most notably in Paris, where policemen were 'trained as motor car drivers and specially allocated to supervising motor traffic'. When eventually the Victorian force did use motor vehicles it was at first only for the transport of people and property, and it was some years later (in 1922) that policemen actually used motor vehicles for traffic and patrol work. Yet policemen were among the earlier motoring fatalities; two constables from the Police Band died in December 1911 at Camperdown, when a Rolls Royce in which they were passengers lost a wheel and crashed during a band visit to the district. The first fatal accident involving a police patrol vehicle occurred in 1926 when a Lancia car overturned near the Alfred Hospital, killing the wireless operator, Constable Arthur Currie.[6]

The intensity of the hostility between policemen and motorists abated but never disappeared. Regulation of motor traffic was a new and ongoing duty that increasingly occupied police time and distanced the force from large sections of the community. Many traffic laws were absolute, and people were liable to prosecution and conviction even if they did not know they were doing wrong. Constables had traditionally pursued bush-rangers, footpads, vagabonds and others of similar ilk, and few honest people questioned that police role. With the coming of the motor car, constables were also required to pursue the likes of the local magistrate, mayor, bank manager and parson. To the policeman anyone who drove a motor vehicle was a potential law breaker, and to the motorist all police-men were potential prosecutors. The rules had changed. Something was lost in police and community relationships when the sand boxes disappeared from busy street corners.

A National Existence

Nationhood and federalism were developments of little direct significance to the Victoria Police Force until World War I, when the police of
all states were inextricably caught up in the national war effort. The Great
War, like the advent of the motor car, altered the relationships of policemen with large sections of the community and forced policemen to alter
their thinking and their methods, in order to meet the mixed demands of
the domestic policing needs of a state and the pressing federal needs of a
nation at war. In a rousing and patriotic oration at the Melbourne Town
Hall on 15 August 1914, Chief Commissioner Alfred George Sainsbury
plunged the force into the war effort by declaring that 'we were fighting
with the gloves off a deadly and determined enemy, fighting to the death
. . . we were fighting—not for the sake of Jingoism or even patriotism but
for our national existence'. The loss of the war, he went on, would mean
'the establishment of a German Police Force, and in fact the Germanising
and controlling of all city and country institutions by the enemy'.
Sainsbury advocated the formation of 'a regiment of one thousand well
disciplined and drilled men, comprising police and police pensioners';
and boasted that 'if the police had to face the foe they would show that
they were as courageous and game as any'. Although Sainsbury offered
his services as commander of such a unit, and suggested that 'the Commonwealth arm us and the State pay us', it was not a practical proposition:
he was in effect pledging more than half of his men to the expeditionary
force. The idea was not accepted, but the Government did allow policemen to volunteer, and the first to enlist did so within days of the outbreak
of a war in which 139 members of the force enrolled for active service,
twenty-seven of them either being killed in action or dying of wounds.
Military promotion was earned by seventy-nine members, and decorations conferred on some of them included the Distinguished Service
Order, Distinguished Conduct Medal, Military Medal and Croix de
Guerre.[7]

The number of policemen who went to war fell well short of Sainsbury's
envisaged regiment, and when the fervour of his oration began to die so
too did the level of support given to those men who enlisted—a failure of
action to match ardent rhetoric that was not confined to the police. Nevertheless, policemen contemplating enlistment were beset by a confusion
of bureaucratic haggling over wages, life insurance premiums, reinstatement rights and other entitlements. Many people, including policemen,
were unprepared for the onset of war and in the absence of contingency
planning the precedent for decision-making was often the Boer War. So
the first policemen to enlist were discharged from the force by compulsory resignation, paid in full, instructed to hand in their kits, requested
to pay increased life insurance premiums in advance and dropped as
much as 5s 2d a day in wages. Representations were made to the govern-

142

ment on behalf of policemen wanting to enlist and, as the war progressed, conditions of enlistment were made clearer and more attractive. In 1915 it was decided that the positions of all policemen who went to war 'would remain open for them on their return to Victoria'. If, under ordinary circumstances, they would have been granted increased pay during their time in the army, that was granted to them on their return to police duty: they were 'simply regarded as being on leave'. The Government also agreed to maintain the compulsory police life-assurance policies for those who went to war, but this was not matched by insurance companies, who demanded higher premiums paid in advance because policemen were engaged in active service abroad, not just for the defence of Australia. The Government refused, when asked, to follow the lead of 'private firms and banks' in making up the difference between the 7s 6d a day paid to constables and the five shillings a day they earned as privates in the expeditionary forces. Patriotism had its price: at least one constable returned from service overseas to be refused reinstatement in the force because his pre-war police record was not good. But sometimes patriotism was rewarded: 178 civilians who went to war, and returned home fit and well, were given preferential recruitment into the police force for serving King and Country.

In *Sunday at Kooyong Road* Brian Lewis suggests that for young boys like him in 1914–18 'The police are enemies for they are Irish and the Irish are opposed to the war ... The Irish police show a reluctance to change the dark-blue uniform of the State for the khaki of the Commonwealth; the police become more and more Irish as the war goes on'. He is both right and wrong. Only one Irish member of the police force is known to have enlisted in the army during World War I but of 250 men who joined the police force during that period only six were Irishmen, the only perceptible increase in the Irishness of the force being in the minds of those harbouring prejudices.

For many policemen the most important battle was fought on the home front where a depleted force served both a state and a federal master, with a variety of added wartime responsibilities. The routine work of policemen escaped the notice of many people, including the war historian Ernest Scott who, apart from one favourable passage of seven lines, spares the police only several curt mentions in his 922-page tome, *Australia during the War*. The essential nature of much police work was not overlooked by everybody, however, and Major General Sir John Gellibrand drew on his military experiences when he wrote, 'It cannot be too strongly urged that police are in a sense a force on active service in a continuous campaign . . .'[8]

A police recruiting poster, pre-World War I

The man who headed the force during its 'continuous campaign' from 1913 to 1919 was Alfred George Sainsbury, who succeeded Thomas O'Callaghan as Chief Commissioner on 1 April 1913. O'Callaghan's retirement, like much of his police career, was topical and public—being debated in parliament and featured in the daily newspapers, the *Argus* in particular urging his resignation and applauding its acceptance. According to that paper, the force under O'Callaghan was 'utterly demoralised', 'suffering from a kind of moral dry-rot' and lacking 'morale and tone'. It is true that police pay and work conditions had deteriorated, fostering discontent throughout the force. This was due more to a lack of government funding than to O'Callaghan's administration, yet his rigid discipline and brusque manner made him a focal point for disaffection. The moves toward police unionization that he sparked and extinguished in 1903 were again ignited in 1913. At the age of sixty-seven and after a decade at the top, his administration was stultified, lacking innovation and a sense of direction. He did leave the force in a rundown state and the men in it disenchanted, and he continued his enigmatic ways during retirement: he visited police departments in Europe and North America and, on his return, encroached on Sainsbury's administration by submitting a report to the Government, suggesting police reforms of a sort that he should have implemented himself while Chief Commissioner. He then went on to sit regularly as a Justice of the Peace at the Melbourne Court of Petty Sessions and became a prominent local historian, serving as president of the Royal Historical Society of Victoria and publishing several articles about early Victorian history. In 1923 he made a searing public statement, denouncing the police strikers in Victoria, whose refusal to work was largely rooted in decisions taken under him.[9]

Sainsbury was a moderate achiever, although generally overlooked by historians. In each of three works touching on Victorian police history, Sainsbury rates a scant paragraph and is generally squashed between O'Callaghan and his successor with comments like 'Sainsbury's administration, possibly due to the war, was not particularly distinguished'. On the contrary, because of the war and the social and industrial turmoil of those years, his term of office ranks among the most testing of the pre-1939 era. Sainsbury was a native of Heidelberg, Victoria, and after working as a farrier he joined the force as a mounted constable on 17 May 1878 at the age of twenty-four. He worked his way through the ranks, serving in different parts of the state as a detective and in uniform, and along the way he amassed twenty-six commendations, including a famous one for 'elucidating a north-eastern mystery, in which a baby was murdered and the body was thrown to the pigs to eat'. Unlike O'Callaghan's record, Sainsbury's was exemplary; he was never charged with misconduct, nor made the subject of an inquiry. When appointed Chief Commissioner, he held the rank of Inspecting-Superintendent

Chief Commissioner
A. G. Sainsbury

and, at fifty-seven, was the oldest man in the force. An unassuming type, he always wore 'a battered hat' and 'spurned the use of cars', preferring to ride to work in trams. He was the first Chief Commissioner to have been born in Victoria and, following Chomley and O'Callaghan, was the third successive career policeman to be appointed to the senior post. Sainsbury was selected for the position from an initial list of seventeen applicants that included policemen, soldiers and lawyers, but only three serving members of the force. The decision to appoint Sainsbury 'was received with marked approbation by practically every member of the force, as it was recognised that the order of seniority was being maintained'. Indeed, not only did most of the force approve of Sainsbury's promotion, they held meetings prior to his appointment and publicly lobbied on his behalf. In unprecedented fashion, policemen of all ranks were

145

party to the passing of resolutions that 'the position of Chief Commissioner of Police, in the event of such office becoming vacant, should
be filled by the appointment from within the force of the officer next in
rank and seniority'. It was indicative of the times and the moves toward
employee combinations that policemen organized to press home a
demand such as this. It was also indicative of the conservative nature of
the force, in that rank was their guide, and seniority their yardstick, in
seeking to maintain the status quo through all levels of the force. The
Argus had strongly urged the appointment of an eminent young administrator from outside the force, but that was not to be. Adherence to the
seniority system was good for morale, enhancing promotion prospects
and fuelling ambition. However, it did not necessarily secure the best
available person to head the force, and a preoccupation with seniority
meant that good luck rather than good management made Sainsbury the
force's wartime leader. Luck, however, this time produced an acceptably
solid Commissioner.[10]

Against a background of world conflict, Sainsbury experimented with
motorcycle patrols, training classes in lifesaving, first aid and ju-jitsu, purchased a motorized prison van, phased out many troop horses and
replaced them with bicycles, and supported the introduction of Sunday
rest days for police. It was also during his command, but not due to it, that
the Victoria Police Association was formed and two women were allowed
to join the force. He was also the first Chief Commissioner to make statements about the inadequacy of some criminal laws and to suggest legal
reforms. He criticized the role of juries in criminal trials and commented
'that what was an excellent thing in the time of King Alfred the Great,
possesses no virtue at all at the present time'. Sainsbury, like his immediate
two predecessors, was a conservative leader but, unlike Chomley, he was
not reactionary and, unlike O'Callaghan, he was not fractious. He was a
cautious man who often, as with the introduction of women into police
work, adopted a 'wait and see' attitude and watched closely the course of
such experiments when they were tried interstate and overseas. He was
not destined to be in the vanguard of police reform but neither was his
always a rearguard action. Most of Sainsbury's reforms reflected broader
changes in technology and social values within the Australian community, such as motorization and the suffragette movement, which is true
of almost all police reform.

Still, senior police administrators in Victoria had a record of resistance
to change, and Sainsbury was in a position to encourage or reject new
ideas. It is to his credit that he ventured to accept the changes that he did.
His principal errors lay in his rejection of two new policing ideas that later
gained almost universal acceptance throughout the police world. He
refused to use police dogs because he felt 'man could beat the dog every
time . . . I do not think their services as a whole would be worth the time,

trouble and money', and he decided not to introduce electric patrol boxes because they 'might mean undue interference with promotion, for if constables mechanically record their own movements it would be hardly worthwhile keeping Senior Constables to watch them too'. Mostly, though, Sainsbury recognized the changed needs of the community and the necessity for the force to offer new skills and services. Under his leadership there began a gradual shift in the emphasis of police work. Instead of focusing almost exclusively on brawny beat constables and distant mounted troopers, the operations of the force were adapted and extended, so that police—men and women—applied new skills to traditional roles and became more active in community welfare work. Less emphasis was placed on the physical size and equestrian ability of recruits, and more attention was given to preparing police to deal with twentieth-century people and problems. After thirty-five years experience, and at fifty-seven years of age, Sainsbury coped well with the stresses of war and proved a loyal servant to both the state and commonwealth governments, for the horizons and loyalties of the force were extended beyond the traditional geographic boundaries of the state and, in some respects, police work on the home front did become a fight for national existence.[11]

Before the outbreak of war, work undertaken by policemen in Victoria on behalf of the Commonwealth Government was limited and passive, deriving principally from the presence of federal parliament in Melbourne. There was no commonwealth police force, so state policemen provided security at the Federal Treasury, Federal Parliament House and other commonwealth offices. War quickly transformed this picture and, in addition to those Victorian policemen who went overseas on active service, most members of the force at some time found themselves engaged on commonwealth duties. Ernest Scott described the wartime role of policemen as one where they worked as 'useful police allies' to military authorities. Such a description understates the nature and extent of the role of state police who, rather than being merely 'useful allies', were the key front-line element in commonwealth efforts to safeguard Australia from the 'enemy within'. It was the scattered presence of ordinary policemen that made the nation's internal defences operative. The threat from within was often more imagined than real but counter-espionage work, intelligence work, translating, surveillance, alien registration and internments were some of the duties undertaken by police on behalf of the commonwealth. In an air of wondrous expectation, police in the remotest corners of the state were alerted to 'watch for aerials of enemy agents transmitting messages', and to watch for and report by telegraph the flights of any aircraft. These duties were different, and were seen as important enough to be tinged with excitement; certainly they were national duties done for the people of Australia.[12]

The main commonwealth duty that fell to the lot of policemen was the registration of aliens under the War Precautions Act. Police were appointed Registration Officers, and a proclamation by the Governor-General ordered 'all persons who are subjects of the German Empire and who are resident in the Commonwealth' to report themselves to their nearest police station, and to notify immediately any change of address. Several days later, Austrian subjects were included. Duties in connection with the registration of aliens meant 'a large amount of work' that was 'greatly increased by the aliens constantly changing their addresses'. By 1917 the number of registered aliens in Victoria was twelve thousand.

Policemen were also required to 'arrest and detain all German Officers or Reservists as prisoners-of-war', and to effect the internment of enemy subjects. A total of 6890 people were interned in Australia, and in Victoria 889 were allowed on parole under police supervision. These duties drew a mixed reaction to and from policemen, who were often required to investigate or arrest local residents of long standing. It was sensitive work where people could be easily offended, and policemen sometimes erred or over-reacted, letting suspicion supplant fact. Generally, however, they trod warily and Scott suggests that,

> The cool, good sense of an experienced police sergeant with a knowledge of the people living in his district, saved many a person of German origin from interference, or even from removal to a concentration camp, when reports tinged with hysteria or malice might otherwise have brought discomfort upon him.[13]

Some policemen worked in sensitive areas on secret work. Constable F. W. Sickerdick and a number of detectives were transferred to the Military Intelligence Section for duties that included translating documents and undercover investigation. Sickerdick proved so adept at this type of work that the Defence Department asked for his retention at an increased rank and higher wages. Another policeman whose services the commonwealth sought to retain after the war was Detective R. P. Brennan, who was sent to Egypt and London on 'special duty'. The Egyptian authorities had requested the services of Australian police, and after consultations between the Acting Prime Minister, G. F. Pearce, and the Premier of Victoria, Brennan sailed aboard the RMS *Malwa* on 21 March 1916. He remained in Egypt until July 1916, when he transferred to England, and he did not return to Victoria until 1920. Brennan was selected for work overseas because he had a 'full knowledge of Victorian criminals', and most of his time abroad was spent tracing Australians who were wanted for criminal offences committed in Australia or while serving abroad with the AIF. For this duty he was specially mentioned in despatches.

Defence work undertaken by policemen was shrouded in varying degrees of secrecy, but undoubtedly the most clandestine was the part played by policemen in founding the Australian Secret Service. First formed in 1916, and called the Counter Espionage Bureau, the secret unit was directed by Major George Steward and staffed by one agent and a detective from Victoria. Steward was then private secretary to the Governor-General and the CEB office was reputedly in Government House, Melbourne. The secret service was established 'at the request of the Imperial Government' and was 'worked in co-operation of [*sic*] the British Counter Espionage Bureau' as 'an important link in the Imperial scheme for countering enemy activities within the Empire'. Sainsbury was made a member of the bureau, and direct communication was established between him and Steward, but not even the superintendent in charge of detectives was told of the bureau's existence or of the fact that one of his men was a CEB operative. In a secret despatch, W. M. Hughes acknowledged that the success of the bureau 'must always depend in a very large measure upon the co-operation of the State Commissioners of Police', and to this end Steward organized a wartime conference of all Australian police commissioners in Melbourne, where an 'efficient system of interchange of information' was developed for such matters as

> the control of traffic through the sea-ports of Australia; investigation of cases of espionage; the circulation of warrants and descriptions of suspects; the countering of the activity on the part of hostile Secret Service agents and the tracing and recording of the personal histories of alien enemy agents and suspects.

The CEB was the 'central point' for Australian counter-espionage activity, but ordinary policemen were its principal source of intelligence data and served as its eyes and ears in the community. In *The Origins of Political Surveillance in Australia*, Frank Cain comments, 'The police forces were essential to the carrying out of surveillance . . . The police possessed the skilled investigators, they knew how to maintain comprehensive record systems, they had skills in conducting prosecutions and getting convictions . . . They were important cogs in the machine of the political observation of Australian radicalism'. The integral involvement of policemen with the CEB heightened the national consciousness of disparate state police forces and brought them together on a united front that transcended state boundaries. It also set a precedent that served as the forerunner to the Australian Security Intelligence Organization and state police Special Branches, taking police clearly into the realm of secret agents, clandestine operations and political surveillance. Early targets of the CEB were politically disaffected individuals and groups such as 'the Revolutionary Industrial Workers of the World', and Irish Republican Brotherhood sympathizers.[14]

The hunt for enemy agents was a secret, exciting but small part of the total police war effort. Policemen performed a wide variety of other federal duties like the investigation and arrest of military deserters (which earned them a bounty of £1 a head for each capture), passport and naturalization inquiries, amusement and betting tax investigations, questions relating to maternity allowances and soldiers' allotments to dependants, checking federal electoral rolls, manning federal polling booths, providing money escorts and guarding the prime minister. These extra duties combined with the absence of men overseas to make the force short of manpower, and this difficulty was aggravated by a lack of recruits. Sainsbury was under considerable pressure not to appoint 'men who will not enlist in the Expeditionary Forces', and eventually he made a public announcement that such men would 'have greater chance of getting struck by lightning than of getting into the police force'. It was good stuff to please the State Parliamentary Recruiting Committee, but not even Sainsbury's patriotic rhetoric could placate the true zealots, who criticized the police retiring age of sixty and argued that it would be better 'if the policeman could be left at his usual necessary occupation, and that the recruit who seeks his position should go straight into the Expeditionary Force'. They were difficult times for Sainsbury, who was clearly committed to the war effort while still bound to hold his police force together and maintain peace at home. He closed quiet police stations and transferred men to areas of great need, and actively sought to fill vacancies by recruiting returned soldiers. Yet circumstances were against him. As his shortfall of men moved into the hundreds, those policemen still on duty worked extended hours, and as late as 1920 were owed 1600 days in leave and rest days accrued during the war and armistice periods. Men were refused leave to assist with the harvest on family farms, and police pensioners were employed as guards to release policemen (and soldiers) for other work. At war's end an influenza epidemic in Melbourne further taxed the force's resources so that the city 'was being guarded by a body of men less than one-half of the minimum recognised strength'. In government papers marked 'strictly secret', 'secret' and 'urgent' the under-recruiting and undermanning of the force was described as 'very grave', and secret steps were taken to bolster the strength of the force so as not 'to create any alarm' and to prevent 'a very serious outbreak' of crime. Policemen were indeed fighting a battle.[15]

The involvement of state police in the national war effort exposed policemen to a kind and degree of federalism that they had never before experienced. Most of their wartime duties were not lasting but, even when W. M. Hughes formed his own token Commonwealth Police Force, the new-found police nationalism did not dissipate. A great deal of what policemen actually thought and did during the war was clouded in secrecy, and somebody's subsequent culling of the wartime files has added to the density of that cloud. Cryptic index entries tell us that a census was conducted of policemen of enemy birth, but that file is missing, along with many others relevant to the police force at war. Because of the absence of so much important archival material, any account of police activities during the war is impressionistic and sketchy. Nevertheless, sufficient traces have survived to show something of the force during war, certainly enough to show that the 10 per cent of policemen who went to war were a very small part of the police war effort. Duty on the home front did not carry with it the mortality rate of duty abroad, but neither was it a haven for the fearful or indolent. Sainsbury himself shouldered enormous responsibilities, and in the shadow of war few people could have realized the many fronts on which his battles loomed. While the sights of many people were fixed on events in Europe, Sainsbury was fighting at close quarters with elements at home who wanted to unionize the police. It was a legacy inherited from the days of O'Callaghan on the eve of war. Compared with world conflict it was a minor domestic crisis. To Sainsbury and his force it was a turning point of perhaps greater lasting significance than world war itself.[16]

A Union for Policemen

> . . . a policeman is not supposed to desire beauty. At all events, he does not get it . . . Still, he is thankful for small mercies—he obtains free some 20lb of straw with which he may stuff his mattress. He feels that the Government has not entirely forgotten him when he hears that straw crackle under him at night.

The daily regimen for many hundreds of policemen was a spartan one and, in real terms, their work conditions deteriorated as the first years of the twentieth century advanced. Sainsbury inherited a sub-standard, undermanned and demoralized force that was suffering from years of inadequate government support. Most of the responsibility for this lay with a succession of conservative governments, but Sainsbury's predecessor was also culpable, in that he was quick to crush signs of agitation in the ranks and slow to seek increased pay and improved working conditions on behalf of his men. O'Callaghan was a loyal servant of the governments that appointed and kept him in office. He labelled press accounts of the standard of the force and its work as 'newspaper tripe', and vigorously sought to identify and obtain the resignations of any policemen who publicly complained about their lot. A decade of his style of management left the force the poorest of any in mainland Australia, with the result that immediately preceding and during World War I, Sainsbury was engaged in a constant effort to hold the force together in the face of sub-standard working conditions, employee dissatisfaction and, eventually, police unionization.[17]

In 1913, when Sainsbury took command, policemen in Victoria still worked a seven-day week and each day-shift was divided into two four-hour reliefs spread over twelve hours. Men who went on duty at 5.00 a.m. did not go off duty until 5.00 p.m. There were no rest days or public holidays, and the annual leave of seventeen days could not be taken at Christmas or Easter. Ordinary workers subject to Wages Board determinations were paid double for Sunday work, time-and-half for overtime and holiday work, and an allowance for working certain night shifts. None of this was paid to policemen: the starting pay of constables was 7s 6d a day, plus sixpence a day for rent or quarters, and after twenty years service constables were paid a total of ten shillings a day. Promotion to the ranks of senior constable and sergeant took twenty-four and twenty-nine years respectively. With little short-term prospect of promotion or incremental pay rise, junior constables were paid less than tram conductors and a sum equivalent to the minimum wage paid to labourers. However, as well as facing the usual living expenses of a labourer, policemen had to buy and maintain a uniform worth about £12 and pay fivepence a day in compulsory police insurance. On top of all, policemen were expected to 'live in a house better than the house which an ordinary labourer occupies' and 'to keep his family respectably'. The paradox of paying policemen as one class and expecting them to live as another was recognized by some members of parliament, who urged that policemen be paid a 'living wage'. A. A. Farthing, MLA, whose electorate of East Melbourne included the Russell Street Barracks, warned of the dangers of 'placing these men in the greatest temptation' and pleaded that 'they should be paid sufficiently well to enable them to act honestly, and live and bring up their families respectably, educating their children as we expect reputable citizens of Victoria to do'.

Although many people could see the point, the problem was compounded by the fact that constables were still drawn from the working classes. Within the public service the force was regarded as 'the bottom of the ladder' and educational standards for entry were 'not so high as for other branches of the Public Service'. Men who had not progressed beyond fourth grade were accepted as policemen because the main prerequisites were physical rather than educational. Similarly, the eight-week induction period focused on drill and physical activity to prepare men for a constant round of foot-slogging on beat duty. Entrance standards and working conditions in the force prompted the view that it was a 'dumping ground' and that the rewards 'were not sufficiently liberal to attract men of high character and ability when such qualities are in so much demand elsewhere'. Society wanted a force of respectable police, but 'respectable' men of educated and middle-class backgrounds did not join the police force. Of 250 men who joined the force during the years 1914 to 1918, almost 70 per cent were formerly labourers, or rural workers employed on such chores as shearing, dairying, mining, timber-cutting and farm work. Most of the others came from service industries where they had been employed as storemen, salesmen, gripmen, drivers and clerks. Eleven recruits had been tradesmen, one claimed he was an engineer, two claimed to be schoolteachers and one gave his occupation as 'foot-runner'.

Although people seeking to determine the appropriate status and pay for policemen compared them with labourers, teachers, railway workers and public servants, none of these comparisons proved useful. Eventually all parties began to view the police as a distinct occupational group and to look at police forces in other states for realistic comparisons. This was a trend that suited policemen but worried the government; notwithstanding the boast of the Premier, W. A. Watt, that Victorian policemen could 'eat the New South Wales men for breakfast, without pepper or salt', the policemen of his state received the lowest pay and benefits of any in Australia. Per capita expenditure on the police was higher in all the other states, police to population ratios were better, and policemen received more holidays and uniform benefits. Because of its comparable size, similar policing problems and proximity to Victoria, the New South Wales force was the obvious one with which to make comparisons. In New South Wales, policemen received twenty-eight days annual leave, were granted a rest day every second Sunday, worked continuous eight-hour shifts, were provided with free uniforms and were paid an average of two shillings a day more. Per capita expenditure on the police in New South Wales was 6s 7d and the police to population ratio was 1:698. In Victoria the equivalent figures were 5s 1d and 1:795. Because per capita expenditure and police ratios are closely linked to population dispersal, and New South Wales was much larger than Victoria, those 'unfavourable' comparisons are less significant than they might seem. However, the differences in pay and holidays were very real, and they rankled with policemen south of the border. That they were worth as much as schoolteachers in their own state was debatable; that they were worth less than policemen in New South Wales was untenable. [18]

For many decades a succession of governments relied upon the conservatism and 'loyalty' of policemen for industrial harmony. They did not unionize, strike or affiliate with the Victorian State Service Federation, nor were they subject to Wages Board determinations. If policemen wanted increased pay or improved conditions they sent a deputation direct to the government, and if a government wanted to restrict or prevent protests by trade unions they sent in the police. It was an informal but traditional relationship, and government members spoke often of police loyalty. It was reinforced by the hierarchical and disciplined nature of the force and the large body of regulations that governed it. Those policemen who did publicly complain were quickly labelled as agitators or put down as 'younger and more impetuous'. In 1912 an unsuccessful police deputation did approach the government for increased pay and Watt, like many government leaders before him, imposed upon their loyalty when denying their claims, saying in parliament that 'whilst they would like to get higher pay, they are not adopting a disloyal stand'. Such an understanding could continue only as long as the government was reasonably responsive to police deputations. It was at a time of increased worker unionization that the Watt government refused the police pay request, while agreeing to retrospective pay increases for railway workers and a pay rise for teachers, both of which groups had employee unions. A letter published in the *Argus* warned an 'obdurate' government that 'perhaps the police association about to be formed, will bring about reforms and redress; but on the other hand, it is sure to create a fighting spirit in the ranks'.[19]

Apart from that letter, and some parliamentary talk about police 'dissension and revolt', there is no evidence of policemen attempting to form an association in 1912. The first concrete signs of such a movement occurred on 20 August 1913, when Sergeant Michael O'Loughlin of Albert Park submitted a report requesting permission to convene a meeting of police 'to consider the questions of approaching the Government for an increase of pay and the formation of a Police Association'. O'Loughlin was a seasoned veteran of thirty years experience in the force, so he could not be disregarded as 'younger and more impetuous'. On the contrary, he was qualified for a full police pension and promotion to officer rank, and he put both at risk by seeking to unionize the police. His action, like that of Costelloe and Strickland nearly a decade before, was a bold one, but in 1913 the suggestion was not totally radical and did have precedents in police unions formed in South Australia (1911) and Western Australia (1912).

Even so, Sainsbury was caught unawares by O'Loughlin's request and, in a letter marked 'very *urgent*', wrote to the Commissioner of Police in South Australia that he was 'anxious to learn' if the police association 'tends to the welfare of members of the Force without clashing with the best interests of the Service'. The South Australian Commissioner declared to Sainsbury, 'Personally I am not very sweet on Police Associations', and he heartened the Victorian Chief Commissioner when he reported,

> The Association was formed during the regime of the Labor Ministry ... immediately a Liberal Ministry came into power the Chief Secretary, our Ministerial Head, intimated he was not in sympathy with the movement, and in fact made it clearly understood the Government did not intend to recognize the Association in any shape or form, and though still in existence I have not since heard much of it. When first formed it rather looked as if the Association was to manage the Department, but now of course all that is a matter of the past.

Sainsbury liked the South Australian Liberal approach to police unions and, in a memo dated 1 September 1913, informed the Under Secretary that 'it would not matter much if a police association existed as long as the government took the view which the South Australian Government has taken'. O'Loughlin's report, together with the correspondence from South Australia and Sainsbury's comments, went before State Cabinet on 4 September 1913, but if a decision was reached on that day, it was not then made public, nor was the urgency with which Sainsbury and the Government treated O'Loughlin's request intimated to him. Although he submitted additional reports in September and December, he was not given the courtesy of 'either an acknowledgment or reply'. It was not until 10 February 1914, when the subject was raised in the Legislative Assembly by John Lemmon, a staunch Labor man and MLA for Williamstown, that the matter was publicly aired for the first time and O'Loughlin got his reply. The Chief Secretary, John Murray, told Lemmon that he had considered but not answered the application from O'Loughlin because it 'was addressed to the Chief Commissioner of Police', and that in any event he 'did not think it was advisable to grant the application'.[20]

The curt and seemingly confident manner in which Murray dispensed with O'Loughlin's application and Lemmon's questions belied the trepidation with which the conservative Government viewed the formation of a police association. O'Loughlin's reports had not simply prompted a flurry of urgent activity behind the scenes, followed by intransigent silence, but had provoked the Government into doing something. In the months after O'Loughlin submitted his first application, and before Murray gave his answer in parliament, the Government sought to defuse the issues behind police moves to unionize by easing two long-standing grievances. On 5 September 1913 Murray announced that 'members of the force are to be given one Sunday off in every four on full pay'. This announcement was made only four days after O'Loughlin's report went before Cabinet, but the rest-day issue was one that had been under government consideration since 1911, when Murray had said, 'If we could only persuade the wicked in our midst—and there are not very many—to cease from troubling on Sunday, the police then might have the day off'. Given that the wicked had not ceased troubling on Sunday, it would seem that Murray was more troubled by O'Loughlin than by evil-doers on the Sabbath. The rest-day scheme started on 1 October 1913 and ended the practice begun in 1836 of policemen being on duty every day of the week. The monthly day of rest fell well short of the weekly rest day granted to policemen in England since 1910, but it was an important concession, a milestone in the quest for improved working conditions. There was still a way to go, however, as the system devised by Murray and Sainsbury was introduced without employing any extra men and at 'no increase in cost to the State'. It was made workable by those men on Sunday duty who, as well as walking their own beats, patrolled those of men on a rest day.

The introduction of a monthly rest day was met with general approval from politicians, policemen and the press, and it allayed some of the dissension within the force. O'Loughlin, however, was not silenced by a day off each month, and his reports of 19 September and 7 December pressed for a pay increase. Perhaps Murray and the Government were influenced by O'Loughlin's doggedness; at any rate, on 5 February 1914, Murray announced a police pay increase of 6d a day. Then five days later, on 10 February, he announced that he was not prepared to agree to O'Loughlin's application for permission to form an association. As with the rest-day announcement, Murray's moves of February 1914 were a timely piece of political work, clearly designed to stifle police unionization. By partly satisfying the immediate needs of many policemen, Murray sought to remove O'Loughlin's basis of support and to shore up the eroding, tacit understanding that policemen would be looked after.[21]

Still the efforts to unionize policemen did not stop. In April 1914 the annual conference of the Political Labour Council resolved to 'take steps to form the police into an industrial union', but members of the force were unanimous 'that, while a union similar to the Public Service Association would be welcomed, any affiliation with the Trades Hall or other political body would be in every way inimical to the police and the public generally'. Policemen were wary about an alliance with the labour movement because they feared it would jeopardize their role 'in preserving order' at industrial disputes, and they were also concerned at the prospect of being called to strike in sympathy with trade unions. It was not an unexpected response from an occupational group as loyal and conservative as the police, but it was one that might well have troubled many thinking labour leaders. Policemen—those brawny toilers drawn from the working classes, and whose work conditions lagged well behind those of the general labouring community—were ready when on duty to intervene on behalf of capital in dispute with labour but unwilling off duty to join with other workers in trying to improve work conditions. In the early years it was a stance voluntarily adopted and maintained by policemen, but since the police strike of 1923 it has been a position reinforced by law. Either way, the division between policemen and the labour movement has proved enduring.

Although policemen resisted efforts to align them with industrial unions, they still wanted a union of their own. Later in 1914 a proposed meeting of policemen 'to consider matters in their own interest' was prohibited by Sainsbury because 'practically it was for a political purpose'. This last movement to convene a meeting had barely gathered momentum when war was declared, inducing a pause in agitation as policemen threw their energies behind Sainsbury and the war effort. Apart from the two concessions granted at the time of O'Loughlin's stirrings, the Government had done nothing to improve conditions for policemen, so that even after the outbreak of war there was an undercurrent of dissatisfaction. National expectations of loyalty and personal sacrifice during the war rendered open agitation by policemen imprudent, but during 1915 city policemen interested in improved work conditions held secret meetings to plan the formation of an association. To avoid infiltration by 'the other side', notice of these meetings was spread by word of mouth and the meeting place was frequently changed. Usually they met in a hotel, but on at least one occasion their meeting was 'held in a timber yard in South Melbourne at nearly midnight'. To this day the identity of the activists has remained secret, but the clandestine gatherings ended on 13 July 1916 when over two hundred policemen openly attended a meeting in the Guild Hall, Swanston Street, Melbourne. They elected Constable F. C. Murphy, of the Little Bourke Street Police Station, as secretary of a movement to press 'for permission to form an association for the general improvement of the Service'. Details of the Guild Hall meeting were reported in the *Argus*, and Sainsbury immediately ordered an investigation to ascertain 'who called and authorized this meeting and who were the speakers at it'. Officers interviewed both O'Loughlin and Murphy as suspected organizers but, in a style befitting the classic coterie of conspirators, not one of the policemen who attended the meeting admitted knowing anything of its organization. Using a statement obtained from the caretaker of the hall, Sainsbury's investigators advised him that an unidentified 'tall dark man engaged the hall and paid for it . . . He said he required the hall for a meeting of the Police Union'.

Although those men who attended at the Guild Hall were tight-mouthed about the original organizers, they went boldly into subsequent action. On 13 July 1916 Murphy wrote to the Chief Commissioner, asking him to receive a deputation 'of the Members of the Force with a view to forming a Police Association . . . Such association to be non-political'. Sainsbury refused this request and Murphy wrote again on 7 August, appealing to the Chief Secretary to receive a deputation because 'the police have always been a loyal body and are not now endeavouring to show any disloyalty'. Murphy pointed out that the penal warders and state school teachers had their association, and the police wanted one 'for their own mutual improvement and defence'. Murphy's second request was approved, with the proviso that 'only members of the force will be heard'—a clause no doubt intended to exclude former policemen, politicians, the Victorian State Service Federation and other union organizers. Policemen filled the Guild Hall on 21 August to elect the members of their deputation, and a conference with the Chief Secretary, Donald McLeod, was held two days later. McLeod viewed the prospect of a police union with the same disdain as had his predecessors and, after raising spurious objections to the police proposals, agreed only to 'consider the matter of allowing the Police to form a Club for their own "Social

Improvement and Mutual Benefit"'. Not surprisingly, Murphy and his colleagues were unhappy with such a response; then, just as their movement began to falter, they were given new and added impetus. On 28 December 1916 the Constitution Act was amended to give all public servants, including policemen, the right to 'take part in the political affairs of the State of Victoria'. Generally termed the Political Rights Bill, the amendment was 'highly prized by the service' and, in giving policemen 'full citizens rights', promoted a surge of interest in state, political and union matters. This legislation enabled policemen to be far more open in political and industrial matters, and soon the Victorian State Service Federation joined with a Police Executive Committee to agitate for the right to form a police association. By 1917 the force was the only sizeable section of government employees without an association, and Gordon Carter, general secretary of the VSSF, acted on behalf of policemen as 'Honorary Special Representative' to press for parity. Under his guidance the police committee lobbied with renewed vigour and framed a model constitution and rules for their proposed association. On 3 April 1917 perseverance was rewarded when McLeod agreed 'to permit of a social club being formed, and to assist it as far as possible'. Some men spoke of a union, some of an association and the government of a social club; but that was all semantics. What policemen had attained was the right to form an employee organization to protect their interests. On 10 May Sainsbury presided over a general meeting of six hundred men who 'decided by a unanimous vote that an Association be formed', and on 27 June an executive committee was elected. One man who no doubt derived a great deal of personal pleasure from the events of 1917 was Michael O'Loughlin. He was prominent in all police agitation from 1913 to 1917 and, after being promoted to officer in 1917, was elected president of the Association on 31 January 1918.

The objects of the Association at the time of its formation were: to affiliate with the Victorian State Service Federation; to conserve and further the interests of the Victoria Police Force; the promotion of good fellowship and social intercourse among its members; and the promotion of efficiency and assistance to the administration. They were benevolent objectives suggesting that the Government was successful in restricting the role of the Association to one of a benign social club. It was a false impression. Behind the façade of smoke nights and billiards was an active and growing police union. Within months the Association, supported by Sainsbury, was successful in obtaining government approval for policemen to work continuous eight-hour shifts and, from 14 January 1918, police hours of duty were 6 a.m. to 2 p.m., 2 p.m. to 10 p.m. and 10 p.m. to 6 a.m. This change removed a long-standing grievance of metropolitan policemen and brought their hours of work into line with those of policemen interstate and overseas. Some months later the Association added to this success with a surprising coup, when the Government responded to its wage deputation by granting all policemen 'an increase in pay of six-pence per day and an allowance of another sixpence per day for uniform'. At a time of national austerity, and with war still raging in Europe, these were considerable achievements. Other matters dealt with included trav-elling and mountain-station allowances, extra leave, pensions, a khaki uniform for summer wear and the individual grievances of policemen regarding transfers, sick pay and legal expenses. The prospect of paying legal fees was a source of concern to most policemen, and the Association was active in seeking compensation on their behalf. A typical case in 1917 was that of Constable Matthew Burke, who was charged by the Kew Council with misconduct 'in not removing disorderly persons from a ref-erendum meeting as instructed by the Mayor'. At a cost of £20 Burke engaged a solicitor to act on his behalf, and the board of inquiry that subsequently heard his case dismissed the charge and found that Burke had acted with 'tact and forbearance'. Though he was innocent of an alle-gation that arose directly from his duties, the Government adhered to normal policy in not providing Burke with legal counsel and refused to pay his legal costs of £20 because 'he could have conducted his own defence'. Burke's expenses in this case were equivalent to almost two months pay, and highlighted the injustices that existed, in spite of the presence of a concerned union.[22]

Although the Association was much more than a social club, it was not a militant union and did pay heed to its stated objects of promoting efficiency and providing assistance to the administration. In this regard the Association was instrumental in having a board appointed 'to investi-gate the alteration of ages of members of the force'. It was an issue peculiar to police, and involved men who gave false birth details to gain admission to the force and then, at the other end of their service, tried to have those details corrected to improve their retirement prospects. The board devised a satisfactory solution and reported that the alteration of ages was due in large measure to 'the connivance of those who had to choose the future members of the Force', and who 'winked at' incorrect statements of age 'in order that they might not have to reject the best material offering'. The board's findings highlighted an irregularity in police recruiting methods dating back to the mid-nineteenth century and in the light of these findings the system was changed. The decisions reached by the board were in the best interests of the force and met with approval from the Association, even though some individual policemen lost retire-ment advantages. It was an early indication of the potential of the Associ-ation to influence the administration of the force.

Another important action taken by the Association was the monthly publication of the *Police Journal*. A modest publication of sixteen pages, it quickly became established as essential reading for all policemen and,

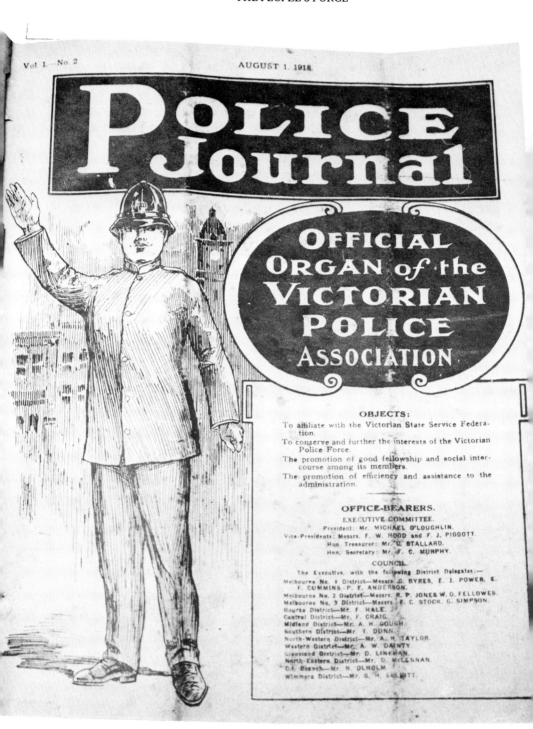

Vol. 1—No. 2

AUGUST 1, 1918.

POLICE Journal

OFFICIAL ORGAN of the VICTORIAN POLICE ASSOCIATION

OBJECTS:

To affiliate with the Victorian State Service Federation.

To conserve and further the interests of the Victorian Police Force.

The promotion of good fellowship and social intercourse among its members.

The promotion of efficiency and assistance to the administration.

OFFICE-BEARERS.

EXECUTIVE COMMITTEE.

President: Mr. MICHAEL O'LOUGHLIN.
Vice-Presidents: Messrs. F. W. HOOD and F. J. PIGGOTT.
Hon. Treasurer: Mr. C. STALLARD.
Hon. Secretary: Mr. J. C. MURPHY.

COUNCIL.

The Executive, with the following District Delegates:—

Melbourne No. 1 District—Messrs. G. BYRES, E. J. POWER, E. F. CUMMINS, P. E. ANDERSON.
Melbourne No. 2 District—Messrs. R. P. JONES W. O. FELLOWES.
Melbourne No. 3 District—Messrs. F. C. STOCK. G. SIMPSON.
Bourke District—Mr. F. HALE.
Central District—Mr. F. CRAIG.
Midland District—Mr. A. H. GOUGH.
Southern District—Mr. T. DUNN.
North-Western District—Mr. A. H. TAYLOR.
Western District—Mr. A. W. DAINTY.
Gippsland District—Mr. D. LINEHAN.
North-Eastern District—Mr. D. McLENNAN.
C.I. Branch—Mr. N. OLHOLM.
Wimmera District—Mr. G. H. ELLIOTT.

as well as association news, it included law notes and items of general interest. The journal was particularly aimed at men who were 'remote from a friendly comrade', and articles on police topics of current interest reached the 'backblock constable' and filled an important need that had never been met by the department. After receiving his first issue, Constable F. A. Rawlings, stationed in the mountains at Walhalla, wrote to express his appreciation and approval. In doing so he expressed a common sentiment and gave a hint of how the force had unwittingly isolated many of its members by failing to provide them with police news and comradeship. Rawlings wrote, 'we in the back parts seldom meet the city men. As for myself, I seldom come in contact with adjoining stations. My nearest neighbour is some 26 miles distant, through bad roads and hilly country'.

The gratitude felt by Rawlings for the Association was not shared by his Chief Commissioner. At the Association's first annual meeting a letter from Sainsbury was read, in which he put the view 'that what was intended was bringing into existence of a social club only, and not a body formed to work together towards securing justice for itself'. His lament was, however, too late and although he and the Chief Secretary tried to restrict the Association's activities by censoring its business papers, it continued to gain strength. Years of government neglect had left policemen ripe for unionization, and the substantial early gains made when they did combine served to increase their enthusiasm. The Association ended its first year of existence with an 'optimistic outlook' and 1346 financial members, who had attained better hours, increased pay and a uniform allowance. 'There were only 70 to 100 members of the whole Police Force who had not thrown in their lot with the majority.' Not included in this minority were two new additions to the force who might have joined the Association if they could, but were not eligible. They were women. While O'Loughlin fought officialdom and Sainsbury fought unionization, the Trades Hall Council was among those groups that had successfully supported the entry of women into the police force.[23]

Women and Warriors

In his early resistance to police unionization, Sainsbury displayed a real fear of having his power and authority usurped by an association that wanted to 'manage the Department'. It was a fear that proved groundless, as did his fear that, if women were appointed to the force, 'trouble could be expected and the question of deciding who is "the boss" might soon have to be determined'.

The first women police were conservative and steady workers, who

More than social intercourse: the
Victoria Police Association Journal, 1918

proved loyal despite the facts that they were not given uniforms or vested with powers of arrest, and were paid less than male members. Miss Beers and Mrs Madge Connor were a token female presence in a force of more than fifteen hundred men and were regarded as police agents, rather than as police constables. Their appointments were nevertheless generally regarded by women's groups as a watershed that ended an eighty-year tradition of total exclusion of women from the police ranks.[24]

Since 1902 the National Council of Women had pressed for the appointment of female warders and searchers, and from 1914 their plea for women police was supported, not only by the Trades Hall Council, but also by such proponents as the *Argus*, and the Women's Political Association, who all agreed that women police were an 'absolute necessity for the protection of women and children'. The suggestion was met by senior policemen and conservative government members with the same loathing with which they viewed the prospect of a police union. In 1915 Sainsbury wrote of 'self-advertising and self-seeking females' wanting to be police, adding that it was 'no time for innovation and increased expense anyway, and I would hasten slowly'. Much of his ire was directed at activists like Adela Pankhurst and Vida Goldstein, and it was expressed in time of war, but at no stage was he enthusiastic about women police. The closest he came to being positive was the suggestion that, if it was decided to give women police a trial, they should be 'relatives of our soldiers who have fought for their country'. In 1916 the police mood had not changed, and in separate memos three senior officers reported tersely to Sainsbury: 'women police would be of little if any use'; 'grave danger is to be apprehended from such an innovation'; and, 'I cannot bring to memory any instance in which a woman could have done more than what has been done under the present system'. The police position was clearly negative. Policemen did not even concede that there was a place in the force for women to perform such duties as the care and interview of female rape victims. The political position, dependent as it was upon the electoral process, was slightly more positive; the Chief Secretary, Donald McLeod, promised to appoint women police on a trial basis, but deferred doing so because 'the need for economy is greater than the need for policewomen'.[25]

But the tide of change was against that view and, as with the unionization question, the authorities were dealing not with a situation peculiar to police, but with a strong international movement toward extensive social reforms. In addition to successes in the fields of education, the arts, the workplace and politics, women's lobby groups adduced evidence that women were working successfully as police in South Australia, New South Wales, England and North America. For a time the Victorian force stood as a conservative all-male bastion but, in the face of mounting pressure, it was decided to employ policewomen as an 'experiment'. Over ninety women applied even before the positions were advertised, but such was the uncertainty about the role women could or should play in the force that no physical, medical or educational standards were prescribed for applicants, other than the desire that they 'must be physically capable, in good health, and be possessed of good sound common sense'. Similarly, no effort was made to define the duties of police women in the way that the Police Code defined them for men, and upon the appointment of Beers and Connor on 28 July 1917 it was decided that their duties were to 'undertake enquiries and take action in cases in which women and children are immediately concerned and generally to supervise public places with a view to the protection of women and children and the prevention and detection of offences by or against females'. So the work of women police was to be restricted to dealing with females and children, in a welfare capacity; it was not intended that their duties would be interchangeable with those of policemen in general police duties. Beers and Connor did not get the rudimentary drill and self-defence training given to male recruits, nor were they incorporated into the police seniority list. In all respects they were unique.

The success and ultimate place of women in the force surpassed the expectations of both their supporters and opponents. Their work was rated by their superiors as 'highly satisfactory', and the women themselves as 'most valuable'. Equipped with a warrant card and lapel badge, the women were attached to the Plain Clothes Branch and worked day duty. At first most of their time was spent tracing women with venereal disease, escorting female lunatics and Aborigines, helping families in distress, and rescuing 'young women who were either leading immoral lives or verging on immorality'. Gradually they gained the confidence of their male colleagues and, by building upon personal successes, extended their range of duties to include the detection of brothels, illicit liquor selling, abortionists, unregistered dentists and Chinese herbalists posing as doctors. The women were cast and fitted readily into the role of *police de moeurs*. They did not undermine Sainsbury's authority, but successfully accepted the challenge of working in an organization that had been comprised solely of men since its inception.[26]

The appointment of women police and the formation of a police union were the last significant changes of the Sainsbury era, and both were made in spite of Sainsbury's reluctance. They were not reforms that he rejected totally, but were ideas that he regarded as a threat and a diversion from his unerring commitment to the war effort. He coped well with the strains imposed by World War I, but as that conflict drew to a close it became increasingly clear that Sainsbury was experiencing difficulty adjusting to social changes at home. His sentiments lay in another era that was fast vanishing. A policeman since 1878, and Chief Commissioner since 1913, the bulk of his career preceded the age of the motor car, unionization and women's rights movements. Always loyal, he agreed to a government request to remain in office after he turned sixty, and retired in February 1919 at the age of sixty-two, fading from public life with neither fanfare nor accolades. In many respects Sainsbury is a forgotten man, over-shadowed by his times.

Like Chomley and O'Callaghan before him, Sainsbury fought hard to maintain the status quo and appeared not to notice much of the changing world around him. Sainsbury and his two immediate predecessors in the office of Chief Commissioner were career policemen who served in the force for fifty, forty-six and forty years respectively. They had all been above-average policemen and were able administrators, but none of them was an outstanding leader. In each case they had attained the top post by virtue of seniority, and all three had spent almost their entire adult lives working seven days a week as policemen. Their formal educational levels were low, their personal knowledge of interstate and overseas police oper-ations was negligible, and none of them had graduated from military com-mand colleges, or had what is now called management training. Their style of leadership was what the American writer Bernard Cohen classifies as 'tradition-oriented': men 'successfully indoctrinated into the police subculture' who continued 'to identify with traditional aspects of the job' and were 'apt to defend the status quo in most areas, to fear and stubbornly resist change'. Thirty-six years of 'tradition-oriented' leader-ship was not good for the force, and left it bereft of a sense of future. There was no overall scheme and no notion of preparing for the years that lay ahead. Growth had been *ad hoc*, change often forced and the decision-making process autocratic. The practice of using the police seniority sys-tem as a basis for appointing Chief Commissioners was not designed to secure the best men available. Chomley shied away from big undertakings, O'Callaghan was a difficult autocrat who bore the stigma of corruption, and in all things but patriotism Sainsbury hastened slowly. Each in his own way had performed the task adequately, but that was all. There was nothing of the dynamic leadership shown by their contemporaries, like August Vollmer in America or, to a lesser extent, by Sir Edward Henry and Sir Nevil Macready in England, and James Mitchell in New South Wales. Those men were innovators who dared to reorganize police forces and who, with an eye to the future, established police training schools and introduced into their forces such things as the study of modus operandi, criminal statistics analysis and specialist policing. By comparison, the Victoria Police Force was a languid victim of its own seniority system.[27]

When Sainsbury resigned in 1919 the conservative Government led by Harry Lawson saw what was wrong and, without advertising the vacancy created by Sainsbury's retirement or opening it to members of the force, appointed Lieutenant-Colonel Sir George Steward, the wartime director of the Counter Espionage Bureau, as Chief Commissioner. He was the first outsider appointed to head the force since Standish was appointed in 1858, and his appointment was opposed by the Labor Party on the grounds that he 'did not possess qualifications for the position'. This argument was probably a pretext; a more likely reason for Labor opposition being Steward's close ties with the Secret Service and its political activities. A number of policemen also objected to Steward's appointment, but their opposition, based on the view that the position of Chief Commissioner was their own preserve, was quickly dispelled by Steward's performance.

Steward was the most highly qualified and successful public administrator ever appointed to the force. His background included service as Under-Secretary for Tasmania, Secretary to the Federal Executive Council, Official Secretary to the Governor-General, twenty- one years continuous service in the Australian Military Forces, and he was founding Director of the Australian Secret Service. In that last position, Steward made a study of police operations in a number of overseas countries, and had regular contact with all police forces in Australia. He was an eminent candidate for the position of Chief Commissioner, yet personally humble. Steward described himself as 'simply and solely a public servant' who revelled in his work, but who 'from a social point of view' was 'a comparatively unknown man'.[28]

Steward's difference was apparent from the start. He exuded leadership qualities, and his communicative style quickly won the confidence of the force. In all his dealings with policemen he abided by the motto, 'I do not want you to take me on trust; I want you to allow me to prove myself'. Shortly after assuming office he held a conference with superintendents from all over the state and actively encouraged their participation in the formulation of departmental policy. He also welcomed discussion with officials from the Police Association and met with them regularly. These meetings were not an idle placatory gesture and, when necessary, he was quick to either admonish or support the Association's stand. On several occasions he personally championed the cause of improved working conditions for his men, and a popular action taken early in his administration was the decision not to accept anonymous complaints about alleged police misbehaviour. Steward set about meeting with as many policemen as he could; on one country tour spanning fourteen days he travelled 1500 miles and visited fifty-seven police stations. He was keenly interested in the welfare of the force and on his initiative were formed a Police Amateur Athletic Association and a Police Life-Saving and Swimming Club. He was also instrumental in promoting the provision and use of a police gymnasium, and in securing new police hospital quarters. These efforts to rally the force were not hollow acts of showmanship but genuine attempts at leadership by consensus, and they

Chief Commissioner
G. C. Steward

were underwritten by a realistic and substantial plan for reorganizing the police. Steward accurately sensed the traditionally conservative mood of the force. Without being apologetic he offered policemen support, while urging them to accept that it was impossible for him to be innovative and 'please everybody'. In a supportive climate he exposed policemen gently to his basic idea that 'Any great public organization had to keep abreast of the times, and, in the case of the police force they had to anticipate it'. To a man of Steward's background this notion was fundamental. To the men of the force it was unheard of.[29]

Steward's plans for reorganizing the force made it clear that he envisioned a future built upon youth and education. His reports were punctuated with terms like 'new blood', 'new methods' and 'the Young School', and he expressed a conviction that 'good education and a natural aptitude are more desirable than athletic proportions . . . We shall have to provide courses of instruction on a scale not, so far, anticipated'. In his brief time as Chief Commissioner, Steward instituted many important changes including the expanded use of finger print analysis and formation of a Finger Print Bureau, decentralization of the CIB, promotion based upon merit, expansion and restructuring of the Plain Clothes Branch, and the introduction of a caseload management scheme for detectives, which divided reported crime into major and minor categories.[30] These were all innovations that placed him in the vanguard of

166

international police reform, but he is best remembered for his outstanding contributions to police education. Although only in office for fifteen months, he is rightly regarded as the founder of police training in Victoria. Before Steward's appointment the training of police recruits 'consisted of about a fortnight's drill and an occasional lecture by an officer on police duties'. There was no training for women police, and no in-service training for detectives or members of the higher ranks. O'Callaghan and Sainsbury had toyed with the concept of police training but never tackled it in earnest. Steward raised the educational entrance standards for police recruits, then personally supervised the implementation of a seven-week training course at the Police Depot, which included classes in law and police procedure, 'squad and section drill, physical culture, instruction in the care and use of rifles and revolvers, first aid, swimming and life saving, and how to manage a boat and drag for a body'. He also introduced a second phase into this training, where recruits who successfully passed the Depot examinations were assigned to work with experienced beat constables at Russell Street to determine their 'fitness for duty'. The *Argus* applauded Steward's efforts with the announcement that 'Brute strength is no longer the primary qualification for admission to the police force'. This type of training was not new, just new to Victoria. Steward, however, went farther and introduced a four-week in-service training course for prospective detectives, where they were instructed and examined in methods of detection, the taking and analysis of finger and foot prints and the making of clay casts at crime scenes, which in 1920 placed the force to the fore in the field of police training. It was not to last. On the morning of 11 May 1920 Steward collapsed and died while driving to work. His death not only left the position of Chief Commissioner vacant in a tragic manner but also drained from the force much of that collective vision and motivation with which he had imbued it. Basic training for police recruits has continued as a feature of police life since 1919, and serves as a vital monument to Steward's faith in youth and education, but much lapsed after his death, including in-service training for detectives, which was only reintroduced by Alexander Duncan in 1938. In many respects Steward was a man ahead of his time.[31]

The void he left was not an easy one to fill, and in the interregnum the Government appointed Sydney Arthur Heathershaw as Acting Chief Commissioner. Heathershaw was Chief Clerk of the Police Department and its most senior public servant, but he had never been a policeman. His appointment was clearly a stopgap measure while the Lawson government again tackled the vexed question of whether the Chief Commissioner should come from the force or be appointed from outside. The fact that the Government had opted for Heathershaw, and not one of the senior policemen, was perhaps an indication of a want of capacity among them. After four months it was finally announced that Major General Sir John Gellibrand would be the next Chief Commissioner.[32]

Gellibrand was of a similar stamp to Steward but, whereas Steward was 'a comparatively unknown man' who had fought his war in the obscurity of the secret service, Gellibrand 'was one of those officers whose bravery was conspicuous even according to the standards by which gallantry was judged in the early days at Anzac'. A well-educated man and a graduate of the Royal Military College, Sandhurst, Gellibrand has been described by C. E. W. Bean as having 'one of the brightest intellects' in the AIF and with being 'the finest trainer of young officers' in that force, although 'unconventional in the extreme', with tastes 'entirely Bohemian'. He was also blunt.[33]

Gellibrand, as Chief Commissioner, would not wear a police uniform, did not mince words and always led from the front. It was a style that made him immediately popular with policemen and moved the Police Association to observe, 'the same ideas of discipline and comradeship which he carried out in France are being applied to the lesser army which he now controls'. With widespread support from his men, Gellibrand sought to consolidate the work started by Steward and prepared his own plans for reorganizing the force. It was his abiding belief that all changes needed to form part of a 'considered whole', and he was positively opposed to piecemeal reforms. In this regard his plans were an advance on and refinement of Steward's work. They began with the determination of a realistic police to population ratio, followed by determination of the proportions of ranks required for supervision and control. Gellibrand was alarmed at the shortage of police, and asked that an extra 250 men be recruited, so that he could match the national average of 133 police for every 100 000 of population, and provide a control span of 'one officer to seven sub-officers to thirty constables'. Even had the Government acceded to his demands for more men, however, recruits were not forthcoming because the conditions of police service compared 'unfavourably with those of private life'. The force was paid below the national police average and was the only one in Australia and New Zealand without a comprehensive police pension scheme. In the interests of recruiting, industrial peace and quality of life, both Steward and Gellibrand strongly urged the Government to reintroduce a pension scheme and reiterated the theme that:

> it is hopeless to anticipate recruiting this Force to its proper strength while the existing rates of pay obtain, *and in the absence of a general pension scheme*. Counter attractions within the City are such that even unskilled labor carrying with it practically no responsibility, eight hours work a day performed wholly in the daylight, and quite immune from the personal dangers which are inseparable from the life of a police constable, are so strong as to entirely preclude desirable individuals from entering the Force.

Chief Commissioner
J. Gellibrand

The balance of Gellibrand's planning took two directions as he tried to rectify the ills of past years and introduce innovations on which to build the future. Along with Steward, he was one of the earliest police administrators to regard motorization, extensive street construction and changed social values as variables to be considered in police planning. He inherited an antiquated armoury, a lack of remounts and an excessive number of low-standard, rented police buildings, and he set about trying to update equipment and premises, while also seeking funds to buy motorcycles and cars for traffic and patrol work. He formed a successful Wharf Patrol to prevent pillaging in the docks area, devised a supernumerary scheme to offset the numbers of men working on extraneous duties, and planned the restructuring of the Melbourne Police district, to provide a more equitable distribution of the workload among officers. Gellibrand was also a firm believer in the future of women police and approached the Government for a tenfold increase in the number appointed. It was not to be.

Beginning with Gellibrand's first proposals for reform in October 1920 the conservative Lawson government adopted a niggardly and obdurate stand. His requests for funds, decisions and policy formulation were denied, delayed and obstructed. During his first year in office Gellibrand

169

submitted no less than seven comprehensive proposals to the Government and invariably the Lawson ministry responded with delaying tactics, such as the request for him to justify his ideas by providing detailed statistical data for the years 1913-14, 1917-18 and 1920-21. The Government's other tack was to suggest *ad hoc* reforms that were politically expedient and designed to meet particular pressures from the electorate, such as increased police control over street hawkers. Steward had also been obstructed in this way, even though the early stages of his reorganization of the force were not costly and reflected credit on the Government. Steward, a career bureaucrat accustomed to the machinations of governments, quietly reminded the Lawson ministry that without their assistance his 'endeavours to give the State an efficient and satisfactory service must be proportionately defeated'. The forthright Gellibrand could not conceal his frustration with the Government's intransigence and did not bother with subtle language. He wrote to the Chief Secretary, 'If my proposals are not accepted as a matter of policy I ask that I may be informed in what respect they are held to fail'. The Chief Secretary remained mute. For Gellibrand, the Government that appointed him was the most reactionary obstacle to his work of reform and, in December 1921, he took his leave and returned permanently to Tasmania.[34]

When Gellibrand resigned, fears were publicly expressed that his successor would be 'an officer already in the department' and the force would 'go back further from the standard aimed at' by Steward and Gellibrand, and an editorial in the *Argus* proclaimed that 'The duties of the commissioner are such that they cannot be adequately filled by an officer of police, who in the ordinary way of promotion has reached the rank of superintendent late in life'. The worst expectations of the pessimists were more than fulfilled. Although personages like Brigadier Generals T. A. Blamey, T. H. Dodds and J. Bruche were mooted as candidates for the job, Gellibrand's successor was the oldest and most senior policeman in the force. Alexander Nicholson, a 59-year-old superintendent and lay Presbyterian preacher from Ballarat, was appointed Chief Commissioner on 11 April 1922. After experiencing the generalship, strength of character and reformist zeal of the Steward–Gellibrand era, the conservative Lawson ministry chose to return to the malleable mediocrity of the police seniority list. It was a decision that proved to be a prelude to disaster.[35]

The Police Strike

Nicholson... would show that it was only men in the service who could perform the work attached to the duties of Chief Commissioner... if he made mistakes it would not be the fault of the head, but of the heart.

The appointment of Alexander Nicholson as Chief Commissioner was greeted by many policemen and the police association with a rash of laudatory remarks and an unwarranted degree of smug optimism. They anticipated—wrongly—that he would better understand their needs and complaints, and would be an influential ally in their quest for improved conditions of service. It mattered not to them that he was an ageing country policeman of mediocre ability. What mattered was that he was one of their own—a career policeman. Although on the surface it appeared to be an attitude at odds with the earlier popularity of Steward and Gellibrand, and the support given to them by policemen, it was not. Most policemen shared the belief that Chief Commissioners should come from within the force because such appointments not only created opportunities for promotion and helped maintain the status quo, but were seen as the ultimate reward for many years of loyal service. This belief did not blind policemen to the worth of men like Steward and Gellibrand, or diminish the level of support and respect given them when they were in command of the force. However, it did lead many policemen to openly express a preference for the appointment of one 'of their own', when the opportunity presented itself. Nicholson for his part encouraged this sentiment and resurrected the 'baton in the knapsack' theory, explaining that although Gellibrand was 'a perfect gentleman' there was a 'deep feeling in police circles' that the position of Chief Commissioner 'should be filled by a member of the force'. Remarks of this sort were a veiled criticism of Gellibrand's abrupt return to Tasmania and there was a feeling among some policemen that 'one of their own' would not have abandoned the task in the way Gellibrand did. Nicholson's comments might also be regarded as an oblique rejoinder to Gellibrand's statement when Chief Commissioner, that the system of automatic promotion by seniority was 'indefensible', and that although it was 'supported collectively and publicly' by policemen, he had not 'met a member who believed the system to be sound or fair'. Given the undoubted leadership skills and administrative talents of Steward and Gellibrand, and the energy expended by them to improve the lot of policemen, the smug view that Nicholson would better their efforts was naïvely ingrown.

Nicholson was a country policeman who had spent almost his entire service in the Ballarat district, at stations such as Wendouree, Sebastopol, Ballarat East, Ballarat and Beaufort. His city experience as a policeman was limited to unavoidable sojourns lasting only a matter of months, and none as an officer. He did not complete primary school; he had never worked as a detective or performed other specialized duty; he had no experience of police operations outside Victoria; and he had not been a military commander. He was, however, an active Freemason, a prominent member of the Australian Natives Association, a much-publicized recipient of the Valour Award and a good friend of Major Matthew Baird, MLA for Ballarat West and the minister responsible for the police force.

*Chief Commissioner
A. Nicholson*

In canvassing reasons for Nicholson's appointment, the *Argus* ventured to suggest that perhaps 'Nicholson's police experience' and 'knowledge of Victorian conditions' gave him a 'decided advantage' over applicants from the Australian Imperial Forces, Scotland Yard and the Royal Irish Constabulary. But his main advantages lay in being the personal friend and local superintendent of the Chief Secretary, and the intention of a conservative government not to be again subjected to pressure from a progressive and demanding Chief Commissioner. Steward and Gellibrand had both made many changes, repeatedly requested more men, money and equipment, and queried government decisions. Nicholson was not the sort of man to make demands of his political masters or to query their actions.[36]

When Nicholson left Ballarat the mayor presented him with a gold-mounted umbrella, but the new Chief Commissioner needed more than that to shield him from the storm lying ahead. In the manner of many conservative disciplinarians, Nicholson swept into power in an autocratic and forthright manner and generated his own turbulence as he went. He did not agree with the principle of participatory management and scrapped the regular conferences of superintendents because he 'found the time was wasted' and the conferences of 'little utility'. In addition,

172

Nicholson's early plans for the force marked a return to the prosaic style of Chomley. He prepared his own recommendations for improving the efficiency of the force, and they included absurdly small requests for one car, one camera, two extra women police and thirty extra constables, which were all approved by the Government within a month. Nicholson's proposals were not only inexpensive when compared with those of Steward and Gellibrand, whose plans included an extra two hundred men, but they also avoided politically sensitive matters such as a want of pensions, low pay, sub-standard accommodation and insufficient horses. Steward and Gellibrand had tried to remove some of the root causes of police griev-ances, in order to lift morale and make the force more attractive to recruits. Nicholson elected to avoid fundamental questions of this sort and merely put forward proposals for short-term, piecemeal changes. He did not delve into the long-term needs of the force or attempt to formulate police to population or supervision ratios. Gellibrand had aimed at a ratio of one sub-officer to every four constables; Nicholson felt the ideal was about 1:7, but actually worked with ratios ranging from 1:2 to 1:25, with a city ratio of 1:10. The undemanding nature of Nicholson's proposals, and the rapidity with which the Government agreed to them in full, suggest that, if his friend Baird did not have a hand in drafting them, Nicholson framed them to please his political masters.

On 12 May 1922 Nicholson assured the Government of his confidence that he could 'meet all legitimate demands which will for some time to come be made for police protection, and, in addition, raise the standard of efficiency in the force'. It was not long, however, before his confidence began to wane and he expressed concern about a want of supervision and a lack of men. He was also confronted by considerable unrest in the ranks as neither he nor the Lawson government had taken positive steps to improve conditions for ordinary working policemen. At the end of Nicholson's first year in office his force was the only one in Australia with-out a pension scheme, his police to population ratio of 1:902 was the worst in mainland Australia, and expenditure per head of population on police in Victoria was the lowest in Australia. His men worked a seven-day week of forty-seven-and-a-quarter hours, for which the base pay rate for con-stables was twelve shillings a day, rising to 14s 6d per day, with allowances. Victorian policemen were not paid for overtime, were granted one Sunday off in every four weeks and received seventeen days annual leave. Although the starting pay of constables was less than that paid to labourers, the Government felt that general police wages and conditions compared favourably with other 'lower grades of employment in the trades and callings'. This view was disputed by policemen and was of little solace to them, anyway, as they did not aspire to the wages and conditions of lower private employment but wanted wages and benefits equal to those of the New South Wales police, who received 3s 6d a day more than their

Victorian counterparts, and enjoyed twenty-eight days annual leave and two Sundays off each month.

The lack of a general pension scheme was one matter that particularly upset younger members of the force and produced much discussion and lobbying. After the scheme was abandoned in 1902, Chomley, Steward and Gellibrand all—at different times—argued for its reintroduction. Over a period of twenty years deputations of policemen unsuccessfully presented their case for pensions to successive governments, and it was a perennial agenda item at Police Association meetings. The closest they came to succeeding was in 1920 when the Premier, Harry Lawson, promised pensions for all policemen in his election policy speech. He broke his promise. In 1923 the force comprised 1808 men of whom all the officers (39), all the sergeants (101) and 84 per cent (179) of the senior constables were entitled to pensions from the pre-1902 fund. Of the constables, 1308 (90 per cent) were not. Unlike Steward and Gellibrand, Nicholson was entitled to a police pension and did not move for the reintroduction of a general scheme. The issue simmered.[37]

Another subject of contention, tackled by Steward and Gellibrand but ignored by Nicholson, was the dilapidated state of many police buildings. For many hundreds of men, police stations were not just their place of work but their home. Single men were compelled to live in barracks and were governed by strict regulations that forbade visitors, smoking, drinking liquor, card playing, and 'conversations in relation to nationality, religion or party politics'. They were allowed to play dominoes. These rules hardly made for 'a home away from home', but some stations too were squalid, men often finding the food inedible and the ablution facilities so inadequate that they washed at the City Baths. Neither Nicholson nor the Lawson ministry did much about the squalid conditions and it was later observed by a Royal Commission:

> At the St Kilda Road Depot . . . the horses are much better served than the men . . . none of the most ordinary comforts or graces of home life are permitted . . . The whole effect was one of repelling cheerlessness . . .

> If the conditions at the depot were repellent, those found to exist at the station at Bourke Street West were shocking . . . the residential portion . . . is unfit for human habitation . . .

> Shabbiness and congestion were the features most in evidence when we visited the Russell Street Barracks . . . Many of the rooms are badly in need of renovation, . . . while the overcrowding of others is serious enough to constitute a menace to the health of the occupants . . .

> A first essential to a spirit of discipline, a smartness of bearing and a dignity of demeanour, is the environment in which a man has to live and work, and the habits of order, cleanliness, and tidiness which satis-

factory conditions engender . . . The conditions prevailing in those buildings of the Victoria Police Force which we inspected were found to be the very antithesis of these.

The plight of the force was not so much the fault of Nicholson as of frugal governments, nestling comfortably in the knowledge that police pay and conditions were not election issues, and that the police themselves could not lawfully strike, even if they had not been too loyal a body of men to think of doing so. Nicholson's culpability lay in his acceptance of the conditions and his failure to follow the example of Steward and Gellibrand in pressing the Government to improve the policeman's lot.[38] Instead of taking action to settle the general unrest of his force, Nicholson aggravated it on 14 November 1922 when he appointed four senior constables to work in plain clothes and operate in pairs throughout the city and suburbs, supervising men on the beat.

Nicholson's justification for introducing the special supervisors was that there was an urgent need to exercise stricter supervision because he had seen 'men idling about the streets, leaning against lamp posts, gossiping and actually smoking in uniform in daylight'. He had also seen policemen 'drunk at night', and one constable had been detected in uniform committing a warehouse burglary. Given the ratio of sub-officers to constables, and the working conditions generally, some slackness and dereliction of duty are not surprising. Nor is it strange that Nicholson should choose to appoint four special supervisors with a roving commission, rather than press the Government for the necessary thirty additional sub-officers.

The special supervisors soon became known as 'spooks'; in parliament they were described as 'pimps', appointed to 'secretly watch and report on constables'; and in some police circles their work was denigrated as 'humiliating espionage'. Although the presence of the special supervisors upset many policemen, their work was confined primarily to the covert supervision of beat constables in the city and inner suburbs, and did not directly affect more senior men, policemen in rural areas, or those engaged on clerical or administrative tasks. Even within their sphere of activity the 'spooks' reported fewer men than did uniformed sub-officers working in the traditional way, and the animosity directed at them was due more to their secretive mode of working, than to any actual cases of injustice or a dramatic rise in the number of discipline reports. The special supervisors performed an important and legitimate function but the question of their appointment was an emotive one, inflamed because Nicholson's choice of men for the task was 'in some cases injudicious', and included the appointment of his brother-in-law as well as another man who had recently been convicted of being found drunk on duty. The 'spook' system struck a serious blow at police morale, and cost Nicholson dearly among those men who had originally welcomed his promotion to Chief Commissioner.[39]

It is difficult to determine whether or not Nicholson's long spell in Ballarat had left him out of touch with city work, or whether he was just a misguided martinet, but soon after launching his 'spook' fiasco he purged the Licensing Branch and set in motion a train of events that ended with the police strike. On 8 February 1923 Nicholson summarily transferred seventeen plain clothes licensing police to uniform work, and among these men was Constable William Brooks, a normal enough member of the branch, who had never been convicted of a discipline offence and who had three commendations to his credit, including one in the preceding two months 'for displaying zeal and tact in partaking in 846 licensing prosecutions and sly-grog cases in twelve months'. Although Nicholson did not know Brooks personally, he had heard that Brooks was 'unfit' for licensing work, and in spite of the recent commendation, he decided that Brooks had to go. Nicholson's decision incensed Brooks and had the effect of transforming him from a loyal and quiet employee into a vocal dissident. Early in April 1923 Brooks circulated a petition, headed 'Comrades and Fellow Workers', amongst constables in the metropolitan area. It demanded the restoration of police pensions, the immediate withdrawal of the special supervisors and the granting of conditions enjoyed by police in New South Wales. Almost seven hundred men signed the petition and it established Brooks as unofficial leader among many metropolitan constables.

It was about this time that the *Melbourne Truth* expressed the view that:

> At no time in the history of the Victoria Police Force has there been so much discontent as there is at present . . . The men not only complain of being underpaid, but of the treatment they receive from the Chief Commissioner, who has won for himself the unenviable distinction of being the most unpopular officer who has occupied the Commissioner's chair.

It is doubtful that this last piece of journalese accurately reflected the opinion of the force, for although Nicholson's popularity, as well as his confidence, was on the wane, he did have his supporters. At one point during 1923 he received widespread acclaim—including a congratulatory letter from the Police Association of New South Wales—when he flew with the police surgeon, Mr G. A. Syme, in an open-cockpit aeroplane to Swan Hill, in a desperate but unsuccessful bid to save the life of Mounted Constable Joseph Delaney, who had been shot while making an arrest. Nevertheless, the rundown state of the force produced festering discontent of a sort not seen for many years, and during April 1923 there was open talk of a police strike. Nicholson defended his position by describing the strike talk as 'moonshine', and an unmoved government simply pointed out that 'there are 948 applications from men to come into the service'. Brooks's petition and its reference to the 'Prussianism' of the supervisors received wide publicity, with the result that he was capriciously transferred to Geelong 'for special work', and on his arrival at Geelong was further ordered to proceed to Colac for licensing duty. In the light of Nicholson's earlier decision about his fitness for such work, Brooks disobeyed the order in Geelong and returned to his wife and family at Prahran, where he was suspended from duty and charged with insubordination. The public hearing of this charge again thrust Brooks into the limelight and into an open courtroom confrontation with Nicholson. Brooks won. In a court decision divided two to one in his favour, he was cleared of the charge, on the grounds that he was 'under the impression that the Chief Commissioner of police had given instructions that he was not to be employed on licensing duty', and returned to uniform duty without loss of pay or position.[40]

Brooks's personal animosity, and the general discontent among sections of the force, remained near boiling point throughout the winter and into the spring of 1923. The special supervisors were still prowling, there was no pension scheme, and work conditions lagged well behind those of the New South Wales police. The Lawson ministry and Nicholson had done nothing substantial to improve conditions for policemen or to ease their discontent, and because the Police Association was a loyal and patient body, this situation could have gone on for months, but it did not. Authority's hand was forced on the night of 31 October 1923, when Brooks led twenty-eight other constables on strike in protest against the system of special supervision. That night, at 10.00 p.m., the beat men at Russell Street refused to parade for duty unless the special supervisors were removed. It has never been disclosed why Brooks chose that night, but it was the eve of Gala Week, when thousands of visitors were expected in Melbourne for a week-long festival of social attractions, one of them the Melbourne Cup, and Brooks's timing—whether by accident or design—guaranteed him much more than average interest and impact. It was the first and, to this day, the only police strike in Australia.

The strike was not organized or supported by the police association but was organized by Brooks who, only minutes before the men were due to parade, called a meeting in the barracks and had them elect him as their spokesman. The majority of these men were young, unmarried constables with less than twelve months service, and their only strike demand was that the special supervisors be removed. The effect of their action was immediate and salutory; the system of special supervisors was abandoned and has never been reintroduced. On the morning of Thursday 1 November the four supervisors were reassigned to other duties, thereby eliminating the single ground on which Brooks and his followers had refused duty the previous night. This action by the police administration,

177

however, was kept secret and not communicated to Brooks or the other strikers. Instead, Brooks met with the Premier and Nicholson that day and was advised that cabinet supported the Chief Commissioner; the special supervisors were to be retained and the men were to return to duty unconditionally. The outcome of this machiavellian approach was that the strike continued into a second night, when Brooks and the same twenty-eight constables again refused to parade for duty. Again their one and only demand was that the special supervisors be removed: an action which, unbeknown to them, had been taken as a result of their strike the night before, but which was never communicated to Brooks nor made public until it emerged during evidence given to a Royal Commission late in 1924. Nicholson never fully explained his reason for adopting this course, and even when questioned about it by the Royal Commission he was evasive and vague. One can only speculate as to why he did it. The two most feasible explanations—perhaps in combination—are that it was a negotiation tactic that went awry and was then kept secret, or Nicholson was painfully aware of the ill-feeling that his supervision system had caused and abandoned it, but did not tell Brooks lest he be seen as capitulating to the demands of a small group of dissidents led by a renegade constable.

Nicholson's decision cost more than six hundred policemen their careers. On the night of 1 November the Commissioner simply told Brooks and the others to return to duty. When they did not, he curtly told those men present, 'You will all be discharged—you can hand in your kits tomorrow'. He then summarily dismissed Brooks and one other constable from the force and discharged the remainder of the men. A later inquiry described Nicholson's behaviour as 'a surprising *dénouement*' and 'an undignified proceeding . . . calculated to cause resentment and to imbalance the judgement of other policemen, who would soon learn, possibly in an exaggerated form, of this theatrical happening'. On being dismissed, Brooks announced that a meeting would be held at the Temperance Hall the following morning, then departed on a tour of suburban police stations, to rally support for the strike. During his visits to stations Brooks grossly exaggerated the extent of his following by stating that 'all the men at Russell Street are out', and by noon on 2 November he had rallied some six hundred men. The initial stages of the strike were a confused tangle of frantic activity, hopeless inactivity and poor communication; many constables were caught up in the strike movement due to a lack of guidance and leadership from Nicholson and officials of the Police Association. Many of the 634 discharged constables did not refuse duty but 'merely hesitated to report for duty or intimate their willingness to do

One view of the police strike from the Bulletin

This is the shop that Jack built.

These are the crooks that looted the shop that Jack built.

Here is the Hop who left the shop for crooks to loot cigars or suit that lay in the shop that Jack built.

These are the "specials" who made no fuss when foolish Hops deserted us; but grabbed a baton and left their jobs to gaily stoush those hostile mobs who looted the shop that Jack built.

This is the shopman all forlorn, who cursed the day when he was born, the poor old shopman, sad and shorn, who lost the loot that fed the brute, when weak Johns Hop ignored the shop, the desolate shop that Jack built

This is the bloke with nimble tongue, who bade the pleecemen green and young leave crook to kill or work his will—yes, leave his job that crooks might rob the stock of the shop that Jack built.

This is McPherson, canny and close, whose methods made John Hop morose, and loath to curb the evil brute who often times gets in the boot, whose first idea is how to loot the unguarded shop that Jack built.

Tom Glover

NURSERY RHYMES FOR MELBOURNE TIMES.

duty while seeking to ascertain what the situation really was, but honestly desiring to do the right thing'. Many men were dealt with unfairly, one so unfairly that he was taken into the police force in South Australia, but regardless of any injustices not one of the 636 men dismissed or discharged by Nicholson and his officers was ever allowed back into the Victorian force.

The absence of so many men from their posts unleashed a wave of violence and looting on a scale never before witnessed in Melbourne. Two men were killed and hundreds more were injured as mobs of roughs fought and looted in an orgy of violence. A tram was stopped and set on fire, and dozens of shop fronts were shattered by brazen looters who tried garments for size before clearing shops of all stock. The uniformed constables still on beat duty were helpless against the unruly mobs, and were themselves jostled and manhandled; while the detectives, who all remained on duty and hovered in the darkness on the outskirts of the city, could not cope with the swarm of laden looters fleeing to the suburbs.[41]

The frenzy of lawlessness that accompanied the police strike so alarmed the Lawson government that, in seeking rescue, it by-passed Nicholson and turned to those men it had overlooked when appointing him in 1922. Lieutenant-General Sir John Monash was given the task of restoring order to the beleaguered city, and the famous soldier soon surrounded himself with a cadre of loyal and outstanding officers from his army days and formed a Special Constabulary Force numbering five thousand men. Monash recognized the ineptitude of Nicholson, and the paralysis that afflicted his diminished force of regular police, and chose to establish and maintain the SCF as an independent peace-keeping unit. When the 'specials' were sworn in each man was equipped with a baton, a brassard and a hat band with the letters SCF, and the motley force of amateur policemen moved in to quell the rioting mobs. They were successful. By Melbourne Cup Day, Tuesday 6 November, relative calm had returned to Melbourne and the people of the city went about their business. For most of them the police strike was over.[42]

The strike in Victoria followed seven other police strikes that had occurred overseas between 1918 and 1921, including major strikes in England and Boston, USA, during 1919, but there is no evidence linking these events overseas with the strike by Victorian policemen and no suggestion that Brooks or his supporters were knowingly copying an international trend. If they were, the overseas experience was a poor precedent for them to follow. The issues in dispute overseas were different from those in Victoria, and in England and Boston they centred on police demands that governments recognize their right to form and join unions. Although both strikes were the final phase in organized and protracted disputes, they were quickly crushed. In England and Boston, a combined force of loyal policemen, special constables and soldiers soon restored order and every policeman who went on strike—2300 in England and 1117 in Boston—was dismissed and never reinstated. The English experience led to the formation of a police federation, which was an official substitute for a police union and was dubbed 'the goose club' because of its 'incapacity to do anything but march in step with the authorities'. In the United States a national backlash against the striking policemen in Boston resulted in 'the complete destruction of the policemen's trade union movement'. In the aftermath of the Victorian police strike the Police Association escaped such retribution because it did not organize or support the strikers, nor was union recognition or affiliation then an issue.[43]

The strike cost the State Treasury £78 263 and 636 policemen their jobs, one-third of the force's manpower. Many hundreds of serving and former policemen were left reeling in bewilderment, as they tried to comprehend the whirlwind of events that was the strike. Many of the discharged men formed themselves into a Police Strikers' Association and lobbied for reinstatement in the force, while others simply obtained alternative employment and put the strike behind them. A high level of public and political interest in the force culminated in the appointment of a Royal Commission on 28 August 1924 to inquire into:

1. (a) The general state, efficiency and condition of the force prior to November 1923;
   (b) As to whether any and what grievances were complained of by members of the Force prior to the month of November, 1923;
   (c) The cause or causes moving certain persons then members of the Force to refuse duty in the month of November, 1923;
   (d) The consequences arising from such refusal of duty;

2. The present standard of efficiency of the force and the best method of securing efficiency, if found to be impaired;

3. As to whether further and better police protection throughout the State, or any part thereof, is necessary; and, if so, what would be the most effective means for ensuring such protection.

The Commission was appointed by the Labor Government led by George Prendergast, who came to power on 18 July 1924. When in opposition the Labor Party had promised to reinstate all 636 police strikers. It was a promise easily made by a political party in opposition and without the means to fulfil it, but the subject was so contentious and hotly debated that when they were elected to govern the Labor politicians shied away from the issue and used the appointment of a Royal Commission as a stalling tactic. The chairman of the Commission was General Sir John Monash, who had so astutely broken the strike and restored order to Melbourne. He was assisted by Superintendent John Martin, an officer subordinate to Nicholson and a former president of the Police Association, and Charles McPherson, Chairman of the Public Service Board. Before these three completed their inquiry the Labor Government was voted from office and saved the anguish of making a decision about reinstatement of the strikers. The new conservative Country Party Government of Premier John Allan amended the Commission's terms of reference to exclude the reinstatement question. The restricted scope of the inquiry diminished the value of its findings accordingly and few people except historians have derived any benefit from its work.

Although the ostensible reason for the strike was the presence of special supervisors, the commission found that 'if pensions had been restored, there would have been no refusal of duty by any considerable section of the force'. Of the 636 men involved in the strike only two had the contingent right to a pension. The lack of a general pension scheme created a situation 'in which, and in which alone, a general strike in the police force became a possibility'. However, notwithstanding the importance of the pension issue, the Commission found that 'the immediate cause of the strike was the agitation engineered by ex-constable Brooks, using as a pretext the system of Special Supervisors', and that 'the generally unsympathetic attitude of successive Governments to the rectification of grievances within the force created a feeling throughout the force which predisposed it to exploitation by an agitator such as Brooks'. The Commission was also severely critical of the actions and administration of Nicholson, who by then was 62 years of age and past the normal police retiring age. His autocratic behaviour and abandonment of conferences, his introduction of the special supervisors, his behaviour during the strike and his age, were just a few of the issues which worried the Royal Commission.[44]

They were not, however, matters of such grave concern to the succession of conservative and Labor Party ministries that held office from 1923 to 1925. Nothwithstanding Nicholson's mismanagement before and during the strike, he was permitted to remain in office and he served as Chief Commissioner while efforts were made to rebuild the force. Unlike 636 other policemen, he survived the night the police went on strike with his source of income—if not his reputation—intact.

5

Good Men are Needed at the Top

The police strike and the events that followed it highlighted the importance of having capable leaders in the senior ranks of the force. It was not enough that they had a sound record of police service; as well as being able to earn the respect and support of subordinates, they had to be at least receptive to new ideas and adaptable to pressures for change. After the strike, the Government appointed Major General Sir James McCay as head of a Special Constabulary Force, to help maintain law and order while the regular force was rebuilt. The two forces co-existed for a few months before the SCF was disbanded, but it was long enough for McCay to overshadow Nicholson and show that there was a wealth of management skills available to the police from outside their ranks. Nicholson was not up to the task and, partly due to his failings, he was the last Chief Commissioner to be appointed from within the force for almost forty years. The three successive Chief Commissioners were all 'outsiders': Brigadier General Thomas A. Blamey, Alexander M. Duncan and Major General Selwyn H. Porter.

The role of the Commissioner was one of the most important factors affecting the fortunes of the force—second only to the influence of the general community itself. This importance was not only in the era of Blamey, Duncan and Porter, nor only in the twentieth century, but it was during and after the police strike that the subject of police leadership became an important public issue, inflamed by Blamey's controversial activities and the importation of Duncan from Scotland Yard.

Blamey, Duncan and Porter worked without the support of deputy or assistant commissioners and, aided only by small personal staffs, they shouldered enormous responsibilities. They were the force's main public figures and spokesmen, and their decisions touched almost every facet of the force's operations. In addition to superintending all manner of internal changes and duties, the personal influence of the three men was to be found in broader social issues, such as police attitudes and activities during the depression, the police war effort and the force's approach to changed juvenile behaviour during the 1950s.

When the Chief Commissioner was vibrant, introduced reforms, and enjoyed public support, the force as a whole generally reflected it. When he waned the force waned with him.

Reconstruction

The police of Victoria are still under the control of the Chief Commissioner. The special police, a special body, existing only for special purposes, and for a limited time, are under the control of Sir James McCay.

By 17 November 1923 the violence and mayhem that marked the early days of the police strike had passed, and the attention of many people turned to the ongoing need to maintain public order and the urgent need to rebuild the police force. Never before in Australia had a community been so 'let down' by its police and so obliged to take the protection of lives and property into its own hands. Such was the loss of confidence in Nicholson and his depleted force that many people in Victoria looked again to someone of Monash's type for succour, and approved of Sir James McCay's appointment as commander of the Special Constabulary Force, which was briefly the larger of Victoria's two police forces and had the finest commander. Nicholson found the role of second fiddle an ignominious sequel to the strike, but McCay was a highly educated lawyer, an experienced military commander, and had added status in his knighthood; his knowledge of people and network of contacts were beyond the reach of the plain man from Ballarat. McCay fitted readily into the role of leader, and not only commanded the SCF but also joined his efforts with Nicholson's to rebuild the regular police force, and there were some expressions of concern that he had 'superseded' or 'displaced' Nicholson, but this was temporary. The SCF was only an interim force, and Nicholson was not destined always to work in McCay's shadow: he remained in office until mid-1925, whereas McCay and the SCF had gone by mid-1924. Nevertheless, that short-lived special force deserves scrutiny.

The headquarters of the SCF was located in the repatriation building at Jolimont. Theoretically an independent adjunct to the regular police force, the SCF became the gateway to the regular force. By government decision, and much to the chagrin of Nicholson's recruiting officers, no man could join Nicholson's force without first serving in McCay's. Officers from the regular force conducted an intensive statewide recruiting campaign that netted an average of one hundred recruits a month, but these men were not immediately available to Nicholson as they were all first inducted into the SCF. As McCay reminded Nicholson, 'I will supply such number of recruits each week as you wish. But of course my supplying them to you is entirely dependent on your first supplying them to me, as we both know'. This arrangement existed to minimize the risk of SCF members being ostracized as a 'scab' minority when they joined the regular force, but it also inflated the importance of the SCF, which had its own corps of officers, its own uniform, its own code of police conduct and which, with a strength of 1380 men, was the third largest force in Australia. Unlike the thousands of men who rallied to Monash's side and volunteered for service as special constables during the police-strike emergency, the men of McCay's SCF were paid employees, whose wage of fifteen shillings a day was higher than the twelve shillings paid to junior constables in the regular force.

The duties and arrest powers of the SCF were almost identical to those of the regular force, and men from both forces worked together at suburban police stations. The main differences between them lay in their degree of public acceptance and their levels of efficiency. The Labor Party viewed the SCF with distaste, and this view was matched by many people in working-class suburbs, especially Collingwood and Northcote, where it was not considered safe for specials to venture alone. The authorities had trouble finding living accommodation for specials in these suburbs, and at certain times they were compelled to patrol in groups of four to ensure their personal safety. The labour movement generally supported reinstatement of the police strikers, and it was felt that 'scabs' of the SCF were thwarting that objective. Some of the specials themselves did little to enhance their collective image. Complaints of officiousness and excessive use of force were common, and two of them were involved in a widely publicized case of attempted extortion. The Labor Party expressed alarm at what it regarded as a 'large number of grave offences committed by special constables' but, given the size and nature of the SCF, the extent and degree of Labor criticism were unwarranted. Ninety-eight specials (about 7 per cent) were discharged for misconduct, but thirty-six of them were for being absent without leave and twenty-one for being 'undesirable'. Much of the trouble with members of the SCF was due to their hasty recruitment and lack of training, and the transitory nature of their role that often saw them go from civilian, to special, to constable, all in the space of fourteen days. Members of the regular force were instructed to treat the specials 'on the same basis as they would treat raw recruits', and were advised that as 'these specials have not had any training in police duties, mistakes and errors of judgment in the performance of their duties must necessarily arise'. Taken overall, the work of the SCF was creditable and, while Nicholson rebuilt his force, the auxiliaries added useful weight against further outbreaks of serious crime and violence. Opponents of the SCF levelled many criticisms at it but never suggested that it was ineffective. It was an expedient for putting 'policemen' on the streets and, on occasions like New Year's Eve, the bolstering of regular police ranks with specials was the salutory difference between a night of rejoicing and a night of rioting.

Andrew Moore is one historian who has looked at the role of special constables, but he approaches the question in doctrinaire fashion and views them as the sinister manifestation of some secret right-wing movement. There is more point of view than hard evidence behind such a proposition, and Moore appears unwilling to accept as a real possibility that the formation of the SCF was a spontaneous and even natural reaction when a community was in crisis, and was forced by the unprecedented breakdown of its regular police force to take steps to secure the order and safety desired by most people. One review properly describes Moore's argument as over-dramatized and his sources as 'sparse', and says of his secret army theory, 'one needs something more substantial than suspicion of an "unseen hand"'. Certainly some working-class areas showed even more active dislike of the specials than they normally did for *any* policemen, and many unionists were resentful of them on good union principles; but probably most Victorians simply wanted to feel safe by having sufficient 'policemen' on the streets, which might be conservative but is hardly sinister. If police militancy suffered a sad blow, that was quite in harmony with the accepted views of a great many Victorians, including non-union wage-earners and their dependants. If it was a plot, it was singularly ill-planned: so unprepared for it was everybody, that even the supply of boots and batons to the specials caused acute problems.

During the period from December 1923 to May 1924 a total of 694 men transferred from the SCF to the Victoria Police Force, which was thus brought back to full strength in only six months. The remaining members of the SCF, including McCay, were demobbed during mid-1924, and on 1 August 1924, a special meeting of justices of the central bailiwick formally disbanded the SCF, when they decreed there was 'no further cause to apprehend that ordinary constables and officers appointed to preserve the peace, are insufficient for the purpose'. From that date Victoria again had one police force and Nicholson stood alone as the state's most senior policeman.[1]

Although at full numerical strength, the force was not regarded as being up to its pre-strike standard. The average length of service of the strikers was five years, and service in individual cases ranged up to twenty-five years, with 135 of them having served for more than ten years each. It was not possible in the space of a few months to impart this level of experience to new recruits, and although former officers were retained as instructors, it was not even possible to give each recruit the standard seven-week training course. The Monash Royal Commission acknowledged that one consequence of the strike was a 'lowering of efficiency' that would take 'two or three years entirely to repair', but it was also acknowledged that the general education level of the new men was higher than that of the police strikers they replaced. Reduced efficiency was a difficult variable to measure and was not at once obvious to many people. A matter of greater concern to the public was 'the number of young constables of small stature to be seen on duty in the city'. In order to bring the force more quickly back to full strength after the strike, and to open the force to more returned soldiers the minimum height requirement was reduced by one inch to 5 feet 8 inches. Throughout efforts to rebuild the force, first preference was always given to returned soldiers, and they comprised 56 per cent of the SCF. A one-inch reduction was not unreasonable but it did run counter to police tradition. Long before they introduced minimum education standards, police forces had minimum—and arbitrary—height requirements: in London 5 feet 7 inches, in Victoria 5 feet 9 inches, and in New South Wales 5 feet 10 inches. In 1924 tradition dictated that 'a foot policeman in uniform should by his obvious physical proportions and strength command a respect for his capacity to deal with every situation demanding a physique well above the average'. The post-strike recruits were criticized for being 'jockey-size', and their 'small stature' so worried many people that in April 1925 the minimum height was restored to 5 feet 9 inches.[2]

Although the police strike may have had some damaging effects on the efficiency and physical appearance of the force, it did bring about significant improvements in the work conditions of Victoria's police. (The only men not to benefit from the strike were the strikers.) In the wake of the strike, the Government and the force administration introduced a series of reforms designed to attract recruits and to reward those men who remained loyal. The strike prompted more improvements in police work conditions than constitutional means had achieved in the previous quarter of a century, and these reforms served as the corner-stone of efforts to rebuild the force.

On eight separate occasions during the period 1903 to 1921, members of the force made formal representations to the Government for the reintroduction of police pensions. All of these were unsuccessful, the best that the police could elicit from the Government being Lawson's 1920 election promise that was broken. However, within weeks of the strike, a Police Pensions Bill was rushed through parliament and became law on 1 January 1924, providing all police with comprehensive pension entitlements, including disability payments and allowances for widows and children. Also, police were given a small increase in pay that raised their minimum yearly salary to £220, and brought them closer to the New South Wales police. A good conduct scheme was introduced, so that 'during the seventh to eleventh years of his service' a constable could 'twice receive an annual increment of £10 for good conduct, special zeal, general intelligence, general proficiency, or by passing a qualifying examination in education and police matters'. Promotion, too, was made quicker and easier; the service period for qualification was reduced from seven to two years, and some other short cuts to promotion became possible. There was a big stick in the background: no man dismissed for misconduct—including going on strike—was entitled 'to any pension or gratuity', and this could mean the loss of a pension of up to £250 a year for a man with thirty years service. Pensions, pay rises and promotion prospects gave police better career goals, a greater sense of personal security, and more money in their pockets. Nor did the rewards for loyalty stop there. In May 1924 all loyalist police were granted seven days extra leave, and in 1925 and 1927 respectively the annual leave for all police was raised to twenty-one days, then twenty-eight days, a great advance on the previous entitlement of seventeen days, and one that brought the force into line with New South Wales.

The Government improved police surroundings with a massive increase in spending on police equipment and buildings. A new depot was built on land fronting St Kilda Road, the Russell Street barracks remodelled, the Bourke Street West Police station renovated and dozens of other lesser works completed at police stations throughout the state. Table 4 shows the scale and rate of this increased capital expenditure. Given the nexus established by the Monash Royal Commission between the squalid state of many police buildings and the propensity of men living in them to strike, it is unfortunate that the frugal Lawson ministry did not spend some of this money before the strike.[3]

TABLE 4

Capital expenditure on buildings and works for police

Financial year	Amount spent (£)	% up or down on *strike year
1918–1919	2891	−66%
1919–1920	2879	−66%
1920–1921	5752	−33%
1921–1922	6681	−22%
1922–1923	8597	*base year
1923–1924	20 997	+144%
1924–1925	20 109	+133%
1925–1926	24 565	+185%
1926–1927	31 637	+268%
1927–1928	39 292	+357%

Victorian Government Expenditure in Division 1 sub-division 2—Police Buildings (includes buildings and works for police, land, furniture, repairs and additions and fencing). (Source: *Victorian Parliamentary Papers.* Treasurer's Financial Report for years 1918–1919 to 1927–1928).

Buildings and manpower were not the only matters to occupy Nicholson in the last months of his career, and after the strike he resumed consideration of three developments that were initiated before October 1923 but temporarily pushed into the background by the strike. They were the use

*The Wireless Patrol: P. C. Bully on running board
and F. W. ('Pop') Downie at extreme right*

of dogs and wireless in police work, and an expanded role for women police. And that is the order of importance in which Nicholson viewed them. In 1922 the force acquired two 'fine young liver-and-white pointers' and during April 1923 they were taken on patrol to test their utility for police work. The trials were a favourite project of Nicholson's and he was firmly committed to the idea that the dogs would prove a 'great success', reduce crime and save 'police from being maltreated'. During 1924 he obtained information about the subject from a number of overseas sources, including the South African police, and initiated a breeding programme at the Dandenong police stud depot, using bulldogs, pointers and airedale terriers. But their handlers lacked expertise, the dogs were not properly trained and were a failure. The scheme gradually faded from existence, but not before an airedale-bulldog-cross named P.C. Bully acquired considerable fame as a night rider with the wireless patrol. As a working police dog Bully was a flop, but perched on the running board of a police Lancia travelling at 50 miles an hour he was the meanest motor car mascot in Melbourne.[4]

Nicholson's keenness to give police dogs a trial set him apart from Alfred Sainsbury, who rejected the idea in 1914 as not worth 'the time, trouble or money'. On another issue both men agreed: women had only a very limited role to play in police work. When women first entered the force in 1917 it was against Sainsbury's wishes and, although many police-men, including Steward and Gellibrand, were pleased with the work of the women, Nicholson remained unimpressed. In 1922, after five years service as 'police agents', Victoria's two policewomen asked if they might be paid equal money for doing equal work. It was a valid plea by women, not subject to any entrance standards or training, but doing the same long hours and shifts as the men, and similar duties. The women took their own case to the Chief Secretary and the Chief Commissioner, arguing that they had all the usual living expenses to meet, plus special police 'out of pocket expenses', and the requirement to 'maintain dignity' and be 'decently dressed' at a time when 'women's clothing had increased in cost by leaps and bounds'. In August 1922 the policewomen were granted a daily plain clothes allowance of 1s 6d, but this still left their pay at least five shillings a day below that of their male colleagues. Because they were not members of the Police Association that body did not support their claim, but the women did have a friend in John Cain, Labor MLA for Northcote, who aired their case in parliament. The moves by and for women police to improve their lot were accompanied by sustained lobby-ing from community groups, like the National Council of Women, to increase their strength; and the number of policewomen was increased to four by the appointment of Mary Cox in September 1922 and Ellen Cook in September 1923. The movement to give policewomen greater recognition was gaining momentum and was given valuable impetus dur-ing the police strike, when the women loyally remained on duty through-out the crisis. After the strike there was talk of recognizing the women's efforts by extending the proposed pay rises and pension scheme to include them, but the moves were stymied by Nicholson. He publicly and pri-vately opposed equal rights for women police and, at the height of dis-cussions in December 1923, he wrote to the Under-Secretary:

> If policewomen were made members of the force, they would be entitled to the pay and privileges of male members, unless special pro-vision to the contrary was arranged. Their degree of usefulness to the government does not, in my opinion, justify their being placed on the same footing as the police, their sex hampering their usefulness.

In a separate press statement Nicholson even went as far as to suggest that if the women were to 'be entitled to the same status as ordinary members of the force' he could see 'no alternative but to dismiss the four women'. A. J. O'Meara has generously assumed that Nicholson adopted this stance in the interests of women, 'as a bluff to focus attention on the fact that, since they were not sworn in as constables, they could not be eligible for all the privileges to which that rank was entitled'. Yet such a claim is based on Nicholson's tacit support for women police *in a restricted welfare role*. The truth is that Nicholson opposed the full entry of women into the force. His opposition to equal rights for policewomen, rather than serving as a ploy to highlight and remedy their plight, actually prolonged it. The conservative government of Harry Lawson accepted Nicholson's recommendations, and it was not until after the Labor Ministry of George Prendergast came to office on 18 July 1924, that Victoria's four women police were sworn in, on 12 November 1924, and legally vested with the same powers of arrest, pay and pension rights as their male colleagues. O'Meara fails to mention the crucial change of government. The Labor Party had always supported efforts to improve the lot of women police, and when they used their brief spell in government to give legal effect to this policy it was not done with Nicholson's concurrence.[5]

Women still had a long way to go. In 1924 there were only four of them among more than eighteen hundred men, and within the force were many sections destined for decades to remain all-male bastions. One of them was the newest and most exciting area of police work—the Wireless Patrol.

> A powerful touring car slips along decorously in the early morning quiet of Melbourne. Externally it is the property of some eminently respectable suburbanite homewardbound.
>
> Inside it, beside the driver, are a dog and four men, one of whom wears a leather helmet and wireless headgear.
>
> The headgear buzzes . . . Dot-Dash-Dash-Dot-Dot . . . 'Thieves in warehouse, Lygon Street, Carlton', the operator reads. At a word the driver accelerates, and the rest of the message is taken at 50 miles an hour.
>
> The wireless patrol, which nightly guards thousands of lives and millions of pounds worth of property, is on the job.

That is the style of journalistic eulogies of the wireless patrol found in the pages of Melbourne newspapers throughout the 1920s and 1930s. The 'Patrol', as it became more colloquially known, was the brainchild of Senior Constable Frederick William 'Pop' Downie, who was described in later years by Sir Thomas Blamey as 'the most intelligent, uneducated man' he had ever met. The hitherto unknown sight of six burly policemen together in a sleek motor car with a dog and a wireless set enraptured the public and proved a revolutionary turning point in modern policing. Members of the patrol were able to boast that 'the average time taken to get to the scene of a crime is 4.4 minutes', and their arrest record was unchallenged by any other police in Australia. Indeed, they were the envy of the international police community, and were the first police in the world to put wireless in a touring car.

Today, police use of sophisticated communications equipment is an essential feature of every force, but in 1920 the mere idea of police wireless was so novel that it attracted wonder, incredulity and sometimes scorn. At that time Downie was serving with the Motor Patrol, which used a Palm car built from model-T-Ford parts to patrol at night, checking such places as post offices and railway stations. To receive and give information, this unit would call at police stations each half-hour and telephone Russell Street for news. It was an inefficient means of communication. Around 1921 Downie began working with the idea of providing wireless for police patrol cars, and by November 1922 had developed his concept to the stage where he was able to persuade Nicholson to take part in experimental transmissions. Initially these experiments were conducted using wireless telephony but it was decided to switch to wireless telegraphy, which involved the use of morse code, and this remained the basis of the police wireless network until April 1940. The force's first Marconi receiving set was hired from Amalgamated Wireless for £1 a week and fitted to the force's one Hotchkiss car in May 1923, and this was followed by the purchase of two new Lancia patrol cars later in 1923, and the progressive purchase of a fleet of Daimlers from August 1926. In the space of five years Downie's wireless patrol was a revolutionary reality. From these small beginnings the combined use of motor cars and wireless by police slowly developed, resulting in the removal of constables from suburban beats and their encapsulation in patrol cars. In the period before World War II it was not a problem, it

Dot-Dash-Dot: telegraphist Clifford Allison and the Wireless Patrol

The men behind the Wireless Patrol: Chief Commissioner A. Nicholson, front centre (seated), F. W. ('Pop') Downie, extreme right (seated), and Constable F. W. Canning (standing second from right).

was progress. However, by the 1970s a 'revolutionary new direction' in police work was 'Operation Crimebeat', a scheme to take policemen from motor cars and put them back on the streets to patrol on foot—with portable radios in their pockets. In 1921 when Downie developed his idea after attending the Melbourne Marconi School of Wireless, not even he could have foreseen the impact that his experiments would have on the future of policing.

What was Nicholson's role in this? Downie's son argues that Nicholson was unenthusiastic about the idea and forced Downie to 'go it alone', while Nicholson's son, and the newspapers of the period, credit Nicholson with appreciating the full possibilities of Downie's vision and with supporting it totally. The real position was more probably as surmised by two of the original wireless telegraphists who worked with Downie: that Nicholson was an ageing and conservative man, approaching retirement, beset by the problems and costs of the police-strike era, and confronted by an inventive senior constable with a bold but expensive plan for police wireless, which had never before been tried in the world. In such circumstances, a cautious response on the part of Nicholson would not only have been reasonable and prudent, but would have been in keeping with his character.[6] In any event, Nicholson did finally facilitate the introduction and development of the wireless patrol, and it served as his swan-song. Before Downie had completed his work, Nicholson became ill and was admitted to hospital in May 1925. He never returned to duty and was succeeded as Chief Commissioner by Brigadier General Thomas Albert Blamey on 1 September 1925. Post-strike efforts to rebuild the force were largely complete, but on the recommendation of the Monash Royal Commission, Blamey was offered a salary of £1500 a year, £600 more than that paid to Nicholson, and he was expected to consolidate Nicholson's work of reconstruction. It was thus that Monash's former Chief of Staff 'embarked on the most tempestuous eleven years of his life'.[7]

On the Edge of a Volcano

One thing at least is certain about Thomas Blamey: he was complex. Sir John Monash said that Blamey 'possessed a mind cultured far above the average, widely informed, alert and prehensile. He had an infinite capacity for taking pains . . . Blamey was a man of inexhaustible industry, and accepted every task with placid readiness. Nothing was ever too much trouble'. Yet David McNicoll is no less right in seeing Blamey as 'without doubt one of the most controversial generals in history. During his lifetime he was accused of perjury, nepotism, larrikinism, faulty judgement, drunkenness, lechery, deceit and even—by a couple of his more dedicated enemies—cowardice'.[8]

Blamey, who was to become Australia's first Field Marshal, is still heralded as its 'greatest soldier' and 'unrecognised hero'; yet in 1936 his career was seemingly in ruins, when 'almost friendless' and 'widely vilified', he was asked to resign from the police force. As Chief Commissioner, Blamey was a controversial figure, uniquely embodying the reformist generalship of Steward and Gellibrand, the fractious authoritarianism of O'Callaghan and the scandal of Standish. His commissionership spanned eleven stormy years, beginning in the wake of the police strike amid calls for an inquiry into police corruption, and ending during the 1930s, following a Royal Commission inquiry into the shooting of Superintendent J. O. Brophy. During his police career Blamey survived five changes of government and an unprecedented challenge to his tenure of office, and confronted—some would say precipitated—a series of personal and professional crises that included the notorious 'badge 80' affair, a provident fund controversy, a running feud with the press, the shooting of demonstrators by police, the break-up

Chief Commissioner
T. A. Blamey

of the Police Association, and several police inquiries. Some of these troubles were primarily of his own making, and others were largely political in origin, but rarely was Blamey an innocent bystander. He was an outspoken man—politically conservative, with a dislike of the Labor Party—and displayed an intense personal interest in the suppression of communism, working-class radicalism and public protest. His reactionary politics he shared with his predecessors in the office of Chief Commissioner, but Blamey served for several years under Labor governments. Against a background of economic depression and unemployment, his personality and politics made a difficult task even harder. In the words of John Hetherington, Blamey's years as Chief Commissioner were spent 'on the edge of a volcano'.

Blamey was initially appointed Chief Commissioner by the conservative Country Party ministry of John Allan, after Sir Harry Chauvel mooted the idea with the Chief Secretary, Dr Stanley Argyle, during an early-morning stroll in the Botanic Gardens. Blamey's appointment was well received by the more conservative and propertied elements in the community, who had been so troubled by the police strike and the seeming inability of policemen like Nicholson to ensure the security of their lives and property. He was only forty-one when he arrived at police headquarters to take charge, but he was a graduate of the military staff college at Quetta, who had earned high praise from Monash for his war work, and had already in the post-war period held such positions as Director of Military Operations, Deputy Chief of the General Staff, Colonel (General Staff) at the High Commissioner's Office, London, and Australian representative on the Imperial General Staff. When he swapped his soldier's sword for the policeman's baton, Blamey was Second Chief of General Staff and right-hand man to Chauvel, then Inspector General of the Australian Military Forces.[9]

So highly was Blamey regarded in some circles that his appointment as Chief Commissioner was of itself enough to end moves for an inquiry into alleged police corruption and maladministration. In the months between Nicholson's hospitalization and Blamey's assumption of command numerous allegations of corruption were levelled at members of the force, particularly the Licensing Branch. Mr H. H. Smith, MLC for Melbourne, moved for a select committee 'to inquire into and report upon the administration of the police department' because there was 'no place on earth' where licensing supervision was 'so lax'. He added that sly-grog selling and two-up games flourished because certain police had accepted bribes. His allegations received some publicity and support, particularly from people concerned about illegal trading by hotels, so his calls for a public inquiry gathered momentum and prompted the Government to demand explanatory reports from senior members of the force. Being then without a permanent Chief Commissioner, the force lacked its traditional spokesman, but the mere announcement that Blamey was to get the post was enough to undo Smith's work. Government members conceded to Smith that there was a 'great deal to deplore in connexion with our police force', but they urged him to drop his calls for a public inquiry because 'the right man' had been selected and the force under Blamey would 'be squared up and cleaned up'. The pro-Blamey lobby persuaded Smith to declare that he would not embarrass Blamey and to withdraw his call for an inquiry. Instead, he would place his evidence of lax liquor control before the new Chief Commissioner. There is no suggestion that the Government hastily appointed Blamey with the intention of silencing Smith; the allegations were not as important as all that, and Blamey's name had been connected with the top police post since 1922. The timing of the announcement was fortuitous, even though it was also fortunate for the Government that the new Chief Commissioner was a well-known and respected general, not an ageing and obscure country police superintendent. The aura of Blamey took effect even before he had taken office.

Yet it was foolish to put such trust in Blamey. The new Chief Commissioner—to whom drinking was an innocent and indispensable element of everyday social life—openly flouted licensing laws, and his presence after hours at fashionable hotels provided fellow illegal drinkers with a guarantee against police raids. It is not known how his predilection for liquor after hours influenced his handling of Smith's complaints, but it did highlight a grave flaw in his police command. He viewed the police force with a soldier's eye, and never really understood the unique responsibilities and obligations attaching to his position as the state's most senior policeman. In matters such as training, supply, personnel management and organizational planning, where his army background could be readily applied to the police, Blamey was a fine leader. Beyond lay many other aspects of police life, and here Blamey ran into trouble. He publicly told implausible lies out of misplaced loyalties, he openly broke licensing laws because he disagreed with them, he smashed the Police Association because it disagreed with him, he disliked and openly haggled with newspapermen, and he never understood the 'indivisibility of the private and official lives of the man in public office'.[10]

It was never more evident than during the 'badge 80' affair, which broke only weeks after Blamey joined the force and cast a shadow of doubt over his veracity and the force he commanded. On the night of 21 October 1925, three members of the Licensing Branch raided a brothel in Bell Street, Fitzroy, where one of the amorous male visitors produced to them a police badge numbered '80' and announced, 'That is all right, boys. I am a plainclothes constable. Here is my badge'. Badge '80' was Blamey's. It took several weeks, but reports of this encounter gradually filtered along the passages of police stations, into the corridors of parliament and on to the pages of newspapers, fed all the while by anonymous letters to the Government, such as this one:

Do you know that the Commissioner of Police was found in a sly grog shop at Fitzroy last month naked and in bed with a naked woman and that the police who found him there are in terror as to what he will do to them. How is the cursed drink to be put down if the head of the police is an adulterer and a drunkard? Good men are needed at the top, pure and honest, (Rom. xiii XI-XIV).

The 'badge 80' affair was a daunting test of character. With such a spectre as the Chief Commissioner wearing naught but his badge, the press had a field day, and during debates in parliament it was suggested that Blamey had been framed (though no one suggested by whom or for what purpose), and calls were made for a full public inquiry. Such an inquiry was never held but, at Blamey's direction, some detectives did conduct an investigation of sorts, the findings of which were inconclusive on all but one point. It was determined, to the satisfaction of Blamey and the Government that appointed him, that Blamey was not the man who produced badge '80' in Mabel Tracey's house of ill repute. That man was never identified or located. The three raiding constables attested that Blamey was not the man, Blamey produced an alibi proving evidence of his whereabouts elsewhere at the crucial time, and Tracey agreed that Blamey was not her amorous customer. Beyond this point the police inquiries went nowhere. It was claimed by Blamey that his police badge was 'surreptitiously removed' from his key-ring the day before the Fitzroy raid, and found by him three days later in his letterbox at the Naval and Military Club. Superintendent Daniel Linehan, the senior officer next in line to Blamey, disputed this story and claimed that he saw the badge on Blamey's desk only seven hours before the Bell Street raid. Linehan's candour caused considerable embarrassment to Blamey and the government, and prompted the Chief Secretary, Argyle, to brand him as 'disloyal'. However, some weeks later, Linehan reached the pension age and retired from the force, whereupon his statement was conveniently forgotten. Many years later, credence was given to Linehan's version by John Hetherington who, in his biography of Blamey, claims that Blamey privately admitted to making up the 'surreptitious removal' story. Blamey allegedly confessed that he gave his key-ring and badge to a visiting friend from Sydney, on the night of 21 October 1925, but would not tell the truth when the furore finally broke because he did not want to implicate his old army colleague who 'was married and the father of three children'. If one accepts Hetherington's account, and it is more plausible than the inconclusive police report released publicly at the time, then one accepts that Blamey lied and embroiled the force in a public scandal, out of a 'quixotic sense of personal loyalty' to an old army mate. Enduring personal loyalty can be an admirable trait, but a man of Blamey's intelligence should perhaps have appreciated that the office of Chief Commissioner, by its very nature, at times demanded a degree of public accountability and personal integrity transcending even that ordinarily expected of a general.[11]

Yet there were great strengths in Blamey. Like Steward and Gellibrand, he could motivate other men. He was frightened of neither change nor challenge, and he quickly applied his many ideas and talents toward improving the force. He gave unqualified support and encouragement to Downie and the wireless patrol team, which developed into a key branch of the force. Some years later he and Downie combined to create an Information Section, for the systematic collection of criminal records and modus operandi analysis. Without reservation Blamey supported the place of women in police work, and he was responsible for increasing their number and expanding their role. He sent two officers to Europe and North America to study the latest developments in criminal investigation and traffic policing; formed a bicycle patrol section, for special anti-crime duties; reorganized the criminal investigation and plain clothes branches; and established a traffic control group, of sixty constables, equipped with thirty motorcycle-sidecar outfits. The formation of a statistics section, the greater utilization of fingerprints and criminal photographs and a police mapping programme, were all matters to which Blamey devoted his seemingly indefatigable energy. He pursued all these projects along with the routine running of the force, and during his first five years in office took a total of only six days leave.

In his approach to police administration Blamey had much in common with Steward, and in one particular area their combined efforts stand as a vital contribution to the force they helped to shape. Both men had an unwavering commitment to the need for police education. Steward began police training; it waned under Gellibrand and Nicholson; Blamey revived it, expanded it and set it on a course from which it has never deviated. Blamey, a former schoolteacher and a product of military discipline, extended the period of basic police training from thirty-five days to three months, and expanded the curriculum to include 'lectures on sex hygiene, the way to live, hints on general behaviour, attitude towards the public, etc.', as well as 'instruction in general education including arithmetic, English, geography, civics, grammar, etc.'. He acknowledged that most police recruits were 'young working men' who were 'not mentally fitted' for an exclusive diet of law lectures, so he determined that one-third of all recruit training classes would be devoted to 'general educational subjects', and 'a highly qualified teacher' from the education department was appointed for the purpose. A qualified teacher from outside the force was unprecedented and his presence exposed police recruits to the wider world of human knowledge existing outside the pages of their law books, and vital in helping them understand the institutions and the people they would be expected to deal with.

In addition to this recast basic training, new regulations effective from 1 August 1926 required recruits graduating from the depot to enter a twelve-month probationary period, at the end of which they sat a retention examination; unless candidates obtained a 60 per cent pass they were not entitled to any increase in pay. The scheme was designed to encourage further study by working police, in their own time, and to facilitate it Blamey scheduled a series of free day and evening instruction classes, covering all the subjects tested at both the retention examination and the promotion examinations for higher ranks. Blamey later claimed that the result was an educational standard 'considerably higher than it ever was before', and an obvious 'improvement in efficiency'. Blamey's mild boast was quite justified; some measure of his success is found in the fact that his basic concept of broadened and in-service police education has survived him and is the corner-stone of modern police training.

Blamey also acquired a deserved reputation as an irritable autocrat who 'enforced his will relentlessly', but his empathy with the welfare needs of the force was greater than that of his predecessors, save perhaps Steward and Gellibrand. In many things touching upon the morale and well-being of the force Blamey had a clear notion of sharing and fairness to all. An element of 'equal opportunity' was introduced into the procedures for filling vacancies in the CIB and plain clothes branch, and into the general system of awarding commendations. Previously the plum jobs and the commendations were something of a 'closed shop', and many qualified members missed out because they had the 'wrong' contacts or did not have the 'right' boss. Blamey changed this for the general good of all members, with beneficial results in morale and efficiency. He also introduced a new grade of first constable, which ranked between those of constable and senior constable, and afforded constables with less than ten years service the chance to gain promotion and increased pay. It was taking constables up to twenty-six years to gain the rank of senior constable, and Blamey's new intermediate grade sustained ambition and morale by providing a chance to earn increased status, responsibility and pay. Blamey also saw the police hospital as a place for treatment and caring, rather than as a hospice for suspected malingerers, and he upgraded its facilities and staffing to include 'three trained nurses with a matron in charge', who took over from the one male dispenser who previously had sole care of patients. Blamey was also very keen on the idea of a police holiday home by the sea, where members and their families could rest and recuperate, and he went so far as to purchase the necessary land at Mornington. Here Blamey was ahead of his time, and it was not until many years after he left the force that his concept was given effect.[12]

Healthy bodies, healthy minds and healthy wallets might well have been Blamey's recipe for the making of a contented force: he devoted considerable energy towards these things. He encouraged the use of new gymnasiums at the police depot and the Russell Street police station, so that men could 'keep themselves fit', and he established a Police Institute 'to allow members of the force to buy good articles at low prices'. Limited credit was allowed to police shopping at the institute and all profits were 'devoted to police welfare objects'. In conjunction with the Police Institute, Blamey started a Police Provident Fund to assist 'policemen who were financially embarrassed owing to illness or other ill-fortune' and to 'prevent young constables from getting into the hands of moneylenders'. Blamey firmly believed that police were underpaid, and he was known to lend those in financial trouble up to £300 from his own pocket, repayable at the rate of five shillings a week, interest free. The provident fund scheme—modelled on similar funds in London—was an extension of this belief, and was a positive attempt to alleviate the financial difficulties of many policemen. After 1925 the post-strike improvement in police working conditions had lost momentum, and the pay of junior constables fell behind the basic wage. Blamey sought in particular to ease the plight of these men, without simply adding his voice to the never-ending and seemingly ineffective chorus asking for increased wages. The provident fund was started in June 1927 with a donation of £100 from the Commonwealth Bank, and was quickly added to when, in July, the philanthropic J. Alston Wallace made a gift of £1000, in recognition 'of the hourly danger to which members of the police force are exposed in their work of protecting the lives and property of the citizens of this state'. Wallace's gesture, like that of Blamey's in establishing the fund, was well-intentioned, but their combined actions prompted a public outcry and drew severe criticism from both the press and the Government. Both men were forced to publicly defend their actions, and for Wallace this meant disclosing his identity and motives, after initially making the gift anonymously. Considerable public pressure was exerted on Blamey to return the money, lest a 'dangerous precedent' be set of police accepting 'gifts of dubious propriety', which could 'hamper them in the execution of their duties'. Blamey, however, proved that he was a man to be reckoned with. Much to the annoyance and embarrassment of Ned Hogan's newly elected Labor government—sections of which labelled the gift as 'practically bribery'—Blamey kept the money and the provident fund, and closed the subject by reporting that he was 'unable to return the money' as he had been legally advised 'that the contribution became the property of every member of the force directly it was accepted'. Blamey's establishment of a police institute and provident fund were not uncharacteristic ventures into socialist co-operativeness but were typical examples of his paternalistic leadership style. He exercised firm control over both ventures. There were no committees, no elected office-bearers, no audits, the balance of accounts was kept secret and disbursements were dependent upon the personal good will of Blamey. Incidents like this rankled with the Labor Party, annoyed the press, and kept Blamey on the edge of a volcano. In doing so he won the wholehearted support of many policemen and a common sentiment among them was that 'all Blamey was ever guilty of was sticking to his men'.[13]

Not all Blamey's troubles ended as resolutely and smugly as the provident fund controversy, nor were the issues in conflict always as straightforward. The most controversial administrative action of his police command involved the virtual destruction of the original Police Association, and the substitution of a puppet organization, over which he retained control. Blamey's attitude was that of a military man: there was no room for a 'trade union' in a disciplined police force. Almost from the time he assumed office, he embarked on a course destined to end in a showdown between himself and the Association. For Blamey it was an immutable question of principle, and he was unmoved by the Association's claims that it had existed since 1917 as a properly constituted body, had not taken part in the police strike, and had over the years made a worthwhile contribution to the well-being of the force.

Before Blamey's appointment the Association had worked with Sainsbury, Steward, Gellibrand and Nicholson, and, although disagreements often arose, there was never any serious conflict of wills. Blamey was in office for less than eight weeks when, on 26 October 1925, he wrote to the Crown Solicitor seeking an opinion about the legality of certain of the Association's activities, including determination of the legal status of its secretary who was 'not a member of the police force'. The Crown Solicitor decided in favour of the Association and no prosecutions were made, but it was an early sign of things to come nearly three years later.

During August 1928 Blamey held the inaugural Victoria Police Conference at the police depot, where twenty-nine elected delegates, who represented all grades and branches of the force, discussed 120 agenda items 'of importance to the force', including pensions, pay, travelling and uniform allowances, accommodation, long service leave, hours of duty, 'bedding for troop horses' and—a clear indication of Blamey's personal influence on the proceedings—a recommendation 'for the removal of the press representatives' from the press room at Russell Street. One delegate represented the Police Association, but his was a token presence for Blamey had effectively established his own system: his conference duplicated a number of the Association's activities and gave him the basic structure of a forum that he later used to supplant the Association. Blamey's conference was modelled on the English police federation instituted in 1919, after the English police strikes, 'as part of the official campaign to destroy an independent union movement, by providing some measure of the right to confer'. The federation was designed to 'act as a means of containing police dissatisfaction, by allowing 'elected representatives of each rank' to 'consider and bring to the notice of police authorities . . . all matters affecting their welfare and efficiency other than questions of discipline and promotion affecting individuals'. Blamey adopted the same sort of forum, even down to incorporating the same words into its charter, and providing for a disproportionately high level of representation by the senior ranks, to minimize the influence of constables, 'the most numerous and militant rank'. Even so, the conference was a valuable arena for debate, encompassing a greater range of delegates and discussion points than did the Association. Blamey's system provided a forum for the previously unheard opinions of the policewomen (who were allowed a delegate of their own) and policemen who were not members of the Police Association. Initially only an annual event, the conference system still had serious implications for the future of the Police Association, so it troubled the Labor government, which first read of Blamey's scheme in the *Age*. In his inimitable fashion Blamey again affronted the Labor Party by setting out to undermine a union of workers without telling his political masters.[14]

Shortly after Blamey's first conference, the conservative McPherson ministry was returned to office and, in a favourable political climate, his conferences were no longer a problem. With the support of McPherson,

Blamey then introduced new promotion regulations that placed emphasis on examination results and ability, rather than seniority. It was a sound idea in principle and had been spoken of by Blamey's predecessors, but he was the first commissioner bold enough to try to shift the emphasis in promotion from seniority to merit. Among often reactionary policemen, Blamey's scheme was widely viewed with disdain; it threatened not only the status quo but also the prospects of policemen of mediocre ability. Merit is hard to define, and Blamey's plans were not foolproof, but he had two good reasons for wanting to change a tradition dear to the hearts of many policemen. First, the many hundreds of men who joined immediately after the police strike were permanently disadvantaged by their lack of seniority. Secondly, Blamey wanted ability promoted. It was his view that:

> The police force of Victoria today is suffering very greatly in its efficiency. . . It can never become a really efficient force until the most able men are given opportunity to attain the highest positions without having to wait for the passing on of men of poorer abilities. Since the rewards in the higher ranks are considerable, the state should have the right to the full value of the services of the men of greater ability in the higher ranks. The seniority system of promotion is the worst factor in the police system of this state.

Blamey had succinctly stated a strong position: a police promotion system should give value to the public who pay for it, not sinecures to ageing and indifferent policemen. Many policemen regarded Blamey's view as heresy, and it has been debated perennially.

The Police Association was quick to oppose his plans, and the subject rapidly escalated into a heated political issue. As the debates warmed up, the parties became increasingly polarized. The Association and its supporters argued that 'the regulations had created discontent, uncertainty, unrest, and suspicion throughout the force, and . . . were undermining the spirit of comradeship and esprit de corps', whereas 'long and faithful service was entitled to rewards'. Blamey, his supporters and even the newspapers reasserted that there 'should be no obstacle to prevent the progress of the brilliant man, and no mechanical advancement for the mediocrity whose only distinction is length of service . . . Those who insist that promotion should be governed exclusively, or even chiefly, by seniority put themselves in the position of defending entrenched incompetence against the pressing claims of ability'. The new regulations were first given legal effect by the McPherson ministry on 1 July 1929 but, before they had any real impact, the Association succeeded in making them an issue during the November 1929 state elections. The Association firmly believed that a change of government was its 'only hope' of having the new promotion scheme modified or abandoned, and during the election campaign it lobbied every candidate for parliament and urged all its mem-

A Plain Clothes Branch muster on the occasion of the visit of the Duke and Duchess of York in 1927: Chief Commissioner Blamey in uniform; Policewoman E. Cook,

bers to vote for 'candidates who have signified their intention of assisting us . . . make sure that all your relatives and friends vote as you intend to on polling day'. This stand came close to being an open endorsement of the Labor Party, and Blamey was so incensed at the Association's defiant and partisan display that he again sought the advice of the Crown Solicitor as to the legality of the Association and its conduct.

Before Blamey had time to take any further action, and to the glee of the Association, the Labor Party won the election and the Hogan ministry again took office. The tables were turned on Blamey. The Association's honorary solicitor, Mr W. Slater, MLA, was sworn as Attorney-General in the new ministry; the Hogan government agreed to defer and review Blamey's promotion plans; and applications were invited for the position of Chief Commissioner. Blamey was told he could reapply for the job if he so desired, but he was—and remains—the only Chief Commissioner

*standing extreme right, and J. R. Birch, standing extreme left, second row. Birch
later founded the Special Branch*

to have his position advertised, against his wishes and while he was still
serving under contract. Blamey was paying for his alienation of the Labor
Party.

The uncertainty of tenure attaching to his position diverted Blamey's
attention away from the promotion regulations and the behaviour of the
Association—for a time. A different man might have resigned, but
Blamey successfully devoted his considerable energies to securing
reappointment and, after months of haggling, he emerged battered but
victorious. The Labor government, having caused Blamey undoubted
anguish of an unprecedented kind, reappointed him on a limited three-
year contract and on a depression salary drastically cut by one-third, from
£1500 to £1000 a year.

Having secured his base again, Blamey sought full and swift retribution
on the Association that had so openly defied him. His new contract began

on 1 September 1930; on 4 September he declared the Association an 'illegally constituted body' and directed all members of the police force 'to dissociate themselves from it'. His action was supported in a petition organized by his personal staff and signed by over three hundred police-men who, although constituting less than 15 per cent of the force, com-prised its most senior members and was backed by a legal opinion from the Crown Solicitor that the existence of the Association 'in its present form' contravened the Police Regulation Act. During October 1930 Blamey used his Third Victoria Police Conference to form a new 'legal' Police Association, modelled closely on the lines of the English police federation. This Association, with teeth drawn, was firmly under his influence and gave him 'complete control of all the members in their sporting and social undertakings'. Some vestiges of the original Associ-ation remained, while the secretary and executive fought for its survival, and for a time the two Associations, differentiated simply as the 'old' and the 'new', existed in spite of each other. Blamey, however, was also quick to end the duplication. Victor G. Price, the civilian secretary of the old Association, was charged and convicted with 'inciting members of the force to commit breaches of discipline' and sentenced to one month in gaol. On appeal to the court of General Sessions his sentence was varied to a fine of £10 but he was refused leave to appeal to the High Court. The police office-bearers of the old Association were reprimanded and trans-ferred from Melbourne to distant rural centres—known colloquially as Siberia—at Mildura, Tallangatta, Portland, Wangaratta and Horsham. By the end of July 1931 Blamey had accomplished the total destruction

Blamey's 'Siberia' transfers

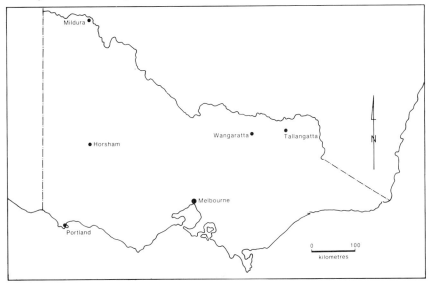

of the original Association and supplanted it with a tame-cat organization of his own making. Eventually, the new Association returned to its 'old' mould and became a genuine union of employees, but that was not for many years, long after the iron-fisted general had left the force.[15]

And what of the new promotion scheme that sparked this affray? It disintegrated like the old Police Association. Blamey tried to develop his idea, but not even the new Association and a return to conservative government could save it from the passive resistance of a force committed to promotion based upon seniority.

The ructions between Blamey and sections of his force were conflicts that at times seriously upset the well-being of the department. However, for many people outside the force they were little more than internal rumblings, although they were symptomatic of more serious and violent activity directed by Blamey against trade unionists, suspected communists and others who dared engage in public protest. During Blamey's commissionership police were involved in a series of conflicts with demonstrators, including one notoriously bloody, large-scale clash, and numerous complaints were made about alleged violence and harassing tactics used by policemen against the unemployed and unionists. The depression years were tough, lean years for many thousands of Victorians—including the police who voluntarily underwent pay cuts—and many people gave vent to frustration in public protests and violence. It was an unsurprising phenomenon in an age when many doubted that the meek would inherit food, clothing and shelter, let alone the earth. Blamey's task was not easy, but he did not make it easier. In contrast to Chomley's discreet policy in the 1890s depression, Blamey was quick to side with capital against labour and quick to crush public protest. He issued a direction that any unemployed people marching through Melbourne and causing a breach of the peace were to be 'hit over the head' with batons, and in a personal battle waged against suspected communists he formed the genesis of a special branch and regularly petitioned the Government for special powers to 'deal with communists'. In his loathing of working-class radicalism and communism Blamey was far from alone, but his repressive zeal was extreme. It prompted an officer of the Investigation Branch of the federal Attorney-General's Department to complain that Blamey 'more than any other' was responsible 'for giving the public something to talk about and exaggerate to hysteria and nonsense'.

Yet Blamey's campaign seemingly had as many supporters as detractors, being backed by a large body of public opinion and the conservatives in parliament. However, the particularly violent clash between police and strikers had even his most loyal backers groping for explanations to justify the shooting by policemen of four unarmed demonstrators. On 2 November 1928 a group of twenty-three armed police, under the command of Sub-Inspector Mossop, were detailed for duty at Prince's Pier 'to protect' strike-breaking volunteers from possible assault and harassment by striking members of the Port Phillip Stevedores' Association. The protection of strike-breakers was a routine police activity, but on this day a large group of strikers stormed the pier and the police line. In the mêlée that followed, the police fired their revolvers into the surging mob, wounding four unarmed stevedores. Three of them received only minor wounds but one was was hospitalized with a serious gunshot wound to the face. The storming strikers stoned the police with blue metal, seriously injuring two constables, one of whom 'fell unconscious, and was kicked as he lay on the pier'. Blamey defended the shootings as being an act of last resort, and added that it 'would have been a tragedy to have allowed the mob to gain possession of the pier'. The labour movement greeted Blamey's statements with anger and derision. Many people harked back to the 'Tom Price incident' of 1890, and the waterfront was alive with the story that 'Inspector Mossop had not adopted the command of Tom Price, "Fire low and lay them out". He had told his men to fire high and be sure to kill'. In 1873 when Standish's men at Clunes drew their guns to protect Chinese strike-breakers from protesters, Standish was castigated by the Government for intervening in 'a dispute between employer and employed'. In 1928 there was no such censure for Blamey. No policemen or strikers were charged over the incident, and the conservative Argyle ministry resisted calls for a public inquiry into the shootings, on the ground that they were justified, and pointed out that Mossop's men were heavily outnumbered by hundreds of angry, burly stevedores. Many people acknowledged that this last point had some relevance, but in the absence of a full public disclosure of the facts some questions remained unanswered. Why did the police not retreat instead of shooting? Why did the police have guns at the scene of a public demonstration? Why were there so few policemen on the pier, with no reinforcements in reserve, to contain such a situation without using firearms? Blamey and the Government remained mute in a stand that did little to help the image of the police or placate a seething waterfront population. Hetherington says that although Blamey was 'authoritarian', he knew that his force was 'not at war with the citizens'; and yet Hetherington adds that in the 'economic depression of the early 1930s the police had to maintain public order in Victoria when thousands of men who wanted work and could not get it were clamouring for the right to earn their daily bread. The problem of how to keep the peace without using violence now and then would have baffled Solomon'. There is truth in this defence of Blamey, but it could be said with equal validity that Blamey's style of dealing with public protest was confrontationist, readily violent, and generally ruthless.[16]

In 1932 serious allegations of violence were again levelled at Blamey's men after they used batons to stop a peaceful protest of 150 unemployed workers marching along Flinders Street. This time the Labor Hogan ministry appointed Mr A. A. Kelley, PM, as a one-man board of inquiry to investigate the incident. Kelley eventually exonerated the police and found—according to the newspapers (copies of the report itself seem not to exist)—that they were 'justified in using force'. During the investigation Blamey defended the actions of his men and advised Kelley that 'unchecked demonstrations' were a 'real danger', and that to combat them he had formed a special section to 'watch communist propaganda, and to attend to all matters, such as evictions, which tend to mass lawlessness'. Sergeant J. R. Birch was the head of this special section, and he told Kelley that the protest march was stopped because he had 'heard from a reliable source' that the marchers 'proposed to demonstrate at Parliament House'. Not surprisingly, Kelley's finding and the evidence of Blamey and Birch alarmed many working-class people and the Central Unemployment Committee denounced the outcome as 'white-washing'. The Hogan government too was concerned at the train of events, and paid the legal expenses of the unemployed men involved, but before Hogan could take the matter any further his government was voted from office.[17]

Much to the relief of Blamey, May 1932 saw a return to office of a conservative ministry under Argyle, the friend who appointed Blamey in 1925, and who now restored his salary to its original level and gave him security of tenure for life. Yet the volcano was not extinct. During 1933 allegations of corruption continued to be levelled at Blamey and some other members of the force, primarily in connection with the recovery and restoration of stolen motor cars, and Kelley was again appointed to investigate. The inquiry generated some bad publicity for the force but, after sitting publicly for twenty-seven days and examining 146 witnesses, Kelley exonerated all the police, including Blamey, and the matter ended.[18]

There is no evidence of impropriety on Kelley's part, but he proved a good friend to Blamey when it counted most. In 1930 it was he who gaoled Price and finally broke the spirit of the old Police Association; in 1932 it was he who condoned the use of police violence to stop a peaceful protest march; and in 1933 it was he who dismissed thirty corruption allegations levelled against members of the force. The 1932 and 1933 Kelley inquiries have a relatively insignificant place in Victorian police history. All the police involved were exonerated and the matters were quickly forgotten. No published work on the force has even mentioned them.

During Blamey's time the exoneration of policemen accused of wrongdoing was not unusual. It is also not unusual to find that the relevant reports and other important documents are missing. Large amounts of archival material from Blamey's commissionership cannot be found; all the Chief Commissioner's correspondence for the period 1921–34 is missing and registered by the force as 'destroyed'. The Chief Secretary's inward correspondence for the years 1933–35 is missing, as are the

Premier's secret papers for the years 1929–37. Included amongst these papers are most of the documents relevant to Blamey's anti-communist activities, the formation and work of his 'special section' and complaint files about alleged police corruption, violence and harassment during the depression years. The destruction of such a large volume of police papers is unique to the Blamey era.

A key link in the chain of troubles leading to Blamey's ultimate downfall was his bitter and constant battles with the press. He shared the opinion held by many regular army officers that 'newspapers were irresponsible, mischievous and often ill-informed', and he believed that they 'ought to be regimented'. From the beginning of his police command Blamey took steps to thwart what many other people accepted as the legitimate activities of newspapermen. He stopped policemen giving information to journalists, he delayed and vetted crime reports that were released to the press, he had surveillance police follow reporters to check on their activities, and he closed the press room at police headquarters to all police roundsmen and prohibited their entry beyond the public inquiry counter. Blamey's initial idea was the sound one of trying to bring some measure of control into the relationships between police and journalists, to stop policemen leaking information to favoured journalists—usually for payment—and to stop the lionization of individual detectives by friendly journalists. Regulation of such practices has since been adopted as an important part of the relations between police and press, but Blamey went beyond reasonable control and embarked on an individual crusade against newspapermen, for their 'insufferable disposition' to intrude upon 'strictly personal affairs'. Apart from the *Star*, which he sued for libel, Blamey did not single out any particular journalist or paper for his wrath, but labelled them collectively as the 'Modern Moloch'. For their part, the newspapers responded with a range of journalistic retorts, including one prophetic line in an *Argus* editorial, satirically headed 'Atten-Shon!', that criticized Blamey's position as that of a man in 'the Indian summer of a fading autocracy'. Blamey's attitude has since been described as 'resentment of press criticism carried to an extreme', and although a number of his close friends warned him that his stand was unwise, he dismissed their misgivings with a gruff, 'I'm not afraid of the press'. It was unfortunate for him that he was not. He had whipped the Police Association, the Labor Party, the communists, and anyone else who dared defy him, but in his battle with the newspapers was himself about to be whipped and pilloried by a united press, keen to see him squirm. Although he could not guess it in 1935—the year he was knighted—Blamey had less than twelve months to serve as Chief Commissioner and was soon to stand vilified and shamed at the hands of the press: living proof of Napoleon Bonaparte's epigram that 'Four hostile newspapers are more formidable than a thousand bayonets'.[19]

Or, to revert to another metaphor, Blamey's volcano was about to erupt.

The Third Degree

In 1936 a popular comic strip in a Melbourne newspaper was 'King of the Royal Mounted', by Zane Grey, which featured a member of the Royal Canadian Mounted Police, magnificent in every way, using dog sleds and ski-planes to track dangerous criminals, and always getting his man fairly. The successful adventures of the scarlet-clad hero contrasted sharply with the prosaic efforts of Victoria's own police, who were then actively engaged in efforts to apprehend boys kicking footballs 'to a height of more than fifteen feet, within fifty yards of any portion of an electric line'. Constables were paid a reward of £1 for each child they successfully prosecuted for this offence, and children's court officials complained that they were 'sick and tired' of courts jammed with budding league footballers whose only crime was kicking the magic fifteen feet under the watchful eye of a constable. Internationally the Royal Canadian Mounted Police benefited greatly from the fictional image makers, and Blamey might well have contrasted it with his own force, and pondered why his men could do no better than feature as obese John Hops in satirical newspaper cartoons. The force numbered 2281 men and eight women, and with a police to population ratio of 1:809—the worst in mainland Australia—was generally regarded as being undermanned and declining in efficiency. Its low public image was helped neither by the antics of policemen chasing young footballers, nor by Blamey's poor relations with the press. Blamey's stagnation and the state of the force were not surprising. They conformed to the broad pattern that police development in Victoria had followed since 1836. The general trend was positive but the size, image and performance of the force were prone to rises and falls, and the force itself was a constantly changing parade of people, whose conduct, efficiency and worth to the organization varied. Blamey had been Chief Commissioner for more than a decade and, seemingly inured to the shortcomings of his own administration, no longer produced the energy, ideas or reform that had earlier made him such a valued leader. His best years as a police administrator were behind him. Many people felt that a particularly low ebb in force morale was reached when a trainee constable died in a suicide pact with a fellow trainee, who survived his own attempt. However, the worst was still to come, and while 'King of the Royal Mounted' remained the favourite policeman of local schoolboys, the government was soon to turn its attentions to the equally famed sleuths of Scotland Yard, in a bid to rejuvenate a discredited and ailing Victoria Police Force.[20]

The end of Blamey's police career began in the darkened precincts of Royal Park on the night of 22 May 1936, when Superintendent John O'Connell Brophy, head of the CIB, was allegedly shot and wounded by bandits, while he was seated in a chauffeur-driven motor car, in company with two lady friends. Brophy was shot three times—in the right arm, the cheek, and above the heart—but notwithstanding the seriousness of his wounds, there was no immediate flurry of urgent searches and inquiries, as would normally be expected to follow the shooting of the state's most senior detective. Instead, a cabal of senior police, including Blamey and Brophy, set about deceiving the public by concocting and releasing to journalists an untrue announcement that, 'Superintendent Brophy was accidentally shot in the right forearm whilst handling his revolver'. Given the nature of Brophy's wounds, this account was implausible and, under pressure from incredulous journalists, police officials later altered their public position and announced that Brophy had been shot by bandits. In this version of events it was claimed Brophy went to Royal Park to meet someone with information about 'hold-ups that had taken place in that locality recently'. No mention was made of Brophy's two female companions. Brophy was a famous detective, immortalized—along with another—in the underworld ditty 'Ashes to ashes and dust to dust; if Brophy don't get you then Piggott must', and this degree of personal

A BOBBY DAZZLER

Fact and fiction

212

THE STORY SO FAR.—King, an officer of the Royal Canadian Mounted Police, is trying to save Betty Blake and her brother, the Kid, who are heirs to a fortune, from Rod Lash, Betty's guardian. The Kid is lost, and King and Betty, with the pilot Laroux, set out by plane to find him. They crash. King is held up by Lash and imprisoned. Lash takes Betty and the pilot to his own shack. Meantime, Corporal Richards finds the Kid. Lash kidnaps Betty. King breaks free and sets out after Lash and rescues Betty from drowning. Lash appears and holds King at rifle-point.

No. 60
GOT HIS MAN

KING OF THE ROYAL MOUNTED by Zane Grey

KING, HAVING RESCUED BETTY FROM THE ICY WATER, PLANS TO TAKE HER BACK TO THE ALDER CREEK CABIN TO REJOIN KID, LAROUX AND RICHARDS, AND THEN GO OUT ALONE IN PURSUIT OF LASH. HAVING FIRST STOPPED TO DRY THEIR CLOTHES, HE AND BETTY ARE ABOUT TO LEAVE FOR THE CABIN, WHEN LASH SUDDENLY APPEARS FROM BEHIND.

I'LL TAKE YOUR GUN - YOU WON'T NEED IT

LASH TURNS HIS BACK ON BETTY TO FOCUS HIS ATTENTION ON KING.

NOW BEAT IT!

BETTY GRASPS A HEAVY SNAG

AS KING MOVES AWAY BETTY ATTACKS LASH

KING LUNGES AS LASH SNAPS A SHOT AT BETTY.

THE BULLET MISSES AND THEY GO DOWN IN A HEAP.

OH, IF I CAN ONLY GET A CHANCE TO STRIKE!

ALL OF THE FURY OF WEEKS OF FRUITLESS PURSUIT KING THROWS INTO THE BATTLE.

I'VE HAD ENOUGH!

UNARMED, THE OUTLAW IS NO MATCH FOR THE POWERFUL MOUNTED POLICEMAN.

GRAB LASH'S GUN, BETTY. KEEP THE DROP ON HIM UNTIL I GET HIM HANDCUFFED.

LASH, YOU RIDE ON THE FRONT OF THE SLED. BETTY, YOU HOLD THE GUN ON HIM. IF HE TRIES ANYTHING, LET HIM HAVE IT.

KING STARTS FOR CIVILIZATION WITH HIS PRISONER AND BETTY WHO SECRETLY LOVES HIM. THE LONE CHASE IS ENDED. THE ROYAL MOUNTED AGAIN GETS HIS MAN.

I HOPED TO GIVE YOU A VACATION AFTER CLEANING UP THE LASH GANG.

I COULD USE ONE.

A WEEK LATER KING GETS ANOTHER ASSIGNMENT

NO ONE HAS EVER SEEN HIM - HE ONLY MET HIS MEN AT NIGHT - EVEN THEY DON'T KNOW WHO HE IS.

notoriety guaranteed more than average public interest in his shooting. The awkward police posturing on the subject inflamed rather than suppressed public curiosity and provided Melbourne newspapermen with their long-awaited opportunity to vilify Blamey. Melbourne's four main daily newspapers—the *Age, Argus, Herald* and *Sun*—pursued the subject relentlessly and within days several state politicians added their voices to the chorus, all wanting to know what really happened to Brophy and why lies were told. The ruling Country Party ministry of Albert Dunstan was called upon to investigate the incident at cabinet level, and sections of the Labor Party wanted a Royal Commission to inquire into what they regarded as a public scandal. The parliamentary position of Dunstan's government was not as secure as Allan's had been at the time of the 'badge 80' crisis, and Dunstan could not afford to shield Blamey from a full public inquiry, as Allan had in 1925. Dunstan was dependent upon Labor Party good will for continued political survival and knew that a Royal Commission would ease the pressure on his government and please many of Blamey's long-time adversaries in the Labor Party. On 5 June 1936 Judge Hugh Macindoe was appointed as Royal Commissioner to investigate the alleged shooting of Brophy, and the subsequent statements issued by Blamey and his officers.[21]

Macindoe opened his inquiry on 10 June and sat for eleven days, taking evidence from forty-four witnesses, including Blamey and Brophy. Much of the inquiry's time was devoted to routine matters and to refutation of suggestions that the 'scandalous' Brophy was shot by an enraged husband, and was guilty of improper conduct in taking female companions with him to meet an informer. The actual evidence, allegations and counter-allegations do not warrant repetition or analysis here. Of singular significance is the fact that the Royal Commission provided Blamey with a public forum to honestly explain his own position and restore faith in his administration. He did not. Macindoe has since admitted that he was impressed with Blamey and that he tried during the taking of evidence 'to steer him to the true story' but could not 'save him from himself'. Macindoe's partisanship is shown in his euphemistic report that Blamey 'gave replies which were not in accordance with the truth, with the sole purpose of secreting from the press the fact that women were in the company of Superintendent Brophy'. As at the time of the 'badge 80' affair, Blamey again failed to satisfy the standards of public accountability and personal integrity that his position demanded, and this time he did not have unqualified government support. Macindoe submitted his report on 2 July 1936 and within a week the Dunstan ministry asked Blamey to resign. He did so on 9 July and was replaced immediately by Superintendent W. W. W. Mooney, who was appointed Acting Chief Commissioner. Blamey's police career ended abruptly, in the controversial and public fashion that was the hallmark of his commissionership, and he then entered what was for a time 'the bitterest, and most sterile, period of his life'.[22]

The Brophy incident was not, of itself, anywhere near as important a social issue as some of the earlier crises Blamey had survived, such as the waterfront shootings and his anti-union activities, but it nevertheless became a vital test of personal credibility for him, and he failed. His supporters argued that his behaviour was not 'unchristian' and that he treated Brophy sympathetically because, in the words of Macindoe, he was 'jealous of the reputation of the force' and thought that it 'might be endangered if the whole truth was disclosed'. Although the Brophy case was the second occasion on which serious doubts were publicly cast over Blamey's veracity, his supporters' pleas might have succeeded but for the case of the 'third degree'. On 18 June 1936, while the Macindoe Royal Commission was still sitting, another exposé further shook public faith in the police, when Sir Frederick Mann, Chief Justice of the Victorian Supreme Court, denounced improper police practices, known colloquially as the 'third degree'. Published accounts of Blamey's police career attribute his resignation exclusively to the Brophy shooting and Macindoe's inquiry, but the 'third degree' was a second, much less publicized but far more socially significant matter that undoubtedly figured in Blamey's forced resignation. Mann described the force's criminal investigation work as the crude and unbridled doings of untrained investigators, who depended too much on informers and physical coercion, and who too often failed to give due regard to the rights of suspects. Mann's calls for police reform were supported by many others, including lawyer groups and the newspapers, and were studied by the Government. The timing of Mann's allegations placed added pressure on Blamey and almost certainly blocked any chance he had of continuing as Chief Commissioner in the wake of Macindoe's report. Mann and the 'third degree' controversy are not mentioned in several works touching upon Blamey's resignation, yet when he resigned he did not mention Brophy or Macindoe, but said that he was standing down 'to give the government freedom of action' to undertake 're-organisation of the police department'. Blamey's insistence that he was simply clearing the way for reform was probably not genuine: Brophy, Macindoe and political pressure had to be key elements in his decision. However, important reforms to criminal investigation procedures did follow his resignation, and the Mann denunciation of third degree tactics clearly added weight to the pressure exerted upon Blamey to resign, and added stimulus to moves toward reform.

The third degree is epitomized by that bullying style of police interrogation often depicted in movies. In a dingy, smokefilled room, lit only by a bare globe and minus windows or home comforts, several large, mean detectives badger and bludgeon a suspect for hours, until the innocent wretch breaks down and confesses. In Victoria things were not usually as bad as the celluloid image, but Mann was concerned about people being interrogated in a way that 'might elicit false confessions of guilt', and about detectives being allowed 'to cross-examine suspects in private, in their own way and for an unlimited time'. In the absence of departmental guidelines to regulate the conduct of criminal investigations, individual policemen were left to their own devices: under pressure to solve crimes and apprehend criminals, but not specially trained for the work nor provided with forensic science assistance. In the words of an *Argus* editorial, it was 'a temptation to inefficient police to procure convictions by the rough-and-ready method of extorting confessions rather than ascertain the truth by painstaking investigation'.[23]

That members of the force were using third degree tactics was not so much an indictment against individual policemen as an indicator that the force as a whole, and the community it served, had not kept pace with overseas thinking and developments in the fields of criminal law reform, criminal investigation techniques, detective training and forensic science. In Europe and North America the combined forces of scientific knowledge and humanist thought were forging a new police professionalism that saw academics, scientists, lawyers and policemen working together to improve the quality of police investigations, while safeguarding the rights of suspects. By modern standards, the technological aspects of this police reformation—such as comparative ballistics—were still at a primitive stage and Victoria was actually not so far behind, but the level of community awareness and debate about the humanist aspects was much higher overseas. As early as 1918 the judges of the Queen's Bench in England formulated the Judges' Rules for the guidance of police in an effort to eradicate practices like the third degree, and a decade later a police commission again reviewed the question of police investigations and individual liberties.

The Victorian police did have a fingerprint branch founded by Lionel Potter in 1903, a photographic section started by Fred Hobley in 1930, and an information section established by Frederick Downie in 1934, but these were small, nascent units, heavily dependent upon the skills of a few self-motivated individuals, and were not typical of the force or generally available to it. In major cases Hobley did call upon the 'big three'—Dr Mollison, the government pathologist, Pat Shea, the government surveyor, and Charles Taylor, the government analyst—but these specialities were not reflected in the everyday work of ordinary policemen. In Victoria, as in England, 'the idea that science could aid [police in solving] the more ordinary crimes . . . was slow to develop'.[24]

The force's crude criminal investigation efforts might have centred on the third degree indefinitely if Blamey's resignation had not opened the way for reform, and Mann pinpointed one area where it was urgently needed. Scotland Yard was then renowned as the home of the world's finest detectives and it was to it that the Dunstan government turned for assistance. Previous governments had looked to military men—Steward, Gellibrand, Blamey—to reorganize the force, but in 1936 the need was different. It was no straightforward task of organizational efficiency but the need to transform a force of antipodean John Hops into something like a professional body of investigators. No doubt many young boys would have preferred Corporal King of the RCMP, but on 12 October 1936 Chief Inspector Alexander Mitchell Duncan, head of Scotland Yard's famous Flying Squad, arrived in Melbourne with the daunting task of inspecting and improving the Victoria Police Force.

A native of Scotland, and 48 years of age, Duncan had behind him an illustrious police career spanning twenty-six years, during which he had received forty-five commissioner's commendations for solving murders and other major crimes, and he had taught at the Scotland Yard school for detectives. His forte was criminal investigation, a fact that adds weight to the suggestion that Mann's public statements about the third degree had influenced the Government at the time of Blamey's sacking. Duncan's brief from the Victorian government included the specific request that he examine Mann's criticisms and the question of the third degree. Duncan began by looking closely at the criminal investigation work of the force and, one month later, he submitted an interim report to the Government. He was not prepared to wait until he had completed a full appraisal of the general force because he was 'convinced that certain changes . . . should be put into effect as soon as possible'. Duncan was critical of all aspects of the force's criminal investigation work. It was his view that detectives were not 'playing the game', but were 'free and easy' and took the view that 'tomorrow will do'. Their methods were 'crude', and untrained men were 'left more or less to their own resources'. Even more troubling were the numerous 'serious allegations made against members of the police force', and the instances of police being success-fully sued for damages. Duncan suggested extensive changes to the CIB, and emphatically proposed detective training courses and scientific investigation.[25]

Mooney made some sort of start on these reforms while Duncan went on to inquire into the administration and operations of the general force. He completed this job and submitted his final report on 22 January 1937, with recommendations for changes ranging through the promotion sys-tem, buildings, equipment, supervision and the traffic branch. Like those 'outsiders' before him—Steward and Blamey—he stressed the need for police education.

Mooney was only Acting Chief Commissioner and due to retire. As had been the case with Nicolson and Heathershaw, many years earlier, Mooney was not a serious contender for the permanent position of Chief

*Chief Commissioner
A. M. Duncan*

Commissioner. Duncan himself, his plans for reorganizing the force made and submitted, was offered the position of Chief Commissioner and, after resigning from the London Metropolitan Police, he took up the position on 7 February 1937. The Labor Party, with a history of opposition to the appointment of 'outsiders', was again vocal in its criticism of Duncan's appointment, mockingly wanting to know why Charlie Chan—a fictional policeman of some fame—had not been offered the job. The Laborites wanted a local man promoted, and suggested that there was 'ample talent available in the Force'. They were wrong. The police system of promotion by seniority, the lack of any formal management training, and the shabby state of the force generally, all meant that the Chief Commissioner had to be an 'outsider'.[26]

In the years preceding World War II, the former Flying Squad commander lived up to his popular image as an envoy from Scotland Yard. He possessed the drive and organizational ability of men like Steward and Gellibrand, but it was enhanced by twenty-six years with the London Metropolitan Police. He implemented many of his own recommended reforms, but was most noted in the pre-war period for his efforts to make the force's criminal investigation methods professional. He introduced a comprehensive set of instructions to regulate 'the questioning of prisoners and suspected persons, methods of identification and interrogation of women and children'. These new standing orders were not all original, since they embodied both the Judges' Rules and other instructions complied with 'throughout the British Isles', but as a code of conduct they were unprecedented in Victoria. Not only did Duncan introduce rules designed to ensure that suspects were treated fairly; he also introduced procedural safeguards to give police a measure of protection against untrue allegations, and provided guidelines dealing with the special needs of children and female victims. It would be naïve to suggest that Duncan's instructions put an end to police malpractices, and indeed such allegations have proved an omnipresent feature of police life right up to the present. However, Duncan did provide a procedural framework within which police could work and which, if adhered to, did afford a greater measure of fairness and protection to victims, suspects and police.

In 1938 Duncan obtained special government approval to promote Hobley to the rank of Brevet Sub-Inspector, and gave him the task of establishing a scientific section and a detective training school. The Government then spent £750 to equip the force with scientific and photographic equipment that included an analytical lamp, an optiscope, a cine camera and several microscopes. It was basic stuff, but Hobley was a police pioneer in the true sense and Duncan boasted that his scientific section was then equal to any police laboratory in the world.

Detectives are now taught that 'physical evidence is the best evidence', and this dictum was first stressed to Victorian detectives on 17 October 1938, when Duncan opened the inaugural course at Australia's first detective training school—known disrespectfully as Bonehead College. Located at the police depot in Melbourne, the school provided instruction in chemistry, physics, ballistics, photography and other subjects relevant to the 'scientific detection of crime'. The school was modelled on courses overseas and was a significant advance on the rudimentary detective training that Steward introduced for a short time in 1920. Hobley was the senior of three police lecturers at the new school, and guest lecturers included the government pathologist and analyst, the crown prosecutor, and the chief officer of the fire brigade. Duncan also lectured at the school and was always present on the oral examination boards. As with the instructions governing the conduct of investigations, the detective training school could not guarantee that all its students would work in accordance with its teachings, but it did expose detectives to the philosophy of scientific detection and provided them with a basic knowledge of its workings.

The reformation that had so altered the course of policing in other parts of the world had arrived in Victoria, and scientific analysis was permanently adopted as an integral part of the force's operations. The police scientist has never supplanted the street policeman as the key figure in criminal investigation work, but science has afforded detectives the support of highly credible physical evidence, not easily discredited by allegations that it was produced by the third degree. Indeed, in a fit of journalistic euphoria prompted by Duncan's work, the *Argus* labelled science as 'the most efficient and effective member of the Victoria Police Force . . . the one unimpeachable witness'.[27]

In only three years Duncan had indelibly made his mark on the force and silenced those critics who originally claimed that his lack of local knowledge rendered him useless as Chief Commissioner. He was a principal agent of change and the efficacy of his work was recognized in the public press, which moved from a position of vilification of the police to one of support for the 'scientific policeman'. A great deal of reorganization still remained to be done when in 1939 Duncan was forced to lay aside his blueprint for police reform and don the helmet of Chief Air Raid Warden for Victoria. Australia entered World War II in September 1939 and all things—including Duncan's plans—were rendered subservient to the war effort. During the next six years Duncan and his force went to war on the home front, while former Chief Commissioner Blamey emerged from bitter sterility to become Commander-in-Chief of the Australian Military Forces, and operational commander of the Allied Land Forces, South West Pacific Area.[28]

The Home Front

Your work is not spectacular, but let there be no misunderstanding of the fact that it is a national service appreciated by the community . . . We should regard it as a privilege to be permitted to give the best that is in us, knowing we are making a contribution of incalculable value to our national war effort.

This Christmas message from Duncan to his force in 1941 gave police work in wartime its due importance without resort to the euphoric orations of Sainsbury during World War I. It hinted at the problems Duncan encountered, convincing his men—most of whom were young, fit and disciplined—that police duty performed in the relative safety of the home front was an appreciated national duty as essential as combat in the front line. In World War I police were allowed to enlist in the armed forces, and Sainsbury roused his men with talk of 'fighting to the death' to prevent the 'Germanising' of Australia. Almost 10 per cent of his men did enlist, and the force became dangerously depleted because able-bodied young men were not recruited as policemen while the army wanted them. Certainly the police who were left were encouraged to feel that they were direct participants in the war, and were afforded opportunities to work with the secret service, watch for enemy agents, and secure

Australia from 'the enemy within', but the emphasis had been different in 1914 from that in 1939.

'Materially and spiritually' the Australian people—including the police—were 'unprepared for war' in 1939, and in the wake of the depression there was evidence of 'some bitterness, resentment, and a cynical lack of enthusiasm'. Police were openly discouraged from enlisting; there was no jingoism, no euphoria and no talk of death or glory. Instead, official policy decreed that police 'should take no part in hostilities', and even in the event of enemy invasion police were not to take up arms but were to 'act as intermediaries between the enemy and the civil population' and 'alleviate the position of the latter'. Police were not permitted to leave the force to enlist for military service unless the defence department requested the services of specific men, and only then if they were 'essential for military purposes' and 'of more value to the Empire as such'. As a result, during the six years of war, only fifty Victorian policemen were granted extended leave to join the armed forces. Another fifty-six did enlist, but they did so against the wishes of Duncan and were compelled to resign from the force, forfeiting their pension entitlements and having no guarantee of re-employment. Indeed, Duncan required each of them to give the statutory three months notice of resignation, in order to maximize their services and in the hope that during that time they might be dissuaded from leaving. A number of policemen who enlisted gave false occupation details, for fear that the armed services would reject them if they knew their true occupations. Many found police duty on the home front irksome when the nation was at war, and many policemen who enlisted made it clear that they wanted to be combatants, not 'coppers'. Of the first eighty-one Victorian policemen to enlist in the armed forces, well over half refused to serve in the provost corps. Less than 5 per cent of the police force went overseas on military service.[29]

As the war progressed, police throughout Victoria assumed responsibility for a wide variety of wartime duties that became more numerous, more pressing and more earnest from December 1941—when Japan entered the war. Shortly before the outbreak of war Duncan was appointed Chief Air Raid Warden for Victoria, whereupon the technical and manpower resources of the force became key elements in the state's ARP organization. The National Security Regulations vested police with duties that included alien registration and supervision; control of firearms, explosives, rubber and liquid fuel; impressment of motor vehicles, boats and guns; counter-subversion work and the guarding of vulnerable installations; enforcement of lighting regulations and 'blackouts'; and the investigation and arrest of escaped internees, prisoners of war and military deserters. The police became society's wartime odd-job men. They did everything and anything that other people could or would not do. With a network of 397 police stations, the force was well placed for this type of work and it was to these stations that people went if they wanted such things as authorization for urgent petrol supplies, permission to obtain new rubber tyres, advice on 'blackout' methods, or the registration of motor vehicles fitted with charcoal gas-producers.[30]

Many hundreds of policemen also voluntarily assumed responsibility for tasks that were often foreign to them in peacetime, and neither obligatory nor measurable. As women and men from across Victoria left home to 'do their bit', their public positions in local communities were sometimes filled by police, who were also encouraged to spend their annual leave working as paid labourers 'handling the wool clip or assisting with the wheat harvest'. First Constable James Chester Draper, of Heyfield, was regarded by his peers as the model local policeman, and during wartime he became the hub of the community he served. Friend and confidant to all who would have him, his list of wartime community activities grew to include the role of Sunday School teacher, scoutmaster, fire brigade captain, school bus and ambulance driver, school committee secretary, shire delegate, and a host of other *ad hoc* positions. He drilled the local Volunteer Defence Corps unit—which paraded with broomsticks because there were no rifles—and on Sundays, by special request, he gave a 'unit' of fourteen local, ageing farmers a course in Light Horse drill: a task that provided him, as a mounted trooper, with both satisfaction and mirth. It was a time when you not only went to the police station to get booked, bloodied, or browbeaten—for that still happened to some—but when to 'ask a policeman' took on new meaning. Whether the worry was about God, tying reef knots, or Light Horse drill, his door was usually open. This work later earned Draper a Chief Commissioner's Certificate for 'excellent policemanship', and a street in Heyfield was named after him.[31]

The police force also legitimized the covert work of the Special Branch and—along with the war itself—gave it a degree of public acceptance and permanence that it had never before had. This branch and its work were the antithesis of the friendly local constable: a body of faceless bureaucrats, working behind closed doors on who knew what, a continuation of the section established by Blamey in 1931, and originally part of his crusade against communism and working-class radicalism. Labelled by its detractors as the 'political squad'—which it was—the branch worked in the shadows of police and political life, gathering and collating 'evidence against subversive elements in the community'. Now the original squad of three men was given branch status and, under the supervision of Inspector J. R. Birch, grew to number twenty-one police and twelve public servants, handling almost 20 000 'files' a year. Much of the branch's war was routine and involved the control of aliens, investigating applications for the transfer of land and 'the checking of the suitability of applicants for enrolment in the various armed forces and their auxiliary services'. However, Special Branch's heavy involvement in supervising 'foreign clubs', watching 'persons of enemy origin' and investigating 'persons with alleged anti-British sympathies' was not necessarily routine work. In 1942 the branch became an adjunct to the Commonwealth Security Service, a move largely due to the influence of Duncan, who had worked in the Special Branch at Scotland yard, and who in 1941, at the request of the Prime Minister, Robert Menzies, undertook a secret investigation of both the Military Intelligence Service and the Commonwealth Security Service, and assisted in their wartime reorganization. From that time the Special Branch in Victoria never returned to its earlier position as a fringe element of the force. After the war it retained branch status and continued its 'special' work: a source of concern to many people—especially communists, political activists and civil libertarians—until it was finally disbanded in 1983.[32]

To support the 2200 members of the regular police force in their war work, the Government recalled all able police pensioners and also formed two separate auxiliary police forces. The first of them, the Police Auxiliary Force, was formed in July 1940 and numbered 2718 men over military age—preferably between 45 and 60 years—who were attached to police stations throughout the state, 'issued with a badge, baton, arm-band, book of instructions and a note book', and trained in 'police and ARP work'. These men were drawn from all sections of the community—labourers, tradesmen, bankers, merchants, agents, salesmen—and all were nominated by regular policemen, who became responsible for their on-duty activities. The spare-time work of the PAF not only freed regular police from the responsibility for many routine tasks, but also 'had the effect of creating more friendly co-operation between the regular police and members of the public'. Initially many regular policemen were sceptical about the worth of amateur auxiliaries, but soon the Police Association hailed the PAF as a 'tower of strength—2500 real friends . . . willing and anxious to share our difficulties and labours, to be in the thick of whatever has to be done'. The PAF enabled many men, who would not otherwise have had the chance, to experience at first hand the working world of policemen. The auxiliaries, who previously 'had very little knowledge of the police force and its doings', appreciated their new insight into the force and often took the force into the community in a way that regular police had rarely done. The Association was aware of it, and reminded its members that the auxiliaries 'occupy all kinds of positions in life . . . they all have friends and those friends will be our friends'. Auxiliaries did spread the word, and it was not uncommon to hear them speak of their 'surprise' at the 'wonderful service' the taxpayers got from the police: 'The amount of advice, help and protection . . . has to be seen to be believed'. Few records of the PAF remain and little else is known of their actual work. Although the group was 'specially formed to give assistance in the event of air raids and blackouts' (and had no air raids to cope with), R. G. Menzies had a slightly different view of the possibilities. In a secret telegram he said that bodies of 'loyal citizens'—like the PAF—could 'assist in combatting fifth column and subversive activities in Australia', and 'would afford justification for prohibiting formation of voluntary bodies whose existence or activities might and almost certainly would become embarrassing'. There is no evidence that they were ever used as such. In Great Britain the auxiliary police (full and part-time) numbered 35 000, and their exemplary work during German bombing raids earned them a noted place in British police history. The Victorian PAF worked in relative safety and obscurity, and it remained obscure, but its formation probably produced a mutual respect and understanding between regular police and auxiliaries, with a useful flow-on among their families and friends.[33]

The other arm of the auxiliary police was the Women's Police Auxiliary Force, which also fostered a spirit of co-operation and understanding between the regular police and sections of the community. The WPAF was formed shortly before Japan entered the war and, along with other groups like the Australian Women's Legion, Country Women's Association Land Army, and Women's Auxiliary Service Patriots, offered Victorian women a clear and active part to play in the national war effort. The WPAF was comprised of two hundred sworn volunteers and fifty full-time paid members, trained in police communications and ARP work, and available in the event of an air raid or other emergency. However, like their male colleagues in the PAF, most female auxiliaries were never fully put to the test, and little is known of their work. The fifty full-time members worked as car drivers, clerks, typists, receptionists, telephonists, lift and weighbridge attendants, so releasing 'male members of the force for active police duty'. They were also different in that they were not disbanded at the end of the war, but continued working within the force until 1953, when many of them joined the force as regular women police and public servants. Throughout their service these women operated as a distinct body within the force and were issued with a uniform and badge. It was the first time that women employed by the force appeared in uniform, and it was done to the chagrin of the regular policewomen who, from their inception in 1917, had always worked in plain clothes. The regulars objected to uniforms for 'auxiliaries who were doing clerical work', and described the paid auxiliaries as a 'glamour force of heroines'. So intent were they on glamour that 'the wearing of the uniform had come to be more often honoured in the breach than the observance'. The rationale for putting auxiliary policewomen in uniform,

Women police in the post-World War II years

224

when regular policewomen worked in plain clothes, is not known. The historian of the women police, A. J. O'Meara, suggests that it was done as a 'recruiting aid', and it is a feasible idea because women who formed or joined wartime auxiliary groups did show a penchant for wearing uniforms, and competition between groups to attract recruits might have necessitated a 'police' uniform. When it came to 'social life', however, many young women preferred to wear something more feminine than a uniform; so, if the grumble was true about the auxiliaries not wearing uniform on duty at all times, it was due to a simple conflict of interests.

O'Meara has suggested that 'the war seems to have retarded the development of the [regular] women's force', and he attributes this, in part, to the formation of the WPAF. But, in fact, it was during World War II that women in the force notched up several firsts, and the notion of retarded development is more a matter of unfulfilled expectation on O'Meara's part than a lack of actual achievement on theirs. During the war the number of regular women police was increased from eight to twelve, and between 1945 and 1949 was further increased to eighteen. The wartime increase was the first since 1928, and was especially significant because those four recruits were the first women to undergo the regular four-month police training course. Also during the war, women were allowed for the first time to undertake promotion examinations for sub-officer rank, and Katherine Mackay was subsequently promoted to senior constable. She then not only headed the force of regular women police, but also worked as counsellor to women in the WPAF. Before the war, women were not permitted to drive police vehicles, but they moved quickly from being allowed to drive in 1942, to being issued with their own motor car shortly after the war. Similarly, in 1947, the regular women police were issued with a uniform and commenced working foot patrols and performing other preventative police work. The gains made by women police during and in the immediate wake of World War II were not temporary wartime measures but were lasting developments. In view of this, it is not accurate to describe the war as retarding their development. As O'Meara's own analysis shows, the acceptance and development of women police from 1917 onwards was a slow process, but the 1939–45 war was far from making it slower. O'Meara clearly has as his basic premise the fact that during the war women made major inroads into the general workforce and entered 'hitherto all-male preserves', but women had broken into that all-male preserve, the police force, as early as 1917 (during World War I) and, for them, World War II was a time of modest consolidation. Indeed it could be said that the war, rather than retarding the development of women police, gave some of their sisters outside the force a chance to catch up.[34]

The war certainly had a big effect on two other important aspects of police activity. The first was in the field of communications technology, where wartime demands precipitated a lasting revolution. The other was in the field of police-community relations, where the police assumed new attitudes and social responsibilities that they have been developing—slowly but inexorably—ever since.

The war and the appointment of Duncan as Chief ARP Warden for Victoria produced a massive and costly transformation of the police communications system. Police were responsible for all the precautionary air raid warnings issued in Victoria and for public lighting control. Armed service police units, essential services and lighthouses were all connected to the police control room, which was even used by the navy to recall their ships' personnel on leave. At the outbreak of war only six police vehicles, from a fleet of more than eighty, were equipped with wireless and operated by the special wireless patrol. Apart from an increase in the number of calls and arrests, things had changed little since the 1920s. All transmissions were made using morse telegraphy and wireless patrol crews were heavily dependent upon the skills of wireless telegraphists who were their 'ears and voice' to the outside world. The force did not use wireless telephony, and there was no central police control room or emergency telephone number.

From 1939 to 1946 things changed spectacularly: £19 000 was spent on communications equipment for the force, and the world of wireless—for seventeen years the sole preserve of the élite wireless patrol—was opened to the police, and the public, generally. In December 1939 the now famous police communications centre—D.24—was established, and in April 1940 the force switched from wireless telegraphy to wireless telephony, making trained wireless operators unnecessary. Once this switch was made, two-way and one-way radios were fitted to almost seventy police vehicles, putting detectives, traffic police and general duties men, as well as the wireless patrol, in constant radio contact with D.24. In addition, mobile units from all Australian and United States armed forces were linked to D.24, and those citizens of Melbourne with a domestic radio receiver were also able to 'twiddle the dials' and hear the police at work. The D.24 broadcasting call sign was 'VKC', and its popularity came to rival that of the commercial radio stations. For many people the voice transmissions from D.24 were an exciting link with crime and adventure, while to many lonely and elderly people they served as a source of personal comfort. D.24 took the police force to the firesides of thousands of Melburnians.[35]

It was a time of swift invention, and radio communication was not the only police technological advance of the war era. Other developments included the successful radio transmission of fingerprints between D.24 and Scotland Yard; the establishment of an interstate police wireless service with Sydney and Brisbane; the introduction of direct telephone lines to D.24, including a free emergency number; the purchase of two mobile

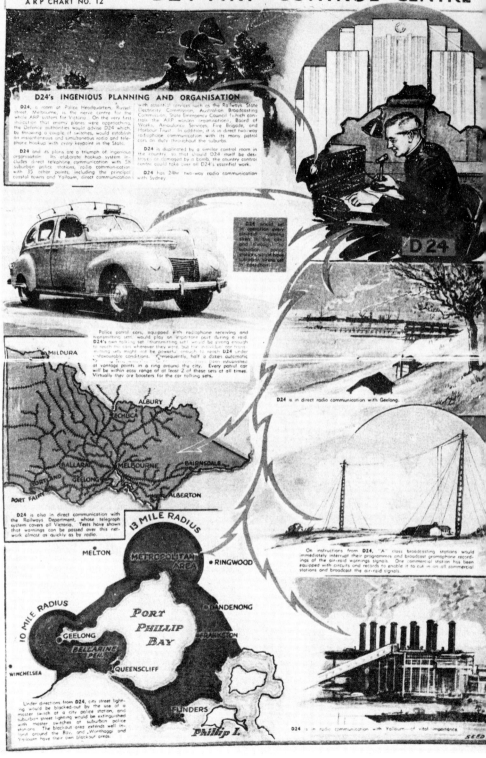

wireless vans fitted with transmitter-receiver equipment, for use in rural areas during searches, floods and bushfires; the installation of direct telephone lines to metropolitan police stations; and the provision of radio receivers to those in the country. The war years also witnessed the opening of a new ten-storey police headquarters at Russell Street, part of which housed an enlarged D.24 complex. The headquarters and the Melbourne skyline were dominated by a 146-ft radio tower, on top of and equally high as the actual building. The building and the mast still stand, symbols not only of the force itself but of the cataclymsic war years that permanently transformed the force's communications system and its approach to policing.[36]

Before the war, members of the force were not noted for their community activities, partly because their one rest day a fortnight gave them limited spare time, but mostly because the force was prepared to 'stand aside and merely keep the peace whilst other bodies—business, private and governmental—promoted the social welfare of the community'. Some individual policemen did involve themselves in local community groups, but apart from the community work of the police bands and the police carnival, they were not actively encouraged to do so, and there was no co-ordinated police–community relations effort. In the decade before the war the force severed relations with the press, Special Branch monitored the activities of unemployed people, and policemen chased young 'footballers'.

The years after 1939 saw a steady development in the official police position and a favourable shift in the state of police-community relations. One area where this was most evident was in the field of youth welfare work. In the 1930s police involvement in boys clubs was virtually non-existent, and it was much more common for children to feel the toe-cap of a size-ten police boot on their rump than to meet its wearer at gym class. The war changed that, and policemen were implored to remember that 'every man was once a boy'. Members of the force became actively involved in the National Fitness Council and were encouraged to undertake youth leader courses of up to five months duration. The Government supported police youth workers by recognizing any injury received in the course of youth work as being on duty, and the police Association joined in by publishing a series of articles on boys clubs and related community activities. The theme was reiterated that police should offer children 'assistance and guidance' because 'prevention is better than cure'. They were encouraged to act as paternal counsellor and friend to children whose fathers were away at war, and to show 'these lads that we are human and feel as they feel'. The *Police Journal* put it this way:

The home front

229

Give them a place for innocent sport
Give them a place for fun,
Better a playground plot than court
And a gaol when the harm is done.

It was a notion in striking contrast to the football rewards of earlier years.

The activities of hundreds of policemen like James Draper, the youth work of many of his colleagues, the influx of more than three thousand auxiliaries into the force, and the broadcasts of D.24, were all part of a broader move that brought the force closer to the community it served. The increased range of police wartime duties, the pressures of war, the increased contact between police and ordinary people and the policeman's position as a pillar in many rural towns, all combined to create at last a general police awareness that they had to participate 'in the efforts of other bodies and authorities working for the general uplifting of the moral, physical and social well-being' of all. It is difficult to quantify this metamorphosis in terms of pounds spent or souls saved, but at war's end it was claimed by the police, with some justification, that the wartime transition in the character of the police service rendered 'any isolation of this civilian in uniform from the rest of the citizens retrograde and out of date'.[37]

Tenez le Droit

The years following World War II were one of the most paradoxical times in the history of the Victoria Police. The force ended its involvement in the war effort on a seemingly positive note: only three policemen were killed on active military duty, and most returned home to adulatory greetings, two even with the rank of lieutenant-colonel. The police communications system was at its most sophisticated and efficient level ever, and relations between police and community were at an all-time high. The force, with a changed character forged by the pressures of war, stood optimistically on the threshold of a new peacetime era. Between 1945 and 1959 it adopted a new motto, badge and uniform, and introduced important changes in the fields of public relations, recruiting, training and traffic control. The police were on the move—changing, adapting, experimenting and generally coming to grips with the social and technological advances of the mid-twentieth century. Or was it quite like that? Behind a façade of 'development' lay more cramped and cramping conditions. Limited wartime recruiting had left the force grossly undermanned, and after the war candidates for the force were scarcer than they had been at any time since 1850; the force in fact remained understrength well into the 1960s. Suitable young men found a police

Russell Street Police Headquarters

career 'unattractive', and it was 'disturbing' to police recruiters that 75 per cent of all men who did apply were unacceptable because they could not meet educational or physical requirements. Police pay and work conditions—though substantially improved from 1946—were still the poorest of any force in Australia and New Zealand, and lagged well behind those of the general workforce. One example serves to illustrate this point. In 1946 the state public service and the Board of Works staff were granted a five-day working week. At the same time it was announced that the police would get one extra rest day each fortnight, giving them a six-day working week, 'when the exigencies of the service permitted'. Indeed, much of what might be called 'development' in the post-war years was in reality a desperate bid to keep the force functioning: the focus on 'police image', the improvement in work conditions and the introduction of junior trainees and a police reserve were not the experiments of an enlightened administration so much as the actions of officials struggling to recruit, train and retain police. In bouyant employment times the police force was not an occupation to which educated young people aspired, and the waiting lists of bygone days were but a memory in the minds of ageing police who reminisced about the pre-war years. The pressures of modern policing, built up by ever-increasing numbers of migrants, motor cars, traffic accidents and crimes, together with shift work, weekend duty, poor pay and long hours, were part of the paradox of the force that was 'on the move' yet deteriorating under strain. The new badge and uniform were symbolic of a progressive front, behind which often lurked the troubled minds of policemen with deep concerns about their personal security and destiny. Dressed in blue, with new badge and motto, their updated public image belied much about the true nature of the force they served, and the service they offered.[38]

In 1939, before war was declared, the force was 2333 strong and had a police to population ratio of 1:816. It was then the most undermanned and lowest paid police department in Australia, and lacked the leave, rest day and uniform entitlements of many interstate and overseas police forces. The Police Association was negotiating with Duncan and the conservative Dunstan government for work conditions on a par with those of other forces, but progress was slow and by the outbreak of war the Association had not been successful in its bid to have police pay rates raised to the pre-depression level. An allowance of sixpence a day, which was voluntarily surrendered during the depression, was never restored. No adjustment was made in police salaries from 1933 to 1941, although the cost of living during those years rose by 18 per cent. It was a situation that prompted many sympathetic people to reiterate an *Argus* theme, that the force was awarded 'first place in efficiency' by 'many competent judges', but remained 'the lowest paid in Australia and New Zealand'. As a 'wartime gesture' the Police Association followed the precedent set by police during World War I and agreed not to harry the Government over such matters as long service leave and hours of duty. For six years the Association limited its action to moderate requests for cost of living adjustments. The combined result of police industrial passivity and wartime austerity was that Victorian police were worse off in 1945 than they had been in 1939. The police strength had dropped to 2131, and the police to population ratio had worsened to 1:946. They were working harder and longer on less real pay and without the benefits enjoyed by police in other states— more rest days, long-service leave, uniform allowances and access to an independent industrial court or similar body. The result was a spate of resignations not matched by recruits. The post-war economic climate provided returned servicemen and others with a different El Dorado from that of the nineteenth-century gold rushes, but the 1940s were like the 1850s in that the police administration could not match the lucrative incentives offering to potential and serving policemen outside the police force.[39]

A Labor government led by John Cain came to office in November 1945 and was quick to appreciate and act upon the problems besetting the force, a quickness of action no doubt aided by the fact that the honorary solicitor of the Police Association, William Slater, MLA for Dundas, was also Chief Secretary, Attorney-General and Solicitor-General in the new ministry. The Police Association—as distinct from the police administration—justifiably saw the Labor government as an ally, and expressed disillusionment with the string of conservative ministries which, for more than a decade, had neglected the policeman's lot. It was a neglect that aroused working-class sentiments in the police ranks, even prompting occasional public claims by their union leaders that policemen were 'only workers' who served as 'the guardians of "big business"' while '"big business" denied them so much as one crumb from their table of plenty'. In a tone that would have made former Chief Commissioners like Blamey wince, Association leaders spoke ill of capitalism, proposed police affiliation with the Australian Council of Trade Unions, and talked of 'doing away with the old order'. It was heated and radical rhetoric of a sort not heard since the days of the police strike. And it worked.

Within a year of taking office the Labor government met many of the Police Association requests. Among other things, the Labor government established an independent Police Classification Board 'to determine the wages and general conditions of service of members of the police force'; it established an independent Police Discipline Board 'to provide for inquiries into police misconduct', and included provision for appeal to a County Court judge if a member was dissatisfied with a decision of the Chief Commissioner or the Board; all police were provided with long-service leave of six months after twenty years; section 81 of the Police Regulation Act was repealed to allow the police association 'to affiliate with any federation of police associations or police unions of Australia'; and all police were granted a weekly rest day. These conditions most other Australian and New Zealand police forces already had, and the police Association had been asking for them since the 1930s, but their introduction in Victoria was not taken for granted by the Police Association executive, which was generous in its praise of the Cain government and described Slater as 'a man's man', and urged all police to make themselves known, 'give him your hand' and 'thank him for yourself, wife and family'.[40]

Governments in Victoria had so long denied police the privilege of a weekly rest day because of its cost to the taxpayer. When introduced in 1946 it required an increase of 380 men in the authorized strength of the force, just to maintain police service to the community at its existing level, but this number of recruits could not be found, so many policemen were compelled to work extra duty to compensate for the loss of those who were on days off. Two years later this shortage was worsened when the Police Classification Board granted an Association claim for a forty-hour, five-day working week, following New South Wales, Tasmania, the Federal Capital Territory police and the state public service. It was a radical improvement for those many men still serving, who had joined in the 1920s when they received one rest day a month, and worked alongside 'old hands' who had joined before 1913, when policemen worked the full year without any rest days. The forty-hour week resulted in an increase of 299 men being permitted, and also in a revised classification of stations and police members throughout the state. Duncan hoped that it would stimulate police recruiting, but it did not. Despite the most massive recruiting campaign in the force's history, the police to population ratio worsened, and at the end of 1948 the force was 390 men under strength. Duncan anticipated it would take three years to make up the leeway, but the loss of manpower caused by the introduction of the forty-hour week was still a problem in the 1960s.

The shortened working week placed further stress on the ability of the force to meet the public demand for its services, and prompted Duncan to observe that 'the true conception of police duty—*the prevention of crime and protection of life and property*—is being lost sight of and, as a matter of expediency, police duty to the public has tended to become simply a matter of attendance at the spot after an offence has been committed'. Duncan was right. The forty-hour week, even after allowing for an increase in the size of the force, meant that fewer policemen were available for duty at any given time, forcing a change in the level and style of police service, from the traditional system of patrol and prevention, to one that increasingly focused on responding to calls for assistance and investigation. Given that shorter working hours were generally available to other workers, their extension to policemen was to be expected. However, few people have realized the negative impact that they have had, not only on police availability but on the nature of police services generally. The universality with which this factor has been overlooked is highlighted by its omission from S. K. Mukherjee's pioneering study, *Crime Trends in Twentieth-Century Australia*, which discusses the correlation between police staffing levels and the crime rate, without reference to the fact that during the period spanned by his study, the time that policemen spent on duty in Victoria dropped by more than one-third, a reduction of 976 hours a year for each member of the force.[41]

Nevertheless, it was not working hours but the formation of the Police Classification Board that produced a furore. Since the 1920s the Police Association had pressed for the creation of an independent tribunal to determine police wages and work conditions, and cited forces in other states as evidence that access to an independent body was the rule, not the exception. Police in Victoria had always been forced to go 'cap in hand' to the Chief Commissioner and the Government of the day for any alteration to their pay and conditions, and as a 'loyal' body were not affiliated with any union group or prone to industrial action. So police claims were not judged on their merits but were neglected while governments considered demands from larger, militant, unionized groups. Determination of police pay and conditions had to be removed from the partisan and capricious arena of state politics and entrusted to an independent tribunal. The Labor government agreed with the Police Association on that, and one of the first acts of the Cain administration was the extensive reform of the Police Regulation Act to set up a three-man Police Classification Board, made up of a county court judge as chairman, a representative of the Government and an elected representative of the police force. The Board handed down its first determination on 13 November 1946 and has had continuous existence ever since—although now known as the Police Service Board. It gave the missing element of dignity to police wage bargaining, and ended the days of policemen lobbying in the corridors of parliament for an extra sixpence a day or the right to wear beards. The Classification Board responded quickly and favourably to claims for higher pay, special duties allowances, and compensatory allowances for weekend, night and public holiday duty, thereby bringing the benefits available to Victorian police closer to those offered interstate and overseas. The Board was also quick to approve of a new police uniform and, in a commensense gesture that set the Board apart from the old system, with its stuffiness from a past era, authorized policemen to remove their heavy woollen tunics in summer. It took an independent board to do it, but finally—after 110 years—police were allowed to appear in public in shirt-sleeves. It symbolized the sense of relief with which many policemen in the street greeted the arrival of the Police Classification Board.[42]

Until the creation of the Board, police wages and conditions of work in Victoria almost always lagged behind those of other Australian police forces. No comparative research to determine why this was so has been undertaken, and the answer, perhaps entwined with the reasons why the only strike by policemen in Australia occurred in Victoria, lies well beyond the scope of this study. The Police Classification Board went part of the way towards giving Victorian policemen parity with those interstate, but it was not a panacea and the previous absence of such a tribunal could never be regarded as being the main reason why Victoria lagged behind. Policemen in Western Australia, Queensland and South Australia had access to independent arbitration boards, well before they did in Victoria, but policemen in New South Wales did not and they were the national pace-setters in attaining higher pay and better conditions. There is no simple explanation why Victorian policemen—Australian leaders in such things as the use of wireless, fingerprint analysis, forensic science and detective training—trailed the nation in matters of pay and conditions, but key elements in a complex answer appear to be the conservative nature of policemen and Victorian politics. For most of its existence the force was subject to the rule of conservative governments that exploited police conservatism and loyalty, and relied upon their ingrained reluctance to affiliate with or support trade unions. The police force was the last group of government employees to be allowed to vote in parliamentary elections, the last to be permitted to form a union, and the last to be granted access to an independent board for the determination of salaries and conditions. Such factors as these kept many policemen subjugated for a long time and made them dependent upon the personal interest and good will of politicians for improved conditions. Paradoxically, it was usual during the time of Labor governments for significant improvements to be made and the creation of a Classification Board was one of these.

The marked improvement in police wages and work conditions was associated with a recruiting campaign and, for the first time, police recruiters used a whole repertoire of devices to attract candidates. Recruiting drives were conducted in all suburban and country areas; advertisements were placed in newspapers; police broadcast shows on commercial radio stations; a press liaison officer (later a personnel and public relations officer) was appointed; police processions and exhibitions were held, and all serving police were told to 'approach the prospective recruit'. All these efforts met with such limited success that the police force widened its pool of prospective recruits by reducing the minimum joining age from 20 to 19, and raising the maximum age for returned servicemen from 27 to 33. Still only a trickle of recruits resulted, so the police training period was reduced by seven weeks to get constables more quickly on the streets. The Government was not prepared to reduce the height limit for recruits because of 'the nature of the duties they are called upon to perform', even though many men of 5 feet 8 inches who joined after the police strike were then working successfully as policemen. The lack of suitable local applicants for the force so worried Duncan and the Government that they looked overseas and sought to recruit trained policemen from England and Palestine. The Victorian Agent-General in London was hired to recruit English policemen, and Duncan went on a personal tour of English police forces to tout for likely candidates. The overseas campaign netted more than three hundred men, but doubts were expressed about their worth when almost one hundred resigned after arriving in Victoria—including 58 of the first 129 to sign up. Many of those who resigned did so because they were disappointed with police wages and conditions in Victoria and could earn more money doing 'seasonal work, such as wheat harvesting'. Indeed, the high rate of 'desertions' by English recruits—who had their full fare paid to Australia—so alarmed Victorian authorities that migrant ships with English police on board were met in Port Phillip Bay and the Englishmen were taken ashore as a group to be sworn in, lest they 'jump ship' to find work elsewhere.

The importation of such a large number of police from the United Kingdom had not been undertaken since the recruitment of the 'London Fifty' in 1852, and the two distant instances provided a parallel. In both cases the Englishmen were imported to bolster an ailing force, and both times many of the new arrivals were disillusioned with what they found in Victoria. In 1853 two of the English recruits were charged with insubordination for refusing to cut firewood and procure water for the cook. The men refused to do this work because they were experienced police and, although their refusal had some justification, they were chided and told that 'soldiers were not degraded by doing fatigue duty'. In 1948 it was declared in parliament that recruits from overseas with up to 'six years experience in the London force' were put to work 'cleaning floors' and 'peeling potatoes'. Many people wondered how a force that was so undermanned could afford this luxury, but at least one observer aired the sentiment of 1853 and remarked, 'recruits in the army are called upon to do menial jobs'. The comparison between police recruits and those in the army was not altogether unfair. Both groups underwent training in drill, self-defence and the use of firearms, and in both cases the training process, including fatigue duty, was used to initiate young civilian men into a disciplined and hierarchical work environment, where uniforms, parades, salutes and barracks were part of everyday life. However, though the Englishmen were undoubtedly in need of some introduction to Victorian laws and police procedures, they were not callow rookies in need of an initiation into disciplined police life. They were experienced policemen who had trained and served in forces overseas. More efficient managers might perhaps have devised a means of integrating the

Englishmen into the force, without subjecting them to basic police training, in every respect identical to that given to rookies. A more enlightened approach might perhaps have got urgently needed policemen on to the streets quicker and minimized their disenchantment with things in Victoria.[43]

Notwithstanding such problems, the administration tried to promote a sense of *esprit de corps* internally and to improve the external image of the police. Much of this was a flow-on from wartime community work, some of it as internal staff relations and much of it as part of the recruiting campaign. A key element was the introduction of a motto and badge, and a change in the style of uniform. The Police Association had lobbied for several years for a change of uniform, particularly something more suited to the Australian climate. Several patterns were studied, including one of a khaki uniform, to be worn with a white helmet and tan boots, but it was not until 1946 and the creation of the Classification Board that a final decision was made to introduce a lapel-fronted tunic of blue cloth, to be worn with a collar, tie and cap. This outfit replaced the old high-collar tunic and polished black leather helmet, on issue since 1877, and was a popular choice with all but a few men, who were worried that the tie would give assailants something to throttle them with in a brawl, or who lamented that the summer uniform had a belt but no braces. There is, however, no record of any constable being strangled with his tie (often clip-ons, anyway), or losing his trousers in a fight.

Also, the force for the first time adopted an official badge. It incorporated the service number of the wearer and a motto in French: *Tenez le Droit*, or 'Uphold the Right', which was almost a direct copy of the motto of the Royal Canadian Mounted Police, *Maintiens le Droit*. The badge was designed by Robert Peacock, a noted expert in heraldry. No longer were the Victoria police 'the only force in Australia and the Empire' without a distinctive symbol, and the adoption of the badge from 1946 onwards—when it started to appear on clothing and, as a logo, on publications, correspondence and elsewhere—had a real effect on the outward image of the force, and helped promote a sense of identity.[44]

Duncan, who superintended most of the changes to the force in the post-war decade, was due to retire in September 1953 at 65 years of age, but his term as Chief Commissioner was extended so that he could head the force during the Royal Visit of Queen Elizabeth the Second, during 1954. The Police Association was eager that Duncan be succeeded as Chief Commissioner by a career policeman from Victoria, and well before the time of Duncan's retirement the Association wrote to the Cain government and lobbied publicly for the appointment of a 'serving member of the Victoria Police Force who has come up through the ranks'. The member that the Association clearly had in mind was Inspecting-Superintendent A. A. Webster, the man next in seniority to Duncan.

Chief Commissioner
S. H. Porter

Webster had joined the force in 1915 and had risen through the ranks, with an impressive record that included interchange duty in New South Wales and South Australia, service as a foundation lecturer at the Detective Training School, several stints as Acting Chief Commissioner in the absence of Duncan, and successful completion of the executive training course held at the British Police College, Ryton-on-Dunsmore. The Police Association lobbying was to no avail, however, and Webster was superannuated on 9 October 1954, his sixtieth birthday, and Major General Selwyn Porter was appointed to succeed Duncan from 1 January 1955.

At the time of his appointment Porter was staff manager for the large Melbourne-based retailing firm of Myer, but he had a distinguished military record and this was his principal qualification for the top police post. The Association was disappointed about the appointment of another 'outsider' to head the force, describing it as a 'bombshell' that ended the 'hopes' of career policemen. Porter was appointed by John Cain's Labor ministry and it was reported that only 'two ministers out of thirteen supported the appointment of a man from within the force'. It was a bitter blow to the Association, which strongly censured the Government and expressed concern about a general tendency toward the promotion of men on the basis of 'merit'. Even so, the Association pledged its loyalty to Porter, who was 'deserving of co-operation' as a man who had 'served his country with distinction', although the strong contrary feelings never entirely disappeared during Porter's period in office. Although he was a generally popular leader—and one who devoted considerable attention to internal and public relations—his personal emphasis on police training and the establishment of a police college prompted a meeting of one thousand police to pass a vote of no-confidence in his 'administration of the police force, and his system of promotion'. He was the first Chief Commissioner to be made the subject of such a motion, which was largely the work of reactionary elements within the force. These men were worried that 'any member wanting to become an officer would have to attend the college for seven months and live-in away from his wife and family', and were also concerned that higher education requirements would favour younger men. Porter easily survived the trials of the no-confidence vote and, in a volte-face, many of the men who were party to the vote later supported a Police Association communication to the Government, asking that Porter be given a pay rise because: 'As a result of the many training schemes and other programmes initiated by the Chief Comissioner since the 1st July 1955 . . . the efficiency of the force as a whole, individual standards of education and the capacity to perform exacting duties have advanced to a marked degree'.[45]

Porter worked as understudy to Duncan during the last months of 1954 and assumed sole charge in January 1955. Duncan left the force in much better shape than he had found it, particularly in the areas of criminal investigation and detective training, but it was still a force with big problems. On the eve of Porter's appointment the force had a worse police to population ratio than it had in 1939 and, although the authorized strength of 3100 was the highest ever, the combined effect of the forty-hour week and an inability to recruit men was that the actual strength was only 3021 and the total hours police were available for duty in 1955 were less than in 1939. Porter estimated that the force was two thousand men below the level needed to attain optimum efficiency and was also of the opinion that his men had a 'pushbike age' approach to policing, and failed to match the 'accelerated tempo of living', increasing mobility and 'general advance' of the Victorian people. He undertook his police command with zeal and was quick to appraise the force, determine its shortcomings and, in systematic fashion, set out about instituting positive changes.

Porter's opinion of the force and his quickness to change it were not surprising. It had happened before. In common with those other 'outsiders'—Steward, Gellibrand, Blamey and Duncan—Porter was a strong leader, and a thinker whose ideas on the force were not blinkered by previous service in it, but were enhanced by overseas travel and a knowledge of people gained by working and living outside the police environment. When first appointed, each of them firmly took command. They were dissatisfied with the force as they found it and quickly put many of their own ideas into effect. There was an element of the 'new broom' in much of this and even mediocre leaders—Chomley, O'Callaghan, Sainsbury and Nicholson—displayed that trait, but Porter and the others were chosen especially for their management skills, and with considerable fanfare were appointed on the understanding that they would significantly improve the force. However, none of them completed the job and it is primarily for this reason that the pattern of police organizational development was a recurring sequence of a change in command leading to a spate of reforms followed by a period of relative stagnation and decline. Each of them in turn left for his successor an organization that was in need of rejuvenation and new ideas, and these needs were seemingly incapable of being filled by the general run of policemen themselves, who suffered from a collective lack of desire and ability to work in that direction. It was a perennial problem and one that eventually engulfed Porter. He started with a burst of ideas and energy but his drive waned and he later died while still in office.

During his commissionership, Porter paid considerable attention to recruiting, training, public relations and the road toll, and in addition was openly critical of the way political considerations—rather than legitimate public need—had traditionally determined the location and level of police services. Porter was the first Chief Commissioner to adopt a business approach to public relations, recruiting and personnel management, and he linked these previously separate areas of police activity and co-ordinated efforts to improve police performance in each area and promote a better police 'image'. He cultivated good relations with all sections of the news media and fostered police appearances on radio and television. Lasting innovations he made in this field include the appointment of a senior member as personnel and public relations officer, publication of an official monthly police magazine, *Police Life*, and the introduction of a Chief Commissioner's Certificate as an award for sustained good service, filling the gap between the formal commendation of members and the issue of a medal or bravery award.[46]

Porter dropped the minimum height requirement for police recruits by one inch to 5 feet 8 inches, and further extended their maximum age, from 33 to 35 years for ex-servicemen, and from 27 to 30 years for other men. Like the earlier concessions of Duncan, they were insufficient to fill the police ranks, so Porter obtained government approval to form both a corps of junior police trainees (cadets) and a police reserve. The force had not recruited cadets since the manpower crisis of the 1850s, when

Sturt had recruited 'eduated young men from the upper classes' as the nucleus of an *officer* class. Porter's scheme was aimed at preparing youths aged sixteen and above for entry into the force as *constables* when old enough. He hoped to attract those who 'at the time of leaving school, have ambitions to become members of the police force but cannot do so until they attain the age of nineteen years'. Porter argued that many potential policemen were lost as youths by being absorbed into commerce and industry. In the years between the cadet schemes of Sturt and Porter, both Blamey and Duncan had tried to introduce cadets, only to fail because of government indifference in Blamey's case and Police Association opposition in Duncan's. The first squad of thirty cadets recruited by Porter began training on 2 May 1955 and the scheme proved a successful and prolific source of police recruits. From 1955 to 1982—when the scheme ended—almost three thousand young men joined the force as cadets.[47]

As an alternative means of easing the personnel shortage, Porter also formed a police reserve comprised of 'able and experienced' retired constables and first constables, to be used for 'sedentary tasks', thereby 'freeing fit men for active police duty'. For almost a decade, first Duncan, then Porter, supported by many parliamentarians and members of the public, had pressed for the formation of a permanent police auxiliary force. The work of the PAF during World War II, especially its positive influence on police-community relations, had left an indelible mark in the minds of many people, who envisaged a permanent reserve of trained civilians to assist in such major emergencies as floods, bushfires and riots, by relieving regular police of administrative and communications work for active duty. Duncan had believed, as had Menzies during World War II, that if 'loyal-minded citizens' were denied the 'active expressions of their citizenship' they might 'be attracted to other unauthorized organizations whose professed aims have a specious appeal'. He regarded an auxiliary force as a realistic alternative for men who otherwise might join vigilante groups or private armies. Yet the prospect of civil auxiliaries alarmed the Police Association, which declared the proposed reserve a 'fascist strike-breaking body', inimical in every way to the interests of the regular police. From the end of World War II until 1956 the debate about auxiliary police raged, until the Government, Porter and the Association finally agreed on a modified scheme, using retired Victorian police in a restricted capacity, simply to free younger policemen from clerical and administrative work. Porter's 'reserve force' was not a reserve at all, and was a far cry from the civilian auxiliary force proposed by Duncan, but it did allow some flexibility of manpower deployment and, during its first year of operation, almost one hundred retired men were recruited. The 'retired police reserve' has continued as an adjunct to the regular force ever since, and more than five hundred men and women have joined. It provided some relief for the manpower shortage confronting Porter in the 1950s, but in a later time of high unemployment probably denied young people potential careers in the force and public service.[48]

This implementation of a cadet corps and police reserve was Porter building on foundations laid by Duncan in the 1940s, and Porter's efforts to combat the rising number of deaths in motor accidents also followed Duncan, who had been the first Chief Commissioner seriously to consider the mounting road toll as a joint community-police problem. In an effort to counter it, he had increased the number and range of traffic patrols and formed a special squad to give lectures on road safety to school children. For Duncan the ever-increasing road toll had been 'one of the major problems' of the time. Porter agreed, and quickly consolidated Duncan's work of making police more professional in traffic work and alerting the community to the carnage on Victorian roads. During Porter's first year in office 540 people were killed and 13 182 injured in 22 672 vehicular accidents, while reported assaults and other criminal offences 'against the person' numbered 3442, including 24 murders. Deaths and injuries due to car accidents of such epidemic proportions troubled Porter, who commented that 'loss of life occasioned by behaviour while using a motor car is not looked at in the same light as loss of life occasioned by other behaviour'. Porter steadily increased the police resources devoted to traffic control work, formed a road courtesy squad, with the objective of promoting good will between motorists, and introduced driver-education lectures, known as the 'motorists hour'. Within the force he established a Vehicle Safety Testing School, Motor Driving School, and Accident Appreciation Squad, to improve police traffic expertise and capabilities, and he appointed as police surgeon Dr John Birrell, who pioneered Australian efforts to curb death and injury caused by drunk drivers.[49]

Porter is generally regarded as being a police leader who was 'adept at innovation', and his list of achievements in the fields of public relations, recruiting and traffic policing supports this notion, but it should be recognized that Duncan was the progenitor of many ideas later successfully implemented by Porter. It was so in the field of education, where Porter exerted his most telling and lasting influence on the force by transforming Duncan's vision of a police college into a reality. Before he retired, Duncan secured premises at Mornington for use as a police college, obtained funding for selected men to attend specialist police training courses overseas, arranged for police instructors to attend teacher training courses conducted by the Education Department, enrolled suitably qualified men from the communications section in courses at the Royal Melbourne Institute of Technology, and actively supported individual policemen who undertook relevant tertiary courses. (Most notable among the last was the police scientist, Norman McCallum; as a serving policeman, he attended the University of Melbourne and obtained a bachelor's and then a master's degree in science.) Duncan's efforts to foster higher education levels within the force were a marked advance on anything undertaken by his predecessors, although it was not to be in his term that the police college finally opened.

The Mornington property acquired by the Government for a college in 1950 proved unsuitable for its intended purpose and the introduction of officer training courses was delayed until 1958, when the first officers course was conducted at a newly acquired Police College, the South Yarra mansion known as 'Airlie'. The course was a residential one of seven months, and its aim was 'to give broadening training to potential officers with the object of equipping them for their administrative and executive roles as police officers'. The college at 'Airlie' was modelled on the English and Scottish police colleges, and was the last link in Porter's three-tiered training system that included 'primary training' for recruits and cadets, 'secondary training designed to fit sub-officers for all postings up to and including station officer', and 'tertiary training' for potential officers. The structured courses introduced by Porter have been retained ever since as central elements in the training system. Porter's changes put the force in the vanguard of Australasian police education development, and the Police College played host to visiting students from other Australian forces and nearby international neighbours, including New Zealand, India, Kenya, Fiji and Malaysia. Indeed, Porter's contribution in this area is the hallmark of his commissionership and marks a turning point. Porter himself aptly observed that 'the task of the modern policeman' had 'progressed beyond recognition as that of P.C. 49'. When Porter was appointed Chief Commissioner—from outside the force—the Labor government gave him as one of his specific tasks responsibility for training his successors from among serving policemen. Some evidence that he did this is found in the fact that all four Chief Commissioners appointed after him, together with all the deputy commissioners, assistant commissioners and commanders, have been career policemen, and all but the earliest few have been graduates of the Police College at 'Airlie'.[50]

Although the 1950s was primarily a time of introspection for the police, when a preoccupation with image, recruiting, training and work conditions produced important internal changes, the decade ended much as it had started and Porter reported in 1959 that 'the staff shortage was desperate'. The authorized strength of the force was then 3772 but the ratio of one policeman to every 733 Victorians was worsening and in some of the rapidly expanding eastern suburbs the ratio was 1:1662. But the seemingly perennial manpower crisis was not simply a question of numbers. It was a dilemma compounded by the nature and rate of social change in an increasingly motorized and mobile society. Those two 'old standards'—the crime rate and the road toll—were steadily escalating but an unprepared police force also had to contend with a range of other problems, reflected in the changing police idiom. Expressions such as 'New Australians', 'expresso bars', 'bodgies', 'the liberty of the subject', 'joy-rides' and 'drug bureau' crept into police parlance. The force still had more pushbikes than it did motor cars. Assaults on police were a rising cause for concern. The incidence of sickness and overtiredness among harried detectives was commented upon. And Porter warned of signs that youths were 'behaving more aggressively and using more violence than in recent decades ... some of the group violence of earlier days is threatening'. It was an age when Porter prophesied of worse to come and lamented that in too many instances, 'both parents in a family go to work during the day and spend their evenings ... watching a television programme in semi-darkness, while their children roam the streets'.[51]

It was the dawning of the 1960s.

6

Towards the Twenty-first Century

Between 1945 and 1984 the force underwent more changes than ever before and experienced an unprecedented rise in almost all areas of work. The combined pressures of change and workload placed the force and its component parts—people—under increasing stress, leading to corruption, maladministration and inefficiency. As usual, sections of the community exposed and tried to remedy these problems, in a process that was at times difficult and embarrassing for policemen, but was essential. In many tangible ways the force went through a significant metamorphosis and broke with the past, yet some old attitudes and practices persisted; indeed, large sections of the force displayed a hostile resistance to change. The force was still not representative of the people it served, which seriously restricted its ability to cope with many of the social problems found in the general community. When 1984 ended, the police and the community were awaiting the outcome of an inquiry set up to point the force more effectively in the direction of the year 2000.

The Thin Blue Line

'The thin blue line' is a cliché often used in police circles; there are too few police compared with the awesome modern scale of organized, white-collar and computer crime, narcotic drug abuse, juvenile delinquency, protest demonstrations and the road toll. The problems are compounded by the increasing complexity of police duties in a multicultural, urbanized society that is in some ways materialistic and in other ways ultra-conscious of rights for women, children, blacks, prisoners, various minorities and even animals. Legislators enact an expanding range of laws, embodying criminal sanctions and police powers, in an effort to control the use of such things as noisy motor mowers, listening devices and obscene video cassettes. Disturbing levels of youth unemployment, poverty, mental illness and social dysfunction cast people into contact with the police, who all too often are expected to serve as the community's social agency of last resort. Since the end of World War II police work has increased in volume and changed in nature to such an extent that the police are often unable to cope. Rising levels of crime preventable by patrols, diminishing crime clearance rates, the selective attendance at

246

crime scenes by detectives (crime screening), and the rapid growth of private security forces, are all indicators that the police do not have the resources necessary to provide proper public protection and service. New technology and higher education have not closed the gap between police workload and ability to cope with it. The commercial sector and the wealthy can respond to a shortfall in police service by turning to private security entrepreneurs, who now have an entrenched role protecting private property and people—for a fee—but that is an alternative only open to those who can pay for it. A different public effort was the initiation of co-operative community programmes, such as Neighbourhood Watch and Safety House, in a bid to ease the strain on the thin blue line and give community members an active part to play in caring for each other.[1]

Figure 2 illustrates graphically the rate at which reported crimes on the major crime index, and the number of registered motor vehicles, outstripped increases in the police strength. From 1945 to 1980 the population of Victoria increased by 94 per cent, the number of police by 261 per cent, the number of registered motor vehicles by 682 per cent and the number of reported major crimes by 767 per cent. During the same period the clearance rate for major crime offences dropped from 39 per cent to 22 per cent, while the number of drink-driving prosecutions rose from 204 in 1945 to 15 757 in 1982. At a glance, the improvement in the ratio of police to population looked good—1:946 in 1945 to 1:482 in 1982— but against this improved ratio must be weighed the massive increases in most facets of police work, and the reduction in police working hours from 52 to 40 hours a week, which produced an actual deterioration in 'standards of law and order' and 'a decline in the ability of the police force to deter crime and to maintain crime clearance standards'. In the words of one retired policeman:

> When I joined the force in 1949 we were solely a law enforcement body . . . our duties were mainly concerned with protection of people and property against law breakers . . . We did not even have one vehicle attached to the station. Every shop door handle was tested and every lane was patrolled. The men were out on the street all the time and I knew every businessman and also every no-hoper in my district personally. But today it is all different.

He was right. The beat constable testing shop door handles had been replaced by the private security guard, who flitted about the suburbs in a motor car emblazoned with his company motif, usually toting a gun and wearing a uniform tailored in the hues and style of a policeman, and whose calling cards littered the doorways of those paying for his service. And what of the constable 'out on the street all the time'? He was still there, working to fulfil the proud claim that 'the Victoria Police is the only organization in society that will answer any call for help—anywhere,

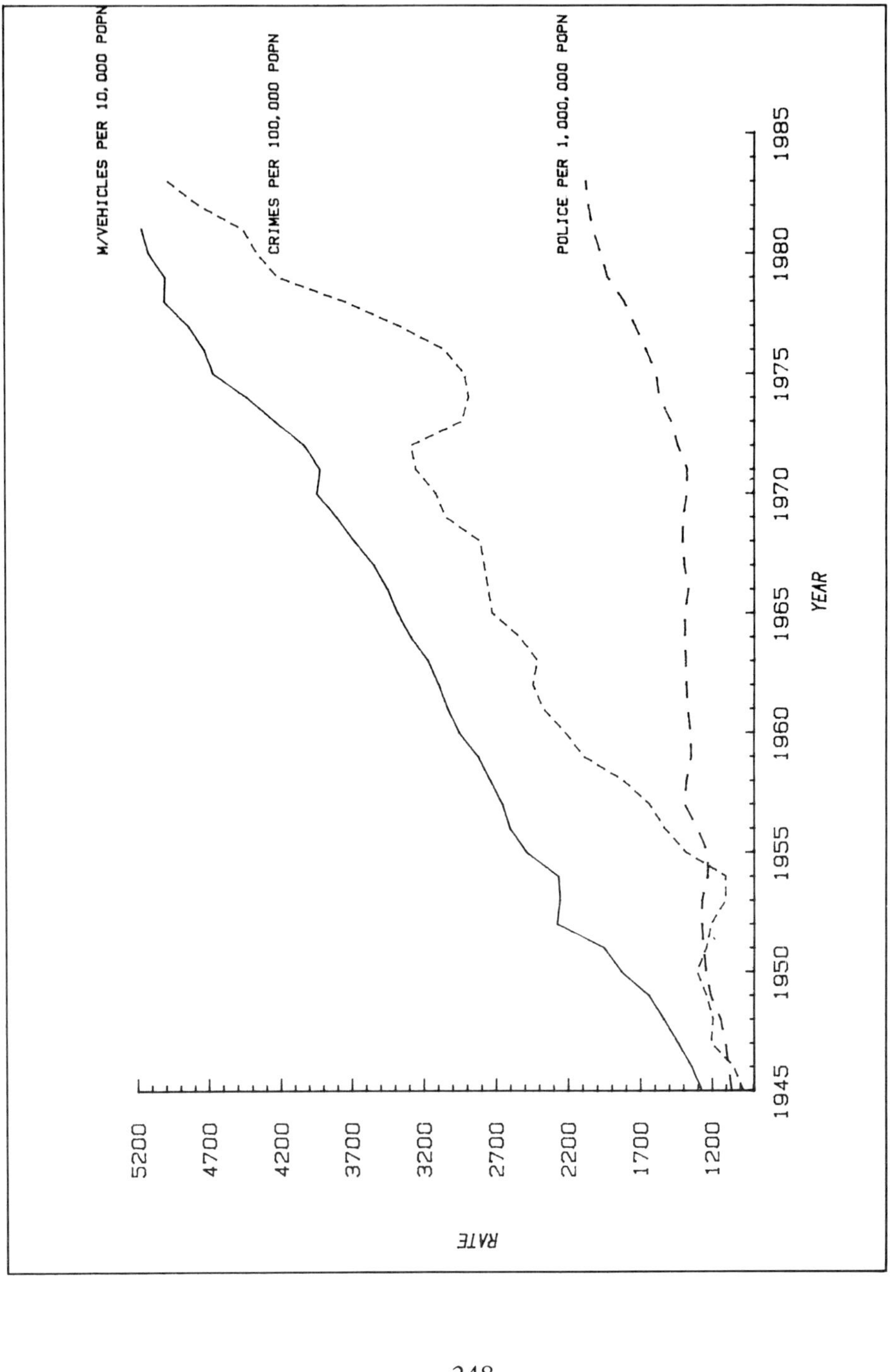

Figure 2: Graph showing increases in motor vehicle

any time'—but he was encapsulated in a motor car. He drove about his sub-district, booking motorists and responding to radio calls for help, and except during the lonely and quiet hours of the early morning—when most motor vehicles were parked, still and silent—no longer had the time to pay close regard to shop doors. Modern social pressures and motorization forced a shift in his horizons and work orientation, away from the traditional 'protection of people and property against law breakers', to the provision of a complex range of general community services and a focus on traffic policing. His presence was symbolized by the 'divisional van', and the fleeting sightings of it in sprawling urban environments was symptomatic of the thin blue line he represented.[2]

The motor vehicle almost absorbed the policeman. He was registering motor vehicles and licensing drivers, directing the traffic flow, booking illegally parked cars, tracing stolen vehicles, detecting and prosecuting errant motorists, and performing a thousand-and-one ancillary tasks: retrieving ignition keys from a locked vehicle, assisting a stalled vehicle in heavy traffic, locating cars 'lost' in the maze of large shopping complexes, or helping unskilled motorists to change flat tyres or manoeuvre vehicles from tight parking spaces. During the 1960s it was calculated that there was 'one vehicle for every three citizens' and a '6 per cent annual increase in road traffic', and it was even estimated that 70 per cent of all police work was in some way connected with traffic policing. A more realistic determination of the police traffic workload was obtained in 1970, when it was calculated that police devoted 22 per cent of their time to traffic work, but that was still the largest single percentage out of ten categories of work, including patrol, crime investigation, public order and civil matters.

From 1910 until 30 June 1981 the Motor Registration Branch formed part of the force, which for all that time was the sole authority for registering motor vehicles, licensing drivers, maintaining traffic conviction records, and performing all the related administrative tasks. In 1970–71 Colonel Sir Eric St Johnston inspected the force and reported that nowhere else in the world had he 'found the police to be responsible for the registering of motor vehicles. It is clearly not a police function'. His study showed that the time then spent by police on motor vehicle registration and licence testing duties was equivalent to the full-time deployment of 295 men 'who would become available for other duties, if they were relieved of these duties'.

Progressively since 1981 they have been mostly relieved of those duties, and the relevant records and public service staff transferred to a newly created Road Traffic Authority. However, the police still had responsibility for traffic law enforcement and accident investigation, occupying large amounts of time and requiring specialists. In 1946 the Traffic Control Branch comprised a Mobile Traffic Section of 101 men equipped with twenty-two cars and seventeen motorcycles, who patrolled 'metropolitan roads and country highways radiating from Melbourne', and a Foot Traffic Section of eighty-one men, who controlled city traffic and supervised 'traffic at race meetings, football matches and other large sporting, etc., functions outside the city area'. In 1983 the Traffic Department under the command of an Assistant Commissioner numbered 727 personnel, or 9 per cent of the force. Members of the operational arm of the Traffic Department—the Traffic Operations Group—worked throughout the state, supported by specialist sections like the breath analysis section, accident investigation section, special motorcycle section and central traffic policy and information section. In addition, most other operational members of the force, including detectives, at some time were called upon to act in a traffic policing capacity, and most uniformed patrols were ever alert for the errant motorist. The police vehicle fleet totalled 1716, a ratio of vehicles to police of about 1:5. Modern technology did not ease the traffic workload of the force but added to it by providing scientific instruments—amphometers, breathalysers, digitectors, radar guns, red-light cameras—that enabled police to obtain higher standards of evidence but generated more work because they produced many more charges, being simple to operate and providing instant evidence. Similarly, aeroplanes, helicopters and high-powered pursuit vehicles were all used to combat the road toll, but they soaked up manpower. The employment of civilians to release trained police from clerical and other non-operational duties was one way of boosting the number of police available for patrol, but it was not fully effective. The number of public servants rose from 108 in 1946 to 1303 in 1983, but the ratio of public servants to police of 1:6 remained fairly constant from the 1960s, and many policemen still performed tasks that could arguably have been done better and more cheaply by civilians. Likewise, the retired police reserve was not a significant means of releasing police for active duty; during the 1970s the reserve strength was only about forty-two.[3]

As the motor vehicle became a principal contact point between police and members of the public, it did the greatest damage to relations. A 1969 study by Chappell and Wilson found that 'resentment towards the police was particularly strong among members of the motoring public', and that 'lack of respect for the police increases with the number of miles driven per year'. They suggested that police–community relationships suffered because of 'frequent and unpleasant encounters with police officers over traffic breaches. Motorists who are booked by police for what they consider to be trivial offences feel that the police should be spending their time on much more serious crimes such as burglary and theft'. The aggrieved motorists might be wrong, but were they entirely wrong? In 1982, of 189 987 major crime offences reported to police, only one-quarter were solved, whereas in the same year police detected 499 825 traffic offences, conducted 110 858 breathalyser and preliminary breath tests and attended to 39 828 road traffic collisions. In a famous *Punch* cartoon a young girl being safely ushered across a roadway by a policeman asks her mother what policemen did before there were motor cars. Prudently her mother does not answer, but she might well have said, 'Protected people and property against law breakers, my dear . . . and tested shop door handles!' She might have missed a point or two, but she also would have made one.[4]

Streetscapes changed after the war, society changed and the pattern of crime changed—and escalated. Crime increased far more than the population growth or the ratio of police to public, and new crime trends emerged, reflecting significant social, economic and technological changes within the community. Narcotic drug abuse, almost unheard of in the 1950s, was rampant by 1983, along with massive-scale organized crime, including murders executed for a fee. Arson was an industry. Armed robbery, rape and other serious crimes of violence were so commonplace as to be barely newsworthy. Burglary more than doubled in ten years, and more than quadrupled in twenty: in 1983 a burglary was committed somewhere in Victoria every seven minutes. In the words of one Chief Commissioner, S. I. Miller,

> armed robbery is an accepted fact of everyday life, everyone's home is vulnerable to burglary, it's not uncommon for women to be raped in their own homes, elderly women are routinely victims of handbag snatchers, it is becoming increasingly unsafe to walk the streets at night and the motoring mayhem continues on our roads.

Figure 3 illustrates just how dramatic some of the increases in reported crime were between 1945 and 1983. The reasons for the rising crime rate were many and complex, but it stretched the thin blue line even thinner. Police were (and are) not coping with crime. They were not preventing its commission or solving enough of it, and they seemed unlikely ever to have sufficient personnel to do so.[5]

Before World War II many towns had their solitary night watchman, who for a small fee rattled doors and exchanged knowing nods with beat constables during the twilight hours. But these services were anachronistic, even rustic, and were more a matter of form than effect. From the 1950s a burgeoning private security industry took up the slack and offered the public—for a price—the close personal security attention that police did not provide. It was estimated that the private security industry in the 1980s employed more people than there were police. If you wanted your shop door tested, your money carried, your house guarded or your life protected, you could pay for it on top of contributing taxes to the police budget. In November 1983 there were in Victoria 5755 licensed private agents, including 3490 watchmen, who were but the front line of a much

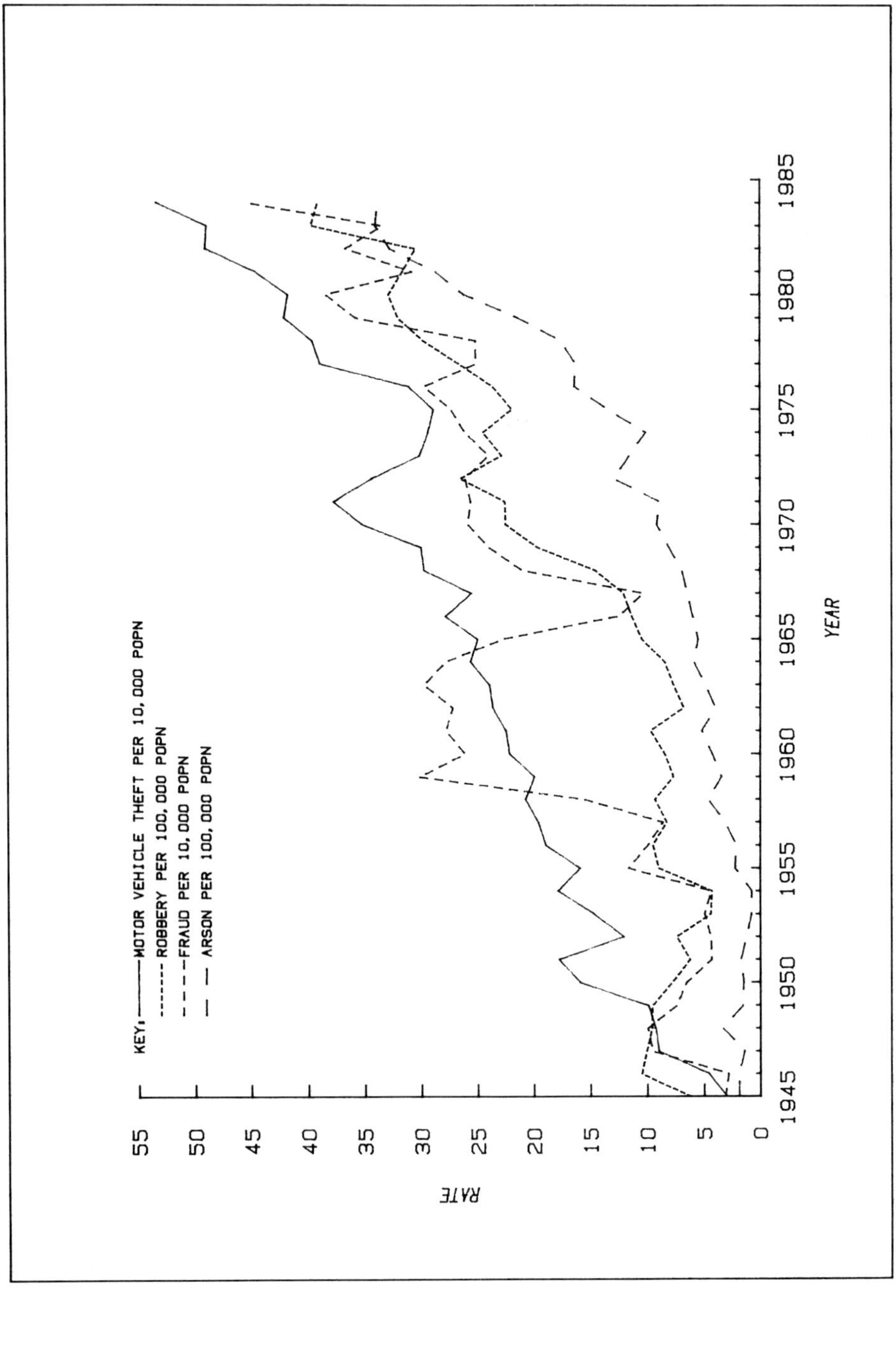
KEY: —— MOTOR VEHICLE THEFT PER 10,000 POPN
------ ROBBERY PER 100,000 POPN
- - - FRAUD PER 10,000 POPN
— — ARSON PER 100,000 POPN
RATE
0
5
10
15
20
25
30
35
40
45
50
55
YEAR
1945
1950
1955
1960
1965
1970
1975
1980
1985

Figure 3: Graph showing increases in selected reported crimes 1945–1984 (Victoria)

Note: no figures available for 1966, 1967 for arson

bigger industry employing thousands of people in the manufacture, sales and installation of alarms, locks, safes, and other security devices, together with security advisers, bodyguards, 'bouncers', store and house detectives, and a plethora of people selling 'peace of mind' to those unable or unwilling to do it themselves and reluctant to trust their security to the police. From the 1950s there also emerged a range of quasi-police and law enforcement personnel in the public sector. The Victorian Railways had long had their own 'investigators', but they were now joined by Education Department security men, university and college security staffs, municipal traffic and by-laws officers and a montage of uniformed, plain-clothed and undercover personnel doing security and investigative work for government and semi-government bodies. So extensive was this network of non-police security people that it was not known exactly how many there were, who they all represented or precisely what they all did. Yet many of them performed tasks once undertaken by police, and for some people they served as a bulwark against the insecurity of modern urbanized living, which fleeting glimpses of the 'divvy van' did little to dissipate.

Although the private security industry was large and constantly expanding, it was operated by entrepreneurs, and its services could never be equated with those of the police force. The industry was not there to support the police but to make money and serve sectional interests. Private security services were available only to the businesses and individuals that could afford to pay. The industry was attracted to those fields where it could profit and its concern about crime and disorder was not general but centred on the special needs and concerns of its customers. Indeed, it is arguable that the growth of private security organizations was not in the best interests of the community as a whole. If in the 1950s and 1960s people had tried to develop community-based responses to the rising crime rate, rather than turning to enterpreneurs, there might have then emerged a more healthy community awareness and a sense of collective responsibility for the problem. Instead, many wealthy people and those in the commercial sector used insurance and private security services in an effort to insulate themselves from the root causes and effects of crime. This boosted the security industry but it did not stop the overall rise in crime or the escalating burglary rate in particular. These problems were left largely in the hands of an overworked police force and it was not until crimes such as housebreaking reached epidemic proportions that positive and non-profit community initiatives emerged.[6]

Two of the main problems underlying the diminishing ability of the police to cope with their mounting workload were their dependence on traditional methods, and the reluctance of large sections of the community to actively support the police. In 1979 a Deputy Commissioner commented that his primary task during the preceding ten years had been 'to grab the police force by the scruff of the neck and drag it into the twentieth century'. His exaggeration was pardonable. It was not until the 1970s that the force first used computers and aircraft, undertook large-scale systematic planning and research, and underwent a programme of innovation and reorganization that went a long way towards finally shattering its nineteenth-century mould. Despite all its changes before the 1970s, the force had still failed to match the rate of social change within Victoria and had not optimized its available resources to meet the challenges. The relative inefficiencies of the force stretched its resources thinner than proper management would have permitted.[7]

The community too had a hand in this. Many people had abrogated their traditional community responsibility. Excusing themselves with 'I don't want to get involved', many people were willing to stand as idle and mute witnesses, while their neighbours' houses were burgled, their friends' children molested, their local shopkeepers' wares pilfered, and their district policemen abused and battered by mobs at local hotels and sporting grounds. Since ancient times all effective forms of maintaining social order have depended upon community involvement. This concept was the essence of Sir Robert Peel's 'New Police' formed in 1829, upon which the Victorian force was in some important senses closely modelled. From the start, Peel's force was to be a democratic body 'understanding the people, belonging to the people, and drawing its strength from the people'. In 1856 Chief Commissioner MacMahon drew upon that idea when he wrote, 'A constabulary force can only obtain complete success with the general support of the community'. The police have never had the full support of the community, and the pace and style of modern urban living, and modern insularity, contributed substantially towards overtaxing the resources of policemen who were all too often expected to do their work without an adequate level of active community support. The fact is that the police never were—never should be—expected to go it alone. The 1980s witnessed a sudden awareness of this when communities rallied to support each other and the police in a bid to combat crime. Neighbourhood Watch, a community-based crime prevention programme, aimed 'to reduce the rate of crime, particularly residential burglary, by involving the community in active crime prevention', is a classic example of a renewed public awareness that 'neighbours' have a role and responsibility to care for each other. Chief Commissioner Miller described it as a 'back to basics approach' that involved 'turning the clock back'.[8]

No one is ever able to turn the clock right back, and the 'good old days'—which arguably never were—are gone. Motor cars, drugs, robberies, burglaries, organized crime, and their attendant misery and violence were entrenched features of modern living. However, some relief might be found whenever people of all hues—political, socio-economic and racial—combine with the police to ensure the security and safety of all. Police alone can never cope. The thin blue line must be part of a rainbow of community involvement, with collective well-being and peace of mind as its pot of gold.

Age of Dissent

On 4 July 1968 two thousand demonstrators congregated outside the United States Consulate in Commercial Road, Prahran, to protest against America's involvement in the Vietnam war. It was not the first street demonstration in Melbourne during the 1960s but it turned into the first major violent confrontation between police and protesters since the depression, and it marked the beginning of a new phase in antagonism between police and sections of the public. Windows were smashed, police cars were damaged, thirty people were injured, including a policeman who was slashed with a razor blade, and twenty-six people were arrested. These arrests prompted further demonstrations outside police headquarters and the city watch-house, where stones were hurled at police. It was a tumultuous chain of events that reflected international trends in student protest and a groundswell of public opposition to the war in Vietnam. Victorian police, like many other sections of the community, were not ready for mass street demonstrations and rallies, and appeared not to understand what was happening or why. The police response was the traditional one of confrontation. In the immediate wake of 4 July the Chief Commissioner, Rupert Arnold, spoke ill of 'so-called intellectuals who want to change the world', and insensitively observed that with demonstrators who 'wanted absolute freedom, it would be a simple matter to drop them on uninhabited desert islands'. Outlining the official police view of 'demonstrations in public places', he warned that police had 'the right to take instant action by way of arrest', and promised to stamp out demonstrations 'with all expedition wherever they occur, using all the force required'. At a police graduation parade he referred to instances of student violence occurring in Mexico, Paris and the United States, but he appeared oblivious to the underlying causes of this global phenomenon, and made the declaration of a parochial policeman, 'So long as I am Chief Commissioner . . . I require it to be crushed in its incipient stages with all the force necessary'.[9]

The strong line adopted by Arnold was hardly surprising. Appointed Chief Commissioner on 15 October 1963, to replace Porter who died in office, Arnold at nearly 60 years of age was the oldest man ever given the position. He was the first serving member since Nicholson (in 1922) to be entrusted with the job, and he stamped it with the same lack-lustre conservatism that had led to Nicholson's downfall. Arnold's term was marked by a relative absence of organizational reform or progress. The principal innovations of his time were not due to his own work but coincided with his appointment; they included a regrouping of specialized districts according to function, and the appointment of H. V. Clugston, Reginald Jackson and Noel Wilby to newly created positions as Assistant Commissioners. In his first Chief Commissioner's message Arnold promised 'that no reforms are contemplated by me' and, as an augury of things to come, he addressed the subjects of hooliganism and young people with the lament that 'justice sometimes is too tempered with mercy'. He was, however, encouraged that a 'recent flaunting of principles of good citizenship' was 'put down' by police in a 'vigorous way'.

Arnold, previously a farm labourer, joined the force in 1924 during the boom recruiting period after the police strike, and was schooled as a constable under Blamey's tough anti-union administration, when protests and marches were things to be quickly crushed. Arnold's experience of public protest, like that of his brother senior officers, was limited. They had all joined in the 1920s and 1930s, when confrontationist policy was in operation against communists, unionists and unemployed. In these

A bloody confrontation: Melbourne, 4 July 1968

struggles burly working men often gave police almost as good as they got, and neither passive resistance nor police restraint was practised. In later years there was a hiatus in much of this activity as Australia entered first the war, then the contented 1950s; apart from crowd control duty at sporting venues, few policemen dealt with large assemblages of people, let alone hostile mobs or groups wanting to 'take to the streets'. Most senior policemen of Arnold's vintage did not have the benefit of formal command training and had no experience of controlling large hostile crowds. The force did not have contingency plans to counter such eventualities and relevant subjects were not taught at the Officers College. The police could not have anticipated the 'youth revolution', student unrest and mass street demonstrations of the 1960s. When the age of dissent did dawn, a generation of police blooded in the pre-war years simply fell back on traditional police practices. York describes the police environment as 'a radical Right milieu, implicitly endorsed and encouraged by government legislation which criminalised certain forms of dissent'. He is a trifle doctrinaire but basically correct.[10]

The confrontation on 4 July and Arnold's hard-line policy caused considerable concern to both conservatives and radicals, for different reasons, but they were really only developmental phases in the emergence of street protests as a legitimate and commonplace community forum—and in the formulation of a fuller and more understanding police response to them. Demonstrations did not begin with the Vietnam war nor end with it. Arnold did not 'stamp them out', nor was it desirable that he should do so. The 1960s and 1970s were decades of changing values and goals, and the force was compelled by social forces to adapt its philosophy and methods, to meet the challenges posed by people who took to the streets in a bid to end wars, save lives, challenge political systems and, in a sense, to 'change the world'.

It was the scale, composition and frequency of the protest groups that made them remarkable in the 1960s. Since the time of the miners' protest at the Eureka Stockade, police in Victoria had been called upon on many different occasions to deal with people gathered in groups to promote a particular cause or protest against some action or inaction. Depending upon the prevailing political climate, the nature of the issue, the mood and size of the crowd, and the degree of violence used, these protests have been variously labelled as insurrections, riots, rallies, marches, meetings, demonstrations, sit-ins, occupations, pickets and industrial disputes. Regardless of the label, all embodied the common factor of people in protest and, until the 1970s, mostly elicited a police response of confrontation and attempted suppression. In 1854 armed police and troopers stormed the Eureka Stockade; in 1873 police drew revolvers to break up a miners' dispute at Clunes; from the 1890s until after World War I militant trades unionists were routed by the police; in 1928 police shot and wounded

Chief Commissioner
R. H. Arnold

protesting dock workers; in 1932 police used batons to break up a peaceful march of unemployed men in Flinders Street; in the 1950s police confronted the 'youth problem' by the formation of a 'bodgie squad' and the use of force; and in the 1960s street protesters were met by barricades and lines of mounted and foot police in confrontations that, like the one on 4 July 1968, ended in ugly violence and personal injury. They were the typical police responses to community dissent over 130 years. The traditional approach was legalistic: if protesters broke laws—even relatively minor ones relating to such things as traffic obstruction—they had to be routed or arrested. This notion embraced the idea that an 'unlawful' but peaceful protest was impossible; the *Victoria Police Journal* once said, 'Let us face it squarely, there is no such thing as a peaceful demonstration, unless, of course, you are home in bed!'[11]

The 1960s protest movement is generally regarded as having its genesis in the student uprisings at Berkeley, California, in 1964, which were emulated in universities throughout much of the western world, including those at Melbourne, Monash and La Trobe. There is no doubt that student unrest and political activism contributed much towards fomenting the more general mass dissent exhibited during the Vietnam war period, but it is important to note, particularly in the context of the police response, that protests had occurred both on and off university campuses in Melbourne before Berkeley, and that from the late 1950s police had trouble understanding and controlling the behaviour of groups of young people around Melbourne. In the police *Annual Report* published each year from 1958 to 1965, first Porter, then Arnold, expressed concern about the trend for teenagers to congregate in groups and misbehave in public places. They regarded this trend as a sign of 'social disorder', the teenagers themselves as 'truculent groups of youths', and their behaviour as 'hooliganism' that needed to be put down by 'summary justice'. This was not new. It had happened before in bygone years when police confronted larrikin street pushes, who wore distinctive attire and had colourful names like the Golden Dragons, the Montague Dingoes and the Richmond Dirty Dozen. Since then, however, police had functioned in a long and fairly quiet phase, and they experienced trouble adjusting to the reality of a suddenly changing society in which there was also a greater proportion of teenagers than ever before. These young people were made all the more conspicuous by increasing affluence and the mobility afforded by motor vehicles. It was the nascent age of television, rock and roll music, Elvis Presley, the Beatles, and youth fads that included bodgies, widgies, rockers, jazzers and denim jeans.

The group behaviour—or misbehaviour—of teenagers was met by police in the traditional legalistic and confrontationist way, in what one writer describes as 'a virtual anti-youth campaign'. Porter advocated the use of 'summary justice' and formed a 'bodgie squad' to rout 'hooligans' from city streets. On a more general level Arnold later authorized 'a drive' of more than one thousand police 'to stamp out unseemly conduct, particularly in the vicinity of dance halls'. It was a generational problem and a precursor of things to come. Along with governments and large sections of the community, the police failed to adapt to shifting demographic patterns, changing educational levels, and the values and goals of young people. In 1967 a study by Chappell and Wilson highlighted the fact that 'people under 25 years of age had much less respect for the police than did older informants'; that both the police and the public considered 'teenagers to be a group in conflict with the police'; and that there was a strong inverse relationship 'between the level of education of the respondent and the degree of esteem held for the police'. Police, on the other hand, expressed 'opinions with a strong anti-intellectual, anti-educational bias'. This was part of the harvest of conflict and dissent, sown by seeds of ignorance in the 1950s.

The teenage behavioural problems that police endeavoured to counter with the 'bodgie squad approach' were not political, and in their efforts to curb the errant ways of budding 'rock 'n rollers' police enjoyed considerable support from middle Australia—parents, teachers, clergy and community leaders—who were concerned about the path Australia's youth might tread. Few people wanted their children to become swashbuckling, leather-clad clones of the sort portrayed by Marlon Brando in the cultist 1954 motorcycle film *The Wild One*. The 1960s introduced a new element: young people, particularly university students, became noticeably active and vocal on a range of political and social issues, such as capital punishment and racism. Labelled as 'radicalization' this movement did not simply involve young people 'at play' or students participating in debates on key social issues. It produced public protests—on and off university campuses—including anti-apartheid demonstrations in 1960, following the Sharpeville massacres in South Africa; demonstrations against the White Australia Policy during the 1961 election campaigns; and protests against capital punishment in 1962, when Robert Tait was sentenced to be hanged at Pentridge Gaol.[12]

It was in 1962 that the Australian Government first sent thirty army advisers to South Vietnam, thereby involving Australia in a war that eventually polarized the nation and cast protesters and police into their most violent, bloody and large-scale confrontations. The related issues of military conscription and the Vietnam war gave full vent to the radicalization of student protest, and the crescendo of demonstrations and violence that spread throughout the community culminated in the largest street demonstration ever seen in Australia, and brought into question the traditional police practice of confrontation. It could not work against one hundred thousand people. And much of middle Australia had taken to the streets in protest or supported those who did—signalling to governments and the police that it was time for a change.

It did not happen overnight. The first anti-Vietnam war protest in Melbourne was staged on 9 August 1964, Hiroshima Day, and only two hundred people took part. This was in the same year that the Menzies government sent another thirty army advisers to Vietnam and introduced a National Service Bill to provide a selective (birthday ballot) call-up of 20-year-old males for two-year periods of military service. Australia's official commitment to the war, and opposition to it, then escalated steadily. In 1965 the Menzies government committed an Australian army battalion to Vietnam, and amended legislation to permit the use of conscripted national servicemen overseas. In 1966 Australia's military presence in Vietnam was increased to 4500 troops, who for the first time included national servicemen; police in Melbourne clashed with hostile demonstrators during the visit of the United States President, Lyndon B. Johnson; and in other confrontations protesters held vigils outside the home of the Prime Minister, Harold Holt, and staged a sit-down during Melbourne's annual Moomba Parade. In 1967 large crowds of demon-

strators and police confronted each other during the visit to Melbourne of Air Vice-Marshal Ky, the Prime Minister of South Vietnam. In 1968 protests against the war were perennial, the Draft Resisters Movement was formed, there was the bloody battle between police and protesters on 4 July and an attempt later to firebomb the United States Consulate. In 1969 the events of the previous year were largely repeated and W. D. Crowley, the secretary of the Police Association, issued a plea on behalf of embattled police, duty bound 'to stand in pouring rain, outnumbered ten to one, facing a howling mob of malcontents [who were] . . . armed with sticks, stones, flour-bombs, bottles and dangerous fire crackers', and expected 'to do so without recourse to counter violence'.[13]

It was on 8 May 1970 that the tide turned. On that day Dr Jim Cairns headed the first Vietnam Moratorium in Melbourne, a march of 100 000 people who sat down in Bourke Street, bringing the city to a standstill. It was claimed to be the largest demonstration in the history of Australia and in that crowd of people—labelled by Billy Snedden, the Minister for Labor and National Service, as 'political bikies pack-raping democracy' —were students, teachers, clergy, community leaders, parents, grandparents and returned servicemen. Over one thousand police—a quarter of the force—were on duty at the Moratorium that day. There was no confrontation, no arrests and no violence. What one senior police officer later described as an anticlimax was in fact a climax, a pinnacle of peaceful protest.[14]

Although the Moratorium was hailed as a success, the war went on, and subsequent moratoriums were held in September 1970 and June 1971. These were smaller demonstrations than the first, but the pattern of non-violence was repeated. There were no more moratoriums of that sort after it was announced in 1971 that all Australian troops were being withdrawn from Vietnam, but they had introduced a new era in public protest. They were massive, essentially non-violent, successful demonstrations, involving 'ordinary people' and were organized and led by people with a strong ideological commitment to peace.

Even so, there could not be eternal peace between police and protesters. Not all protesters supported the idea of non-violence, nor were all political ideologies amenable to it. Not all protest movements involved responsible leaders and 'ordinary people', nor could the police always be relied upon to exercise discipline and restraint. Even at the height of the Vietnam Moratorium Campaign—when peaceful protest could be seen to be working—there were several extremist groups who wanted to provoke a confrontation with the police. During the moratorium on 18 September 1970 Cairns was greeted with derision and jeers from a section of

The moratorium march: Bourke Street, Melbourne, 1970

the marchers, when he avoided a confrontation with police by agreeing to a request to remain in William Street and did not attempt to breach police lines in order to lead the march along Swanston Street. Some splinter groups did attempt to breach the lines but rejected claims that they were a 'disruptive minority' and labelled Cairns as a 'peace phoney'. At times peace was tenuous.[15]

Studies of student anti-conscription activities and the police response to them suggest that police violence 'brought the war home', and protesters whose original civil disobedience focus was anti-war, anti-conscription, and anti-American imperialism, were easily turned by police violence into enemies of the police. This was evident at La Trobe University during September 1970, when the actions of policemen dispersing a pre-Moratorium march prompted students and others to hold two further marches in protest against the war in Vietnam—and police brutality. On 11 September what started out as 'just another pre-Moratorium local activity' involving about one hundred people, ended in a mélée on the fringes of the university where baton-wielding policemen were stoned by demonstrators who had been moved against for traffic obstruction. One policeman was hospitalized with a head wound, three marchers were arrested and students later accused the police of savage brutality and harassment.

Indignant at what had occurred, four hundred students and supporters held another protest march five days later, from the Northland shopping centre towards La Trobe University. Again violence flared in Waterdale Road, West Heidelberg—after the march had peacefully covered several kilometres—when policemen intervened to minimize traffic obstruction, and eighteen marchers were arrested for offensive behaviour, using indecent language and obstructing police. The degree of violence used by policemen to disperse the march and make arrests was criticized by many people including student groups, the university administration, the Victorian Council for Civil Liberties, and the Labor Party. A university chaplain, the Reverend Doctor Ian Parsons, was a witness to the fray and, in a letter to the *Age*, he expressed 'complete disgust at the police behaviour', describing it as 'the cheapening of authority by its radical misuse'. Doctor A. D. Ward, then a senior lecturer at the university, lamented that 'the police broke the spirit of co-operation' by 'the sudden pulling of batons' on the marchers, and 'a sickening use of force'. These feelings were inflamed when the officer-in-charge of police at the march was reported in the newspapers as saying, 'They got some baton today and they'll get a lot more in the future'. A subsequent police internal investigation described this statement as 'ill-considered', and found that an 'apparently inoffensive march' was turned into 'a chaotic situation' by a combination of factors, including the use of batons by policemen 'to shepherd demonstrators from the road', the police being 'insufficiently briefed or organized', 'previous police tolerance' being 'suddenly with-drawn without sufficient warning', and some policemen acting out of a sense of retribution. It was recommended that the force formulate clear policies for action at such marches and that policemen be trained accordingly.

Two weeks after the 'Waterdale Road Riot' five hundred people pro-tested against police brutality by again marching from the Northland shopping centre to the university. In spite of what were generally regarded as deliberate attempts by a militant minority to provoke the police into violence, there was none. The march passed peacefully and there were no arrests. In a second letter to the *Age* Parsons wrote, 'Some students did all they could to provoke a police confrontation . . . [but the police] were not drawn into one. On this occasion the police won the moral victory . . . The forbearance of the constabulary is to be commended'. And Ward endorsed those comments, adding that the police conduct 'revealed skill and restraint of a high order . . . [They] seemed to realise that methods possibly appropriate to a rioting football crowd are not appropriate for a demonstration of deep-seated social protest'. Some police did appear to have learned that much, and had shown by their own actions that violence could provoke retaliation and resentment, whereas non-violence and restraint could defuse it. Old attitudes lingered, however, and one senior officer was worried that tolerance in the face of provocation and disorder 'impugned' the police role 'of maintaining law and order'.[16]

Not all the violence that ensued from public protests was initiated by the police, and there were many instances when protesters provocatively wore protective headgear and clothing and were aggressively armed with rocks, firecrackers, smoke bombs and a variety of home-made weapons to attack the police. In some cases the particular ideology of a protest or a section of protesters precluded peaceful demonstrations because of commitment to confrontation and violence as part of the cause. However, the general police approach to demonstrations before 1970 had been confrontationist, typified by action taken during Blamey's commis-sionership to repress working-class radicalism even when it was expressed in the form of a peaceful street march. The hard line had grown from a concern, still being expressed as late as 1970, that 'tolerance and understanding' might be 'mistaken for weakness and indecision', an unsuitable image for police who saw themselves as 'the last bastion between the community and an unruly mob determined to break the law'.[17]

On 3 July 1971, before conscription and Australia's involvement in the Vietnam war had ended, and while police and protesters were still toasting the success of their different roles in the achievement of peaceful moratoriums, serious violence erupted between police and anti-apartheid demonstrators at Melbourne's Olympic Park Stadium, during a rugby game involving a touring team from South Africa. As a public spectacle and source of media attention the rugby took second place to incidents in the terraces where '650 policemen with truncheons and horses took on about twice as many demonstrators'. There were 139 arrests and many people were injured, including one constable who suffered serious hearing damage when a firecracker exploded in his ear. The level of violence at Olympic Park was described as 'sickening' and was a sad contrast to the peace of the moratorium campaign. The anti-apartheid protest was a poorly organized fiasco that lacked mature leadership and peaceful goals. It had as its object the disruption of the game at any cost. There was no one of the moderation and stature of Cairns to lead the demonstration at Olympic Park, and in the opinion of the Special Branch it was for those reasons that disturbances followed. It was the last bloody confrontation of its type and scale, and precipitated moves to ensure lasting peace between police and protest organizers prepared to negotiate pacts of non-violence.[18]

Around the end of 1971 a series of unrelated events fortuitously came together to defuse the protest situation in Victoria. On 11 October 1971 S. I. Miller was appointed as Assistant Commissioner (Operations), giving him responsibility for the direction of police planning and preparations in cases of demonstrations. Miller had recently returned from Great Britain, where he attended the senior command course at 'Bramshill', the British National Police College. While there, Miller witnessed the civil strife and the police response to it in Northern Ireland, and he came home convinced that police actions in the face of demonstrations should, as far as possible, be low-key, non-violent and non-confrontationist.

On 21 October 1971 the Chief Secretary, R. J. Hamer, convened a meeting of police and citizen groups, under the chairmanship of the Under Secretary, J. V. Dillon, to establish an acceptable set of guidelines for the conduct of demonstrations. York dismisses the conference as 'gimmicky', but the conference unanimously accepted eleven recommended guidelines that have been adhered to ever since. Implicit in the guidelines is the right to demonstrate in public, and their essence is one of co-operation, planning, tolerance and the avoidance of violence. A significant achievement was the adoption of the rule that 'police and organisers should have preliminary discussions in every case. Police should be prepared to take the initiative in making contact with organisers where possible'. Traditionally, and such was the case during the Vietnam Moratorium Campaign, senior police refused to take the initiative in consulting officially and openly with protest organizers to ascertain their plans. Depending upon the mood and available information, police had generally relied upon covert intelligence gathering, or 'unofficial' sources, but insisted that their door was always open should protest organizers want to come to them. The only consultation between police and moratorium organizers before the mammoth march on 8 May 1970 occurred when an inspector 'unofficially' approached Cairns because the two knew each other from Cairns's days in the force.[19]

In the year after Miller's appointment and the adoption of demonstration guidelines, the Labor government led by Gough Whitlam swept into office. The Whitlam government brought the last Australian soldiers home from Vietnam and ended conscription, released all draft resisters who were in gaol and quashed all pending prosecutions under the National Service Act. Another source of community dissension was removed the same year when the Australian Cricket Board of Control decided not to proceed with a planned tour by the South African cricket team. With these changes, much of the vehemence disappeared from political and public life in Australia. For a while street demonstrators became 'less numerous' and were no longer the 'significant police problem' they once were. In stark contrast to the rousing messages of Arnold in 1968, the Chief Commissioner, Reginald Jackson, summarized the mood of 1972 when he addressed the force with the message:

> In a democratic society the right to stage a peaceful protest is accepted . . . In demonstration situations, it is imperative that police act with tolerance, discretion and understanding; and every reasonable effort must be made to avoid violence. Under these circumstances, minor offences which, in other circumstances might warrant arrest, may be ignored in the interests of preserving the overall situation; that is, by exercising tolerance and restraint, we endeavour to keep down the temperature of the situation.

For many people the age of dissent ended in 1972 and they returned to their more usual way of life, university studies and the business of sedate living. In the words of Donald Horne, 'by 1972 it was hard to get a big crowd together about anything . . . excitement that had been vaporised at meetings and marches was distilled into a more humdrum range of conventional political activity'.

This did not mean that dissent was dead. The operative word in Horne's statement was 'big'. What took place from 1972 was the regular occurrence of moderate demonstrations—in terms of both scale and ideology—involving 'ordinary people', who protested about a wide range of industrial, political, social, environmental and economic issues and who for the most part were gently shepherded by small groups of police. People took to streets, parks, shopping malls and city squares throughout Victoria to engage mostly in legitimate protest, but those ideologically committed to violence were still there and during one demonstration, on 21 April 1972, pyrotechnic flares were thrown at police horses. Jackson accurately described such doings as the work of a 'lunatic fringe'—forever present, fortunately a minority.[20]

From 1974 to 1982 the average annual number of demonstrations attended by police in Victoria was more than 150, with a peak of 204 in 1976. The requirement to plan for and respond to such eventualities was recognized in the 1970s as a specialist function, and this realization was one of the factors behind the formation of an Operations Department and an Independent Patrol Group.

Street demonstrations are now an accepted part of community and police life, and rarely do they result in confrontation or violence unless those protesting are committed to such a course or desire to inflame the situation to attract media coverage. It is not uncommon for several auton-omous demonstrations to be held simultaneously in different parts of Melbourne, each one requiring some police supervision. Regular attend-ance at these events is a drain on police resources and at times stretches the thin blue line perilously thin. Even though most demonstrations are peaceful they all require the presence of some policemen to ensure the safe passage of the protesters—as well as other pedestrian and vehicular traffic—and to keep the peace lest bystanders or opposing factions come into conflict with demonstrators. A feature of the police presence at dem-onstrations in recent years has been their conciliatory role, keeping the peace between rival groups such as unions involved in demarcation dis-putes, farmers and meatworkers disputing over meat exports, and pro- and anti-abortion protesters rallying at one location. The largest of these post-1972 demonstrations has required the deployment of up to four hun-dred police, and one typical industrial dispute in 1980 occupied three police cars and seven men for a total of 825 hours. It is the price of peace that most Victorians appear to want and are prepared to pay for.[21]

From the storming of the Eureka Stockade in 1854 up to the shepherding of fifteen thousand anti-nuclear demonstrators on Palm Sunday in 1984, the force has frequently been expected to deal with groups of people in dissent. Each with a cause and all wanting to be heard and noticed. Since 1854 there has been considerable confrontation, viol-ence and bloodshed, and throughout most of that time the police were backed by powerful elements within the community. The police actions have not taken place in an atmosphere devoid of political, legal or com-munity support. The Vietnam war era witnessed a peak in the intensity, frequency and scale of public demonstrations and a radical change in the police response to them, from a position of confrontation and conflict to one of consultation and co-operation. This was not simply a change in police tactics but embodied a change in attitudes and behaviour that was exemplified during 1984 when the 'mountain cattlemen' protested out-side Parliament House, Melbourne: among their number, atop his horse and cart, was an off duty 'mountain policeman'. This change was forced by the people of Victoria, and for the police it was a period of learning and metamorphosis. It stands as one of the clearest instances where the

268

Victorian community has shaped the thinking and actions of its police force. It gives real meaning to the notion that it is a force of the people.[22]

The Policeman's Position

In 1970 the secretary of the Police Association, W. D. Crowley, wrote:

> Currently, the Victoria Police Force is going through one of the most trying periods in its history. It is over forty years since we received anything like the present sensational adverse publicity. Police morale has undoubtedly received its biggest reverse since the police strike. At the same time, it is obvious that many members of the public are making a thoughtful re-assessment of the police 'image'.

The force was generally regarded by its members as being overworked, undermanned, underpaid and under siege. Police morale was in the doldrums and public attitudes to the force were often precariously ambivalent. Police were confronting a rising crime rate and road toll, had been buffeted by violent street demonstrations and other forms of public protest, and were in the full glare of media attention involving sensational allegations of corruption, malpractice and ineptitude. In defensive mood, police were prompted to lament that the 'popular sport of the day seems to be attacking the police force'.

In the years around 1970 the force, although used to being in the public eye, was the focus of an unusually high degree of attention from the media, academics, lawyers, government officials and the public generally. As well as the Vietnam Moratoriums, notable events during 1970 included a Royal Tour, and the collapse of the Westgate Bridge. The massive police presence on these occasions taxed the force's resources and put large numbers of police on display. Public attention was also focused on the force by the publication of *The Police and the Public in Australia and New Zealand* and *Police Killings in Australia*, works by university lecturers that reflected an international trend toward criminological research on police and related subjects. These books were the first of their kind published in Australia and received considerable publicity. In particular, Richard Harding's *Police Killings* was searing on some aspects of police behaviour and aroused the ire of many people, including policemen who contemplated suing him for libel. Harding's work purported to be a detailed analysis of fifteen cases showing 'a pattern of systematic abuse of the rules relating to deaths caused in arrest situations, at least in so far as those rules concerned police'. One police critic simple-mindedly described the study as a use of government monies 'to rubbish their own employees'. It was a common police attitude, and one that did nothing to placate people concerned with civil rights, who were 'left reeling' by Harding's findings. Both positions were extreme and not really justified.

269

Harding's study had considerable academic merit and social significance, and was deserving of serious attention by policemen—who had the option of heeding his message if his hypothesis proved correct, or of suing him if he was wrong. On the other hand, the cases analysed by Harding had all been widely canvassed before his work appeared, and no one should have reeled at his findings, which paled alongside other events that occurred about the time *Police Killings* was published.[23]

In 1969 Mrs Inez Corry died when a motor car driven by her husband collided with a police divisional van at the intersection of Warrigal and Dandenong Roads, Oakleigh. The driver of the police vehicle was later suspended from duty and charged with culpable driving but was acquitted by a county court jury in April 1970. The investigation and legal proceedings following the collision took more than a year to finalize and, during that period, there was some division and bitterness within the force on the subject of paying the accused constable's legal costs. Funds to meet these costs were largely raised by a financial appeal within the force but the Police Association 'made up the balance' in a gesture claimed to be 'the first time ever that the police association has paid for the defence of a member on an indictable criminal charge'. This question of legal support was given publicity in the press and on television in a manner that irked many policemen. There was also bad publicity for the force over the police defence, which was that the divisional van was pursuing a speeding yellow Holden Monaro at the time of the crash. The coroner described this claim as 'improbable' and the yellow Monaro as 'mythical'. Although the constable was acquitted, not all public doubts about the case were dispelled and the coroner's comments lingered in the minds of many people—inflamed by other events of the period. For there came more trouble.[24]

On 26 March 1971 Neil Collingburn, a man well-known to police, was admitted to St Vincent's Hospital in Melbourne with an injured duodenum, after being taken into police custody earlier that day for questioning at Russell Street about possession of a set of golf clubs that were later established to be his own property. Collingburn died in hospital two days later and, following an internal police investigation, two policemen were suspended from duty and charged with manslaughter. As in the culpable driving case the year before, a county court jury acquitted those charged, but not before the death and related events had attracted sensational public attention. Reports of the case filled pages of newspapers, and an *Age* editorial headed 'Why did he die?' echoed the thoughts of many people when it described the circumstances surrounding the death as 'disturbing' and the implications as 'alarming'. In some circles the case became a *cause célèbre*. Demonstrations were held in the city; unionists stopped work and seven thousand waterfront workers went on strike; staff from the law school at the University of Melbourne demanded to know why the policemen were not charged with murder; and a black-painted mock coffin was left on the doorstep of the Russell Street police station. Student political groups linked the Collingburn case with their more general anti-police line during activities directed against conscription and the Vietnam war. The chant of 'Who killed Collingburn?' emerged during anti-war marches and 'assumed a certain vogue with demonstrators' in Melbourne during the early 1970s. The Collingburn case was given prominence in student publications, and broadsheets headed 'Murder' and 'Murderers—they killed Collingburn' appeared in Melbourne streets. One section of such an article reminded readers of the earlier published findings of Harding with regard to police killings, while another assumed the guilt of one of the policemen involved because he had 'an Irish name'. For the force it was far from good press, and moves were initiated by the Police Association to take action for criminal libel to suppress what were described as 'outrageous' publications. It was a pitiful response from the police, who instead of wasting their efforts on the suppression of inflammatory student broadsheets, should have been making a thoughtful reassessment of their own position and behaviour. They would have discovered that the police image had been tarnished by the actions of policemen and that dwindling public confidence in the force was justified.[25]

The Corry and Collingburn tragedies stand as the opening and closing parts of a trilogy that had as its dramatic and prolonged centrepiece the abortion inquiry. Described in the *Age* as 'one of the most sensational and controversial public inquiries and criminal trials this State has experienced', the saga began in earnest during June 1969 when a relatively unknown general practitioner, Dr Bertram Wainer, publicly claimed that policemen were taking bribes from those illegal operators, the abortionists. Wainer was a member of the Abortion Law Reform Association, with a private medical practice in St Kilda. He had migrated to Australia from his native Scotland in 1949 with free passage as an ex-serviceman, and his career after arriving included graduating from the University of Melbourne with degrees in medicine, residency at Prince Henry's Hospital, and service as a medical officer in the Australian army. In a bid to expose police corruption and reform abortion law and practices in Victoria, Wainer throughout the latter half of 1969 made allegations, sought interviews with members of the Government, published notices in newspapers, and issued affidavits. His tirelessness reached a pitch on 9 December 1969 when six affidavits were handed to the Solicitor-General, B. L. Murray, QC, alleging that high-ranking policemen had accepted bribes from abortionists. The Chief Commissioner was directed by the Government to investigate the allegations, but five of the deponents refused to be questioned by him, forcing the Government to appoint an independent board of inquiry.

William Kaye, QC, was appointed as a one-man board of inquiry on 5 January 1970 to establish whether members of the police force had demanded or accepted money from persons connected with abortion in Victoria. The board sat from 12 January 1970 to 28 May 1970, taking evidence from 140 persons. Specific allegations were made against seven former and serving policemen, including a former Deputy Commissioner, and it was generally alleged that corruption had flourished in Melbourne since 1953 and that this activity centred on particular members of the élite Homicide Squad, who were paid up to $150 each a week to look after the interests of abortionists. This was at a time when the weekly wage of a detective sergeant was $122.

Kaye found against four men—Superintendent John Matthews, Inspector Jack Ford, retired Station Officer Frederick Adam and a former detective, Martin Jacobson—and all four stood trial in 1971 charged with conspiring to obstruct the course of justice, in that they had accepted bribes to protect the illegal activities of abortionists. Matthews, Ford and Jacobson were convicted and sentenced to gaol for five, five and three years respectively. When passing sentence Mr Justice Starke commented, 'By your conduct you have severely shaken the community's confidence in the Victoria Police Force, and inevitably I think the morale of the force itself must have been lowered'. He was right. The worst tragedy in this part of the trilogy was not that three policemen went to gaol, but that their activities shrouded an entire police force in a cloud of suspicion and innuendo. Although only three men were proved to have been involved in the scandal, the matter raised serious questions about more general aspects of the force because of the length of time over which the illegal activities had flourished, the seniority of the policemen involved and their prominent positions in police and public life. Some people were also perhaps mindful of the serious allegations of police malpractice made by Brian Latch during the 1960s. There were repeated calls for a royal commission to inquire into the general running of the force and much talk of the need for police reform. Many people did not accept the simplistic notion that all was basically well with the force except for the activities of a few 'rotten apples'. The *Age* was a staunch advocate of moves to review the force, and one editorial arguing the case for police reform warned that 'It would be naive to suppose that responsible Ministers and officials, and successive police chiefs, could have had no inkling of what was going on'.[26]

The minister responsible for the police force from June 1955 until his resignation from parliament in March 1971 was Sir Arthur Rylah, who served all that time in the conservative Liberal Party government of Sir Henry Bolte. The Chief Commissioner from 1 February 1969 until his premature retirement due to ill health in 1971 was Noel Wilby. A career policeman, he joined the force in 1937 and experienced an unusually quick rise to the top, passing from sergeant to assistant commissioner dur-

Chief Commissioner
N. Wilby

ing 1963, in less than nine months. His background included uniform duty at Footscray and Williamstown, service with the wireless patrol, interchange duty in Brisbane and extensive experience in the CIB, including time with the Homicide Squad. Wilby was held in high regard by many who knew him but he succeeded Arnold during difficult times, when the image of the force was already tarnished and his own influence on it was limited by failing health. His commissionership is principally remembered for the action he took during 1970 to phase out the legendary wireless patrol and replace it with a network of smaller crime car squads. Wilby inherited a force in which the vital areas of organizational development, innovation and reform had largely been allowed to stagnate for six years, while Arnold fulfilled his promise of 'no reforms'. He also inherited responsibility for the abortion scandal, and life at the top was made particularly onerous for Wilby when, in his first year as Chief Commissioner, the Bolte government directed him to investigate personally the allegations made by Wainer and others in the sworn affidavits delivered to the solicitor-general.[27]

The concern expressed by the *Age* and others that something was

273

seriously wrong with the force was well founded. It was not limited to police corruption or illegal behaviour, however. The rot undermining the force included these taints, but they existed largely because the force was suffering from a more general and complex combination of political neglect, public apathy, maladministration, demoralizingly low pay and sub-standard work benefits. Conditions within the force were not good enough to attract or retain the best people, nor to ensure optimum performance from serving members. The seniority system stifled ability, opportunity and effort. Policemen worked hard and long for rewards that were so meagre that they would have prompted industrial action from more militant workers, and their pay was not sufficient to place them above the sort of common temptations offered by S.P. bookmakers, hotelkeepers trading after hours and shopkeepers wanting special favours. The force was in urgent need of review, not because corruption flourished, but because conditions conducive to it did, and only a major shake-up could stop the slide. The policeman's position—like his image—was not good.

The force that Wilby commanded numbered 4700 policemen, 122 policewomen and 1500 public servants. There was one deputy commissioner, three assistant commissioners, 152 other officers, 1193 sub-officers and the balance of the force—more than 3400 men and women—comprised first constables and constables. There were 502 members in the criminal investigation branch and 320 in the mobile traffic section, but most policemen performed general uniform duties at one of the 392 police stations located throughout Victoria, including those in remote country towns. Most members of the force were far removed from the back rooms of power at Parliament House and police headquarters by geography, rank and socio-economic status. And the vast majority of them had neither been involved in cases of the sort exposed by Harding, nor personally involved in the abortion racket or any of the other sensational events of that period. Just as the Kelly saga had done almost a century before, the trilogy of events that centred on the abortion inquiry—with their attendant and ongoing sensational publicity—distorted the real picture and obscured from public view the facts that, not only were most members of the force not personally involved in the scandals, but also that they were something of a beleaguered minority group within the Victorian community who, against a demoralizing background of innuendo, were troubled by low pay, poor work conditions and an acute manpower shortage.[28]

In 1970 the starting pay of a constable was $60 per week, or roughly that of a tram conductor. Policemen were not paid incentive, bonus or over-award payments, nor permitted to supplement their incomes by working at a second job during their holidays or in their spare time. From 1955 to 1970 constables in Victoria lost pay relativity with the general workforce to the extent of 27.56 per cent. One study found that policemen were not receiving their 'fair share of the economic cake' and were not paid sufficiently to remunerate them 'for the exacting nature of police work', or to make it 'unnecessary for them to seek additional employment'. In December 1970 the weekly salary of a constable was 21.24 per cent below the average weekly wage.

Policemen were not generally paid for overtime worked; government policy was that they should take time off instead, which depleted scarce manpower resources and caused discontent among policemen who wanted monetary payment. They believed, as did the President of the ACTU, Mr R. J. Hawke, that it was 'inequitable in the extreme' that they were 'abstracted from the labour market' when they could not abstract themselves 'from the operation of the commodity market'. Payment for overtime worked was a universally accepted practice in the general community, and the average adult male employee in Victoria was then receiving overtime payment for 5.3 hours a week. Had policemen shared in that benefit, the average uniformed policeman would have been paid an extra $11 a week.

That the more senior members were paid at a higher rate than the junior ranks was of little consolation to first constables and constables—the two most numerous ranks—because promotion was slow and depended largely on seniority. The average age of sergeants in the force was forty-six and promotion to that rank was taking eighteen years. In 1969 the Chief Commissioner dealt with 1721 vacancies and in all but forty-two cases the successful applicant was the senior applicant. Due to 'the deadening mediocrity' of the seniority rule, relatively well-educated young men were forced 'to wait twenty years or more before reaching even a minor supervisory position'. It was a source of bitterness and a cause of resignations.

Ancillary benefits available to members were better than their basic pay, but were not sufficiently lucrative to attract and retain enough recruits or compensate for the distasteful side of police duties. Every policeman was eligible to participate in the State Superannuation Scheme, and had access to the police provident fund and the services offered at the police hospital. All police were issued free with their first uniform and were paid an allowance to maintain and renew it. Additionally, there was a range of monetary allowances for particularly onerous or specialist work, including the payment of sixty cents a night for working night shift and $3.85 a week for working a one-man police station. Each member received seven weeks annual recreational leave and fifteen days sick leave a year, which was cumulative, but there was no provision for public holidays such as Christmas Day. The police working-fortnight was divided into ten eight-hour shifts and four rest days, one of which was to be a Sunday, but the force was required on a roster basis to be on duty twenty-four hours a day, every day of the year, in all weathers and in the face of all hazards.[29]

Although constables were paid substantially less than other members of the community, much more was expected of them than was often expected of people who, in safe and comfortable surroundings, worked only day shift on weekdays for their much higher wages and better ancillary benefits. The job specifications for police applicants required that they be aged between 18½ and 32 years (35 years for returned servicemen), a minimum of 5 feet 8½ inches tall, 'of impeccable character and good family background' and able to pass a police educational entrance examination and a medical examination. The minimum education standard required of recruits was equivalent to second-year high school and the police entrance examination consisted of tests in arithmetic and English—spelling, dictation and expression—and an aptitude test of sixty-five questions to be answered in thirty-five minutes. The medical examination was one of the most demanding pre-employment medical checks in Australia and candidates were rejected for such things as vision less than 6/6, colour blindness, imperfect hearing, speech defects, and a range of 'disabilities' that included round shoulders, varicose veins, acne and flat feet. Applicants who passed these examinations were required to appear before a selection board and, if deemed suitable, were made the subject of further discreet enquiries, checking their references, previous employers and reputations— including their families' reputations—with local police. The Victoria Police entrance examinations were generally accepted as being the most difficult of any force in Australia, and the general entrance standards as the highest, exceeding those of the armed services and rivalling those of the Australian security organizations.

Candidates accepted into the force commenced their police careers at the Police Training Depot, St Kilda Road, Melbourne, where they underwent a twenty-week residential training course in elementary law and police duties, English, social studies, written expression, typing, boxing, wrestling, swimming, firearms training, physical training, fingerprinting, and first aid. While in training, recruits were subjected to a military-style discipline of parade drill, curfews, and fatigue duty each morning, doing such chores as sweeping floors and cleaning toilets. Uniforms and rooms were regularly inspected, and a demerit points system operated to ensure lots of spit and polish and little sign of dirt or dust. Many young men found the regimen of the training depot hard going and even on weekends, when dressed in ordinary street clothes, police trainees in the age of 'Hair' were made conspicuous and conscious of their new careers by their regulation short-back-and-sides haircuts.

At the end of twenty weeks training, recruits graduated from the Depot as sworn constables and entered a one-year probationary period, during which they were detailed on normal police duties and were required to satisfactorily complete a six-week retention course in law and police procedure, before being confirmed as permanent members of the force. Three separate appraisals of police training in Australia during 1968–71 rated the training system in Victoria as 'the most extensive and highly developed' in the nation.[30]

After they graduated from the Depot all constables were sent to the Russell Street police station where they were introduced to real police work, while they waited for their first suburban or country posting. In some cases this took a few days, in other cases many months. The not so fortunate found themselves 'shanghaied' to postings that more senior men did not want, such as the tougher inner-suburban police sub-districts, the records section and the city morgue. All members were liable to be posted anywhere within the state, at the direction of the Chief Commissioner, for the good of the service. The Chief Commissioner was also empowered to require any single man, widower or divorcee to reside in barracks, and this rule was applied to large numbers of junior constables at Russell Street so that it was both their place of residence and work. Life there was governed by the police *Standing Orders*, which forbade such things as pictures on the walls, alcohol, female visitors and television sets, and much of the regimen of depot life applied to the 126 men who called it 'home'.

Constables at Russell Street spent their working day on much the same routine duties as in police stations elsewhere, including mobile, bicycle and foot patrols, traffic duty, criminal investigation work, watch-house and enquiry-counter duties, paperwork and clerical tasks. Because of Russell Street's unique position as the central police station, men from there also performed security duty at Parliament House, Government House and the United States Consulate, escort duty with prisoners and payrolls, duty at demonstrations and sporting fixtures, patrol duty at Flinders Street railway station and aboard trains on the suburban rail network, and work as mortuary attendants at the city morgue at night.

The working life of policemen away from Russell Street was a continuum of what they did there, except that they generally encountered a greater range of situations and problems and had the benefit of past experience to see them through. Regardless of time or the day of the week, state of the weather or nature of the task, policemen were expected to be there, doing such things as delivering death messages, finding lost children, recovering bodies, quietening noisy parties, attending accidents, brawls and domestic disputes, chasing away prowlers and investigating reports of crime. Policemen, like front-line soldiers, are expected not to turn tail and run, even in the face of overwhelming odds or imminent danger. At the height of the police troubles in 1970 this was borne home to many policemen and members of the public when a mob of about one hundred men attacked three policemen outside the St Kilda football ground. One bystander described the attack as 'murderous' and 'frightening'. 'Speaking for myself', he went on, 'I find it difficult to see why anyone should want to become a policeman in this country'.[31]

There were obviously many who agreed with him. In that year 168 men and women resigned from the force, as 325 had done over the previous two years. The ratio of police to population in Victoria was 1:732—the worst in Australia. Each year from 1960 to 1970 the force failed to attract sufficient recruits to meet its authorized strength and in 1970 the shortfall was fifty-three, although a study of the force's real manpower needs in that year estimated that it was two thousand men below strength. The resignations and lack of recruits so alarmed the authorities that a full-time recruiting officer was appointed, with a committee of senior officers to direct his activities. Funding was allocated for advertising and the recruiting officer, Inspector L. Newell, was sent to England on a four-month recruiting campaign. His tour did not pay: up to 1 October 1971 only seventeen men recruited in the United Kingdom arrived and took up an effective appointment with the force. Some members of the Police Association were critical of Newell's work in England and described it as a bid to import 'cheap labour'. The view was that men could be retained in the force if the Government 'paid enough for the product', and that adequate numbers of recruits could be obtained in Victoria if the Government matched pay rates offered on the open labour market. The pay question ($60 a week, with little short-term prospect of promotion), was seen as vital, so that one research team concluded, 'The first battle in meeting the challenge of crime in the present decade, it seems to us, begins in the Arbitration Court'.

Meanwhile police work did not attract people with higher education. There were only two university graduates in the force, and they had obtained their degrees after becoming policemen. From 1945 to 1969 not one university graduate applied to join the force, and of those recruits who joined between May 1969 and June 1970, only 7 per cent had matriculated. Of the remainder, 76 per cent had either their intermediate or leaving certificates, and the balance had 'achieved form three level'. The occupation of a policeman was then generally ranked above most blue-collar occupations but was regarded as being toward the lower end of white-collar groups. One survey conducted in Melbourne listed seven occupations, policemen, firemen, ambulance drivers, private detectives, architects, plumbers and insurance salesmen, and asked respondents 'what in your opinion is the relative importance to a community of the following occupational groups?' Policemen were ranked first or second by 76 per cent of those people surveyed.[32]

Police Association concern about the financial status, morale and image of its members, and public concern about the state of the force generally, brought about two separate but overlapping investigations aimed at improving the policeman's position and restoring public confidence in the force. The first was initiated by the Association early in 1970 when it commissioned Paul Wilson and John Western, senior members of the Department of Government at the University of Queensland, to undertake an examination of the force to 'fix the policeman's position in the community wage structure'. Wilson and Western looked at such areas as 'the deployment of personnel, police training, promotion policies [and] reasons for resignations', and published their findings in a book entitled, *The Policeman's Position Today and Tomorrow*. The material gathered by them was successfully used by the association in claims before the Police Service Board, to improve the financial and occupational status of its members, and it now remains as a unique record of the policeman's position during the years 1969–70.

The second study was in the form of a tour of inspection conducted by Colonel Sir Eric St Johnston, formerly Chief Inspector of Constabulary for England and Wales, who undertook his work at the request and expense of the Bolte government. Many Victorians, including the Australian Labor Party, the Country Party and the Democratic Labor Party, wanted a royal commission into the force, but the Liberal government decided against such a course because they had seen 'enough dirty linen washed through the press' during the abortion inquiry and 'did not want another serve'. Instead of a public hearing presided over by judges and lawyers, in the presence of a press gallery, the Bolte government chose a much less public course, and one that was arguably just as effective as a royal commission. St Johnston was hired 'to examine the administration and organization of the force', and 'to report and make recommendations as to the means by which the efficiency' could be improved. He arrived in Victoria on 1 October 1970 and travelled throughout the state, inspecting all sections of the force, with particular emphasis on the CIB. He submitted his report to the Government on 22 February 1971, and it contained more than 180 recommendations for restructuring the Victoria Police. Many of St Johnston's findings coincided with those of Wilson and Western, and he described their survey and his report as 'complementary documents' that 'should be read together'.

The studies of Wilson, Western and St Johnston, and the later work of such men as A. H. Coventry, D. J. Swanson and J. R. G. Salisbury in implementing St Johnston's recommendations, combined to usher in a new era of organizational change, improved police salaries and work conditions, and bountiful recruiting. Their work altered the course of the force and, although many problems still lay ahead it was a turning point. It has been suggested by one of St Johnston's staff that had there been no Wainer and no abortion inquiry there would have been no St Johnston Report. In that sense it was like the Kelly saga. For out of the ashes of anguish, vitriol and personal devastation there grew the fruits of reform.[33]

Future Shock

> Change is avalanching upon our heads and most people are gro-
> tesquely unprepared to cope with it. . . . by violently expanding the
> scope of change, and, most crucially, by accelerating its pace, we have
> broken irretrievably with the past.

Change—its nature, scope, rate and effect on people—was the subject of
Alvin Toffler's *Future Shock*, published in 1970. It was not about policemen or police forces; they were not even mentioned. Yet if members of
the Victoria Police Force had studied Toffler's work during the decade
after the abortion inquiry, they would have found in it prescient comment
on what was basically taking place in their own work environment. Traditional practices, institutions and links with the past were being modified, discarded and broken in ways that matched change in the general
community and came from various quarters: officials, academics, men
like St Johnston and some policemen who embraced change (particularly
electronic and technological) and quickly made their mark in communications, computer system and airborne operations, or those who embraced
the prospect of higher education, new management techniques, research
and planning methodology and the notion of professionalism. Many
policemen, however, were resistant to change, and for them it was a difficult time of transition when changes seemed too forced, quick and
frequent—often leaving them reeling in that state of disorientation
labelled by Toffler as future shock.[34]

In a little more than a decade the force increased in size from 4700 to
8365 and its female component went from 2 per cent to 10. New buildings, uniforms, technology and specialist sections were the outward signs
of a much deeper internal reorganization that touched every facet of the
force and every person in it. Some revelled in this, some rebelled, some
resigned, while most coped as best they could and sought to maintain a
sense of balance in a whirlwind of change. Policemen, many of whom
had joined in the 1940s, were coping with satellite surveillance, helicopters, computers, and ranks swelled by university graduates and women.
In many fields, teams of specialists supplanted the individual policeman.

The overseers of most of this change were Reginald Jackson, who succeeded Wilby as Chief Commissioner on 11 October 1971, and Sinclair
Imrie ('Mick') Miller, who was appointed as Assistant Commissioner
(Operations) on the same day, and served under Jackson until he succeeded him on 13 June 1977. Jackson and Miller were of different police
backgrounds and contrasting styles but each of them at different times
had to overcome police industrial actions that were, in part, open displays
of resistance to change: Jackson faced a threatened police strike at the
height of the Beach Inquiry, and Miller a Police Association resolution
expressing a lack of confidence in the administration of the force.

Chief Commissioner
R. Jackson

At the time of his appointment as Chief Commissioner Jackson was 58 years old and had behind him a police career spanning more than thirty-five years, during which his experience included uniform duty at Mildura and service with the CIB at Malvern, South Melbourne, the Breaking Squad and Stolen Motor Vehicle Squad. In 1961 he was appointed as an inspector and served at that rank as officer-in-charge of Public Relations; in 1963 he was appointed Assistant Commissioner (General), under Arnold; and in 1969 he was appointed Deputy Commissioner, under Wilby. In contrast to the antipathy shown toward the police association by earlier Commissioners such as Blamey, Jackson was a former president and executive member of the Association, and as a life member he insisted upon maintaining active membership on taking office as Chief Commissioner. An editorial in the *Victoria Police Journal* at the time described him as a man who had 'come up the hard way through the ranks . . . a man of great integrity and humility, possessing an innate ability to fraternise with subordinates'. Popular and sociable, Jackson was the traditional 'good bloke' and he enjoyed immense personal loyalty. He was not a progressive or an initiator of ideas and his commissionership was buoyed by a team of deputy and assistant commissioners whom he allowed free rein.

Miller was a different type. A former Melbourne High School boy and trooper with the AIF First Armoured Car Squadron, he joined the force on 5 November 1947, at twenty-one, and led a varied career that included uniform duty at Richmond and Fitzroy, service with the Special Patrol at Russell Street, extensive duty with the CIB, including interchange duty in Brisbane, and appointments as officer-in-charge of the Gaming Branch, Vice Squad and Detective Training School. When he was head of the Gaming (Special Duties) Branch, in the 1950s, its reputation for honesty and effectiveness was such that Miller and his men were dubbed the 'untouchables'. In 1967 he was awarded a Churchill Fellowship to study detective training in the United Kingdom, France and the United States of America, where he studied at the Federal Bureau of Investigation National Academy. In 1971, when still a sub-officer, he was selected by St Johnston to undertake advanced police training in England and attended the Senior Command Course at 'Bramshill', the British National Police College. On his return he was appointed Assistant Commissioner (Operations), then in 1976 Assistant Commissioner (Crime), and finally in 1977 Chief Commissioner.[35]

The studies completed by St Johnston, and Wilson and Western, provided Jackson and his senior officers with a blueprint for change and, with government support and funding, they capitalized on it. Some critics complained that St Johnston's report produced no answers that 'could be regarded as revolutionary' and that 'in many cases the solutions had been advocated previously by the force administration', but St Johnson was in fact a genuine agent of change. With Wilson and Western he encouraged reform and the climate in which it could happen. In the wake of such work Jackson labelled 1971 as 'a watershed in the history of the Victoria Police Force'. It was not, but it was a year when police were granted average salary increases of 21 per cent, the level of recruiting was so 'greatly improved' that accommodation was a 'concern', and the force administration was reorganized into six departments—crime, traffic, operations, personnel, services and administration. The first five were each headed by an assistant commissioner, necessitating an increase in their number by two, while the Administration Department constituted the public service component of the force and was headed by a civilian Director of Administration. These changes at command level were followed by a regrouping of departments and a reorganization of the State's police districts, involving the creation of six new metropolitan districts and adjustments to the boundaries of adjoining districts—both metropolitan and country. This rationalization reduced the size of the districts on the outer suburban fringe and made for more effective policing and better internal management.

During October and November 1971 the nascent Information Systems

Division undertook the trial of a computer in recording and checking stolen vehicles; in four weeks, recovery of stolen cars increased by 241 per cent, and the way was paved for the more extensive use of computers within the force.

On 15 December 1971 a new rank structure came into operation, comprising twelve ranks from cadet to chief commissioner. The change did away with grades, such as Superintendent Grade 1 and Inspector Grade II, and the rank of first constable was abolished and replaced by that of senior constable. Three years later the additional rank of commander was interposed between those of chief superintendent and assistant commissioner, to provide for the country and metropolitan co-ordinators based at headquarters. The aim was better control and supervision, and more appealing ranks. Overnight, all first constables became senior constables, all senior constables became sergeants, and all sergeants became senior sergeants.[36]

Whereas major changes in the past had generally been followed by periods of unchanging stability, those in the wake of St Johnston heralded an era of innovation and transience that had not ended more than ten years later. Administrative reorganization mostly took place during 1971–72, with the regrouping of departments and the structuring of districts, but it was very much an ongoing series of changes orchestrated by the Inspectorate and Future Plans Division, largely in accordance with the blueprint prepared by St Johnston. Of St Johnston's 186 recommendations, 63 had been fully implemented by 8 July 1974, another 47 had been varied or were in the course of implementation, and the remainder were either not to be implemented or still to be considered.

The Inspectorate and Future Plans Division was formed primarily to implement the St Johnston recommendations, but was itself transformed. The small unit of three men, with an inspector in charge, more than quadrupled in size and was renamed the Management Services Bureau with a superintendent in command. By the end of 1981 the Management Services Bureau was absorbed into a much larger, newly created department titled Research and Development, which was headed by an assistant commissioner, and had a staff of more than twenty. In the transient nature of Toffler's 'ad-hocracy', staff in the Research and Development Department, and especially in its two smaller forerunners, accepted a relative waiver of hierarchy in order to facilitate decision-making and maximize personal skill levels, adopted the use of transitory project teams, and worked in a changing environment of shifting walls and equipment. Much of what the Research and Development Department and its forerunners did was alien to the self-approved pragmatic world of street policemen, who derisively nicknamed the department 'Fantasyland'.[37]

Many of the changes that the force underwent were not at once obvious to those people not directly touched by them, but most Melburnians could not help but notice when the force shifted its landmarks. For almost a century the Police Depot in St Kilda Road and the Police Headquarters at Russell Street had stood as the two most important bases of police activity in the state. They were symbols of permanence. Although they had altered over the years—like the worn handles of an axe—they were veritable institutions where thousands of policemen from successive generations had joined, trained, lived and worked. It ended during the 1970s when the expression 'the depot' passed from police parlance, the quaint red-brick police hospital fronting St Kilda Road closed its doors, and police headquarters was shifted from Russell Street to the 'other' end of town.

In 1972 the force acquired a former warehouse in Wellington Street, Collingwood, for use as a central store and workshop, and the former seminary, Corpus Christi College at Glen Waverley, for use as a training academy. The following year the Police Depot site—with the exception of the stable complex and police hospital—became part of the Arts complex. In 1981 the police hospital was moved into a new building at the rear of Prince Henry's Hospital. The move from St Kilda Road effectively ended a colourful chapter of police history at a very central and picturesque location within walking distance of the city. The force had maintained a central Police Depot since 1853 and its passing was appropriate to the times: it was swapped for a cream brick building in the outer-suburban middle-class area of Glen Waverley, and was renamed the Police Training Academy.

The other major building change occurred in 1977 when the administrative staff of Police Headquarters were transferred to a modern ten-storey office building at 380 William Street, Melbourne. The buildings at Russell Street were retained by the force and renamed the Russell Street Police Complex, but nevertheless it was a distinct break with the past when the Chief Commissioner, S. I. Miller, became the first of his rank for more than a century to be housed away from Russell Street. Whereas the headquarters at Russell Street had long been known as 'the castle', the new building at William Street was quickly labelled 'the ivory tower'.

The move itself was also a sign of growth. In addition to a training complex, hospital, store and workshops, and headquarters that were all new, the force acquired the former Savoy Plaza Hotel in Spencer Street, a ten-storey building opposite the railway station, for use initially as a cadet school and later as an office complex. The acquisition of modern buildings in the city area was matched by the erection of 'futuristically designed' police stations in the suburbs and country districts and, in a clear break with past practice, more than fifty architecturally modern stations with such features as carpeted floors and landscaped frontages were built at such places as Altona North, Sale, Colac, Doncaster, Mooroolbark and Mallacoota. Many other stations were extended or renovated, and modular station buildings went up at remote localitites such as Buchan, in a post-1970 police building boom that was the most extensive since the gold rushes. The opening of the City West Police Station on the ground floor of the new police headquarters enabled the closure of the Bourke Street West Police station, erected in 1889, condemned in 1924 as unfit for human habitation, condemned again in 1967—while still occupied,—as 'old and dilapidated', and described by St Johnston as 'quite the worst police station I have visited for many years'.[38]

In 1973 W. P. Nichol, a telecommunications expert from London, came to Victoria 'to consult and advise on police communications'. He was quick to warn that 'The century is three quarters of the way expired and we have men walking on the moon . . . time is not on our side and the police must be brought into this modern technological development now'. Moves were already afoot within the force to do so, but his message was not lost. Within a decade the computer system was expanded so that visual display terminals located throughout Victoria gave police almost instant access to such data as motor vehicle registration and driving licence details, criminal records, daily message print-outs and personnel records. Other technological advances included the formation of an Audio-Visual Section, to support the extended use of tape recorders and video equipment within the force; the establishment of a Video Production Unit, with full production and editing facilities, for the making of in-service training films; the construction and equipping of a new communications complex; the general issue of personal radios for use at special events, and by members on foot patrol or away from their vehicle radios; and a general upgrading of the entire communications network, so that police anywhere in the state—whether in the air or on sea or land—could communicate with a police base.[39]

Many things were tried and changed in a decade when the colour of some police cars went from stratosphere blue, to white, to iridescent orange, to bright yellow. Obsolete weapons were phased out and replaced with .38-calibre Smith and Wesson revolvers. A newly formed Instrument Development and Maintenance Section produced flashing blue lights and 'yippee' sirens in ever-changing and dazzling combinations. A nascent Research and Planning Unit introduced a force-wide workload assessment system. The *Police Manual* was completely rewritten and published in two volumes, and for the first time ever was available for public sale and incorporated a comprehensive 'Force Philosophy'. Minibuses and command caravans were purchased for special operations, country members commenced using four-wheel drive vehicles, and a 52-ft steel-hulled displacement cruiser—the *Reginald Jackson*—was commissioned for use as an all-weather patrol vessel on Port Phillip Bay. A new identification pass was introduced, and a section was formed to design and introduce a modern and functional uniform, which moved away from the

English model and incorporated American-style cloth shoulder patches and a belt of sufficient size and strength to carry a holster and gun. The only concessions to English tradition were the retention of blue as the cloth colour and the adoption of a blue and white chequered cap band. With the formation of a design section, police personnel began appearing in all manner of protective and special clothing: white reflectorized raincoats, blue leather motorcycle jackets, insulated snow gear and shortwaisted patrol jackets. Long gone were the days when a change of uniform meant wearing a white helmet in summer and a polished black leather one in winter.

Long gone too were the days when every policeman was a 'Jack-of-all-trades'. The Internal Investigations Bureau, Management Services Bureau, Computer Systems Division, Audio Visual Section, Video Production Unit and Uniform Design Section, were only a few of the specialist groups formed in a large modern police force. A Dog Squad, Air Wing, Independent Patrol Group, Special Operations Group, Court Security Group, Bureau of Criminal Intelligence, Sexual Offences Squad and Psychology Office were added to the specialist squads already in existence. It became increasingly possible for members of the force with appropriate qualifications to specialize in these fields and gain promotion to brevet positions. Individuals were permanently employed as divisional crime collators and district traffic accident record co-ordinators, and task forces were set up for specific investigations. In 1981 a force-wide *Job Description Manual* was compiled that listed over five hundred separate tasks and positions. It had become possible for many policemen and policewomen, who had completed their training phase, to follow a career that at no time necessitated them pounding a beat, working at a police station or making an arrest. Those who did perform traditional duties were able to call upon a wide range of help in times of need and so render a more efficient and effective public service. For many Melburnians the most obvious hint of the direction of change was the almost daily presence overhead of the police helicopter—an Aerospatiale Dauphin SA 365 twin-engine helicopter purchased in 1979 at a cost of almost one million dollars.

The increasing complexity of modern policing—especially the new technology—and the shift toward specialization, necessitated higher levels of education and advanced training. A new system of Promotion Boards, the introduction of a personnel assessment system and the creation of Selection Boards to screen applicants for special vacancies, all combined to emphasize the need for professionalism. The police recruit training scheme was updated and extended, and a range of in-service

The police helicopter above Melbourne

training courses was devised, including a four-wheel-drive course, advanced detective training and crime prevention. Senior police were admitted as adult students into the Diploma of Criminology course at the University of Melbourne, while other policemen commenced part-time studies in arts, science, social sciences, law and behavioural sciences at all four Victorian universities. A specific police studies course was started at the Caulfield Institute of Technology, and other relevant certificate and diploma courses were undertaken by police at suburban and rural colleges. It became common for individual members to be awarded research grants for study overseas and recipients of such awards as the C. J. La Trobe Study Award, Churchill Fellowship and Australasian Police Special Study Grant travelled to the United Kingdom, Europe, Asia and North America to observe, study and return home with ideas that often accelerated the onset of future shock in their colleagues.[40]

While the general trend in the force was toward specialization, one of the oldest and most traditional specialist sections went the other way. The policewomen, since 1917 a separate entity with their own seniority list and specialist duties, underwent a major organizational upheaval that saw a significant increase in their number, an unprecedented widening of the scope of duties open to them and a major shift in their conditions of service. Those former all-female bastions, Women Police Divisions, were 'desexed' and renamed Community Policing Squads in a move that expanded their range of duties and opened vacancies in them to men. In 1978 the women were integrated laterally into the general seniority list so that many of them gained accelerated promotion over their male colleagues. Positions in the general force were opened to women, and before the decade was out they were working as equal partners with men in most areas of the force. The places where women were not found were in senior command positions, small rural police stations and in postings such as the search and rescue squad, motorcycle section and the special operations group, where the tasks performed demanded a high degree of physical strength. The appearance of women in the CIB, Mounted Branch, Vice Squad and Fingerprint Section, and at suburban police stations, was a precursor to a series of individual achievements by policewomen, including receipt of a Churchill Fellowship, qualification as an air observer leader and attendance at the Australian Police College. Their rate of dispersal into almost all facets of police work was exceeded only by their growth in number, which went from 69 in 1970 to 835 in 1984, when the percentage of women in the force was the highest of any force in Australia and exceeded the national averages in England and the United States of America. The rapid changes in the role and number of women police were largely a reflection of changes taking place in the general community. However, specific elements that advanced the lot of women in the force included St Johnston's recommendation that they be more fully utilized, the change of regulations in 1972 that allowed married women to join and remain in the force, and the passing of the Equal Opportunity Act in 1978. There was no limit on the percentage of the total force that women could comprise and few legal or policy restrictions on the work they could do. In the name of equal opportunity, women of 162.5 cm were accepted into the force but men of 173 cm or shorter were not. Policewomen unquestionably had a role to play in cases involving females and young children, and proved themselves capable in most other areas of police work. However, there was a doubt about the ability of policewomen to cope in situations demanding physical presence or strength. Calls to deal with drunken louts, street gangs, brawls, violent demonstrations, domestic disputes and angry incidents in hotel bars were of daily occurrence, and perhaps one reason why 64 per cent of policemen and policewomen surveyed in one study expressed a preference for a male partner when on patrol. The rising number of policewomen and their dispersal throughout the force fulfilled an admirable ideal but was not without problems. Yet the problems—real or otherwise—were not investigated. The integration was not properly evaluated, empirical research was not undertaken, and pertinent data about such things as the incidence of assaults upon and the work injuries sustained by policewomen were not collated. The ostrich-like inaction of those officials responsible for policy formulation and implementation suggests blithe acceptance of the equality ideal, and too little regard for the impact of some changes on the police workforce and the level of its service to the community.[41]

Many policemen did not accept changes gracefully. There were those who disdained higher qualifications as 'academic'. They were troubled by the activities of police researchers, examiners and promotion boards, and were concerned about their own career prospects when they heard others speak about relative merit, education and professionalism. Many were also uneasy about new management methods, advanced technology and working as equal partners with women. It was not uncommon for police in station mess rooms to be regaled with tales of policewomen who could not cope with men's work, researchers from 'fantasyland' who did not understand the 'real' world, and senior administrators in the 'ivory tower' who had not 'caught a thief in years'. A degree of passive resistance, such as mess-room jeers, was to be expected; it even helped people cope with their changing work situation. To many of them the present and the future were threatening, while the past assumed the aura of an arcadia. Yet throughout most of the post-1970 reformation, resistance from within was mild and rarely exceeded that of the sort displayed by a diffident child. In a bid to minimize such diffidence, considerable emphasis was placed on industrial relations and the marketing of new procedures and equipment. An Industrial Liaison Office was created in 1981, Police Association officials were permitted to attend meetings of senior police, and staff from the Association and police administration worked together on joint working parties. The Computer Systems Division paved the way for the acceptance of its wares by programming the noughts and crosses game into the police computer system, to encourage its use and, in the process, build user confidence and dexterity with the equipment. There were occasions, however, when even the diffident became demonstrative.[42]

In October 1974 Dr Bertram Wainer met the Solicitor-General, Daryl Dawson, and the Assistant Commissioner (Crime), W. Crowley, and alleged once more that certain members of the force were guilty of illegal behaviour. Wainer had established a measure of personal credibility when his earlier activities led to the gaoling of Ford, Matthews and Jacobson, so the Government appointed the former South Australian lawyer, Cairns Villeneuve-Smith, QC, to conduct a preliminary investigation into the allegations. Villeneuve-Smith's work led to the appointment by Order-in-Council on 18 March 1975 of Barry Beach, QC, to sit as a one-man Board of Inquiry, and report whether there was 'any credible evidence raising a strong and probable presumption that any and if so, which members of the Victoria Police Force' were guilty of criminal offences, breaches of Standing Orders, or 'harassment or intimidation of any member of the public'. Beach conducted his inquiry over fifteen months, during which time he received 131 complaints against police, and fully investigated 21 of them. The others were rejected as frivolous or vexatious, or for some other reason. During the course of his inquiry Beach took evidence from 240 witnesses and examined 766 exhibits. In the end he made adverse findings against 55 members of the force—alleging that they were guilty of such things as conspiracy, perjury, assault, unlawful arrest, corruptly receiving money and fabricating evidence—and under seventeen headings he made extensive recommendations for reform to a range of police procedures, including the conduct of identification parades, the investigation of complaints, police practice in relation to the interview register, and the interrogation of persons under arrest or other restraint.

Before Beach's recommendations were made public they provoked the most serious display of animosity since the police strike of 1923, when 4200 men and women from a force of 6400 met at Festival Hall on 18 October 1976 to formulate a plan of resistance. They had not seen Beach's report, they did not know what his recommendations were, and they did not know which police he had named or why, but they gathered in what the president of the Police Association, L. J. Blogg, described as 'the greatest demonstration of unity in the history of the Association'. Although there was talk of a strike, that did not eventuate. The Chief Commissioner, Jackson, addressed the gathering and was given a standing ovation, but the meeting sought the resignation of the Chief Secretary, Vance Dickie, requested a Royal Commission be appointed to inquire into the Beach Inquiry, instituted a work-to-rule campaign, and put forward a set of seven categoric demands, including one that 'Any change in police procedures was to be the result of a conference involving the police department, the police association and the government, and not based upon any recommendations made by Beach'. In the face of massive police industrial action, the Government led by R. J. Hamer accepted the seven demands.

Following the meeting at Festival Hall only thirty-two of the fifty-five police named by Beach were charged, and none was convicted. Beach's recommendations for procedural reform met a similar fate when the Government appointed a committee comprising the Honourable J. G. Norris, QC, former Judge of the Supreme Court (chairman), Chief Commissioner Jackson, R. Glenister and R. L. King—the Norris Committee—to review them. It was a conservative group, drawn from institutional backgrounds and predisposed to a cautious approach by careers in legal, government and police positions. It effectively stifled Beach's proposals and recommended a 'steady as she goes' approach, criticized by one observer on the grounds that the 'overwhelming rejection of the Beach procedural proposals by the Norris Committee meant the retention of the *status quo*'.

Criticism of the final outcome of the Beach Inquiry was justified. It was a result that defied common sense. In their massive opposition to Beach's work, many members of the force and their supporters did not think or discriminate. Bonded instinctively by camaraderie and swept along in a whirlwind of rhetoric, they provided legal, financial and moral support for each other, regardless of the merits of individual cases. The corrupt, unlucky and stupid—and all who came near those categories—were gathered under one umbrella and sheltered. It was an emotive cause. Many policemen were turned against the inquiry from the outset by the involvement of the antipolice crusader, Dr Wainer. Some of the complainants and witnesses who gave evidence before the inquiry were infamous criminals and their allegations were often preposterous and unfounded. Policemen also took exception to the sometimes caustic and barbed remarks of Villeneuve-Smith and Beach. Nevertheless, the collective police response was accurately described in the *Age* as a 'gross over-reaction' and along with many Victorians, it regretted that 'in some of the heated harangues from police spokesmen never has there been the slightest admission that any policemen could be anything but perfect'. The force displayed a reluctance to admit to, or cleanse itself of, undesirable elements and was reactionary in its resistance to Beach's recommendations for reform. Lawyers and magistrates played key parts in determining the outcome of prosecutions recommended by Beach and, because of their participation in the legal process, policemen alone could not be blamed for the results. However, more troubling than the possibility that a few crooked policemen might have gone unpunished was the bitter public aftertaste that policemen had displayed a 'collective assumption' that they were 'beyond reproach and above the law'.[43]

Opposition to the inquiry and findings of Beach was led by the Police Association and its success was almost absolute. The successful and vigorous campaign conducted by the Association marked its emergence as a force to be reckoned with. Never before had it been so organized, received so much publicity and wielded so much political influence. Like police unions in other parts of the world, the Association had entered a militant phase and was relishing it. In the aftermath of the Beach Inquiry the Association was brimming with confidence, and that ebullient state produced a series of disputes between the Chief Commissioner, S. I. Miller, and the Association, as Miller tried to make organizational changes and the Association fought to maintain the status quo.

Unlike his predecessor, Miller did not closely identify himself with the Association and was prepared to try to force change where Jackson had not. The disputation between the Association and Miller came to a climax in 1979 when the executive of the Association passed a resolution expressing its 'complete dissatisfaction with and lack of confidence' in the police administration. The resolution claimed to be the result 'of the continual and repeated failure of the Police Department to take due and compassionate consideration of the welfare, safety, well being, efficiency, interests and morale of members of the police association'. In moving the motion J. R. Splatt, a member of the executive, cited twenty specific instances that he described as 'apathetic administration' illustrative of 'a total absence of compassion'. A number of the matters raised by Splatt predated Miller's commissionership and were perennial issues, seemingly included in the list of 'instances' for effect. Another one, 'lack of support by senior officers', was at the root of the feud between Miller and the Association, and stemmed from Miller's belief that the force was accountable to the community for its actions. On three separate occasions he publicly apologized for or rebuked policemen, and in doing so he incurred the wrath of the Association, which felt that his candour showed a lack of support for its members. Miller replied that 'in a society which believes in the rule of law, nobody is above the law . . . where a member's conduct is clearly unsatisfactory or where he has clearly committed a breach of the law, it is unrealistic to suggest that the member should be blindly supported'. It was a truism too often forgotten in some police circles.

Important background elements in the action taken by the Association—and included in Splatt's 'specific instances'—were Executive Instructions nos 94 and 97, which were issued under Miller's command to improve efficiency in the CIB. However, they also altered traditional practice. Instruction no. 94 pooled all detectives from specific squads and divisions into the CIB District, giving the Assistant Commissioner (Crime) greater flexibility with their deployment. Detectives could be moved to where the need was most urgent, inefficient or unsuitable detectives could be shifted away from sensitive or important areas, and transfers could be used to minimize the risk of corruption. This was new and unpalatable to policemen, who liked the old system under which they applied for and were appointed to specific positions, where they could stay regardless of indifferent performance or the level of crime. Instruction no. 94 was challenged before the Police Service Board and declared illegal in 1981. It was cancelled and the status quo prevailed.

Instruction no. 97 was introduced because the CIB was short of experienced detectives and was not providing a satisfactory level of service. Appointees to the branch were serving only comparatively short periods before transferring elsewhere on promotion. Due to the unacceptably high turnover of staff, it was decided to appoint to the CIB only those constables and senior constables from whom a minimum three years service as detectives could reasonably be expected. It was a decision that suddenly ended the anticipated career paths of many young policemen and was universally unpopular in the junior ranks. It was, however, a decision made in the best interests of the community. In the face of opposition from the Association, the implementation of instruction no. 97 was briefly deferred but later became effective.

Eventually the rift between Miller and the Association healed, but the no-confidence resolution and the events leading up to it gave both parties a taste of future shock. In a rapidly changing world the Association experienced pressures for reform in its own sphere of occupational interest, while Miller and his senior management people were subjected to the sting of a changing and increasingly militant police union, prepared and able to organize, speak and act on issues, in ways that were almost unthought of ten years earlier.[44]

Toffler tells us that there is 'no absolute way to measure change', that it is necessarily relative and uneven, and that 'when we speak of the rate of change, we refer to the number of events crowded into an arbitrary fixed interval of time'. Using time—his yardstick for the measurement of change—it is clear that more things, physical and social, changed in the force during the years after 1970 than during any equivalent timespan in its history. During earlier decades policemen experienced administrative upheavals and breaks with past personalities and practices—such as occurred during the Kelly saga, and at the time of the police strike—but those reformations did not approximate the rate and extent of change that began in 1971–72 and continued into the 1980s. Had a time-traveller made decennial visits to the force throughout its history, that person would have found on most visits that the status quo was enduring and that few major changes occurred during any one decade. Not so in the 1970s.

Although many things had altered soon after World War II, the rate of change had accelerated as the twenty-first century drew closer, and the force had never before been subjected to so much concentrated and ongoing change. The decennial visitor in 1980 would have found almost everything different, and a force that had in many things tangible—if not in spirit—irretrievably broken with the past.[45]

1984

1984 is upon us, but there is no sign of George Orwell's totalitarian state—no Big Brother, no Thought Police. On the police front, it seems much the same as any other year.

1984 is where this history ends. The bureaucratized and repressive world feared by Orwell had not come to Victoria, but in changed times Victorian people were troubled by criminals. During 1983 more than 200 000 major crimes were reported in the state, prompting the Chief Commissioner to warn at the beginning of 1984, 'our freedom will not be assailed by the spectre of totalitarian tyranny, but all of us will be confronted by the very real threat of victimization by increasing crime'. And this was in spite of the police force in the 1980s having embarked on a number of community policing initiatives and being regarded as the national model in that field. The force formed Community Policing Squads 'to prevent crime by marshalling communal resources' and concentrating upon situations involving juvenile offenders, children at risk, family counselling, community education and crime prevention programmes. Community Involvement Groups were established at Frankston and Broadmeadows 'to examine and assess areas of social dysfunction in the community and to initiate courses of police action aimed at remedying the underlying problems'. The groups developed close contact with community social agencies, schools, church groups, service clubs and businesses, resulting in an improved understanding measurable, in some areas, by reduction in crime and misbehaviour. By the end of the year the Neighbourhood Watch scheme had been adopted by organized groups of householders in sixty-one separate areas within Victoria, embracing 42 079 households and 128 000 people—and there was a reduction by 10 per cent of the number of burglaries reported during the last eight months of the year.[46] The Safety House Programme was another community-based crime prevention programme, designed to ensure the personal safety of young children in going to and from school. Operation Crime Beat was the return of foot constables to beats in commercial shopping areas, and there was a similar use of foot patrols in high-rise apartment areas. Four separate liaison committees were formed, involving regular meetings between police and representatives from lawyer groups, the media, the Aboriginal community, and Victoria's various

Chief Commissioner
S. I. Miller

ethnic groups. There was, in addition, the development of Operation Ethos, including the appointment of an Ethnic Liaison Adviser, 'to improve relationships and understanding between ethnic communities and the police'. Blue Light Discos were operated by four hundred off-duty police at more than sixty locations throughout the state, and Operation Olympus was introduced to promote the sporting ethic in young people by the award of trophies to those competitors deemed to be 'the most disciplined'.

Due largely to efforts such as these, a Morgan Gallup Poll rated police in Victoria fourth of fifteen occupational groups in terms of honesty and ethical standards. Policemen ranked below doctors, dentists and bank managers, but above accountants, lawyers, schoolteachers, university lecturers and members of parliament. Another survey found that 79 per cent of the public thought the police 'did a good job'. Recognition of this work came from the Parents Without Partners organization, in granting the force its national 'Distinguished Service to Children Award' for police involvement in Blue Light Discos, and the Victorian Fathers' Day Council, when it selected the Chief Commissioner, S. I. Miller, as 'Father of the Year'. Some people might think of these achievements as spurious; in fact, the awards show that the activities of many policemen and policewomen in Victoria in 1984 were not of the sort envisaged by Orwell, that the force was in many ways trying to be responsive to the needs of the people it served, and was in part succeeding.[47]

During June 1984 the strength of the force was 7564 men and 801 women. The police to population ratio was 1:487 (compared with 1:732 in 1971, before St Johnston's recommendations were implemented). There were 348 police stations and the police vehicle fleet numbered 1740. The total annual budget was in excess of $300 million. The Chief Commissioner was supported by two deputy commissioners, six assistant commissioners and four commanders. A seventh assistant commissioner position was created during 1984 when Superintendent Kelvin Glare, a trained lawyer, was promoted to head an enlarged Internal Investigations Bureau. The balance of the force comprised 402 officers, 1953 sub-officers and 5997 senior constables and constables. It was in many respects a force of young people, reflecting both the growth rate of the post-1970 years and the active, physical nature of many police duties. Sixty-nine per cent of the force was aged 35 years or under, and only 8 per cent fell within the age group 51-60 years. Youth was particularly evident in that fastest growing section of the force, the women police, and 93 per cent of their number were 35 or under, with 48 per cent of them being under 26 years of age.

For administrative purposes the force was divided into departments: operations, crime, traffic, services, personnel, research and development, internal investigations, and administration. The largest of these were the operational three—operations, crime and traffic—which respectively comprised 65 per cent, 15 per cent and 9 per cent of the force. For operational purposes the state was divided into twenty-three police districts, eleven metropolitan and twelve country. In addition there existed a wide range of specialist districts, divisions and sections, which were based in the Melbourne area but were available for duty throughout the state if needed. They included the Search and Rescue Squad, Water Police, Air Wing, Dog Squad, Mounted Branch, Special Operations Group, Independent Patrol Group and specialist squads from the Crime Department.[48]

The Chief Commissioner estimated in 1984 that the force was 2383 personnel below optimum level, a deficiency due to government budget constraints, rather than a poor response to recruiting. The waiting list of applicants to join the force was increasing at the rate of seventy per week and, at one stage, applications on hand exceeded fifteen hundred. With jobs hard to get, competition to join the police force was so keen that only two applicants in every hundred were successful. Almost one-third of all applicants were female, and their success rate was reflected in their increasing percentage of the force's overall strength. From 1971 the number of women police increased considerably faster than the growth rate for men. Fifteen per cent of police recruited were from a non-Australian background, and in 1984 there were 421 members of the force who between them spoke forty-one languages. Many applicants to join the force were bilingual, many others had trade qualifications or management experience in the private sector, and it was not unusual for applicants to have tertiary qualifications in Arts, Education, Law or Science.

Regardless of their education qualifications or employment record, applicants were required to meet a number of set criteria and to pass an entrance examination consisting of tests in arithmetic, general knowledge and English—spelling, comprehension, and essay writing. All applicants had to be 'an Australian citizen or else have been granted permanent residence in Australia; of good character, at least 18 years and 6 months old but less than 34 years old; if male, be at least 174 cm tall or 162.5 cm if female'. Applicants who satisfied these criteria also had to pass hearing and vision tests, undertake an agility co-ordination test, satisfy other medical tests and be accepted by a selection panel.

Those candidates accepted into the force were inducted into police life at the Training Academy, where they lived in barracks for eighteen weeks while they studied law, English, human behaviour, police duties, typing and fingerprints, and were trained in parade drill, swimming, lifesaving, restraint and control techniques and the use of firearms. Time spent at the academy was only the initial part of an extensive training programme and upon graduation they continued training for a further seventy weeks under the Probationary Constables Extended Training Scheme. During that time constables received on-the-job training at a variety of stations and participated in a concurrent correspondence course. Those who satisfactorily completed the Extended Training Scheme were admitted as permanent members of the force, and became eligible to apply for transfers to advertised vacancies at police stations or specialized branches.

In 1984 there were thirty-three external and seventy internal courses available to members of the force. In addition a number of tertiary insitutions offered courses of specific relevance to police work and 127 members took study leave to do them. The enlistment of recruits with tertiary education and the provision of tertiary study leave for serving members of the force combined to give the force in 1984 a higher level of education than ever before. More than one hundred police were holders of university degrees in a wide range of fields including Arts, Law, Science, Physical Education, Psychology, Economics and Public Administration. Another 250 were holders of diplomas, and over one thousand members of the force held formal trade or technical qualifications.

Conditions of service for police compared favourably with those offering on the open employment market. The total salary and allowances payable to a first year probationary constable was $18 741 per year. Senior constables received up to $24 849; sergeants $27 459; senior sergeants $30 672; and officers (not including commissioners) ranged from $37 053 up to $49 153. This was at a time when the average annual wage for people in Australia was about $17 400. All police were issued with a free uniform and paid an allowance to maintain it. A wide range of specialist and other allowances were alo paid for such things as working at night and being 'on call'. Leave entitlements were seven weeks annual leave, three months long-service leave after ten years service, and cumulative sick leave of fifteen days on full pay each year. All police were eligible to join the State Superannuation Fund and had access to the police hospital. The Police Association operated a Benefit Fund and Legal Costs Fund, and available for the use of police were a licensed club, two gymnasiums, a ski-lodge and holiday houses at Eildon, Lakes Entrance, Port Fairy and Tawonga South. An Amateur Sports and Welfare Society was run by the force, and its affiliates numbered thirty-two police clubs covering most sports, including flying, sailing, snow and water ski-ing and angling.

Promotions within the force to all ranks from senior constable to inspector depended upon passing written and oral examinations, and satisfactory appearances before Promotion Boards. The first promotion, from constable to senior constable, was the only one requiring a minimum period of service—five years after graduating from the academy. Subsequent promotion opportunities varied considerably depending upon force wastage and individual qualifications. Many members reached the ranks of sergeant with under ten years service, senior sergeant after fifteen years and inspector in under twenty years.[49]

As had always been the way with the force, the majority of its members were posted to police stations and performed general duties in uniform. No amount of technological or other change had altered the fact that the essence of police work was people dealing with people. In a world of robot devices, vending machines and self-service one could still find policemen in person in all corners of the state. Eighty police stations provided a twenty-four-hour service and, in the tradition of the force, there were 111 one-man stations.

The thought of a solitary policeman working in almost traditional fashion in some rugged and remote part of the state had an arcadian appeal for many Victorians, who liked the idea of a masculine and weatherworn outdoorsman dropping in on local folk in his police four-wheel-drive vehicle. (The last country troop horse ceased work in 1961.) Others favoured educated, bilingual and female police, working in multicultural urban environments, and able to understand many of the problems and languages of the people they encountered. The force was tailored to meet many tastes and needs in 1984. However, it would be wrong to suggest that it was everything it could have been—or that it was what everyone wanted it to be. In common with other industrialized and urbanized Western cultures, Victoria was an imperfect society with many social and other problems. The force drew the bulk of its members from that society and, despite screening, it incorporated some of the problems found there; and some members responded badly to some community problems.[50]

During 1983–84 a total of 576 formal complaints were made against members of the force, including allegations of assault, corruption, harassment, and unjustified arrest, prosecution, search or seizure. Most of the complaints were found not to be justified, but forty-three members appeared before the Discipline Board and sixty-five were the subject of counselling, reprimand or disciplinary transfer. In addition, a total of 514 requests were received under the Freedom of Information Act for access to police documents, more requests than those for any other State government agency, and including requests for copies of criminal records and complaint investigation files. A significant number of requests related to Special Branch. The number of complaints against police that resulted in discipline or legal action was evidence that the force was not perfect. Some members were heavy-handed, rude, incompetent or criminal. Their kind had always been there and probably always would be, while policemen were drawn from the community and reflected its broad range of character types, temperaments, degrees of tolerance and standard of honesty. The screening of police applicants minimized the proportion of undesirables admitted to the force but it did not eliminate them. Nor could the selection and training processes take into account all the violent situations, pressures and temptations to which policemen were exposed in the course of careers spanning thirty years.

Of those formal complaints made against members of the force, over half were allegations of assault. The next most common category was 'unsatisfactory performance of duty', but only four people alleged instances of corruption. The level of public dissatisfaction with the force, as expressed through the formal complaint system, was low when ranked alongside the number of contacts between members of the force and members of the public: 286 909 traffic infringement notices were issued, 277 260 crimes were reported, 227 754 drivers were given breath tests, 55 343 vehicles were checked for roadworthiness, 47 392 persons were proceeded against for criminal offences, 41 939 accidents were reported, 38 900 parking infringement notices were issued, and many thousands of police–citizen contacts were never documented or tallied.[51]

During the same period, 92 members retired from the force after being found medically unfit by the Government Medical Officer, and of these 54 were suffering from a nervous disorder. Corresponding figures for the previous year were 114 and 74. The rate of ill-health retirements, particularly those due to nervous disorders, was a source of concern to both the police administration and Association. The Chief Commissioner highlighted 'the pressures of over-exposure and over-work' as key factors contributing to the rate of ill-health retirements, but also lamented that 'there are those inadequate personalities who ought not to have been recruited in the first place'. Moves were made to develop 'an effective psychological screening program', and it was suggested that police medical services be co-ordinated from point of entry to eventual retirement. Given that ill health due to occupational factors was first identified among Victorian policemen during the nineteenth century, it is perhaps an indication of their lowly lot, and an indictment of successive governments and police administrators, that so little was done to remedy the situation until the 1980s. Throughout most of the force's existence much has been made of the physical and mental resilience of its members, in the face of all odds, an attitude reinforced by the emphasis placed on physical prowess and the past practice of awarding a trophy to the 'most promising' wrestler and boxer in each graduating squad and of affording them similar status to the academic dux. During 1984 more than one thousand members of the force were assaulted in the course of duty, so there was a continuing need for self-defence training, and perhaps more of it. Yet many policemen—and policewomen—were not as physically and mentally tough as they were often assumed to be. Tradition had it that they could look after themselves, so preventive medicine and health programmes had been relatively neglected. The spate of resignations through ill health indicated, however, that much more needed to be done in this way to help members of the force cope with their difficult and changed world.

An instance of this sort was the establishment of a Personal Assistance Programme Committee to look at the problem of alcohol and drug abuse among police, and to provide a service to help them. Formation of the committee was prompted by the Chief Commissioner, who expressed concern that, during the four-year period 1980–83, sixteen off-duty members of the force were killed in motor vehicle collisions, including twelve with positive blood alcohol concentrations, and was belated recognition that some police in Victoria—on a continuing basis since 1836—had personal problems with alcohol abuse. The answer in 1854 was to erect extra cells at the Police Depot to accommdate them. In 1984 the Victoria Police Surgeon, Dr J. Peter Bush, acknowledging that there were police 'who use alcohol immoderately—who have an alcohol problem', urged that it be recognized and treated as 'a sickness, a health problem'. The traditional police-force reliance on individual toughness and ability to cope had meant that positive medical help for alcoholic policemen was not forthcoming for well over a century.[52]

In addition to personal problems among its members, the force in the

1980s, in common with other Australian police forces, was forced to recognize that in terms of its sexual, racial and ethnic composition it was not—and never had been—truly representative of the community it served. In the matter of equal opportunity for women, the force had taken great strides, but females occupied mainly lower ranks and still only comprised 10 per cent of the force when they made up more than half of the Victorian population. Similarly, in a multicultural society, most ethnic groups were under-represented and many were not represented at all.

It might be argued that to be professional and efficient a police force need not be truly representative of the community it serves, and there is some merit in that proposition. Yet it could equally well be argued that a greater ethnic and racial mix would have increased multicultural understanding and reduced racial tension. However, the force in 1984 included only one Aborigine, one Asian and only a relative smattering of persons born outside the British Commonwealth. Of the almost 250 000 Victorians born in Italy, Greece or Yugoslavia only thirty-seven were members of the force. Based upon their proportions of the overseas-born population of Victoria, people from these countries were significantly under-represented in the force, whereas people from New Zealand, the Netherlands, Germany, the United Kingdom and Ireland were significantly over-represented in the police ranks. The number of police born in other overseas countries did not exceed eight for any individual nation and the total comprised less than 10 per cent of the overseas-born component and less than 2 per cent of the force overall. Detailed statistics relevant to the parentage and ethnic backgrounds of Australian-born members of the force have never been available.[53]

Policing Victoria in 1984 involved two contradictory—or perhaps, complementary—elements. On the one hand, it was the age of community policing, with members of the public sharing the responsibility for the well-being of their neighbourhoods. On the other hand, it was the era of anti-crime task forces and recognition by governments, police and people that large-scale organized crime had become 'big business'. It was recognized that traditional methods of policing were impotent against criminals, who crossed state and national borders at will and had the financial backing of millionaires. No fewer than eighty members of the force were deployed on eleven task forces, some of which were joint ventures involving the Australian Federal Police, Australian customs officials, and police from other states. During 1984 the National Crime Authority (NCA) was formed to combat organized crime on a national scale, and members of the force were seconded to work for it on a full-time basis. The use of task forces and the formation of the NCA were evidence of the community responding to the challenges of organized crime: they introduced another stratum into Victorian policing, and marked a significant point in the development of law enforcement. Upon formation of the NCA its foundation chairman, Mr Justice Stewart, expressed the hope that his organization and the force would have a 'long and productive history of co-operation'. A similar sentiment had launched the Victoria Police Force as the state's sole policing authority in 1853.[54]

It was appropriate, when the police alone were seen not to be coping with organized crime, that the Government, the police and the people combined to seek a better way. That had been the way of things in Victoria for almost 150 years, and on that note 1984 ended. A Committee of Inquiry headed by Mr Tom Neesham, a barrister and former deputy ombudsman, was preparing a report on its examination of the organization and administration of the force. The committee of five men was appointed in September 1982 by the newly elected Labor government led by John Cain Jr, which had pledged such an inquiry during its election campaign.[55]

Conclusion

Underlying this book, and running through it, is the notion that the police force was shaped by the community it served—the people of Victoria. It is an adaptation of the adage that the community gets the police it deserves. Some people may question this, on the grounds that the population of Victoria has never been a homogeneous whole, with one set of ideas, attitudes and influences. The diversity and conflicts within society are acknowledged, but that only makes it more true that the force is a force of the people. In different ways it has been influenced by the mosaic of interest groups that is the Victorian community. John Batman and members of the Port Phillip Association, Peter Lalor and the Ballarat miners, Francis Longmore and the Kelly gang, Adela Pankhurst and the suffragettes, Sir Thomas Blamey and the Labor Party, Dr Jim Cairns and the Vietnam Moratorium Committee, and Dr Bertram Wainer and the Abortion Law Reform Association are just a sprinkling of the thousands of individuals and groups who have influenced the development of policing in Victoria. They have taken different forms, exerted their influence in a variety of ways and have often disagreed with the police and each other. However, the net result of debate and compromise has been a general shaping of the force by the community.

Successive generations of Victorians have collectively influenced the force in ways that have ensured it a significant level of public support and good will, and themselves a tolerable police service. There have been fluctuations in the levels of public good will and police acceptability, sometimes due to errant or outstanding police conduct, and often because the social standards, tolerances, and expectations of different generations have varied. On many occasions policemen have enforced unpopular laws or enforced acceptable laws in unpopular fashion; they have angered workers by appearing too ready to side with capital against labour; and at different times individual policemen or groups of them have aroused public indignation, concern and action by behaving corruptly, violently, dishonestly or ineptly, or by failing to meet some widely accepted standards of police conduct and performance. Nevertheless, the system of policing has generally worked for the people, not against them, although it has required community vigilance to ensure it.

It might be argued that 'ordinary people', those individuals without wealth or positions of power, have never been able to exert their will over the police force, but they have. Ordinary Victorians have played a key part in the process of government that has directed the force; they have given evidence at the many public inquiries into policing; they have made their opinions known through the media and in representations to politicians and police leaders; and most strikingly they have banded together in ways that have forced the police to change. On the Ballarat goldfield in 1854, and during the Kelly saga at the end of the 1870s, in the 1890s depression, the 1923 police strike and the moratorium marches of the 1970s, the collective will of ordinary people began to change the police force. Clearly, individual levels of influence have never been equal, and in many cases they have been negligible, but that is not the point under debate here. The central question is: has the police force autonomously determined the course of its development, or has it been decided outside, in the community?

Since 1836 almost every important decision and action on the development of policing in Victoria has come from beyond the force. The police have generally been a conservative, often reactionary, group of public servants who, on low pay and under poor working conditions, have ambled along at the behest of the public. On a personal level, policemen— confident, large, authority figures—might appear to have had the upper hand, but as a force they have generally been a slow, timid and erring bureaucracy, floundering or stultifying when left too long away from the gaze and influence of the community. Technology and world events have been important in determining the course of the force's development, but its responses have often been reluctantly made under external pressures. The motor car revolutionized policing, yet in the beginning it was shunned by policemen who had to be convinced of its permanence and potential. The use of photographs, forensic science, computers and aircraft were technological aids either that the force was relatively slow to adopt, or which met with resistance from sections of the force when introduced. Unless prodded by the community, policemen often failed to comprehend the international scale and social significance of such things as the unionization of workers, the activities of suffragettes and women's rights movements, and the spread of student protests and the peace movement. The most notable exceptions to this trend, and they were few, were the production of Barry's *Police Guide*, the introduction of fingerprint analysis, the establishment of the wireless patrol, and a number of the post-1970 policing initiatives, which were all the work of policemen and later sanctioned by the Government.

The traditional and principal factor governing the activities of policemen has been the law, and from the beginning they have worked within a framework of law that has regulated almost every aspect of their duties.

General criminal offences and procedures, unlawful conduct, powers of arrest, search, seizure and prosecution have been decreed by law, and policemen themselves have always been subject to a Police Regulation Act covering such matters as appointments, dismissals, superannuation, tenure, and misconduct. Policemen have always been individually liable at law for unlawful acts or actions committed in the course of their work and have been investigated, sued, charged, convicted, fined and gaoled for things they have done on duty. It is not hard to see why many policemen have been conservative, thinking in terms of duty, obedience and regulations. They have always been men *under* authority. The source of law is the Government, and from 1856 to 1984 the force worked under fifty parliaments and more than sixty separate ministries, each appointed 'democratically' and together spanning a broad spectrum of political labels and ideologies. The force has always been answerable to a ministerial head, traditionally the Chief Secretary, but since 1978 the Minister for Police and Emergency Services; and, until the establishment of the Police Classification Board in 1946, the Government determined police wages, duties and conditions of service. The performance of the force has always been significantly affected by government policies, the level of government funding and interest, and the general ability of its ministerial head and his colleagues. The abysmal performance of governments caused serious police unrest in the 1860s, then stagnation in the 1870s, and contributed substantially to the police strike in 1923. On the other hand, positive government action in the 1920s enabled Blamey to boost the force, and in the 1940s dramatically improved police morale and work conditions, averting serious industrial problems. It was unpopular laws or government policies that cast policemen into open conflict with sizeable sections of the community during such times as the gold era, the economic depressions of the 1890s and 1930s, and the Vietnam war period, and then resulted in changes to the force. From both sides— people in power, and other people demanding to be heard—pressures were put on the police, who were to some extent moulded by them.

One important aspect of the democratic process and an important forum for public debate has been the series of Royal Commissions and other inquiries that different governments have appointed to inquire into the force. There were more than fifteen of these between 1839 and 1984, and most of them proved worth while. The 1852 Select Committee inquiry was responsible for unifying the disparate police forces in Victoria and establishing the basic structure of the Victoria Police Force. The important Royal Commission appointed to inquire into the Kelly outbreak cleansed the force of some of its least efficient and more discreditable elements, and gave it new direction. Other inquiries brought about the resignation of Blamey, curbed Wren's gambling empire, rid the force of corrupt policemen and provided blueprints for change. More importantly, they gave hundreds of Victorians an opportunity to speak out and criticize the force in a constructive way, and opened the force to general scrutiny and debate. Even the Beach Inquiry, the end result of which was a farcical victory for an uncharacteristic police militancy, opened the workings of the police for close examination and increased public awareness. Most inquiries since 1839 showed some individual policemen to be ineffective or guilty of wrongdoing, and highlighted the need to probe and prod the force as a whole, to make it publicly accountable and give it impetus and direction.

Police leaders, particularly the Chief Commissioners, bore a heavy responsibility for giving the force direction. Some gave it, some did not. When the force languished, as it often did, the community through the agency of government appointed men from outside the force to take charge and reorganize it. The periods of the force's history most marked by important reforms, public approbation and high levels of police performance, almost universally coincided with the commissionerships of 'outsiders'. Steward, Gellibrand, Blamey, Duncan and Porter were all extremely capable administrators, appointed in the face of opposition from serving policemen, and given the task of improving police performance. In its choice of these men the community vitally influenced the force and served itself well. Although an appointment to the top position from within the force has been known to work well (Miller was a notable example), on the whole the outsiders were the more stimulating.

Other outside elements that significantly affected the force include the news media and the legal profession. Victoria's newspapers always provided an extensive coverage of police matters, and proved particularly vigilant in bringing instances of corruption, misconduct and ineptitude to public notice. In the 1850s pressure from the *Argus* for a proper civil constabulary was a key factor leading to the formation of the Victoria Police Force, and since then newspapers closely followed, and helped determine, its fortunes. This fact was recognized by the establishment of formal links between policemen and pressmen, culminating in the formation of a Press Liaison Bureau, and the importance of the press was well illustrated by the way in which newspapers contributed to the downfall of Chief Commissioner Blamey. A number of public inquiries, including the Longmore Royal Commission into the Kelly outbreak, the Monash Royal Commission into the police strike, and the Beach Inquiry, were preceded by extensive newspaper coverage of the relevant events and allegations. Although representative of different commercial and political interests, the various forms of news media have collectively served as a vital link between the police force and the community, and have displayed a distinct willingness to help keep policemen honest.

The role of the legal profession was not always as overt as that of the press, but in many respects it has been as telling. Lawyers played a significant part at most of the inquiries into the force and proved adept at probing and exposing errant police behaviour. They also served to articulate the questions, concerns and allegations of 'ordinary people' in a way that often they could not do themselves. It is arguable that lesser men than Sir John Monash, Hugh Macindoe, William Kaye, Cairns Villeneuve-Smith and Barry Beach, would not have had the capacity or the fortitude to conduct complex and lengthy public inquiries into the actions of policemen. Lawyers and members of the judiciary also had the daily task of overseeing police behaviour in the courts, and they have often reprimanded, reported, or taken action against policemen for improper actions. Mr Justice Mann's denunciation of the police 'third degree' method was one instance of judicial comment that produced significant changes to criminal investigation procedures.

The degree to which the community determined the course of police development might suggest that policemen were a rather ordinary bunch. In many respects they were. Throughout most of its existence the force was largely comprised of men drawn from the working classes into one of the lowest strata in the public service, and paid and treated accordingly. Generally, policemen favoured the seniority system, with its hope of eventual promotion—and never mind about its inbuilt mediocrity. Mainly (though not always) they were reluctant to make trouble over wages or conditions of service. Their hours of work, leave, rest days and other benefits had a tendency to lag behind those of the general workforce and police in other states, and Victorian police have been housed in buildings declared unfit for human habitation. Often rough and needing to be tough, policemen were expected to work alone, confronting all manner of situations, including births, deaths and many of life's events that fell between. Police work rarely attracted the genteel, wealthy, highly educated or faint-hearted. Had it so desired, the community could have developed a police force from such types, but it did not. Working-class men were cheaper and arguably more suited to the physical, outdoors and often onerous nature of police duty.

The ordinariness of the force might be seen as a retardant that limited its actual and potential growth. However, there were also benefits to be found in its ordinariness. It made the force heavily dependent upon community involvement, always a desirable element in policing. It kept the force 'democratic', in the sense of understanding 'the people', belonging to them and drawing its strength from them. The fact that policemen were neither autonomous nor progressive pace-setters meant that they did not dictate to the Victorian people the sort of police service there would be. K. S. Inglis concluded his book, *The Stuart Case*, by writing that, 'The line from Australia to a police state is long. It is nevertheless continuous'.[1]

It would be equally true, and almost certainly more apt, to radically change that perspective. The line from Victoria to a police state is long—so long that it has never been properly surveyed, let alone made. It is so discontinuous, and leads in such an unaccustomed direction, that most policemen never think of trying to follow it. It is not their way. They are ordinary people, guided almost entirely by what is wanted by ordinary people and the people's government. Police complain if they are not given the powers to do the work they are asked to do—but that is so far back along the track that arriving at a police state is not in their itinerary. Anyway, so far the Victorian community has always managed—though in fits and starts—to move its police force in the directions chosen by majority opinion. It should continue to do so.

Yet many policemen over the years were far from being just ordinary. In different ways their individual achievements, ideas and bravery lifted them above the average, not only when judged alongside their colleagues but also when judged by those standards used to measure personal achievement and courage in the general community. More than fifty policemen were killed or died on duty, in a range of shootings, stabbings, drownings and accidents. All too often they were quickly forgotten and no one knows precisely how many there were or how they all died. The murders of Joseph Delaney, George Howell, Bob Lane, Stephen Henry, and others, received sensational publicity and they are well remembered in a way that highlights a particular aspect of police work and the sacrifices it sometimes demanded. Many others, however, died in more obscure, yet nonetheless courageous circumstances, such as William Harnetty, who drowned while attempting to rescue flood-bound sheep at Bet Bet in 1956, and Constable William Benbow who was killed at Richmond in 1971, when a building wall collapsed while he was trying to ensure the safety of others. In addition to those policemen who died on duty, hundreds of others were commended for placing their own safety at risk to save or protect other people. Between 1874 and 1984, more than four hundred policemen received bravery awards that included the George Cross, George Medal, Queen's Gallantry Medal, Royal Humane Society awards, and Valour Award. Constable Michael Pratt received the George Cross after being shot and wounded while trying to prevent the escape of three criminals from the scene of a bank robbery. His award was the highest honour for bravery available to a civilian in Australia and was perhaps the most publicized. In many less known cases policemen endangered themselves to secure the safe return of hostages, rescue people from drowning, find others lost in the bush, evacuate those threatened by bushfires, prevent people from committing suicide, and to apprehend armed and dangerous criminals or mentally disturbed persons. They were special feats accomplished by ordinary people; perhaps people like the man in the anonymous poem, 'I'm just a man like you':

I have been where you fear to be
I have seen what you fear to see
I have done what you fear to do
All these things I have done for you.

I am the man you lean upon
The man you cast your scorn upon
The man you bring your troubles to
All these men I have been for you.

The man you ask to stand apart
The man you feel should have no heart
The man you call the man in blue
But I'm just a man, just like you.

And through the years, I've come to see
That I am not what you ask of me
So take this badge, take this gun
Will you take it?—Will anyone?

And when you watch a person die
And hear a battered baby cry
Then do you think that you can be
All these things that you ask of me?[2]

Notes

Introduction

[1] John McQuilton, *The Kelly Outbreak*; John Molony, *I Am Ned Kelly*; John Meredith and Bill Scott, *Ned Kelly After a Century of Acrimony*, for bibliography; Les Blake, *Young Ned*, for school days; Doug Morrissey, 'Ned Kelly's Sympathizers', *Historical Studies*, vol. 18, no. 71 (October 1978), pp. 288-96.

[2] Niall Brennan, *John Wren: Gambler*; Hugh Buggy, *The Real John Wren*; Frank J. Hardy, *Power Without Glory*; Hugh Anderson, *Larrikin Crook: the Rise and Fall of Squizzy Taylor*; Mitchell Library, *Dictionary Catalogue of Printed Books*, for police bibliography.

[3] For twenty years the only published reference on the police was G. M. O'Brien, *The Australian Police Forces*. It lacks notes and bibliography, the style is journalese, and the author was a serving member of the Victoria Police public relations staff. John O'Sullivan, *Mounted Police of Victoria and Tasmania*, is a light work, without proper notes or bibliography, and is restricted to its narrow subject. Victoria Police, *Police in Victoria, 1836–1980*, is a booklet of 125 pages prepared by members of the force. A. J. O'Meara's thesis was written for La Trobe University, in 1977. The honours theses were written by J. McCahon, University of Melbourne, 1962; Gregory Coish, La Trobe University, 1971; R. K. Haldane, La Trobe University, 1981.

[4] D. Chappell and P. R. Wilson, *The Police and the Public in Australia and New Zealand*, p. 35.

1 Redcoats, Bluebottles and Alligators

[1] *New South Wales Government Gazette*, 9 September 1835, p. 627, for proclamation re trespassing; Letter from John Batman to Sir George Arthur, 23 October 1835, Mitchell Library, Papers of Sir George Arthur, vol. 33, manuscript A2193, pp. 40-7.

[2] A. K. Jackman, Development of Police Administration in Tasmania 1804-1960, for Tasmanian experience; Leon Radzinowicz, *A History of English Criminal Law and its Administration from 1750*: Volume 2. *The Enforcement of the Law*, for English experience. The 'Hue and Cry' was the old common law process where all members of a community had an obligation to join in the pursuit of a felon — with a view to apprehension — and alerted each other to the pursuit by raising a hue and cry with horns and voices.

[3] Correspondence from H. C. Wilson to Colonial Secretary, 4 May 1836, quoted in Pauline Jones (ed.), *Historical Records of Victoria*, vol. 1: *Beginnings of Permanent Government*, pp. 19-20, for appointment of Stewart; pp. 39-43, for Stewart's report.

[4] *New South Wales Government Gazette*, 14 September 1836, pp. 180 and 182, for appointments; Ernest Scott, 'Captain Lonsdale and the Foundation of Melbourne', pp. 97-116, for Lonsdale's background; Civil instructions from the Colonial Secretary to William Lonsdale, 14 September 1836, Mitchell Library, Despatches from the Governor of N.S.W. to the Secretary of State, 1836, A1267-14, pp. 1687-93.

5 VPRS 4, unit 1, item 36/1, for military instructions; Charles Reith, *A New Study of Police History*, pp. 121-287, for English principles.

6 Thomas O'Callaghan, 'Police in Port Phillip and Victoria, 1836-1913', p. 181, and Victoria Police Force, *Police in Victoria* 1836–1980, p. 3, for claims of former Sydney Police service and dismissal for drunkenness. Considerable misinformation about Day, Dwyer and Hooson is in print and is the subject of oral tradition. The primary and most inaccurate source of much of this false data is Edmund Finn, *Chronicles of Early Melbourne*, which among other things credits Hooson with being the first and only police official in Melbourne. The above material is drawn from an unpublished study by Linda Barraclough, who has undertaken research on the three men in Victoria, New South Wales and Tasmania. A copy of her work is held by the writer.

7 VPRS 1, vol. A, p. 1, no. 1, for Lonsdale's report of *Rattlesnake* arrival; Jones, p. 79, for Steel's appointment and salary; VPRS 51, vol. 1, pp. 35-168, for details of punishments.

8 VPRS 1, vol. A, p. 5, for appointment of Buckley; John Morgan, *The Life and Adventures of William Buckley*, for Buckley's story; Port Phillip Police Court Register, VPRS 51, vol. 1, pp. 2-6, for Steel's case.

9 Correspondence from William Lonsdale to Colonial Secretary, 13 March 1837, VPRS 1, vol. A, pp. 48-52, for cases to Sydney.

10 Correspondence from Francis Fisher to Colonial Secretary, 12 December 1836, quoted in Jones, pp. 185-6, for oath.

11 VPRS 1, vol. A, for dismissal of Dwyer (p. 19), Day (p. 22) and Hooson (p. 136).

12 *Age*, 16 August 1980, p. 5, for first police being drunks T. A. Critchley, *A History of Police in England and Wales*, pp. 51-5, for account of New Police; Correspondence from Colonial Secretary to William Lonsdale, 15 September 1836, Mitchell Library, A 1267-14, pp. 1686-7, for wage rates.

13 Correspondence from H. C. Wilson to Colonial Secretary, 17 February 1837, quoted in Jones, p. 187, for Tomkin's appointment; Correspondence from William Lonsdale to Colonial Secretary, 8 January 1838, VPRS 1, vol. A, item 38/1, p. 161, for Tomkin's death; ibid., 8 July 1837, VPRS 1, vol. A, item 37/59, p. 88, for Batman's appointment; ibid., 5 August 1838, VPRS 1, vol. A, item 38/100, p. 263, for Batman's suspension.

14 Ibid., 23 May 1837, VPRS 1, vol. A, p. 115, for Rogers and Allsworth.

15 See Edmund J. B. Foxcroft, *Australian Native Policy: Its History Especially in Victoria*; Barry Bridges, 'The Native Police Corps, Port Phillip District and Victoria, 1837-53', pp. 113-42; Les Blake, *Captain Dana and The Native Police*.

16 Correspondence from William Lonsdale to Colonial Secretary, 24 August 1836, VPRS 1, vol. A, item 38/115, p. 277, for uniforms; ibid., correspondence, 23 February 1839, for rules.

17 Petition from Western District Settlers to Sir Richard Bourke, 8 June 1837, quoted in Jones, pp. 219-21; Petition from Goulburn River Settlers to Colonial Secretary, 21 August 1838, quoted in Jones, pp. 270-1; Petition from Ovens River settlers to C. J. La Trobe, 20 November 1839, quoted in Jones, pp. 271-2; Mitchell Library, A1267-14, pp. 1871-4, for pledge to defray costs.

18 *New South Wales Government Gazette*, 13 September 1837, p. 625, for Geelong appointments; Correspondence from Foster Fyans to Colonial Secretary, 24 May 1839, N.S.W. State Archives 39/6957, for extraneous appointment; *Report of the Committee on Police and Gaols*, Sydney, T. Trood, 1839 (hereafter cited as the 1839 Police Report), p. 35, for recommendation.

19 *Police in Victoria*, p. 5, for number of police; Correspondence from William Lonsdale to Colonial Secretary, 5 August 1838, VPRS 1, vol. A, item 38/100, p. 263, for appointment of Wright; W. A. Sanderson, 'Mr John Waugh's Reminiscences of Early Melbourne', pp. 1-18, for 'Tulip'.

20 Correspondence from William Lonsdale to Colonial Secretary, 5 August 1838, VPRS 1, vol. A, item 38/100, p. 263, for mark of improvement; O'Callaghan (1928),

pp. 186-7, for quotation and efficiency; Finn, pp. 51-5, for reputation as thief-taker.

21 Correspondence from William Lonsdale to Colonial Secretary, 13 December 1838, VPRS 1, vol. A, item 38/169, p. 326, for new gaol; ibid., 12 June 1838, VPRS 1, vol. A, item 38/73, p. 240, for powers and manual; *New South Wales Government Gazette*, 28 November 1838, for proclamation.

22 1839 Police Report, pp. 16, 34-5, for details of mounted police; John O'Sullivan, *Mounted Police of Victoria and Tasmania*, p. 13, for police at Broken River.

23 N. M. O'Donnell, 'The Australian Career of Henry Fysche Gisborne', pp. 112-36, for Gisborne's work; 1839 Police Report, pp. 17 and 37, for Border Police; Edward M. Curr, *Recollections of Squatting in Victoria*, p. 92, for killing; O'Sullivan, pp. 22-35, for an account of Border Police work, including murders.

24 Thomas O'Callaghan, *List of Chief Constables, District Constables, Police Cadets, and Police Officers in Victoria 1836 to 1907*, pp. 5-6, for Falkiner, Brodie and Sugden.

25 *Report from the Select Committee on Police*, 1852 (hereafter cited as 1852 Select Committee on Police), Evidence, p. 56 (Sugden), for appointment of detectives and their work; ibid., (Ashley), for ideal type; David Ascoli, *The Queen's Peace: The Origins and Development of the Metropolitan Police 1829–1979*, pp. 118-121, for English detectives.

26 1852 Select Committee on Police, Evidence, p. 8 (Sturt), for enlistment of emancipists.

27 O'Callaghan (1907), p. 5, for police service dates of Bloomfield; ibid., p. 24, for police service dates of Sturt; *Argus*, 11 May 1853, for assault and Merrijig Hotel; VPA, O'Callaghan Papers (unpublished manuscript), for Sturt's early days with police; *ADB*, vol. 6, pp. 215-16, for Sturt biography.

28 D. R. G. Packer, 'Victorian Population Data, 1851-61: A Preliminary Analysis', pp. 307-23, for population data; Geoffrey Serle, *The Golden Age*, pp. 9-36, for the early goldrushes; J. Sadleir, 'The Early Days of the Victorian Police Force', pp. 73-9, for quotation.

29 *Argus*, 14 August 1852, for quotation; Serle, p. 382, for population doubling; Packer, pp. 322-3, for V.D.L. immigrants; Correspondence from Superintendent E. P. Sturt to Colonial Secretary, 15 January 1852, VPRS 1189, unit 16, folio 2, file 52/180, for police to goldfields. From the available police archives it has not been possible to determine precisely the nature and rate of the growth in police numbers from the mid-1840s up to the early 1850s.

30 VPA, O'Callaghan Papers, for uniform details and quotations.

31 Serle, p. 97, for majority of ex-convicts; *Argus*, 14 April 1852, for pay rates; Correspondence from Superintendent E. P. Sturt to Colonial Secretary, 15 January 1852, VPRS 1189, unit 16, folio 2, file 52/180, for police as day labourers.

32 VPA, O'Callaghan Papers, for police drunks and gaolings; W. R. Morrison, 'The North-West Mounted Police and the Klondike Gold Rush', pp. 93-105; Western Australia Police Department [author Andrew Gill?], 'Some Aspects of the Western Australian Police Force 1887–1905', p. 29; J. P. Martin and G. Wilson, *The Police: A Study in Manpower. The Evolution of The Service in England*, pp. 23-4, for nineteenth-century police drunkenness in Canada, England and Western Australia; *Argus*, 20 January 1852, for police robbers; ibid., 21 January 1852, for dog rewards.

33 VPRS 1189, Box 16, for Sturt's despatches; Legislation providing moieties of fines for police included: 15 Vic., No. 12 (1852), an Act to Restrain the Practice of Gambling and the use of Obscene Language, section 2; 15 Vic., No. 15 (1852), an Act to Restrain by Summary Proceeding Unauthorised Mining on Waste Lands of the Crown, section 7; 15 Vic., No. 14 (1852), an Act to Consolidate and Amend the Laws relating to the Licensing of Public-houses, and to Regulate the Sale of Fermented and Spirituous Liquors in New South Wales, section 1.

34 15 Vic., No. 12, section 1, for penalty of up to £5 for persons convicted of using obscene

language; *Argus*, 5 June 1852, for conspiracy case and criticism of incentive system; ibid., 12 April, 3 and 8 May 1852, for criticisms; ibid., 17 February 1852, for price of gold; 1852 Select Committee on Police, Evidence, pp. 2-3 (Sturt), for comments on moiety system, including difficulty deploying men and jealousy; ibid., p. 41 (Templeton), for Mounted Police Corps experience and quotation; VPRS, vol. 1, item 161, p. 512, for La Trobe letter; C. Rudston Read, *What I Heard, Saw, and Did at the Australia Goldfields*, pp. 85-6, for £1000 in six months.

35 The amended vagrancy legislation, 16 Vic., No. 22, An Act for the better prevention of Vagrancy and other offences, section 20, was one act that provided for payment of half-shares of fines into the Police Reward fund; VPRS 1189, unit 16, folio 2, file 52/214, for disbursements from fund, including payments for injuries and excessive hours; 1852 Select Committee on Police, Evidence, *passim*, for lack of support for fund.

36 1852 Select Committee on Police, Evidence, p. 9 (Sturt), for quotation; VPA, O'Callaghan Papers, for active men shunning the service; *Argus*, 2, 18 February, 4 June, 16 August, 9, 30 October 1852, for vigilante groups. The term 'bluebottle' was used to derisively describe those men who did join the constabulary during the gold rushes.

37 Correspondence from La Trobe to Colonial Secretary, 22 February 1852, VPRS 1084, vol. 1, item 33, pp. 226-8, for arrival of pensioners; *Argus*, 8 January 1852, for Barrow's work; ibid., 20 February 1852, for 'half-horse half-alligator'; 1852 Select Committee on Police, Evidence, p. 8 (Sturt), for drunken set of men.

38 Correspondence from La Trobe to Secretary of State, 3 December 1851, VPRS 1084, vol. 1, for request for soldiers and warships; VPA, O'Callaghan Papers, for arrival of Valiant and his men; *Argus*, 19 February 1852, for 'we want thief-catchers'.

39 VPA, O'Callaghan Papers, and *Argus*, 3-20 April 1852, for account of *Nelson* robbery. Vandemonians were generally regarded as being responsible for much of the crime committed in Victoria. See VPA, O'Callaghan Papers.

40 J. Sadleir, 'The Early Days of the Victorian Police Force', pp. 77-8, for formation of cadet corps and former occupations; John Sadleir, *Recollections of a Victorian Police Offi-cer*, pp. 24-8 and 298-308, for cadets, including location of camp and personnel listings; VPRS 1189, unit 16, folio 1, file 52/3459, for cadet duties; ibid., unit 145, for Mitchell quotation; *Police Life*, December 1980, p. 16, for Chomley's career; L. E. Hoban, *New South Wales Police Force 1862-1962*, pp. 22-3, for Fosbery's career; *Argus*, 19 February 1852, for 'Brains, brains, brains'.

41 VPRS, Despatches from the Secretary of State, 1852, vol. 2, pp. 1047-72, 1187-1205, for correspondence relating to police from United Kingdom and the London Fifty; VPA, O'Callaghan Papers, for additional material; MS. Material from Superintendent Jack Scully, Curator Royal Ulster Constabulary Museum, dated 11 July 1983, for account of Irish Constabulary formation and uniforms; Hilary Idzikowski, Internal Colonialism and the Emergence of the Irish Police, for workings of Irish Constabulary; Sadleir (1911), pp. 78-9, for quotation.

42 1852 Select Committee on Police, Report, p. ii, for Snodgrass motion; ibid., p. iii, for state of policing in Victoria; ibid., Evidence, *passim*, for matters considered. Robin Walker, 'The New South Wales Police Force, 1862-1900', pp. 25-7, for New South Wales system; R. M. Lawrence, *Police Review 1829-1979*, pp. 9-15, for Western Aus-tralian system; Jackman, pp. 1-101, for Tasmanian system; Queensland Police, *The Queensland Police Force*, pp. 9-13, for Queensland system; Critchley, *passim*, for Eng-lish System.

43 1852 Select Committee on Police, Evidence, p. 4 (Question 70), for showy uniform; Critchley, pp. 168-71, for English police pensions.

44 1852 Select Committee on Police, Report, p. iii, for criticism; ibid., p. v, for rec-

ommended inducements; ibid., p. vi, for hope; Walker, pp. 25-7, for consolidation in New South Wales.

⁴⁵ *Argus*, 11 November 1852, for debate and speculation; 16 Vic., No. 24 (1853), An Act for the Regulation of the Police Force, sections 2-4, for Victorian legislation; 10 Geo. IV, c. 44 (1829), for London Metropolitan Police Act; S. W. Horrall, 'Sir John A. Mac-Donald and the Mounted Police Force for the Northwest Territories', pp. 179-200, for RCMP formation and Irish military influence.

⁴⁶ 14 Vic., No. 38, for New South Wales legislation; 16 Vic., No. 24, section 5, for ranks and appointments; ibid., section 7, for quotation; ibid., sections 15 and 19, for discipline matters; ibid., sections 21-5, for pension provisions; 17 Vic., No. 24, section 7, for repeal of scheme; VPA, 1853 Oath sheets, for unqualified men; Critchley, p. 52, for Peel's standards; *Argus*, 8 March 1853, for objections.

⁴⁷ *Victoria Government Gazette*, 12 January 1853, p. 20, for provisional appointment of Mitchell; ibid., 24 August 1853, p. 1246, for confirmation; *ADB*, vol. 5, pp. 262-3, for Mitchell biography; *Report from the Select Committee on Captain MacMahon's Case* (hereafter cited as Captain MacMahon's Case), Evidence, p. iii (Mitchell), for conditions under which Mitchell took up appointment.

⁴⁸ *Victoria Government Gazette*, 2 February 1853, for list of officer appointments; Captain MacMahon's Case, Evidence pp. 13-14 (Mair), for Mair's background; ibid., pp. 2-12 (Mitchell) and pp. 108-11 (MacMahon) for MacMahon's background; 1852 Select Committee on Police, Evidence, pp. 10-12 (Dana), and *Report from the Select Committee on the Police Force*, 1863 (hereafter cited as 1863 Select Committee on Police), Appendix G, Evidence 1861-2, p. 78 (Dana), for Dana's background.

⁴⁹ VPRS 1189, unit 145, file C53/10.442, for Mitchell's manpower figures and comments; Serle, p. 382, for population figure; *Commonwealth Year Book*, 1910, p. 894, for twentieth-century figures.

⁵⁰ VPRS 1189, unit 145, file C53/10.442, for 2000 men in 1854 and Mitchell's complaints; Packer, p. 323, for migration data; Serle, p. 390, for downturn in gold production; *Argus*, 1 April 1853, for Falstaff's troop.

⁵¹ *Argus*, 12, 18 February, 8 March, 30 April, 25 May, 9 June, 2 July, 24 December 1853, for letters and concern about pay delays.

⁵² VPRS 1189, unit 145, file C53/10.442, for arrival of the London Fifty and Mitchell's comments; *Argus*, 10 May 1853, for letter; ibid., 23 May 1853, for twenty-one men in a room; ibid., 10-11 August 1853, for wood-choppers' case, including Sturt's comment.

⁵³ *Argus*, 20 July 1853, for work of detectives; ibid., 10 October 1853, for mounted city patrol; VPRS 1189, unit 145, file C53/10.442, for Mitchell's opinion of detectives.

⁵⁴ VPA, 1853 Oath sheets, for details of 168 recruits. The birthplaces of those born in the United Kingdom were Ireland 65%, England 26%, Scotland 8%.

⁵⁵ *Argus*, 11 February 1853, for illiteracy; Critchley, p. 209, for English police gazette.

⁵⁶ *Victoria Government Gazette*, 31 May 1853, for Mitchell's proclamation; ibid., 21 February 1854, p. 502, for appointment of MacMahon as Acting Chief Commissioner; *Argus*, 25 November 1853, for quotation. Mitchell was Honorary Minister and Leader of the Legislative Council in the first Haines Ministry (November 1855–March 1857); Minister of Railways and Roads in the O'Shanassy Ministry (December 1861–June 1863); Chairman of Committees, Legislative Council (1869–1870); President of the Legislative Council (1870–24 November 1884). He was knighted (KB) in 1875.

2 Drunks, Soldiers or Policemen?

¹ *Report from the Select Committee on Captain MacMahon's Case* (hereafter cited as Captain MacMahon's Case), Evidence, pp. 2-4 (Mitchell); and *Report from the Select Committee on the Police Force*, 1863 (hereafter cited as 1863 Select Committee on Police), Evidence 1862-3, p. 174 (MacMahon), for MacMahon's military background. In *ADB*,

vol. 5, p. 189, Suzanne G. Mellor claims MacMahon 'joined the Royal Irish Constabulary in 1851'. However, the Irish Constabulary was not given the prefix Royal until 1867, and in the 1863 Select Committee on Police, Evidence 1862-3, Q.4226, p. 174, MacMahon stated that his only personal knowledge of the Irish police was 'merely from casual contact with some of them'. In Ireland he was a soldier — never a policeman, an important distinction in light of the models adopted by the force under his command; *Argus*, 1 July 1854, for objection by the public; *Report of the Commission appointed to enquire into the State of the Police (Melbourne Police)*, 1855 (hereafter cited as 1855 Police Commission Report), p. 4, for quotation.

2 1855 Police Commission Report, p. 14, for military titles; 16 Vic., No. 24, for police legislation; VPRS 1189, unit 150, file F54/1368, for details of men and weapons.

3 G. Serle, *The Golden Age*, ch. 4, for government attitude to miners; *Census of Victoria — 1854*, p. vii, for population data; VPRS 1189, unit 150, file E54/5132, for figures on police strength and firearms.

4 *Report of the Commission Appointed to Enquire into the Conditions of the Gold Fields of Victoria*, 1855 (hereafter cited as 1855 Gold Fields Commission), p. xiii, and Evidence, p. 343 (MacMahon), for policy and practice of police deployment on goldfields; *Returns of Committals, Trials* from 1 July to 31 December 1853, and 1 January to 30 June 1854, for committal figures; Serle, p. 81, for Valiant and Clarke quotations; *Argus*, 13 November 1854, for 'unlitigious' place.

5 1855 Gold Fields Commission, Evidence, pp. 90-2 (Johnstone), and p. 343 (MacMahon), for police administration on goldfields.

6 Ibid., Report, pp. xii, xiii, xxvi, for Commission's view of the Camps, and quotations; *Argus*, 4 November 1854, for 'real enemy's country'; Ballarat Historical Park Association, Sovereign Hill, for Plan of Camp Defences; VPRS 1189, unit 16, folio one, file 52/1215, for police residing among community; ibid., unit 150, file E54/3941, for police on Yarra banks; 1855 Police Commission Report, pp. 8-13, for police system of working in Melbourne.

7 1855 Gold Fields Commission, Report, p. xii, for prudence and good temper; ibid., p. xxvi, for Hotham's order; ibid., Evidence, p. 92 (Johnstone), for lucrativeness; 17 Vic. No. 4, section 24, for half-share; *Report of the Board appointed to enquire into circumstances connected with the late Disturbances at Ballarat*, 1854 (hereafter cited as the 1854 Ballarat Riots Report), p. xiii; Henry Gyles Turner, *Our Own Little Rebellion*, ch. 1, for contemporary accounts; Francis Augustus Hare, *The Last of The Bushrangers*, p. 14, for iniquitous law.

8 1854 Ballarat Riots Report, p. xiii.

9 1855 Gold Fields Commission, Report, pp. xxii-xxiii, for Scobie murder, Eureka Hotel riot, final digger hunt and reading of Riot Act; ibid., pp. xxiv-xxv, for Eureka Stockade; ibid., Evidence, p. 346 (MacMahon), for halving of police; VPRS 1189, unit 153, file K54/2592, for wagon request; Turner, p. 70, for account of events at Stockade; Dr H. V. Evatt, quoted in R. D. Walshe, 'The Significance of Eureka in Australian History', pp. 103-27, for 'Australian democracy was born at Eureka'.

10 1855 Gold Fields Commission, Report, p. xxiv, for first quotation; ibid., p. xi, for other causes of events at Ballarat; Turner, p. 74, for second quotation.

11 1855 Police Commission Report, loc. cit; *Report of the Chief Commissioner for the Year 1859* (hereafter cited as *1859 Police Annual Report*), for lessons of Eureka and impetus to reform; Austin McCallum, *The Eureka Flag*, for King and the Eureka Flag; Hume Dow, 'Eureka and the Creative Writer', pp. 87-102, for Eureka writers and for Daley's ballad that follows.

12 *Victoria Government Gazette*, 3 January 1954, p. 16. Burke was appointed to the Victoria Police Force on 1 April 1853 with the rank of Acting Inspector. In 1860, when he took leave to lead an expedition to the Gulf of Carpentaria, he was Superintendent at Castlemaine.

13 State Library of Victoria, La Trobe Collection MS. 8718, Order Book for B Division of City Police (hereafter cited as La Trobe Collection MS. 8718), entry dated 24 January 1854, for hand trucks; 1855 Police Commission Report, p. 9, for labouring classes; ibid., pp. 10-11, for lightness of the labour, and hours of duty; *Manual of Police Regulations for the guidance of The Constabulary of Victoria*, 1856 (hereafter cited as the *Police Regulations*, 1856), p. 36, for hours of duty.

14 La Trobe Collection MS. 8718, for cases of police drunkenness, special instructions and church parades; 17 Vic., No. 25, section 12, for permitting any constable to become intoxicated; *Argus*, 7 July 1854, for eating an oyster; ibid., 7 October 1854, for trouble for publicans; *Victoria Government Gazette*, 29 August 1854, p. 1943, for police prison; ibid., 12 September 1854, p. 2034, for Visiting Justice.

15 F. T. West Ford, 'The Vital Statistics of the Police Force of the Colony of Victoria for the last ten years', pp. 193-6, for sickness and injury among police; *Maryborough and Dunolly Advertiser*, 5 February 1858, for Barnett's murder; *Police Regulations*, 1856, *passim*, for transfers and duties; La Trobe Collection MS. 8718, for parades and wives willing to cook and wash.

16 17 Vic., No. 25, section 14, for disenfranchisement; *Victoria Government Gazette*, 18 July 1854, p. 1599, for appointment of MacMahon to Legislative Council.

17 1855 Police Commission Report, p. 7, for need of a code; *Police Regulations*, 1856, p. 5, for quotation.

18 *Victorian Hansard*, 1858, vol. 3, p. 305, for murder accusation; Captain MacMahon's Case, Report, p. iii, for committee's exoneration; ibid., Evidence, p. 12 (Mitchell); ibid., p. 73 (Roche), for coroner's comments; ibid., p. 111 (MacMahon), for right to pursue private business; *Police Regulations*, 1856, pp. 9-13, for controls governing activities of constables.

19 *Papers relating to the Retirement of Captain MacMahon from the Government Service*, pp. 1-15.

20 In 1861 MacMahon was elected to the seat of West Bourke in the Legislative Assembly and during the next three decades served almost continuously as a member of parliament. He was twice elected Speaker of the Assembly and was knighted in 1875. In 1862 MacMahon was a member of the Select Committee that inquired into the police force, in 1870 he was instrumental in changing police recruiting procedures, and in the 1880s he was one of those who inquired into the Kelly outbreak.

21 1855 Police Commission Report, p. 7, and *Police Regulations*, 1856, p. 13, for conditions of police service and promotion opportunities.

22 State Library of Victoria, La Trobe Collection MS. 9502, Private Diary of Frederick Charles Standish (hereafter cited as Standish Diary), for opening quotation, hedonism and gambling; *Victoria Government Gazette*, 3 September 1858, p. 1701, for appointment of Standish as Acting Chief Commissioner; and ibid., 10 December 1858, p. 2488, for appointment as Chief Commissioner; *ADB*, vol. 6, pp. 172-3, for Standish biography; 1863 Select Committee on Police, Evidence 1862-3, p. 185 (MacMahon), for humble office; ibid., Appendix G, Evidence 1861-2, pp. 137-8 (Standish), for Standish's account of Selwyn incident.

23 John Sadleir, *Recollections of a Victorian Police Officer*, p. 267, for quotation; *Royal Commission on the Police of Victoria, Ad Interim Report*, (hereafter cited as the 1881 Police Commission, Ad Interim Report), p. iv, for details of Winch's transfer; ibid., p. ix, for details of his discharge; 1863 Select Committee on Police, Report, pp. ii-vi, for recommendation that Standish be replaced by a Board; ibid., p. v, for police hospital as grog shop; ibid., *passim*, for account of Winch's offences; ibid., Evidence 1862-3, p. 94 (Mair), for Freeman suicide; ibid., Appendix G, Evidence, 1861-2, p. 102 (Smith), for fighting cocks; *Police Annual Report*, 1859, p. 17, for flagrant evil; Standish Diary, for dinner parties.

24 Sadleir (1913), p. 267, for 'a strange mixture'; *Police Annual Report*, 1858, Appendix

A, for strength and distribution of force; 1863 Select Committee on Police, Appendix G, Evidence 1860-1, pp. 1-7 (Standish), for evidence of charges; *Police Annual Report*, 1859, pp. 6-19, for innovations by Standish; ibid., for quotation re electric telegraph.

25 *Police Annual Report*, 1858, p. 3, for police districts; ibid., 1859, pp. 5-6, for separation of powers; ibid., pp. 13-15, for demeaning work and quotation re servant-of-all-work; 1863 Select Committee on Police, Appendix G, Evidence 1860-1, pp. 4-5 (Standish); ibid., Evidence 1861-2, p. 30 (Standish); and ibid., Appendix J, for extraneous duties.

26 *Police Annual Report*, 1858, pp. 5-6, for HMCSS *Victoria*.

27 *Police Annual Report*, 1859, p. 8; *Progress Report of the Commissioners Appointed to Consider the Best Mode of Carrying out the Recommendations of The Defences Commission of 1858*, p. 5; and 1863 Select Committee on Police, Evidence, 1862-3, p. 106 (Standish), for militarism in police force and Standish's comments.

28 *Age*, 10 February 1862, p. 5, for 'A Melbourne Constable'.

29 *Report of The Commissioners appointed to Inquire Into and Report Upon The Civil Service of The Colony*, 1859 (hereafter cited as the 1859 Civil Service Commission Report), pp. 48-55, for proposed cuts in police numbers and wages; *Police Annual Report*, 1859, p. 5, for annual wastage. Population figures obtained from Victorian population censuses conducted in 1854 and 1861. Police strength figures obtained from 1855 Police Commission Report; *Police Annual Report*, 1858; ibid., 1859; and 1861 Return showing the distribution of the police force.

30 1859 Civil Service Commission Report, pp. 48-9 and 55, for amended pay scales and reasons; *Police Annual Report*, 1859, p. 5, for incomplete, anomalous and unadvisable; 1863 Select Committee on Police, Evidence 1862-3, pp. 22-4 (Standish), for account of pay cuts; ibid., Appendix G, Evidence 1861-2, p. 54 (Standish), for hand to mouth; *Victoria Government Gazette*, 5 April 1855, p. 898, for good conduct pay.

31 1863 Select Committee on Police, Appendix G, Evidence 1861-2, pp. 66-72 (Mair), for figure of one-quarter; *Age*, 14 February 1862, p. 5, for telegrams and refusals; ibid., 24 February 1862, p. 5, and *Ovens and Murray Advertiser*, 13 February 1862, for editorial comment.

32 1863 Select Committee on Police, Evidence 1862-3, p. 137 (Standish), for dangers and exposure; ibid., p. 41 (West Ford); and ibid., Appendix G, Evidence 1861-2, p. 19 (Standish), for opinions on police pay position; ibid., p. 71 (Mair), for hours of work and leave; *Age*, 11 February 1862, p. 7, for police and railway labourers; *Victorian Hansard*, 1862, vol. 8, p. 585, for O'Shanassy and p. 577, for Woods; *Argus*, 11 February 1862, for police being paid more; *ADB*, vol. 6, pp. 434-5, for Woods biography.

33 1863 Select Committee on Police, Evidence 1862-3, pp. 192-3 (O'Shanassy), for O'Shanassy's comments; ibid., Appendix H, for hospital statistics; ibid., Appendix G, Evidence 1861-2, p. 58 (MacMahon), for level of police pay.

34 1863 Select Committee on Police, Appendix G, Evidence 1861-2, p. 42 (Standish), for comments on police training.

35 1863 Select Committee on Police, Report, pp. iii-vi, for Kelly and Browne case, including finding that Standish be replaced by a Board; ibid., Appendix F, p. 217, for O'Shanassy minute; Appendix G, Evidence 1861-2, p. 145 (Standish), for beard petition; *Petition to the Legislative Assembly for the Colony of Victoria signed by 440 Inhabitants of Richmond*, for appeal by Richmond residents.

36 1863 Select Committee on Police, Report, p. iv, for Committee's criticism of special list; ibid., Evidence 1862-3, pp. 2-5 (Bookey), for working of special list; ibid., Appendix E (No. 2), for record of 1862 special list appointments; ibid., Appendix G, Evidence 1861-2, p. 22 (Standish), for his part in scheme. See *ADB*, vol. 5, pp. 378-82, for background on O'Shanassy, who was prominent in Victorian politics from the 1850s to the 1880s. A native of County Tipperary, Ireland, he was leader of the Catholic interest in the Victorian parliament and in 1866 the Pope appointed him a Knight of the Order of St Gregory.

[37] 1863 Select Committee on Police, Evidence 1862-3, pp. 4-5 (Bookey), for comments on Irishmen; ibid., p. 175 (MacMahon), for recruitment of Englishmen and Scotsmen; ibid., Appendix G, Evidence 1861-2, p. 71 (Mair), for men from Irish Constabulary; *Argus*, 12 February 1862, for 99 per cent Irish.

[38] Thomas O'Callaghan, *List of Chief Constables...*, pp. 10-26, for service dates of pioneer officers.

[39] G. R. Vazenry, *Military Forces of Victoria 1854–1967*, pp. 1.15-1.16, for departure of Second Battalion.

[40] *Report of Colonel Anderson, dated 4 July 1870, on The Defences of The Colony*, for Anderson plan; VPRS 3991, unit 504, file 71/Z10797; and Report from the Select Committee upon The Artillery Corps, 1871 (hereafter cited as 1871 Select Committee on the Artillery Corps), for formation of Artillery Corps.

[41] *Victoria Government Gazette*, 21 October 1870, p. 1553; *Victoria Police Gazette*, 25 October 1870, p. 250; VPD, 1870, vol. II, p. 241, for conditional recruitment and standing army.

[42] 1871 Select Committee on the Artillery Corps, Evidence, pp. 6-16 (Standish, MacMahon, Stubbs, Anderson); Police Regulation Statute 1865, section 7; VPRS 3991, unit 504, file 71/Z10797; Vazenry, p. 19.5, for formation and operation of artillery corps. (A number of married men and men aged over thirty did enter the force after September 1870 in an apparent relaxation of the original guidelines.)

[43] *Royal Commission on the Police of Victoria, Evidence 1882-3*, (hereafter cited as 1881 Police Commission — Evidence 1882-3), p. 53 (Mulcare), for 'a nursery for the police'; ibid., General Report, p. x, for effect of barrack life on morals; 1871 Select Committee on the Artillery Corps, Evidence, p. 2 (Anderson), for benefits of scheme; ibid., p. 5 (Standish), for 50 police candidates agreeing to join the artillery and 33 not agreeing; VPD, 1870, vol. II, pp. 239 and 245, for parliamentary comment. An examination of records in the Victoria Police Archives for the six-year period 1 May 1868 to 30 April 1874 — the last three years of the open recruiting system and the first three years of the artillery corps system — shows that 140 men joined under the open system and 175 via the artillery corps. An analysis based on their ages, previous occupations, nationalities and marital status, disclosed no significant variation between the two groups.

[44] 1871 Select Committee on the Artillery Corps, Evidence, p. 8 (Standish), for warning; ibid., p. 10 (MacMahon), for army concept; 1881 Police Commission, General Report, p. xi, for police failings during Kelly hunt.

[45] VPD, 1873, vol. 16, pp. 873-8, for Electoral Act Amendment debates; ibid., vol. 17, pp. 2127-44, for superannuation debates; ibid., for plaudits, p. 873 (Cope), p. 2134 (Jones), p. 2135 (Kerferd), p. 2135 (Richardson), p. 2133 (Patterson); *Police Regulation Statute* 1873, Part 3, for police superannuation details.

[46] VPD, 1873, vol. 16, p. 874 (Francis), p. 875 (Curtain), p. 875 (Smith), p. 877 (MacMahon), for four quotations.

[47] Ibid., p. 875, for police political activities; William H. F. Mitchell (MLC North-Western Province) was President in the Legislative Council and Captain MacMahon (MLA West Melbourne) was Speaker in the Legislative Assembly. Both were elected to these positions during 1871; *Report of The Royal Commission appointed to enquire into the state of the Public Service and Working of the Civil Service Act*, re police submissions. A police superannuation scheme was created in 1873, a new Manual of Police Regulations was published in 1877, promotional examinations were introduced in 1883, and a non-monetary merit award was introduced in 1899.

[48] On 8 January 1878, 'Black Wednesday', the radical-liberal-protectionist government of Graham Berry dismissed large numbers of senior public servants from the civil service in Victoria. The list numbered hundreds and included all the county court judges, coroners and police magistrates. Not one policeman was dismissed and the force was

the only government department untouched by 'Berry Blight'. The good fortunes of the police have since been attributed to their knowledge of the indiscretions of one of Berry's men. See Sadleir (1913), pp. 179-81; Alfred Deakin, *The Crisis in Victorian Politics 1879–1881*, pp. 16-20; Second Supplement to the *Victoria Government Gazette*, 8 January 1878, pp. 71-2, and VPRS 3995, Unit 1.

[49] The account of the Lothair Mine dispute is drawn from the following sources: *Ballarat Star*, 10 December 1873, pp. 2-3, 12 December 1873, pp. 2-3, 13 December 1873, p. 2, 15 December 1873, p. 2, 17 December 1873, pp. 2-3. *Age*, 10 December 1873, p. 3, 11 December 1873, pp. 2-3, 12 December 1873, pp. 2-3, 15 December 1873, p. 3. VPRS 3991, unit 716, file 73/D16598, for official papers, including correspondence between Francis, Standish and Superintendent Hill; Standish Diary, entry dated 20 February 1874, for comments about Francis.

3 Erinmen, Wren and O'Callaghan's Men

[1] Ned Kelly, 'Jerilderie Letter', quoted in Bill Wannan (ed.), *The Wearing of the Green*, p. 197.

[2] J. F. Hogan, *The Irish in Australia*; P. S. Cleary, *Australia's Debt to Irish Nation Builders*; C. H. Currey, *The Irish at Eureka*, for Irish-Australian writings. For anecdotes, see Cleary, pp. 193-4; Wannan, pp. 142-4; J. B. Castieau, *The Reminiscences of Detective-Inspector Christie*, p. 23; John Sadleir, *Recollections of a Victorian Police Officer*, pp. 278-9. Sadleir is one who credits Dalton with larrikin.

[3] Neil Coughlan, 'The Coming of The Irish to Victoria', pp. 84-5, for quotation and evidence of Irish-Australian outlawry; Niall Brennan, *John Wren: Gambler His Life and Times*, pp. xi-xii, is one example of the use of Coughlan's material in myth-making; VPA, Oath sheets. 1874 Re-sworn series, for Irish-born police; Oliver MacDonagh, 'The Irish in Victoria, 1851-91: A Demographic Essay', for Irish-born attorneys-general and solicitors-general. The numbers of Irish prisoners and police are based on a comparison of criminal statistics published in Victorian *V & P*, 1871, v. 3, p. 12, and the figures in Table 2 (p. 82).

[4] For misleading comments, see Garry Disher, *Wretches and Rebels*, p. 69; John McQuilton, *The Kelly Outbreak 1878-1880*, p. 67. For the public statements, see *Report from the Select Committee on The Police Force*, 1863 (hereafter cited as 1863 Select Committee on Police), Evidence 1862-3, p. 3 (Bookey); Appendix G, Evidence 1861-2, p. 71 (Mair); and *Victorian Hansard*, 1862, vol. 8, p. 577. *T'othersider*, 10 April 1897, p. 15, quoted in Western Australia Police [author, Andrew Gill?], 'Some Aspects of the Western Australian Police Force, 1887-1905', p. 29.

[5] R. B. Walker, 'Bushranging in Fact and Legend', *Historical Studies*, vol. 11, no. 42 (April 1964), p. 211, and R. B. Walker, 'The New South Wales Police Force, 1862-1900', *Journal of Australian Studies*, no. 15 (November 1984), pp. 30-1, for New South Wales figures; 'Some Aspects of the Western Australian Police', pp. 43-64, for Western Australian research.

[6] Seamus Breathnach, *The Irish Police from Earliest Times to the Present Day*, pp. 60-2. Sir Charles Jeffries, *The Colonial Police*, pp. 29-32; Theodore N. Ferdinand, 'Politics, The Police, and Arresting Policies in Salem, Massachusetts Since The Civil War', pp. 572-88. Wilbur R. Miller, *Cops and Bobbies*, James Q. Wilson, 'Generational and Ethnic Differences Among Career Police Officers', pp. 522-8. Arthur Niederhoffer, *Behind The Shield: The Police in Urban Society*, pp. 141-4. Nathan Glazer and Daniel P. Moynihan, *Beyond The Melting Pot*, pp. 219-274, for comparative readings on Irish police.

[7] Hilary Idzikowski, Internal Colonialism and the Emergence of the Irish Police, pp. 104-21; and Robert Curtis, *History of The Royal Irish Constabulary*, pp. 136-7, for events in Ireland and closing quotation.

8 MS. letter from Superintendent Jack Scully, Curator Royal Ulster Constabulary Museum, to writer, 11 July 1983, for marriage theory.

9 E. J. Hobsbawm, *Primitive Rebels*, p. 13; Kelly, quoted in Wannan, p. 197, for rogues at heart. See note 3 above, for prison and police figures.

10 MacDonagh, pp. 67-92; Coughlan, pp. 68-86; David Fitzpatrick, 'Irish Emigration in the Later Nineteenth Century', pp. 126-43.

11 Russel Ward, *The Australian Legend*, pp. 46-68, for currency ethos; Walker (1964), p. 211, for ill-repute; *Age*, 21 September 1888, p. 7, for downturn in Irish applications; R. K. Haldane, Victoria Police Strike 1923, p. 93, for ethnic composition of police strikers in 1923.

12 Idzikowski, pp. 104-54, for criticisms; Michael Davitt, quoted in Breathnach, pp. 59-60, for Imperial political force; Breathnach, p. 60, for style of policing; Jeffries, p. 31, for quotation.

13 Members of the RIC were given formal classroom instruction as well as firearms instruction and drill. In 1883, after the Kelly outbreak, a Royal Commission reported that Victorian police were still not given any preparatory training in their duties or instructed how to use the firearms issued to them. *Royal Commission on the Police of Victoria, General Report* (hereafter cited as 1881 Police Commission, General Report), pp. i-xxx, for English model, Irish appearance and reviled.

14 McQuilton, pp. 48-68, for samples of 'Irish' policing in Victoria; *Minutes of Evidence Taken Before Royal Commission on the Police Force of Victoria, 1881*, Pioneer Facsimile Edition (hereafter cited as 1881 Police Commission, Evidence, Pioneer Edition), Appendix I, p. 681, Q.52 (Montfort), for 'an army of occupation'.

15 1881 Police Commission, General Report, *passim*; and McQuilton, pp. 94 and 145, for shortcomings in limelight; 1863 Select Committee on Police, Evidence 1862-3, p. 4 (Bookey), for quotation; 1881 Police Commission, Evidence, Pioneer Edition, Q. 1282 (Hare), for Aaron Sherritt's description.

16 Details of the Kelly outbreak and those police and criminals involved in the saga were obtained from the following sources: VPRS 4965-4969, Kelly Historical Collection, Parts 1-5; The Kelly Papers, Victoria Police Archives; 1881 Police Commission, Evidence, Pioneer Edition; *Second Progress Report of the Royal Commission of Enquiry into the Circumstances of the Kelly Outbreak* (hereafter cited as 1881 Police Commission, Second Progress Report), p. xi, for 'cruel, wanton'; p. x, for no evidence of persecution. Details about the Kelly family as farmers, their selection and their place in the selector community were obtained from Doug Morrissey, 'Pioneer community life, land selection and the Kelly outbreak'; Doug Morrissey, 'Selection in the Kelly Country: Success or failure?'; Doug Morrissey, 'Ned Kelly's World', pp. 29-34.

17 Metropolitan and rural newspapers covered the Kelly hunt in detail and the *Ovens and Murray Advertiser*, 14 December 1878, echoed a common sentiment in suggesting 'four bush boys have outwitted the whole police force'; *VPD*, 1879-80, vol. 32, pp. 2337-9, and 1880-81, vol. 34, pp. 869-73, 911-17, contain debates about the Kelly outbreak and the 'disgrace to Victoria' caused by police inability to capture them; 1881 Police Commission, Second Progress Report, pp. xv-xxiv, describes police bickering during the hunt; *Argus*, 30 October and 1 November 1880, for Kelly trial details, including 'I will see you'.

18 VPRS 3991, unit 1175, file 80/R.9165, for appointment of Nicolson; VPRS 3991, unit 1173, file R. 8866, for details of Standish retirement.

19 VPRS 4967, unit 2, for inquiry requests by Standish, Nicolson and O'Connor; *Progress Report of the Royal Commission of Enquiry into the Circumstances of the Kelly Outbreak* (hereafter cited as 1881 Police Commission, Progress Report), p. 3, for terms of reference.

20 VPRS 1187, vols 56 and 57, and VPRS 3993, vols 41-3, for details of Royal Commission; *ADB*, vol. 5, p. 101, for Longmore biography; Alfred Deakin, *The Crisis in Victorian*

Politics 1879-1881, p. 15, for Deakin's assessment of Longmore. The eight Royal Commissioners were Longmore, W. Anderson, G. R. Fincham, J. Gibb, J. H. Graves, G. W. Hall, E. J. Dixon and G. C. Levey. Apart from Longmore the most prominent were: Anderson, a Scotsman, farmer, ardent Presbyterian and MLA for Villiers and Heytesbury; Graves, Irish Protestant, MLA for Delatite (Kelly Country), who knew the Kellys personally and was noted as the most sinuous and uncertain of fence-sitters; and Hall, a trade unionist and journalist from England, who was proprietor of the *Mansfield Guardian* at the time of the Stringybark Creek killings and who, in 1879, wrote a pro-Kelly pamphlet entitled *Outlaws of the Wombat Ranges*. Hall had agitated for an inquiry into the police force, and was elected MLA for Moira in July 1880.

[21] 1881 Police Commission, Evidence, Pioneer Edition, p. 706, and 1881 Police Commission, General Report, p. vii, for details of Commission's operation; Victoria Police Archives for police figures.

[22] 1881 Police Commission, Second Progress Report, pp. iv-vi, for findings and recommendations of Commission; VPA, for careers of Nicolson and Hare.

[23] 1881 Police Commission, General Report, p. v, for quotation re disgrace; *1881 Police Commission — Charges Against Members of The Police Force (Sir Charles MacMahon)*, for police replies; John Sadleir, *Recollections of a Victorian Police Officer*, pp. 240-2, for his opinion of Longmore.

[24] 1881 Police Commission, Second Progress Report, p. ix., for causes of the outbreak; *Benalla Standard*, 21 October 1881, for press queries of Commission's findings; VPRS Kelly Historical Collection, for Kelly Reward Board papers; 1881 Police Commission, General Report, pp. v-vii, for details of government actions and reluctance of police to give evidence; Studies of the Kelly outbreak include: Max Brown, *Ned Kelly: Australian Son*; Colin Cave (ed.), *Ned Kelly Man and Myth*; John McQuilton, *The Kelly Outbreak*; and Eric Hobsbawm, *Bandits*, ch. 9.

[25] *ADB*, vol. 5, pp. 364-6, for O'Loghlen biography; 1881 Police Commission, General Report, p. vi., for details of Chomley's appointment; VPA, for details of Chomley's career; 1881 Police Commission, Evidence, Pioneer Edition, p. 704, for letter from Standish; *The Cyclopedia of Victoria*, vol. I, p. 189, for additional details about Chomley, including 'in Brisbane'.

[26] Sadleir (1913), pp. 268-70, for descriptions of Chomley; *Royal Commission on Police, The Proceedings, Minutes of Evidence, Appendices, etc.* (hereafter cited as 1881 Police Commission, Proceedings), pp. 399-401, for Chomley's report; 1881 Police Commission, General Report, p. vi, for 'sanguine anticipation'.

[27] 1881 Police Commission, Ad Interim Report, for Winch and Larner.

[28] *Royal Commission on Police Special Report on the Detective Branch* (hereafter cited as 1881 Police Commission, Special Report), pp. iii-v, for descriptions of force and Secretan. T. A. Critchley, *A History of Police in England and Wales*, p. 161, for London model; Sir Robert Mark, *In the Office of Constable*, pp. 110-37, for changes made in London during the 1970s.

[29] 1881 Police Commission, Special Report, pp. ix-x, for account of 'fiz-gig' system; ibid., Second Progress Report, p. xxiii-xxiv, for Sherritt slaying.

[30] Victoria Police Archives, Kelly Papers, for references to secret service money and 'Diseased Stock'; Philip Stead (ed.), *Pioneers in Policing*, for nineteenth-century developments in criminal detection; Critchley, pp. 160-1, for notes on London detectives.

[31] 1881 Police Commission, General Report, Part xxviii — Summary of Recommendations.

[32] Sadleir (1913), pp. 269-70, re examinations; 1881 Police Commission, Proceedings, evidence of police delegates, *passim*, re suggested changes; ibid., Second Progress Report, p. iv, for quotation re Standish.

[33] From the 1850s onward oral tradition suggested that Victoria's police were the best in Australasia and their general reputation resulted in requests for their services in other

colonies, particularly New Zealand. Former Victorian police attained such positions as Inspector-General of Police (N.S.W.), Royal Commissioner on Police Inquiry (Queensland), Commissioners of Police (New Zealand), and Superintendent of Territorial Police (Tasmania).

[34] Sadleir (1913), p. 248.

[35] *Victoria Government Gazette*, 12 May 1882, p. 1059, for police recruiting details; 1881 Police Commission, General Report, p. xi, for recruiting philosophy; ibid., Proceedings, Evidence, p. 23 (Moors), re police literacy, p. 52 (McConville), re disbandment of artillery corps on 31 December 1880, p. 95 (Mayes), re raw recruits, p. 160 (West Ford), re spirometer test; Census of Victoria, 1881. General Report, p. 255, for absence of graduates; VPA and McQuilton, pp. 63, 177 and 183 for Graham details.

[36] 1881 Police Commission, Proceedings, Evidence, p. 2 (Chomley), p. 42 (Rogerson), p. 48 (McEvoy), p. 56 (Hall), p. 57 (Hillard), p. 65 (Perry), p. 66 (Acton), p. 70 (Thomas), re uniform costs and complaints and McEvoy quotation; *Regulations for the Guidance of The Constabulary of Victoria* (hereafter cited as *Police Regulations*, 1877), 1877, pp. 47-8, for dress regulations.

[37] 1881 Police Commission, Proceedings, Appendices F-L, for police pay rates; Evidence, p. 70 (Thomas), re relative pay position, p. 62 (McElroy), re marriage prohibition, p. 42 (Rogerson), re police petitions, pp. 67-8 (Acton), re civil service comparisons; *Argus*, 7 February 1881, p. 7, for prices of consumer items.

[38] *Police Regulations*, 1877, pp. 26-7, for hours of duty, pp. 44-6, for leave regulations; *Employees in Shops Commission, Second Progress Report* (hereafter cited as the Shops Commission), pp. 1-143, for details of work conditions outside police force; *Report of the Royal Commission appointed to enquire into the State of the Public Service and Working of the Civil Service Act*, and the Civil Service Act, 47 Vic., No. 773, 1883, for civil service conditions of work.

[39] 1881 Police Commission, Proceedings, Evidence, p. 16 (Chomley) re married and single men, p. 42 (Rogerson), re petitions and allowances, p. 70 (Thomas), re rental rates, p. 78 (Smythe), re fuel allowance and kettle boiling.

[40] *Victoria Police Gazette*, 8 January 1879, p. 3, for number and locations of police stations; *Police Regulations*, 1877, pp. 3, 34 for transfer policy and rules; 1881 Police Commission, Proceedings, Evidence, pp. 5-6 (Chomley), re transfers and allow- ances; ibid., Evidence, Pioneer Edition, p. 4 (Standish), and p. 139 (Sadleir), re transfers in north-east and travelling allowances.

[41] *Police Regulations*, 1877, pp. 3, 17-29, 59-61, for regulations governing conduct of constables; 1881 Police Commission, Proceedings, Evidence, pp. 7-8 (Chomley), and pp. 161-2 (West Ford), for policy on hospital attendance; p. 40 (Bourke), re animosity to police hospital system.

[42] *Police Regulations*, 1877, pp. 17-29, for beat duty regulations; 1881 Police Commission, Proceedings, Appendix E, for extraneous police duties.

[43] *Police Regulations*, 1877, pp. 13-17, for duties of officers and sub-officers; VPA, 1881 Police Records of Conduct, for details of discipline offences.

[44] *Police Regulations*, 1877, pp. 17-29, 59-61, 95-6, for duties of mounted constables; John O'Sullivan, *Mounted Police of Victoria and Tasmania*, p. 101, for Fane case; A. L. Haydon, *The Trooper Police of Australia*, p. 244.

[45] VPRS 844, Vol. 1, ref. 38/4/2, for Diary of Duty and Occurrences at Mount Moriac; VPA for biographical details of Hagger.

[46] 1863 Select Committee on Police, Appendix H, for illnesses treated at police hospital; *Australian Medical Journal*, vol. 10 (July 1866), pp. 193-6, vol. 15 (January 1870), pp. 1-4, vol. 17 (May 1872), pp. 143-7, for details of police ailments; 1881 Police Commission, Proceedings, Evidence, p. 4 (Chomley), p. 160 (West Ford), for details of ailments in 1881; Shops Commission, Evidence, p. 31 (Fletcher) (Peel), re medical

aspects of shop and factory work; 1881 Police Commission, General Report, p. xviii, for retirement recommendation.

[47] Critchley, pp. 150-9, for police pay and conditions in England; Haydon, p. 245, for pay comparison with Canada; Sadleir, pp. 291-2 and *passim*, for love of work; 1881 Police Commission, Proceedings, Appendices F-L, for pay and conditions in other Australian colonies; *Age*, 21 September 1888, p. 7, for some 1880s recruiting figures.

[48] Haydon, pp. 244, 406.

[49] *Royal Commission on the Victorian Police Force*, 1906 (hereafter cited as the 1905 Police Commission), Evidence, pp. 1-13 (Chomley); *VPD*, 1888, vol. 58, pp. 1599-1601, for comments re police suffrage; *VPD*, 1899-1900, vol. 93, p. 2721, for description of Chomley, and O'Sullivan, p. 162, for 'darling of the state'.

[50] *Victoria Police Gazette*, 13 June 1883, and *VPD*, 1895, vol. 79, p. 4201, for merger details.

[51] 1881 Police Commission, Report, pp. xi-xii, for Longmore findings; Critchley, p. 156, for English experience; *Victoria Police Gazette*, 4 July 1883, pp. 176-7, 19 December 1883, p. 326, 20 February 1884, pp. 51-2, 26 March 1884, p. 85, 9 April 1884, p. 97, 28 May 1884, pp. 144-5, for first examination details; VPA for career details of Philip Commons, who was dux, and Alfred Sainsbury, who became Chief Commissioner in 1913.

[52] John Barry, *Victorian Police Guide*; VPA for career details; *VPD*, 1888, vol. 58, p. 1702, for discussion of Barry's *Guide*; 1881 Police Commission, Report, p. xi, re Longmore suggestion.

[53] An Act to extend the franchise to members of the Police Force (26 November 1888); *VPD*, 1888, vol. 58, pp. 1599-1601, for police franchise debates.

[54] VPRS 937, unit 513, for police papers on Maritime Strike; Sadleir (1913), pp. 259-64, for comments; *Argus*, 30 August 1890, p. 9, and 1 September 1890, pp. 5-6; and *Age*, 29 August 1890, pp. 4-5, for criticism of police; William Guthrie Spence, *Australia's Awakening*, pp. 132-44 (especially p. 142), for account of strike and Price's order; T.A. Coghlan, *Labour and Industry in Australia*, vol. 3, ch. 7; J. E. Isaac and G. W. Ford (eds), *Australian Labour Relations Readings*, ch. 4; *Victoria Government Gazette*, 29 August 1890, pp. 3513-14, for proclamation; Percival Serle, *Dictionary of Australian Biography*, vol. 1, pp. 347-8, for Gillies biography.

[55] VPRS 937, unit 357, for police papers on unemployed and vagrancy figures; Police Offences Statute 1865, No. 265, part 3, for vagrancy law; Barry, pp. 57-72, re warrant execution; 1881 Police Commission, Evidence, p. 40 (Bourke), re warrants; *Age*, 17 June 1892, p. 5, for account of fray at Carlton.

[56] VPRS 6763, vol. 39, for approval to form band; *Argus*, 2 July 1891, p. 10, for football match; *Victoria Police Journal*, January 1932, pp. 110-12, for early band history.

[57] *Police Regulation Statute* 1873, section 51, for retirement clause; 1881 Police Commission, Report, p. xvii, for recommendation; 1905 Police Commission, Evidence, p. 12 (Chomley), for his opinion; *VPD*, 1891, vol. 67, pp. 1233-4, for 1889 Memo; p. 1233 (O'Loghlen); p. 1235 (Taylor); p. 354 (McLean), for recruiting applications; *Argus*, 21 August 1891, p. 6, 3 September 1891, p. 10, for commentary; *Victoria Police Gazette*, 10 February 1892, p. 41, for original retirement scheme. Amended by Order-in-Council, *Victoria Police Gazette*, 18 December 1895, p. 387.

[58] VPRS 677, unit 83, and VPRS 3992, unit 1105, for introduction of bravery award; *Victoria Police Gazette*, 28 December 1899, p. 411, for notice of first three recipients; VPA for details of recipients.

[59] 1905 Police Commission, Evidence, p. 1 (Chomley), retirement details; p. 2, recruit application figures.

[60] Frank J. Hardy, *Power Without Glory*, pp. 152-5, for Callinan; Frank J. Hardy, *The Hard Way*, p. 9, for Wren, and pp. 49-50 for O'Donnell; VPA for service details of

O'Callaghan; *Victoria Government Gazette*, 26 March 1902, p. 1187, and 16 July 1902, p. 3053, for appointment as Chief Commissioner; J. E. Menadue, *A Centenary History of the Australian Natives Association, passim,* for O'Callaghan's ANA record.

61 *Melbourne Punch*, 18 April 1907, p. 532, for 'O'Cally-ghin'; Hardy (1950), p. 153, for enjoying power; *VPD*, 1903, vol. 106, pp. 2247-8, for want of capacity; 1905 Police Commission, Report, p. xvi, for character; VPA for service record; 1881 Police Commission, Special Report, pp. xii and xiv, for comments re O'Callaghan.

62 *Police Regulation Act* 1902, No. 1798, for abolition of pensions; *Victoria Government Gazette*, 31 December 1902, pp. 5060-1, for insurance scheme; *Victoria Police Gazette*, 27 November 1902, p. 409, for retirement age Order-in-Council; *VPD*, 1902, vol. 101, pp. 118-20, for pension debates; VPA for police strength and pension details; 1905 Police Commission, Evidence, p. 12 (Chomley), for warning; *Royal Commission on the Victoria Police Force* (hereafter cited as 1924 Police Commission), pp. 6-11, for link between pension abolition and strike.

63 *VPD*, 1903, vol. 102, pp. 2049-58; vol. 105, pp. 452, 1078-9; vol. 107, pp. 1504-27, 2238-49, for retiring age debates; *Argus*, 20 March 1903, p. 6, and *Age*, 20 March 1903, p. 5, for press comment; pamphlets dated 8 April 1903 and 8 August 1904, seeking support for proposed Association and opposing new retirement age, held by the writer.

64 VPRS 3992, unit 1327, file T 5475, for Police Association papers; VPA for service records of Costelloe and Strickland; 1905 Police Commission, Evidence, p. 642 (Strickland), for his comments; Robert Reiner, *The Blue-Coated Worker*, pp. 19-54, and Allen Z. Gammage and Stanley L. Sachs, 'Development of Public Employee/Police Unions', in Richard M. Ayres and Thomas L. Wheelen (eds), *Collective Bargaining in The Public Sector*, pp. 71-92, for some comparative reading re police union development.

65 *VPD*, 1906, vol. 114, pp. 2259-60, for barrack deputation; 1905 Police Commission, Report, p. vii, for details of deputation.

66 *VPD*, 1903, vol. 106, pp. 2238-65, and 1905, vol. 100, pp. 91, 136, 746, and *Age*, 4 July 1905, p. 4, for debate preceding appointment of Commission; 1905 Police Commission, Report, pp. v-vi for hearing details, pp. xiii-xv for report on gambling and Wren, and Appendix, pp. xxiv-xxv, for recommended law reforms; Lotteries Gaming and Betting Act 1906, No. 2205, for new gaming laws; Niall Brennan, *John Wren: Gambler*, and Hugh Buggy, *The Real John Wren*, for different but inadequate accounts of John Wren's life and times; Bob Bottom, *The Godfather in Australia*, pp. 9-26, and Alfred W. McCoy, *Drug Traffic Narcotics and Organised Crime in Australia*, pp. 11-159, for discussion and definition of organized crime in Australia; John M. Marzorini, *Memoir of The Life and Deeds of the Late Senior Constable Waldron: the Hercules of the Victorian Police Force*, and J. B. Castieau, *The Reminiscences of Detective-Inspector Christie*; MSS. private papers and memorabilia of David G. O'Donnell (nine volumes), held by his great-grand-daughter Kerry Cue, East Ivanhoe, Victoria.

67 1905 Police Commission, Report, pp. vi-xxi, for findings and recommendations; Evidence, pp. 64-5 (O'Callaghan), for fingerprints. Thomas O'Callaghan, *Victorian Police Code*; VPA for service record of Potter; VPRS 3992, unit 1893, file P3368, for Potter's report on fingerprints; David Ascoli, *The Queen's Peace*, pp. 181-2, for Henry and fingerprints; G. M. O'Brien, *The Australian Police Forces*, pp. 124-5, and Victoria Police Force, *Police in Victoria 1836-1980*, ch. 9, for additional details re fingerprint development; *R. v. Parker* (1912) 28 ALR 150.

68 1905 Police Commission, Evidence, pp. 64-5 (O'Callaghan), for anthrometrics; *VPD*, 1906, vol. 114, p. 1683, for motor car debate.

4 Fighting with the Gloves Off

1 National Trust of Australia (Victoria), Research into Victoria Mounted Police Stables, St Kilda Road, MS. notes, 29 March 1976, Ref. No. 3824, prepared by Dr C. Kellaway, and *Argus*, 25 January 1912, p. 9, and 27 July 1912, p. 21, for stable details; H. H. Paynting (ed.), *The James Flood Book of Early Motoring*, pp. 39-143; John Goode, *Smoke, Smell and Clatter*; and MS. notes from Susan Priestley, 11 October 1983, for history of early motoring in Victoria.

2 *VPD*, 1905, vol. 110, pp. 1268-74, 1292-1309, and vol. 111, pp. 1344-61, for debates on Motor Car Bill; A Bill to Regulate the use of Motor Cars, 1905; Goode, p. 37, for chauffeurs; Police Offences Act 1890, No. 1241, Section 5 (xvii), for furious riding; Motor Car Act 1903, ch. 36 3 Edw. 7, for English legislation.

3 *VPD*, 1908, vol. 119, pp. 1206-19, 1325-34, 1549-55, 1909, vol. 121, Second Session, pp. 1085-7, 1151-63, and vol. 122, pp. 1954-63, for debates on Motor Car Act; Motor Car Act 1909, No. 2237; *Victoria Government Gazette*, 23 February 1910, pp. 1518-21, for Motor Car Act 1909 Regulations; *Report of the Royal Commission on Motor Cars*, London, HMSO, Command 3080, 1906 (hereafter cited as Command Paper 3080); *A Report on the Victoria Police Force following an inspection by Colonel Sir Eric St Johnston*, p. 160.

4 *Argus*, 12 July 1910, p. 6, for first registration figures; *Victorian Year Book* spanning years 1910–19, for police to population ratios, accident statistics, registration figures and horse numbers; Victoria Police, *Police in Victoria 1836-1980*, ch. 8, for brief history of Motor Police; VPRS 3992, unit 2426, file W5221, for proposed transfer of registration responsibility.

5 *Royal Commission on The Victorian Police Force* (hereafter cited as 1905 Police Commission), Report, p. xi, for traffic duty comments and Evidence, p. 71 (O'Callaghan), for evidence of stopping horses; personal interview with former traffic constable Thomas Street, for details of sand and shovel duty; VPA award records for details of Valour Badge recipients; *Argus*, 25 January, and 4 October 1910, for prosecutions at Prahran, 17 November 1910, p. 10, for O'Callaghan's comments, 8 February 1911, p. 4, 3 March 1911, p. 10, 18 August 1911, p. 8, and 31 January 1912, p. 10, for police methods; T. A. Critchley, *A History of Police in England and Wales*, pp. 220-1, for English experience.

6 *Argus*, 15 October 1913, p. 12, re safeguarding cars; Hugh Anderson, *Larrikin Crook: The Rise and Fall of Squizzy Taylor*, pp. 25-34, re use of motor car for crime; *Argus*, 3 August (p. 12), 26 October (p. 14), 28 November (p. 8) 1914, for use of motor cars by post office, ambulance and military authorities; VPRS 3992, unit 1314, file T3344, for 1904 offer of car to police; ibid., unit 2426, file W5221, for new form of criminal activity; Command Paper 3080, p. 55, for Paris police experience; Goode, p. 28, for one account of police pursuit and *Argus*, 31 January 1912, p. 10, for checking speed on bicycles; *Argus*, 19 December 1911, p. 7, re deaths of bandsmen; VPRS 807, 14 November 1910, re first request by police 'for authority to purchase a 24-horsepower Star motor prison van instead of an ordinary horse van'; *Police in Victoria*, chs 6 and 8, for brief account of growth in use of motor vehicles by police; personal interview with Clifford Allison, for first patrol death.

7 VPRS 3992, unit 1910, file P7926, for Sainsbury's Town Hall address; VPRS 3992, unit 2229, file G6243, for statistics of police enlistment and awards; VPRS 807, unit 527, file P10783, for details of first police volunteers. A scheme similar to Sainsbury's was implemented in Canada in 1918 and more than 700 police transferred to the armed services, many of them serving in cavalry squadrons commanded by their own officers. See S. W. Horrall, *The Pictorial History of the Royal Canadian Mounted Police*, p. 91.

8 VPRS 807, unit 526, file P11007, and VPRS 3992, unit 1915, file P9372, for assurance policy premiums; VPRS 807, unit 526, file P10225, for loss of wages, insurance premiums, reinstatement policy and reference to Boer War as a precedent; VPRS 807,

unit 557, file S8263, for final government decision re rights of police who enlisted; VPRS 10257, vol. 16, entry U13422, re refusal to reinstate (file missing); VPRS 3992, unit 2229, file G6243, for details of returned servicemen employed and Gellibrand's comments; Brian Lewis, *Sunday at Kooyong Road*, pp. 115-16, for Irish police quotation; VPA for ethnic composition of police force; Ernest Scott, *Australia during the War*.

9 *Victoria Government Gazette*, 1 April 1913, p. 1453, for appointment of Sainsbury; *Argus*, 21 May 1912, p. 6, 29 May 1912, p. 14, 31 May 1912, p. 15, 18 July 1912, p. 12, 2 September 1912, p. 12, 23 January 1913, p. 6, 11 February 1913, p. 6, for campaign re O'Callaghan's removal and discontent; VPRS 3992, unit 2475, file Y12157, re moves to form an association; VPRS 3992, unit 1893, file P3368, for O'Callaghan's overseas tour report; *Evening Sun*, 9 November 1923, p. 7, for comments on strike; L. J. Blake, 'Past Presidents of the Society', p. 11, for RHSV Presidency; O'Callaghan's history work includes: 'Scraps of Early Melbourne History, 1835-1839', pp. 145-67; 'Police in Port Phillip and Victoria, 1836-1913', pp. 181-203; and an unpublished work titled 'Police and Other People'. In 1921 he advertised for 1000 people to subscribe 10s 6d to publish this manuscript as a book but he failed to attract sufficient sponsors and the interesting work, with over sixty illustrations, was never published.

10 *Police in Victoria*, p. 16, John O'Sullivan, *Mounted Police of Victoria and Tasmania*, p. 169, and G. M. O'Brien, *The Australian Police Forces*, p. 63, for treatment of Sainsbury; VPA for career details; VPRS 3992, unit 1833, file N4721, for list of applicants; *Argus*, 22 July 1912, p. 12, for outside appointment, 7 August 1912, p. 12, and 7 January 1913, p. 6, for police meetings and resolution, 16 January 1913, p. 14, for discussion of merits of applicants for Chief Commissioner's position, 8 March 1913, p. 18, for police approval of Sainsbury's appointment and baby case details; Alan Dower, *Crime Chemist*, p. 12, for battered hat and spurned cars.

11 VPRS 807, unit 543, files R2020, R2001 and S1893, for motorcycles; VPRS 807, unit 526, file P10109, re motor prison van; VPRS 3992, unit 1906, file P6923, re bicycles for horses (file missing); VPRS 3994, vol. 64, p. 429, entry dated 15 September 1914, for ju-jitsu classes; VPRS 10257, vol. 15, entry R6837, for swimming and lifesaving; VPRS 3992, unit 2475, file Y12157, for police association formation; VPRS 10257, vol. 17, entry W7583, re appointment of women; VPRS 3992, unit 1869, file 010425, re Sunday leave; VPRS 807, unit 555, file S6894, and the *Police Journal*, vol. 1, no. 1 (July 1918), p. 10, for defective laws; VPRS 807, unit 555, file S6894, re policy of 'hasten slowly'; VPRS 3992, unit 1893, file P3368, for decisions not to use dogs or patrol boxes; *Argus*, 29 May 1913, p. 5, for relaxation of physical standards; A. J. O'Meara, The Establishment and Development of the Role of Women Police in Victoria, for women police and welfare.

12 A token force of Commonwealth police was not formed until 1917, after Prime Minister W. M. Hughes was struck on the hat by an egg thrown during an anti-conscription campaign at Warwick, Queensland. Kerry Milte in *Police in Australia*, pp. 28-9, claims that the Warwick incident did not prompt the formation of a federal force. There is little doubt, however, that Hughes's dissatisfaction with the inaction of Queensland state police at Warwick promoted the untimely and unwarranted formation of a small, personal force of commonwealth officers; Scott, p. 108, for 'useful police allies'; VPRS 807, unit 628, file W12786, for intelligence and interpreting work; VPRS 1172, unit 8, Premier's Secret Papers, 1917, for counter-espionage work, and letters from Prime Minister for aerials of enemy agents and aircraft.

13 *Commonwealth of Australia Gazette*, 10 August 1914, p. 1381, for proclamation; VPRS 1172, unit 8, Premier's Secret Papers, 1914, for directions to police re German residents; *Final Report of the Royal Commission on the State Public Service* (hereafter cited as 1917 Public Service Commission Report), p. 49, for number of alien registrations and comments re workload; Scott, pp. 108 and 116, for comment re police and aliens on parole.

14 VPRS 807, unit 628, file W12786, and VPA for Sickerdick; VPRS 1172, unit 8, Premier's Secret Papers, 1917, and VPA for Brennan; VPRS 3992, unit 2087, 'sealed papers'; and VPRS 1172, unit 8, Premier's Secret Papers, 1917, for activities and formation of CEB including Hughes Correspondence; Richard Hall, *The Secret State*, and Frank Cain, *The Origins of Political Surveillance in Australia*, for CEB formation and operation, and growth into Australian Security Intelligence Organization; ibid., pp. 143 and 185, for Cain quotation. Hall's book does not contain a bibliography or footnotes and needs to be treated with caution. Throughout the text and index Hall refers to Steward as Stewart, a not insignificant error in a work claiming to be 'a sustained critical analysis' and 'the result of over ten years' investigation'. Also, at p. 20, his very brief account of the police strike is wrong.

15 1917 Public Service Commission Report, p. 49, and VPRS 3992, unit 2229, file G6243, for range of commonwealth duties; Cain, p. 184, for £1 bounty; VPRS 3992, unit 1985, file T2694, for men who will not enlist; VPRS 807, unit 558, file R8425, for lightning strike; *Argus*, 28 August 1916, p. 8, and 30 August 1916, p. 7, for police retiring age and war effort; VPRS 3992, unit 2229, file G6243, for accrued leave; VPRS 3994, vol. 66, p. 499, entry R10235, dated 5 November 1915, for refusal of harvest leave; VPRS 1172, unit 8, Premier's Secret Papers, 1914, for use of police pensioners; ibid., 1919, for secret shortage of police.

16 The Premier's, Chief Secretary's and Chief Commissioner's files spanning the war years are now held at the Public Record Office, Laverton. A systematic search of these archives failed to locate many files relevant to the police war effort. References appeared in indexes and registers but the files were not found in the storage area. Archivists at the State and Commonwealth archives are unable to determine the whereabouts of such files, and neither are officers of the originating departments. Reference to a return of police of enemy birth is found at VPRS 10257, vol. 16, entry T2534 but the return cannot be located. Samples of references to other missing files include: VPRS 10257, vol. 14, entry P11369 'police to furnish reports on Germans, Austrians and Hungarians'; VPRS 10257, vol. 14, entry P16214 'police to work for Defence Department'; VPRS 10257, vol. 15, entry R11461 'members killed in action'; VPRS 10257, vol. 16, entry T9567 'ranks and units of police enlisted'; VPRS 10257, vol. 18, entry Y4813 'list of police aged between 18-44 years'; entry Z14069 'return of police wounded, etc. at war'; entry Z6788 'list of police killed in war'.

17 The twentieth-century deterioration of police work conditions included the loss of pension privileges, the extension of the retirement age and a drop in real wages from a level between tradesmen and labourers to one about equal to labourers. *Argus*, 8 July 1912, p. 10, for quote re straw, 2 September 1912, p. 12, for O'Callaghan's attitude, 31 May 1912, p. 15, for 'newspaper tripe'; *Official Year Book of the Commonwealth of Australia*, 1916, pp. 831-3, for comparative statistics of police budgets and strengths in Australia.

18 *VPD*, 1912, vol. 130, pp. 712-23, and vol. 132, pp. 3957-79, for debates and statistics on police wages and work conditions, p. 718 for education standards, p. 722 for 'bottom of ladder', p. 3961 for Farthing quote, p. 3967 for boast of Watt, and p. 3978 for community expectations; *Argus*, 18 April 1912, p. 6, 29 May 1912, p. 14, 17 July 1912, p. 14, 28 August 1912, p. 15, 19 September 1912, p. 10, 4 December 1912, p. 16, 12 April 1913, p. 19, 27 May 1913, p. 11, and 15 October 1913, p. 7, for police wages and work conditions; 21 May 1912, p. 6, for qualities in demand; 31 May 1912, p. 15, for 'dumping ground'; VPA for figures on previous occupations of police recruits.

19 *VPD*, 1912, vol. 132, p. 3962, for 'younger and more impetuous' and pay rises to teachers and railway workers, p. 3967, for loyal stand; *Argus*, 3 September 1912, p. 4, for letter. The teachers and public servants in Victoria formed unions in 1885; see R. M. Martin, *Whitecollar Unions in Australia*, p. 3.

20 *VPD*, 1913, vol. 132, p. 3967, for 'dissension and revolt'; VPRS 3992, unit 2475, file Y12157, and unit 1854, file 07788, for O'Loughlin reports and papers relevant to for-

mation of Victoria Police Association. O'Loughlin was born at Yackandandah, Victoria, on 3 August 1859. Roman Catholic and a labourer by occupation he joined the force on 1 May 1883 and served thirty-five years, until superannuated at the rank of Inspector on 3 August 1919. He worked at stations in both metropolitan and country areas and his service record was excellent. Details obtained from VPA; *VPD*, 1914, vol. 135, p. 3831, for questions by Lemmon; Bruce Swanton, 'Origins and Development of Police Unions in Australia', pp. 207-19, for comparative material relevant to S.A. and W.A.

21 *VPD*, 1911 Second Session, vol. 129, pp. 253-63, for debate on Sunday rest day, p. 261, for Murray's comment; *VPD*, 1913, vol. 133, p. 625 and pp. 671-7, for renewed discussion; *Argus*, 8 January 1912, p. 6, for statement by Murray re Sundays off duty, 12 September 1912, p. 5, for letter supporting Sunday leave for police, 6 September 1913, p. 19, for Murray's announcement of rest-day scheme, 6 February 1914, p. 11, for pay rise announcement; VPRS 3992, unit 1869, file 010425, for Sainsbury's report on the introduction of the scheme and its cost. The complete official file on the subject of Sunday leave for policemen was not found. The archives searched without success were VPRS 3992, units 1725, 1806 and 1851, and the missing files sought were numbered L1139, N728, N7350; Critchley, p. 171, for English weekly rest day.

22 VPRS 3992, unit 2475, file Y12157, for all correspondence relating to the formation of Association; *Argus*, 15 April 1914, p. 9, for Political Labour Council moves, 14 July 1916, for report of Guild Hall meeting; *VPD*, 1914, vol. 136, p. 1240, for prohibited meeting; *Police Journal*, vol. 1, no. 1 (July 1918), pp. 7-8, for first annual report, including details of meeting on 10 May 1917 and elections on 27 June 1917 and the activities and successes of the Association in its first year, especially the pay rise, continuous shifts and objects; G. I. Westcott, 'The Police Force, 1907-1944', p. 1552, for secret meetings; Section 2 of the Constitution Act Amendment Act 1916, No. 2866, and *VPD*, 1916, vol. 144, pp. 2147-54, for amendments to Section 423(1) of the Constitution Act Amendment Act 1915, No. 2632, generally termed the 'Political Rights Bill amendments'; VPRS 3992, unit 2046, file X3029, for Burke case; *Argus*, 7 December 1917, p. 8, and 5 January 1918, p. 16, for continuous eight-hour shifts, and 22 May 1918, p. 10, for pay rise; Police Pensions Act, No. 3316, Sections 29-31, for ban on union affiliation.

23 *Police Journal*, vol. 1 no. 2 (August 1918), pp. 3-4, for letters from Sainsbury, Rawlings and others, an 'optimistic outlook' and details of membership. (The *Police Journal* has been published monthly by the Police Association since the first issue, vol. 1, no. 1 (July 1918). The force itself did not begin to publish an equivalent official news magazine until 1955.) VPRS 937, unit 513, for Police Ages Commission of Inquiry — 1918. Anthony J. O'Meara, The Establishment and Development of The Role of Women Police in Victoria, p. 9, for THC support of women police. This thesis is the only comprehensive work covering the subject of women police in Victoria and is generally regarded as the authoritative source.

24 VPRS 807, unit 555, file S6894, for Sainsbury quotations; *Argus*, 30 July 1917, p. 8, and 1 August 1917, p. 6, for appointment of Beers and Connor. O'Brien, p. 173, and *Police Life*, December 1959, p. 5, both state incorrectly that Madge Connor and Nell Davidson were appointed as Victoria's first two women police. This error has probably occurred because Davidson replaced Beers on 3 June 1918 and almost nothing is known of Beers's background or record, whereas Davidson served from 1918 to 1941. At the time of appointment Connor, an Irishwoman, was aged thirty-seven. A widow with four children, she had previously undertaken special work for the force in connection with the investigation of fortune-tellers and bookmakers. Ellen Frances 'Nell' Davidson was single, aged thirty-two, and a native of South Australia. She was a member of the Salvation Army and gave her occupation as laundress.

25 Other groups who pressed for the appointment of women police were the Woman's

Christian Temperance Union, the Ballarat League of Honour, the Society for the Prevention of Cruelty to Children and the Sex Hygiene and Morality Council; VPRS 807,
unit 555, file S6894, for Sainsbury's views; VPRS 3992, unit 1951, file S5727, for views
of Inspector O'Sullivan, Inspecting Superintendent Gleeson and Superintendent-in-
Charge CIB; *Argus*, 30 December 1916, p. 10, for McLeod's view. In fairness to
Sainsbury it should be said that the women's movement in Victoria was identified with
radical politics and it was a radicalism that troubled not only him; see Norman Mac-
Kenzie, *Women in Australia*, pp. 45-52.

[26] Sol Encel et al., *Women and Society*, pp. 23-39; Ian Turner, 'Prisoners in Petticoats: A
Shocking History of Female Emancipation in Australia', in Julie Rigg (ed.), *In Her Own
Right*, pp. 3-23, and MacKenzie, *passim*, for early entry of Australian women into such
fields as the arts, education, etc; O'Meara, pp. 1-27, for early women's agitation in Vic-
toria and mention of overseas developments; Edith S. Abbott, *Everybody's Friend The
Inspiring Career of Miss Kate Cocks, M.B.E.*, for South Australian experience; Vince
Kelly, *Rugged Angel*, for N.S.W. experience; *Argus*, 30 December 1916, p. 10, for
ninety applicants; O'Meara, p. 30, for qualities expected; VPRS 3992, unit 2226, file
H4925, for assessment of women police and details of their duties.

[27] *Police Journal*, vol. 1, no. 9 (March 1919), p. 10, for Sainsbury's extended time; VPRS
3992, unit 2145, file D6601, for Sainsbury's retirement, and notification of his death
on 27 February 1920; Bernard Cohen, 'Leadership Styles of Commanders in the New
York City Police Police Department', p. 131, for tradition-oriented leaders; Gene E.
Carte and Elaine H. Carte, *Police Reform in the United States The Era of August Vollmer*,
for Vollmer's work; David Ascoli, *The Queen's Peace*, ch. 8, for Henry and Macready,
and General Sir Nevil Macready, *Annals of an Active Life*, for Macready's work; L. E.
Hoban, *New South Wales Police Force 1862-1962*, p. 24, for Mitchell's work, including
a police study tour abroad, and the introduction of special instructional classes and
qualifying examinations for promotion.

[28] Lieutenant-Colonel Sir George Charles Thomas Steward, KBE, CMG, JP, was born
in Scotland on 17 March 1866. For record of previous service as a civil servant, see
Police Journal, vol. 1, no. 9 (March 1919), p. 10, and *Argus*, 14 February 1919, p. 4;
Victoria Government Gazette, 26 February 1919, p. 669, for appointment of Steward;
Argus, 18 February 1919, p. 5, for Labor protest; *Police Journal*, vol. 1, no. 9 (March
1919), p. 3, for police view; VPRS 3992, unit 2087, file B1940 and 'sealed papers', for
Steward's application, including a letter from the Prime Minister, W. M. Hughes (14
January 1916), and the Premier of Tasmania, J. W. Evans (13 March 1905).

[29] *Argus*, 27 March 1919, p. 4, for superintendents' conference and 28 November 1919,
p. 6, for abreast of times; *Police Journal*, vol. 2, no. 3 (September 1919), p. 5, for motto,
vol. 2 no. 6 (December 1919), p. 4, for initiative in forming clubs, vol. 2 no. 7 (January
1920), p. 5, for debt of gratitude re hospital, vol. 2, no. 9 (March 1920), p. 4, for country
tour and pp. 17-18, for Steward's admonishment.

[30] Steward's plans for reorganizing the force are embodied in three reports. The first is
dated 30 April 1919 and deals with the Criminal Investigation Branch (including the
formation of a Finger Print Bureau). The second report is dated 15 May 1919 and deals
with the Mounted Police, Plain Clothes Police and Foot Police. The third and final
report is dated 11 June 1919 and deals with the administration of the force. All these
reports are located together at VPRS 807, unit 698, file A6842; see also *Argus*, 30 May
1919, p. 7; 25 July 1919, p. 6; 1 October 1919, p. 14.

[31] VPRS 807, unit 695, file B5197; unit 2141, file B13087; unit 698, file A6842; *Police
Journal*, vol. 2, no. 5 (November 1919), p. 3; vol. 3, no. 11 (May 1921), p. 9, and vol. 4,
no. 1 (July 1921), p. 19; *Argus*, 15 June 1921, p. 8, and 31 December 1921, p. 5; and
Annual Report of the Chief Commissioner of Police for the Year 1946, p. 10, for Steward
and police training; VPRS 3992, unit 2142, file C5339; *Police Journal* vol. 2, no. 12
(June 1920), pp. 3-7, and *Argus*, 12 May 1920, p. 10, for death of Steward.

32 *Victoria Government Gazette*, 20 May 1920, p. 1934, and VPRS 3992, unit 2142, file C5339, for appointment of Heathershaw. The government in office at this time was the conservative Nationalist administration headed by Premier Harry Lawson. Along with him the principal obstacles to police reform were the Chief Secretary, Major Matthew Baird, a conservative country lawyer and the Treasurer, Sir William McPherson, who was described as 'a thinker in threepences'. The thrift and conservatism that characterized these three was to prove a bane to Gellibrand.

33 Major General Sir John Gellibrand, KCB, DSO, was born at Ouse, Tasmania, on 5 December 1872, and educated at King's School, Canterbury, and Royal Military College, Sandhurst. He served in the South African War, 1900, with the 1st South Lancashire Regiment and in World War I rose to become Major General commanding the AIF 3rd Division. From July 1919 until appointed Chief Commissioner he was Public Service Commissioner of Tasmania; C. E. W. Bean, *The Official History of Australia in The War of 1914-1918*, vol. 1, *The Story of Anzac*, pp. 79-81, for comments; *Victoria Government Gazette*, 8 September 1920, p. 2848, for appointment; *Argus*, 7 August 1920, p. 20, for sketch of his career.

34 VPRS 3992, unit 2226, file H4925, and unit 2229, file G6243, for Gellibrand's proposals and Lawson ministry comments; *Police Journal*, vol. 3, no. 12 (June 1921), p. 3, for Association view; VPRS 807, unit 698, file A6842, for quote re pay and pensions; *Argus*, 20 December 1921, p. 7; 21 December 1921, p. 10; 28 December 1921, p. 6; 16 January 1922, p. 6; 30 January 1922, p. 6, for Gellibrand's frustration and return to Tasmania; VPRS 3992, unit 2218, file H964, for resignation papers.

35 *Argus*, 2 February 1922, p. 7, for public concern; 14 March 1922, p. 6; 23 March 1922, p. 7; 29 March 1922, p. 10; 7 April 1922, p. 6, and 11 April 1922, p. 6, for speculation on appointments of military men. The complete list of applicants from which Nicholson was chosen is not known. At the Public Record Office it is listed as VPRS 3992, unit 2226, file G4834A, but the documents cannot be located. Given the serious failings of Nicholson's administration it is not unreasonable to suggest that this file was 'lost', stolen or destroyed at the time of the police strike, to conceal the identities of all those men over whom Nicholson was given the appointment, and the reasons why, in order to protect the reputations of those men who appointed him. *Victoria Government Gazette*, 26 April 1922, p. 1096, for appointment of Nicholson. Nicholson was born at Raglan, Victoria, on 25 July 1862. He received a primary school education and worked as a farm labourer before joining the Victoria Police Force on 20 March 1883.

36 *Police Journal*, vol. 4, no. 11 (May 1922), p. 218, for head and heart; *Argus*, 9 February 1922, p. 8, for baton in knapsack; 12 April 1922, p. 99, for Nicholson's advantage; VPRS 3992, unit 2229, file G6243, p. 3, for Gellibrand's criticism of promotion system; VPA and telephone interview with Mr A. M. Nicholson, and personal interview with Mr J. N. Nicholson, for biographical details of Nicholson, who received the Valour Award in 1899 for arresting an armed lunatic and was one of the first three recipients of the award. *Saturday Evening Herald*, 30 October 1925, for Nicholson's account of this incident.

37 *Police Journal*, vol. 4 no. 12 (June 1922), p. 230, for presentation of umbrella; VPRS 3992, unit 2226, file H4925, for Nicholson's recommendation and statement of confidence; *Royal Commission on The Victorian Police Force* (hereafter cited as 1924 Police Commission), Report, p. 8, for abandonment of conferences, Evidence, p. 2119 (Nicholson), for supervision ratios, and p. 2388, for abandonment of conferences. Evidence given before the commission was not published. Typed copies of the transcript are held at the Public Record Office and in the Victoria Police Archives, and microfiche copies are held in the libraries of all Victorian universities and at the State Library of Victoria. *Police Dispute: Case For the Men*, and *The Victorian Police Mutiny: The Facts*, for summaries of police pay and conditions and comparative statistics; R. K. Haldane, Victoria Police Strike, — 1923, pp. 38, 43, 69, for police pension numbers.

[38] 1924 Police Commission, Report, pp. 8-9, for barrack conditions; Thomas O'Callaghan, *Victorian Police Code*, pp. 37-8, for barrack regulations. Personal interviews with Fred Midgley and Lindsay Macphail, for accounts of barrack life in 1923, including inedible food and no showers. Both men are former constables and police strikers.

[39] 1924 Police Commission, Report, pp. 9-10, and Evidence, pp. 2114-18 (Nicholson), for special supervisors; *VPD*, 1922, vol. 163, p. 3380, and 1923, vol. 165, p. 1807, for pimps and secret watching; Haldane, pp. 18-21, for full details of special supervisors and their work.

[40] 1924 Police Commission, Report, p. 10, for licensing purge and petition, and Evidence, p. 2385 (Nicholson), for account of purge; *Argus*, 19 April 1923, p. 12, for talk of strike, text of petition and 'moonshine'; *Truth*, 4 August 1923, p. 7, for Nicholson's popularity; MS. Nicholson family papers in possession of J. N. Nicholson, Box Hill, for account of Delaney mercy flight and letter from N.S.W.; personal interview with Isabella Hutchings (née Brooks), and VPA, for biographical and career details of Brooks. Brooks was born at Port Melbourne on 28 April 1889. A gas stoker by occupation, he joined the force in 1913 and served at Russell Street, Seymour, Prahran and South Yarra, before transferring to the Licensing Branch in 1921. He never publicly claimed membership of any political party or trade union, and no such organization claimed Brooks as a member or representative.

[41] General details of the strike have been pieced together from personal interviews with more than twenty people who witnessed it, including ten former constables who were strikers and eight former constables who remained on duty. One striker interviewed was Fred Midgley, who was one of Brooks's 'original twenty-nine' and who struck on 31 October and 1 November. Other general information was obtained from VPRS 1163, units 559, 563, 566 — Police Strike Papers; 1924 Police Commission Report, p. 11, for surprising *dénouement* and Brooks's efforts to rally support, p. 12, for men wanting to do the right thing; Evidence, p. 2872 (Shelton), for conspiracy of silence; personal interview with James R. Golding, for account of unjust discharge and admission into South Australian Police. Those men *discharged* were eligible for re-employment in the police force, those men *dismissed* were not.

[42] VPA, Melbourne Town Hall Archives and VPRS 1226, unit 123, for special constabulary force papers. The most accurate summary of the activities of the special constabulary force is Warren Perry, 'The Police Strike in Melbourne', pp. 896-935.

[43] John C. Meyer, Jr, 'Police Strikes: A Model to Study Underlying Factors', p. 195, for overseas police strikes 1918-1921; Gerald W. Reynolds and Anthony Judge, *The Night the Police Went on Strike*, and A. V. Sellwood, *Police Strike — 1919*, for accounts of English police strike, including at p. 2 of Sellwood the figure of 2300 dismissed; Francis Russell, *A City in Terror: 1919 The Boston Police Strike*, for one account of that strike and at p. 113, the figure of 1117; Robert Reiner, *The Blue-Coated Worker*, pp. 19-29, for early history and structure of police federation, including at p. 26, 'the goose club'; Sterling D. Spero, 'The Boston Police Strike', in Richard M. Ayres and Thomas L. Wheelen, *Collective Bargaining in the Public Sector*, p. 400, for 'the complete destruction'.

[44] 1924 Police Commission, Report, pp. 1-6, for creation and terms of reference; and pp. 6-12 for findings.

5 Good Men are Needed at the Top

[1] Warren Perry, 'The Police Strike in Melbourne in 1923', pp. 922-3, for brief biography of McCay; *VPD*, 1923-4, vol. 165, p. 2229, for opening quote and Nicholson's displacement; VPA (Police Strike Papers), VPRS 3992, unit 2301, file N2652, and *Argus*, 13-17 November 1923, for all details of SCF, including formation, activities, pay, uniforms,

conditions and politics; Andrew Moore, 'Guns Across the Yarra', pp. 220-33; Raelene Frances et al., 'What Rough Beast?', pp. 72-9, for review; personal interview with Lionel Woodford, for account of SCF formation, lack of equipment and unprepared state. Woodford was on the headquarters staff of the SCF. Those former military officers who assisted McCay to form the SCF included Lieutenant-Colonels D. H. Moors and R. J. Wallace; Majors F. O. Rogers, W. Perrin, J. O'Neill, G. V. Dudley; and Captains A. M. Kemsley, E. J. Ryan, R. Glen, L. T. Jackson, A. E. Wallace, F. P. D. Strickland, J. R. Henderson.

2 VPRS 3992, unit 2301, file N2652, and R. K. Haldane, Victoria Police Strike — 1923, pp. 71-6, for service of strikers; *Royal Commission on The Victorian Police Force*, 1925 (hereafter cited as 1924 Police Commission), Report, pp. 11-12, for physical standards; *Argus*, 16 March 1925, p. 13, and 17 March 1925, p. 10, for jockey-size and higher education, and 4 April 1925, p. 38, for minimum height.

3 *Police Dispute Case for the Men*, for pension agitation history; Police Pensions Act 1923, No. 3316, for pension scheme; *Argus*, 5 December 1923, pp. 21-2, for new benefits; VPRS 3992, unit 2425, file W4414, for good conduct scheme; *Victoria Police Gazette*, 20 December 1923, p. 767, and 13 March 1924, pp. 210-11, for pay increments, 17 January 1924, p. 29, for promotion regulations, 22 May 1924, p. 389, for special leave, 6 August 1925, p. 523, for twenty-one days; VPRS 1411, vol. 80, entries dated 14 and 23 December, for twenty-eight days; VPRS 3992, units 2300 and 2329, files 02142 and Q1772, for capital expenditure.

4 *Argus*, 2 December 1922, p. 10; 9 March 1923, p. 11; 4 April 1923, p. 10; 7 July 1924, p. 19; 9 July 1924, p. 17; 2 August 1924, p. 30, for police dogs.

5 VPRS 3992, unit 2425, file W4414, for equality claims by policewomen; VPRS 3992, unit 2301, file N2652, for signed letter dated 6 December 1923, from Nicholson to Under-Secretary; *Argus*, 13 December 1923, p. 11, and 14 December 1923, p. 11, for Nicholson's press statement, lack of support and Labor support of women; Anthony J. O'Meara, The Establishment and Development of the Role of Women Police in Victoria, pp. 65-7, for his bluff theory. In fairness to O'Meara it should be stated that the vital document, containing Nicholson's denunciation of women police, is so filed at the Public Record Office that a researcher, looking only at the question of women police, would be unlikely to find it.

6 Personal interview with Mr J. N. Nicholson, for Nicholson and wireless patrol. Mr Nicholson is the son of Chief Commissioner Alexander Nicholson. Personal interview with Harry Downie, for work of F. W. Downie. Mr Downie is a former member of the Victoria Police Force and the son of Frederick 'Pop' Downie. Personal interviews with Clifford Allison and Frederick Canning, for wireless patrol history. Both men were wireless telegraphists, and worked with Downie as foundation members of the patrol. Canning designed and built the first truly successful equipment; *Herald*, 15 July 1924, for journalistic eulogy. Background for this section has also come from Downie's scrap book, which contains 100 pages of newspaper cuttings from the *Age, Argus, Herald, Sun* and *Smith's Weekly*, together with original letters and photographs owned by F. W. Downie.

7 *Argus*, 19 May 1925, p. 10, and 30 May 1925, p. 36, for Nicholson's hospitalization; 1924 Police Commission, Report, p. 7, for pay increase; John Hetherington, *Blamey Controversial Soldier*, p. 51, for tempestuous years.

8 Sir John Monash, *The Australian Victories in France*, p. 296; David McNicoll, 'Blamey: controversial but born leader', *Bulletin*, 17 January 1984, p. 24.

9 *Age*, 29 January 1984, for unrecognized hero, and 4 February 1984, p. 12, for greatest soldier; *Bulletin*, 17 January 1984, p. 25, for vilification; Hetherington, pp. 48-50, for pre-police army postings, and p. 64, for edge of volcano. A clearer indication of Blamey's political preferences emerged after he left the police force, when he tried unsuccessfully to enter federal parliament under the banner of the conservative United

Australia Party. He is alleged to have later headed a secret 'White Army', formed to combat communism. See Richard Hall, *The Secret State*, p. 4, and Hetherington, pp. 389-92.

10 *VPD*, 1925, vol. 169, pp. 313-28, 452-64, 656-63, for Smith's allegations; VPRS, unit 2314, file 90533, for official file on Smith's claims, including police reports; *Argus*, 14 March 1922, p. 6, for talk of Blamey being Chief Commissioner; Hetherington, pp. 56-7, for Blamey and liquor, and p. 55, for indivisibility of lives.

11 VPRS 3992, unit 2324, file N14503, for badge 80 police reports, including anonymous letter; *VPD*, 1925, vol. 170, pp. 2845-62, for 'badge 80' debates; *Argus*, 18 November to 10 December 1925, *passim*, for press accounts; Hetherington, pp. 53-5, for Blamey's defence.

12 VPRS 3992, unit 2566, file L5532, for Blamey's reforms; ibid., unit 2405, file T8257, for training curriculum; ibid., unit 2419, file V1577, for first constable scheme.

13 VPA (Provident Fund Papers); *VPD*, 1927, vol. 173, p. 580, and 1929, vol. 180, pp. 1733-4; and *Argus*, 20 July to 27 August 1927, for Wallace donation and provident fund. Telephone interview with Bill King, for Blamey lending money and common sentiment. King served as a constable under Blamey and for a time performed relieving duty as his personal secretary.

14 VPRS 3992, unit 2475, file Y12157, correspondence dated 1925, for legality of association; Hetherington, p. 59, for Blamey on unions; VPRS 3992, units 2402 and 2407, files T7075 and U9481, for police conference, including affront to Labor Party; Robert Reiner, *The Blue-Coated Worker*, pp. 19-29, for structure of police federation.

15 VPRS 3992, units 2419 and 2466, files V1577 and X8729, for promotion scheme, including Blamey's reasons; VPRS 3992, unit 2475, file Y1157, for all papers relevant to end of old Association; VPRS 3992, unit 2566, file L5532, for Blamey's new contract; *Police Journal*, vol. 12, no. 6 (December 1929), pp. 215-16, for claims of ability; *Argus*, 15 January 1930, p. 10, for faithful service; 4-10 October 1930, *passim*, for new Association; 10 July 1931, p. 7, for Siberia transfers; *Victoria Police Gazette*, 4 September 1930, p. 1092, and 13 November 1930, pp. 1305-6, for illegally constituted.

16 Hetherington, p. 63, for Blamey and violence; Hall, pp. 21-2, for hysteria; *VPD*, 1928, vol. 178, pp. 3011, 3191, 3299, 3370-80, for shooting debates; *Argus*, 3 November 1928, pp. 19-20, for account of shootings, including Blamey's defence, and 13 December 1928, p. 7, for Mossop's command. In addition to these two *Argus* references, from which quotations have been taken, background material has come from the very extensive newspaper coverage of the shootings. Although all the official papers relevant to the shootings are registered at the PRO as VPRS 3992, unit 2414, file T12827, it cannot be found. References to police violence and harassment are far too numerous to list here, but can be found in VPRS 1411, vols 80-90. The actual files relevant to Blamey's campaign against communists cannot be found, but these references too can be found in VPRS 1411, vols 84-6.

17 *Argus*, 3 May, p. 10; 4 May, p. 7; 5 May, p. 5; 6 May, p. 9; 20 May, p. 7; 21 May, p. 21; 23 May, p. 8; and 10 June 1932, p. 8, for all details of unemployed march and Kelley Inquiry. The official papers relevant to this incident, including Kelley's report, are registered as VPRS 3992, unit 2517, file C5198, but the file cannot be located. Joanna Monie, *Victorian History and Politics*, vol. 2, p. 598, says of the 1932 Kelley Inquiry, 'that no report can be traced'.

18 *Report of the Board of Inquiry appointed to inquire into Certain Allegations and Complaints made against Certain Members of the Police Force, including the Chief Commissioner of Police*, 1933, for Kelley Inquiry; *VPD*, 1933, vol. 191, pp. 1232-51, for corruption allegations. All the newspapers of the period contain general coverage of the allegations and the inquiry.

19 Hetherington, pp. 64-8, for Blamey and newspapers; *VPD*, 1935, vol. 198, pp. 4933-43, 5001-5, for debates re Blamey and press; *Argus*, 4 December 1935, p. 6, for Atten-shon

and Modern Moloch; VPRS 3992, unit 2554, file L3341, for *Star* libel action; VPRS 3992, unit 2566, file L5532, for Blamey's security of tenure; VPRS 1411, vol. 82, 2 April 1928, and VPRS 3992, unit 2407, file U9481, agenda item 89, for Blamey's early moves to control press; the official papers relevant to the banning of journalists from police headquarters is indexed as VPRS 1411, vol. 88, but the file cannot be found; Douglas Gillison, *A Reporter Looks at his Trade*, pp. 9-12, for Blamey and press, including Bonaparte quote. In addition, all the newspapers of the period contain extensive coverage of the press war with Blamey, labelled colloquially as *Herald* phobia v. Blamey phobia.

20 *Argus*, 1936, *passim*, for 'King of the Royal Mounted'; S. W. Horrall, *The Pictorial History of the Royal Canadian Mounted Police*, pp. 118-27, for Hollywood image; *VPD*, 1936, vol. 199, pp. 248, 291-2, 310-11, 566-7, for football rewards; *Age*, 23 May 1936, p. 22, for suicide.

21 This account of the Brophy case is drawn from extensive reports in the *Age, Argus, Herald* and *Sun*, June–July 1936, and from the Royal Commission file, which includes an unpublished, typed transcript of all the evidence, located at VPRS 2570. Written police reports relevant to the Brophy case are listed at the Public Record Office as VPRS 3992, unit 2561, file M4589, but this file is missing. These sources together with Hetherington, p. 63, also provided material relevant to the political background behind the appointment of the Royal Commission.

22 John Hetherington, *Blamey*, p. 63, for Macindoe on Blamey; pp. 66-8, for Blamey's activities during 1936–39; *Report of the Royal Commission on the Alleged Shooting at and Wounding of John O'Connell Brophy*, 1936, pp. 7-8, for finding re Blamey; VPRS 3992, unit 2567, file L5774, for Blamey resignation papers; *Victoria Government Gazette*, 15 July 1936, p. 1780, for Mooney appointment.

23 VPRS 3992, unit 2590, file L9916, for official papers re third degree, including a newspaper file; *Argus*, 19 June 1936, p. 11, for Mann's comments; 22 June 1936, p. 8, for editorial. Works that attribute Blamey's forced resignation solely to the Brophy incident include, Hetherington (1954), pp. 62-4; G. M. O'Brien, *The Australian Police Forces*, pp. 67-8; Victoria Police Force, *Police in Victoria 1836–1980*, pp. 18-19. The force was publicly accused of using third degree tactics in 1913 and again in 1930, but these accusations did not have the judicial weight of Mann's claims and were quickly 'forgotten'.

24 Telephone interview with Fred Hobley, for forensic science history. Hobley was the foundation member of the photographic and scientific sections and the first detective training instructor; J. W. Cecil Turner (ed.), *Kenny's Outlines of Criminal Law*, pp. 533-4, for Judges' Rules; T. A. Critchley, *A History of Police in England and Wales*, pp. 209-15, for English experience and quotations; *Argus*, 22 June 1936, p. 8, for report of English police commission on police interrogation; Alan Dower, *Crime Chemist*, for a journalistic account of early forensic science work in Victoria; C. R. M. Cuthbert, *Science and the Detection of Crime*, pp. 13-27, and H. J. Walls, *Forensic Science*, pp. 1-5, for overseas developments.

25 *Police Review*, 21 August 1936, p. 164; *Argus*, 13 October 1936, p. 8; and MS. letter, from Commissioner New Scotland Yard to Chief Commissioner Victoria Police, 16 July 1984, for Duncan's career details; *Interim Report of Alexander M. Duncan on the Police Force of Victoria*, 1936, for report and recommendations regarding criminal investigation.

26 *Final Report of Alexander M. Duncan on the Police Force of Victoria*, 1937, for final report and general recommendations; *Victoria Government Gazette*, 10 February 1937, p. 556, for Duncan appointment; VPRS 3992, unit 2576, file M7510; *VPD*, 1936, vol. 199, pp. 568, 1431, 1446-7; *Argus*, 24 July 1936, p. 11, and 24 December 1936, p. 11, for Labor opposition. Charlie Chan, a Chinese-American detective, was the creation of Earl Derr Biggers and was well known through novels and films.

27 *Victoria Police Gazette*, 8 July 1937, pp. 512-14, for Duncan's instructions; *Argus*, 23 August 1937, p. 11; 24 March 1938, p. 1; 17 October 1938, p. 10; 18 October 1938, p. 10, for detective training school; 22 July 1938, p. 10, for purchase of scientific equipment; 24 August 1939, p. 2, for Duncan boast; 11 May 1940, Weekend Magazine, p. 1, for unimpeachable witness. Telephone interview with Fred Hobley, for foundation of scientific section and detective training school.

28 Norman D. Carlyon, *I Remember Blamey*, for a detailed account of Blamey's military career during World War II.

29 *Victoria Police Gazette*, 25 December 1941, p. 671, for Christmas message; Paul Hasluck, *The Government and The People, 1939-1941*, pp. 6-8, for war mood; VPRS 1172, unit 11, file 1942/20, for policy re hostilities; VPRS 3992, unit 3002, file V5748, for discouragement from enlisting; ibid., unit 2988, file V4027, for official enlistment policy, resignation requirement and false occupations; VPRS 5538, unit 1, file 39/6, for provost corps; Victoria Police, *Annual Report of the Chief Commissioner . . . for the year 1946* (hereafter cited as *Police Annual Report*, 1946), p. 13, for police enlistment figures.

30 VPRS 3992, unit 3310, file F5845, and unit 2921, file T6403, for lists and descriptions of police wartime duties; the National Security Regulations are too extensive to list here but those of particular relevance to the police were published in the *Victoria Police Gazette*. Examples of these include *Victoria Police Gazette*, 20 June 1940, pp. 470-3, for firearms amd explosives regulations, and subversive associations regulations; 25 July 1940, pp. 557-61, for lighting restrictions; 11 June 1941, pp. 320-1, for control of photography; 18 December 1941, pp. 652-5, for blackouts; 8 January 1942, pp. 3-4, for charcoal gas-producers; 11 June 1942, pp. 390-1, for unexploded bombs order; 30 September 1943, p. 572, for issue of emergency liquid fuel.

31 VPRS 3992, unit 3107, file Y783, for farm work on leave. Personal interview with James Chester Draper, for account of his wartime police work. Heyfield was a rural service town with a population of about 700. Industry centred on two large cattle yards and the town served a surrounding rural population of 500, mainly in the outlying area north along the Macalister Valley from Glenmaggie to Glencairn, and the Great Dividing Range. Personal interview with Lionel Woodford, for account of police wartime role. During World War II Woodford was a first constable stationed in the City area. He was then secretary of the Victoria Police Association. A veteran of World War I, he was also then on the state executive of the RSSILA and was branch secretary of the state public service sub-branch.

32 VPRS 1411, vol. 88, entry G7401, for political squad; VPRS 3992, unit 2921, file T6403, for special branch wartime work; VPRS 1172, unit 10, ref. 1941/42, for Duncan's secret investigation; *Police Annual Report*, 1946, p. 48, for special branch work 1931-46. News release by Minister for Police and Emergency Services, 5 July 1983, for disbandment.

33 *Police Annual Report*, 1946, p. 28, for brief summary of PAF formation; VPRS 3992, unit 3295, file E4281, for PAF strength figures; ibid., unit 3031, file W9949, for copy of Menzies telegram and related papers; *Argus*, 10 August 1940, Weekend Magazine, p. 3, for PAF occupations; *Victoria Police Gazette*, 12 October 1939, pp. 774-6, for PAF regulations; *Victoria Police Journal*, August 1942, p. 980, for tower of strength; ibid., March 1943, p. 1096, for PAF view of regular police; Critchley, pp. 232-6, for British auxiliary police work.

34 *Police Annual Report*, 1946, p. 27, for development and work of women police; and p. 28 for brief summary of WPAF formation; *Victoria Police Journal*, February 1943, p. 1082, for WPAF graduation; VPRS 3992, unit 3408, file J812, for glamour force; O'Meara, ch. 6, for women police and war years; ibid., p. 118, for retarded development, p. 121, for uniform as recruiting aid; *Victoria Police Gazette*, 11 February 1943, p. 96; 27 May 1943, p. 307; and 24 June 1943, pp. 365-6, for women police promotion examinations

and promotion of Mackay; *Police in Victoria*, pp. 51-3, for summary of women police wartime developments.

[35] The title D.24 was coined in 1939 when the police communications control room was established. Considerable debate surrounds the origin of this title and although there is no documentary evidence to support or refute the theory, oral tradition is that the control room was first meant to be established in room 24, corridor D, of the old Russell Street police buildings. The location was suitable for a broadcasting studio, and the title of D.24 seemed appropriate for at that time a similar control room at Scotland Yard was called D.4. However, room 24 had to be partly demolished during the course of construction of the new headquarters and room 23 was used instead. Nevertheless, the title D.24 was retained. Many letters, cards and personal messages were received at D.24 from sick, lonely, and interested listeners. Every Christmas one elderly lady baked a cake for the D.24 staff.

[36] *Police Annual Report*, 1946, pp. 21-6, *Argus*, 11 May 1940, Weekend Magazine, p. 1; 29 May 1943, w.m. p. 1; 9 October 1943, w.m. p. 3; *Victoria Police Gazette*, 7 September 1939, p. 669, and 25 April 1940, p. 319. Personal interviews with Robert 'Reg' Thomson and Clifford Allison. When D.24 was started in 1939, the staff comprised four senior constables and four wireless operators. Thomson is the only survivor of the original senior constables and Allison is the only survivor of the original four wireless operators.

[37] *Police Annual Report*, 1946, p. 50, for police youth welfare work; *Australian Police Journal*, vol. 1, no. 3 (April-June 1947), pp. 159-61, for shift in police-community relations, including readiness to stand aside, and civilian in uniform; *Victoria Police Journal*, February 1943, p. 1082, for 'give them a chance'; December 1944, pp. 1339, for 'every man was once a boy'; January 1945, pp. 1350-1, February 1945, pp. 1365-6, and April 1945, pp. 1394-5, for examples of 'Boys Club Notes'. Every former member of the force interviewed agreed that World War II was not only a turning point in technological terms, but also in police–community relations.

[38] *Police Annual Report*, 1946, p. 14, for deaths on active war service; ibid., 1953, p. 14, for unattractive career; ibid., 1955, p. 8, for 75 per cent unsuitable; *Argus*, 17 January 1946, p. 6, and 27 February 1946 (editorial), for police returning home; 17 October 1946, p. 4, for six-day week.

[39] *Commonwealth Year Book*, 1951, p. 291, for police strength figures and ratios; *Victoria Police Journal*, June 1940, pp. 488-9, and November 1941, pp. 826-7, for rates of police pay and work conditions in Australia and New Zealand; *Argus*, 5 April 1941, p. 4, for 'first place but lowest paid', and wartime gesture; ibid., 27 February 1946, p. 4, for resignations; ibid., 15 February 1946, p. 3, for post-war police work conditions; *VPD*, 1941, vol. 211, pp. 722, 743-4, 773, for pre-war police wages, including cost of living increase and depression pay cuts; ibid., 1942–43, vol. 213, pp. 50-3, for comparison of police pay and conditions in N.S.W., Queensland and Victoria; VPRS 3992, unit 3342, file G398, for comparative statement of Australian police force strengths, pay and allowances at 9 January 1946.

[40] VPRS 3992, unit 3429, file K8723, for only workers, ACTU affiliate and old order; *Victoria Police Journal*, December 1945, pp. 1527-8, for table of plenty and big business; ibid., June 1946, pp. 1615-16, for list of Labor reforms and 'thank Slater'.

[41] VPRS 3992, unit 2845, file S9533, and *Victoria Police Journal*, December 1939, pp. 316-18, for moves in 1939 to secure police a weekly rest day; ibid., December 1945, pp. 1527-31, for post-war agitation; ibid., August 1948, p. 2069, for true conception of police duty; *Argus*, 17 October 1946, p. 4, for weekly rest day decision; *Police Annual Report*, 1946, p. 10, for extra 380 men; ibid., 1947, p. 11, and ibid., 1948, pp. 5 and 13, for effect of forty-hour week including failure to help recruiting and three-year leeway; ibid., 1949, p. 5, for increase of 299 men and revised classification; Police Service Board

records, Determination no. 7, 16 March 1948, for forty-hour week decision and reasons; Satyansku K. Mukherjee, *Crime Trends in Twentieth-Century Australia*, pp. 27-39.

[42] *Police Regulation Act* 1946, No. 5126, part 1, for Classification Board legislation; VPRS 3992, unit 3370, file G4130, for Classification Board regulations; *VPD*, 1945-46, vol. 220, pp. 625-34, and ibid., vol. 221, pp. 1005-22, 1099-1127, 1423-44, 1477-1516, 1522-4, 1656-62, 1754-66, for debates on Police Regulation Bill and creation of a Police Classification Board; *Victoria Police Journal*, December 1946, pp. 1714-19, and Police Service Board records, Determination no. 1, 13 November 1946, for first determination of the Police Classification Board, including claims and reasons; ibid., Determination no. 2, 13 November 1946, for decision re new uniform, including approval to remove tunic in summer; personal interview with Robert 'Reg' Thomson, for importance of independent board to policemen. Thomson joined the force in 1924 and served until 1963, when he retired as superintendent commanding the Melbourne police district. At different times during the years 1946-63 he served on the executive of the police association, gave evidence at several Police Classification Board hearings and acted as liaison officer between the Board and the police department. The three original members of the Classification Board were Judge G. L. Dethridge of the County Court, Mr C. Turnbull, government representative, and First Constable Delmenico, who was also a member of the Police Association executive.

[43] Police recruiting problems and efforts are chronicled in the *Police Annual Report*, published each year 1946-60, under the heading 'Recruiting and Training'. *Argus*, 11 May 1949, p. 6, for wheat harvesting. *Victoria Police Journal*, November 1945, pp. 1508-9, June 1946, p. 1618, August 1946, p. 1647, July 1948, p. 2034, October 1948, pp. 2093 and 2096, November 1948, pp. 2106, 2110, 2114, for Association and police recruiting, including 'approach the prospective recruit'. VPRS 3992, unit 3469, file 2176, for decision not to reduce height limit; unit 3458, file M9110, for Duncan's recruiting work in Great Britain. Personal interview with Assistant Commissioner P. N. D. Ball, for 'ship jumpers'; Ball was one of those men recruited in England in 1949. *VPD*, 1947-48, vol. 226, pp. 1415-16, for potato peelers.

[44] *Police Annual Report*, 1946, p. 30, for introduction of new uniform and badge; *Victoria Police Gazette*, 21 September 1944, p. 470, for suggested changes to uniform; *Argus*, 19 September 1944, p. 3, for khaki; 20 September 1944, p. 3, for throttling; 21 September 1944, p. 3, for changes wanted; 6 February 1947, p. 6, and 13 February 1947, p. 7, for new uniform details and illustration; *Victoria Police Journal*, October 1944, pp. 1295-7, and October 1946, pp. 1688-90, for association on new uniform; ibid., November 1946, pp. 1700-4, and February 1947, pp. 1753-5, for Classification Board hearing and determination re uniform change; *VPD*, 1946-47, vol. 223, pp. 3592-5, for throttling; personal interview with Robert 'Reg' Thomson, for braces; *Age*, 25 May 1946, p. 2, for only force in Empire; B. Storer, 'Symbol of Authority — Head-dress Badge', p. 5, for history of Victoria Police badge, including a detailed explanation of each of its components and its basic design.

[45] Duncan retired in 1954 and died in a private hospital at Brighton, Victoria, on 1 September 1965, aged 76 years. VPA and VPRS 3992, unit 3510, file P4115, for Webster's personal and career details, including assessment from Police College, Ryton-on-Dunsmore. Porter was born at Tintaldra, Victoria, on 23 February 1905, and educated at the Wangaratta High School and Melbourne University. *Police Life*, March 1981, p. 15, and *Police in Victoria*, pp. 20-1, for Porter's background and work. *Victoria Police Journal*, March 1953, p. 564, April 1953, p. 575, July 1954, pp. 735-6, August 1954, p. 745, for Association views, including choice of Webster, bombshell, censure and pledge of loyalty; VPRS 3992, unit 3816, file D5325, for papers re vote of no-confidence; VPRS 4723, unit 57, file J6192, for pay request.

[46] VPRS 3992, unit 3754, file C12493, for Porter's appraisal of force in 1955; *Police*

Annual Report, 1955, pp. 7-47, for 'pushbike age', strength figures, and innovations; *Police Life*, vol. 1 (May-June 1955), p. 1, for introduction of news magazine; *Police in Victoria*, pp. 20-1, for overview of Porter's work.

⁴⁷ *Police Annual Report*, 1955, p. 8, for height reduction; p. 22, for ages extension; pp. 12 and 23, for introduction of junior police trainees; VPRS 3992, unit 3617, file 6832, for government papers re junior police training corps; VPRS 1411, vol. 89, entry J4917, dated 28 May 1935, for Blamey's cadet proposal; *Argus*, 4 March 1949, p. 1, for Duncan and police cadets; *Victoria Police Journal*, June 1948, p. 2023, for opposition to cadets; *Police Association Victoria*, June 1982, p. 11, and *Police Life*, August 1982, p. 15, for brief history and details re end of cadet scheme.

⁴⁸ VPRS 3992, unit 3650, file B11361, and unit 3509, file P3834, for police reserve papers, including Duncan's ideas, Porter's statement of aims and Association opposition; *Argus*, 25 November 1948, p. 3, and 26 November 1948, p. 7, for strike-breaking body; *Victoria Police Journal*, March 1946, p. 1566; July 1946, pp. 1643-4; April 1950, pp. 60, 71-2; May 1950, pp. 79-80, for examples of association opposition to auxiliary police in peacetime; *Police Annual Report*, 1957, p. 19, for retired police reserve figures during first year.

⁴⁹ *Police Annual Report*, 1946 to 1954, under heading 'Traffic', for chronicle of Duncan's traffic work; ibid., 1955 to 1959, for Porter's innovations; *Police in Victoria*, pp. 81-5, for overview of traffic control work under Duncan and Porter.

⁵⁰ VPRS 3992, unit 3780, file D849, for Executive Instruction no. 27, establishing a Police College, including aims and course outline; *Victoria Police Orders*, 6 February 1958, p. 48; 13 March 1958, p. 89; 8 May 1958, p. 141; 15 May 1958, p. 146; 12 June 1958, p. 166; 30 October 1958, p. 298, for details of Porter's training courses; *Police Annual Report*, 1955, p. 10, for 'P.C. 49'; ibid., 1957, pp. 9-10, for tiered training scheme; ibid., 1958, pp. 8, 10-11, for 'Airlie'; ibid., 1959, p. 9, for first course.

⁵¹ *Police Annual Report*, 1959, pp. 8-9, for staff shortage, strength of force and eastern suburbs; ibid., 1960, pp. 10-11, for aggressive behaviour and roaming the streets. The examples of changing police idiom were drawn from a range of official police documents spanning the years 1950-59.

6 Towards the Twenty-first Century

¹ Richard Broome, Tony Dingle and Susan Priestley, *The Victorians* (3 vols), for the most recent and comprehensive published social history of Victoria, including discussion of immigration, multiculturalism, urbanization, unemployment and social change; Victoria Police, *Statistical Review of Crime*, 1983, for crime figures, 1945-83; Gavin P. Brown et al., *Police Patrol in Victoria*, for patrol-preventable crime; Robert Bayley, *Optimizing Investigative Resources*, for crime screening; A. S. Rees (ed.), *Policing and Private Security*, for growth of private security industry; *Police Life*, August 1983, pp. 16-17, for Safety House; March 1984, pp. 27-30, for Neighbourhood Watch.

² *Police Life*, February 1974, pp. 10-11, for any call, any time; Glenn Withers, 'Police Manpower Adequacy in Victoria', for decline in ability; Paul R. Wilson and John S. Western, *The Policeman's Position Today and Tomorrow*, p. 117, for quotation from retired policeman; MS. report, 6 July 1983, from Force Statistician to Chief Commissioner, for major crime offences clearance rates 1945-83; *Victorian Year Book* and *Victoria Police Annual Report*, annually 1945-83, for population, motor vehicle registration, police ratio and traffic offence figures.

³ *Victorian Year Book*, 1969, p. 614, for 70 per cent; Wilson and Western, pp. 38-65, for 22 per cent; Colonel Sir Eric St Johnston, *A Report on The Victoria Police Force*, pp. 159-64, for motor registration duties; *Annual Report of the Chief Commissioner Victoria* (hereafter cited as *Police Annual Report*), 1946, pp. 39-44, for 1946 traffic oper-

ations; 1983, pp. 17-21, for 1983 traffic operations and fleet figures; 1946–83, *passim*, for public servants and police reserve.

⁴ D. Chappell and P. R. Wilson, *The Police and the Public in Australia and New Zealand*, pp. 120-8, for police and motorists; *Police Annual Report*, 1982, pp. 36-42, for traffic figures; Christopher Pulling, *Mr Punch and the Police*, p. 19, for *Punch* cartoon.

⁵ *Police Life*, January–February 1984, p. 3, for Miller quote and crime figures.

⁶ Telephone interviews with Bill Cherryand Jack Ashby, both former security executives, for account of private security activities in Victoria 1930–84; Rees, pp. 6-7, for 'took up the slack' and estimate of industry growth; Registrar of Private Agents, Ministry for Police and Emergency Services, for licensed private agent figures; Robert H. Smith, 'Private Police Forces', pp. 21-5; 'The growth of private security', *Reporter*, vol. 3, no. 4 (June 1982), pp. 3-6; and *The Report of the Working Party to Review the Operation of the Private Agents Act 1966*, for additional readings relevant to the Victorian situation.

⁷ Quote from the then Deputy Commissioner (Administration), J. R. G. Salisbury, during keynote address at the inaugural annual dinner of the Inspectorate and Future Plans Division. See Victoria Police, *Police in Victoria 1836–1980*, for account of police reforms 1970–84.

⁸ T. A. Critchley, *A History of Police in England and Wales*, p. 52, for force of the people; *Manual of Police Regulations*, 1856, p. 4, for MacMahon's view; *Police Life*, March 1984, p. 27, for turning clock back; pp. 28-30, for Neighbourhood Watch.

⁹ *Police Annual Report*, 1968, p. 6, for events on 4 July 1968; *Police Life*, July 1968, p. 2, and October 1968, pp. 2 and 10, for Arnold's comments. Barry York, 'Police, Students and Dissent: Melbourne, 1966-1972', p. 65, incorrectly attributes the statements of Arnold to Chief Commissioner Noel Wilby, who was not appointed to that position until 1 February 1969.

¹⁰ *Victoria Government Gazette*, 16 October 1963, p. 3211, for appointment of Arnold; VPA, for Arnold's service record; *Police Life*, November 1963, p. 1, and December 1963, p. 3, for promotions of Arnold, Clugston, Jackson and Wilby, and concomitant organizational changes; ibid., p. 2, for Arnold's message; ibid., April 1981, p. 14, for short biography of Arnold; York, p. 65, for 'radical Right milieu'.

¹¹ *Victoria Police Journal*, November 1970, p. 161, for 'home in bed'.

¹² *Police Annual Report*, 1958, p. 13, for summary justice; 1959, p. 10, for social disorder; 1960, p. 10, for truculent youths; 1961, p. 10, 1962, p. 7, 1963, pp. 9-10, 1964, p. 13, and 1965, p. 8, for mention of misconduct by teenagers, hooliganism and visit of the Beatles; James Murray, *Larrikins*, p. 31, for larrikin names; Victoria Police, Office of the Police Statistician, for post-war demographic distribution; York, p. 61, for anti-youth campaign; personal interview with Inspector Robert O'Loughlin, for 'bodgie squad' activities; *Police Annual Report*, 1965, p. 8, for drive of 1000 police; Chappell and Wilson, p. 40, for police anti-intellectual response, and p. 104, for people under 25 and teenage conflict; Patrick Morgan and Warren Osmond, 'The state of student protest', pp. 114-28, for radicalization.

¹³ Details of Australia's escalating involvement in the Vietnam war have been drawn from Peter King (ed.), *Australia's Vietnam*. Additional details relating to street demonstrations and the police response have been drawn from *Police Annual Report(s)* for the corresponding period; *Victoria Police Journal*, August 1968, p. 53, for Crowley's plea.

¹⁴ J. F. Cairns, *Silence Kills*, for a general account of the moratorium on 8 May 1970; *Herald*, 7 May 1970, p. 3, for political bikies; Victoria Police CCB file no. 86-1-228, for official police papers relating to the moratorium, including at folio 14 the opinion that it was an anticlimax. Estimates of the size of the march on 8 May 1970 have varied widely from 15 000 to 100 000, with the police eventually settling on a figure of 70 000. Oral tradition now generally accepts the figure of 100 000, which is found in Cairns, p. 21.

15 Victoria Police CCB file no. 86-1-228, for official police papers relating to moratorium marches in September 1970 and June 1971, including account of splinter group activity and papers labelling Cairns a 'peace phoney'.

16 York, pp. 66-70, and Michael E. Hamel-Green, 'The Resisters: A history of the anti-conscription movement 1964–1972', p. 109, for effect of police violence on protests. Victoria Police CCB file no. 86-1-543, for official police papers relating to marches on 11, 16 and 30 September 1970, including police accounts, witnesses' statements, complaint letters and internal investigation report; *Age*, 22 September 1970, p. 9, for first Parsons letter; 2 October 1970, p. 9, for second letter; and 7 October 1970, p. 9, for Ward's endorsement; *Repression*, 24 September 1970, p. 2, for Ward's initial criticisms of police violence. Additional material was obtained in a telephone interview with the Rev. Dr Ian Parsons, and from student broadsheets and other papers held in the archives, Borchardt Library, La Trobe University. York, one of the leading protesters, in his article, 'Police, Students and Dissent', discusses the march on 16 September and quotes a section of the first Parsons letter in support of his case. However, in his paragraph about the 'final defiant procession' (incorrectly giving the date as 1 October), he does not mention Parsons's second letter or Ward's endorsement of it.

17 *Victoria Police Journal*, November 1970, p. 161, for weakness and indecision, and last bastion.

18 Stewart Harris, *Political Football — The Springbok Tour of Australia, 1971*, pp. 78-90, for account of anti-apartheid violence at Olympic Park, including number of arrests, and 'sickening' violence; Victoria Police CCB file no. 86-1-228, folio 251, for following disturbances; personal interview with Senior Sergeant Ian Miller, for police account of events on 3 July 1971. Miller was the constable downed by a firecracker; he is not to be confused with Chief Commissioner S. I. Miller, who is mentioned in the following note.

19 Personal interview with S. I. Miller, Chief Commissioner of Police, for details of overseas experience and application of low-key approach to demonstrations; personal interview with Sir John Dillon, former Under Secretary; and Police Education Scheme training notes, 'Unlawful Assemblies Demonstrations and Industrial Disputes', pp. 1-2, for demonstration guidelines established 21 October 1971; York, p. 71, for 'gimmicky'; Royal Commission on the September Moratorium Demonstration (South Australia), 1970, typescript of evidence, Superintendent Gerald Hickey, pp. 3932-84, and copy of letter from James Cairns (both unpublished), for police policy of non-consultation with demonstration organizers and 'unofficial' contact before 8 May 1970.

20 *Police Annual Report*, 1973, p. 12, for less numerous and not significant; *Police Life*, May 1972, p. 2, for Jackson's address, 'lunatic fringe', and pyrotechnic incident; Donald Horne, *Time of Hope: Australia 1966–72*, p. 60, for the lack of big crowds.

21 Operations Department, Victoria Police, for figures of street demonstrations in Melbourne 1973 to 1983 and an account of their nature and scale; Victoria Police CCB file no. 36-1-532, for formation of Independent Patrol Group; *Police Annual Report*, 1980, p. 9, for 825 hours. In addition the *Police Annual Report* for each year, 1973 to 1983, includes details of the number, nature and scale of demonstrations and industrial disputes attended by police.

22 In addition to the specific sources cited above, general material for this section has been obtained from the following: each issue of *Police Life* and the *Victoria Police Journal*, published monthly during the years 1963 to 1973; relevant issues of the *Age, Herald, Sun, Australian, Repression, Farrago* and *Moratorium News*, published after the major demonstrations from 1968 to 1972; P. T. Findlay, *Protest Politics and Psychological Warfare*; Paul Ward and Greg Woods, *Law and Order in Australia*; B. York, 'Sources of Student Dissent: La Trobe University, 1967–72', pp. 21-31; *Beginnings: 'a documentary account of student dissent on the La Trobe University campus, and a stylistic coverage of*

the Moratoriums', filmed in Melbourne during June and July 1970; interviews with Dr J. F. Cairns, chairman of the Vietnam Moratorium Committee in Victoria; Reginald Jackson, former Chief Commissioner of Police; Gerald Hickey, former superintendent of police commanding the Melbourne Police District and the officer with overall responsibility for police operations at all the major street demonstrations in Melbourne from 1968 to 1972. The writer was also one of those constables on duty in Bourke Street, Melbourne, during the moratorium marches of 1970–71.

23 *Victoria Police Journal*, March 1970, p. 241, for Crowley quote; ibid., April 1970, p. 270, for 'rubbish . . . own employees'; p. 273, for popular sport of the day; and p. 295, for talk of libel; *Police Annual Report*, 1970, p. v, for summary of year's activities; R. W. Harding, *Police Killings in Australia*, p. 9, for systematic abuse; York, p. 73, for people reeling; D. Chappell and P. R. Wilson, *The Police and the Public in Australia and New Zealand*.

24 Victoria Police CCB file no. 3-6-1958, for official papers on Corry case, including coroner's comments; *Victoria Police Journal*, May 1970, pp. 309-10, for legal support, publicity and defence of member on criminal charge. Background details and newspaper accounts of the case were obtained from a personal inspection of files maintained at the Herald-Sun Library, Melbourne. Fatal accidents involving police vehicles or drivers are not uncommon and the one discussed above was not the worst. Its significance in the context of this work is its timing and place in a trilogy of tragedies, amplified by a high degree of publicity and the suggestion that the Monaro was mythical.

25 Victoria Police CCB file no. 26-2-883, for official papers on Collingburn case, including copies of broadsheets and other published items; *Age*, 30 March 1971, p. 9, for editorial. Background details and comprehensive newspaper accounts of the Collingburn case were obtained from a personal inspection of files maintained at the Herald-Sun Library. York, p. 73, for 'assumed a certain vogue'.

26 Bertram Wainer, *It Isn't Nice, passim*, for Wainer's background details and his personal account of the events surrounding the abortion inquiry. Peggy Berman with Kevin Childs, *Why Isn't She Dead!*; Berman was a key witness at the abortion inquiry and this is her published version of the events. *Report of the Board of Inquiry into Allegations of Corruption in the Police Force in connection with Illegal Abortion Practices in the State of Victoria*, 1971, p. 7, for copy of Order-in-Council; p. 8, for background to inquiry; and p. 152, for summary of findings. *Herald*, 15 April 1971, p. 1, for comments of Mr Justice Starke; *Age*, 2 September 1971, p. 9, for sensational and controversial inquiry, and quote re 'naive'. General facts and background material were obtained from a personal inspection of a five-volume newspaper file maintained at the Herald-Sun Library, Melbourne. For Latch's allegations and how they were dealt with see Brian Latch with Bill Hitchings, *Mr X: Police Informer*.

27 VPA; *Police Life*, December 1963, p. 3, and April 1981, p. 14, for details of Wilby's career; *Police in Victoria*, pp. 21 and 64-5, for Wilby and crime cars.

28 *Police Annual Report*, 1970, pp. 3-10, for police strengths, organization and rank structure.

29 *Victoria Police Journal*, March 1970, lift-out supplement, for police pay scales and allowances; p. 255, for pay of a tram conductor; ibid., May 1970, lift-out supplement, for lost relativity; ibid., August 1970, p. 57, for overtime policy and figures; Wilson and Western, pp. 116-17, for share of cake and Hawke's opinion; St Johnston, *Report*, p. 61, for all but forty-two; p. 66, for deadening mediocrity, wait twenty years and age of sergeants; Determinations of the Police Service Board, kept at the Office of the Service Board, Spring Street, Melbourne, for uniform, allowances and leave entitlements.

30 *Victoria Police Journal*, January 1970, p. 203, for qualifications required of candidates and outline of training, including list of disabilities and reports on families; St Johnston, *Report*, pp. 47-52; Chappell and Wilson, pp. 155-6, for comprehensive description of

police training in Victoria, including highest entrance standards and 'most extensive and highly developed'; personal recollections of the writer, who was a police cadet and trainee at the depot, 1968–70, for fatigues, haircuts and regimen of barrack life.

31 Wilson and Western, pp. 38-54, for analysis of the nature of police work; St Johnston, *Report*, p. 49, for work performed at Russell Street; and p. 95, for 126 men in barracks; Victoria Police, *Standing Orders*, for barrack rules; *Victoria Police Journal*, November 1970, p. 147, for 'speaking for myself'; personal recollections of the writer, who graduated as a constable in April 1970, and was then stationed at Russell Street, Fitzroy and Preston, for description of general duties.

32 *Police Annual Report*, 1960 to 1969, *passim*, for failure to recruit; ibid., 1970, p. 8, for shortfall of fifty-three; and p. 9, for 168 resignations; St Johnston, *Report*, p. 38, for ratio of 1:732 and worst in Australia; pp. 40-1, for 2000 below strength; p. 45, for education levels of recruits; p. 46, for 325 resignations; p. 56, for two university graduates; Victoria Police CCB file no. 78-1-128, for Newell's overseas recruiting tour, including figures; *Victoria Police Journal*, September 1970, p. 99, for cheap labour and Association view; and p. 102, for recruiting committee; Wilson and Western, p. 36, for the first battle; p. 20, for above blue-collar groups; p. 21, for occupational ranking; p. 34, for not one university graduate applying.

33 *Victoria Police Journal*, May 1970, p. 297, for editorial re Wilson and Western study; and p. 299, for ALP wanting a Royal Commission; ibid.; June 1970, p. 9, for DLP wanting a Royal Commission; and p. 11, for explanation of Wilson and Western study; Wilson and Western, pp. ix-xi, for background to their study including original commission, scope and outcome; Eric St Johnston, *One Policeman's Story*, for autobiography, including his visit to Melbourne; St Johnston, *Report*, p. 9, for background of recommendations. Personal interview with Sir John Dillon, former Under Secretary, for Country Party wanting a Royal Commission, 'enough dirty linen' and general background to St Johnston's visit. It was Dillon who arranged it. Personal interview with D. J. McPherson, former Director of Administration, Victoria Police Force, for details of St Johnston's work, report and outcome. McPherson was a member of St Johnston's personal staff during his tour of inspection.

34 Alvin Toffler, *Future Shock*, pp. 1-6, for explanation of term; pp. 12, 17-18, for quotations.

35 VPA; *Police Life*, December 1963, p. 3, and April 1981, p. 14, and telephone interview with Reginald Jackson, for biographical details; *Victoria Police Journal*, November 1971, p. 141, for 'come up the hard way'. Personal interview with S. I. Miller, for his biographical details.

36 *Police Annual Report*, 1971, p. 5, for 'did not produce answers' and watershed year; and *passim*, for reforms undertaken in 1971 including district reorganization, computer trials and new rank structure.

37 Inspectorate and Future Plans Divisions, *Position in regard to recommendations in Report by Colonel Sir Eric St Johnston following his inspection of the Victoria Police Force*, for implementation of his recommendations; *Police Life*, April 1979, p. 8, for brief history of Inspectorate and Future Plans; Toffler, pp. 128-41, for organizational upheaval and 'ad-hocracy'. Personal recollections of the writer who was a member of the Inspectorate and Future Plans Divisions, Management Services Bureau and Research and Development Department from 1979 to 1983.

38 *Police Annual Report*, 1972, p. 6, for purchase of Wellington Street Store and Corpus Christi College; 1973, p. 5, for vacation of St Kilda Road Depot; 1974, p. 7, for purchase of Savoy Plaza Hotel; 1975, p. 11, for purchase of 380 William Street; *Police Life*, 1972 to 1983, *passim*, for openings of new police stations and buildings; April 1973, p. 5, for 'futuristically designed'; May 1983, p. 10, for police hospital. Details of all new police stations, renovations and extensions for the period 1970–84 were obtained from the Victoria Police Services Department, Police Headquarters.

[39] *Police Life*, May 1973, pp. 10-12, for Nichol's warning. Details of technological changes during the years 1973–83 were obtained from the Victoria Police Services Department, Police Headquarters.

[40] *Police Life* and *Victoria Police Gazette*, 1971 to 1983, *passim*, for organizational changes, including details of new squads and equipment; Victoria Police Force, *Manual* and *Standing Orders*, (2 volumes); Victoria Police Force, *Job Description Manual*. Details of in-service training courses, police tertiary student and overseas study tours, obtained from Victoria Police Personnel Department, December 1984.

[41] *Victoria Police Gazette*, 7 December 1978, p. 628, for impact of Equal Opportunity Act and integration of seniority lists; ibid., 11 February 1982, pp. 86-7, for establishment of Community Policing Squads; *Police in Victoria*, p. 56, for individual achievements of women police; *Police Life*, October 1984, pp. 172-3, for growth in numbers and percentages; St Johnston, *Report*, pp. 111-13, for his recommendation; Peter J. Mericka, 'Keeping a Good Man Down', pp. 37-9, for women of 162.5 cm; C. M. McVeigh and V. E. Werner, 'The comparative situations of policemen and policewomen in the Victoria Police Force in the context of career prospects and maintenance of efficiency of the force', p. 13, for 64 per cent.

[42] Personal recollections of the writer based on seventeen years police service for mess-room tales and passive resistance to change. Personal interview with R. W. Stewart, Assistant Commissioner (Research and Development), for history of Industrial Liaison Office, joint working parties and meetings. Stewart was the principal Industrial Liaison Officer.

[43] *Report of the Board of Inquiry into Allegations against Members of the Victoria Police Force* (3 volumes), 1976, pp. 7-16, for appointment of the Board and introduction; pp. 50-8, for findings against individual police; pp. 59-116, for procedural recommendations; *Police Association Victoria*, November 1976, p. 7, for Blogg's statement; pp. 9-49, for minutes of meeting on 18 October 1976; *Report of the Committee Appointed to Examine and Advise in Relation to the Recommendations made in Chapter 8 of Volume 1 of the Report of the Board of Inquiry Appointed for the Purpose of Inquiring into and Reporting upon Certain Allegations against Members of the Victoria Police Force, Part 1 — Police Procedures Relating to the Investigation of Crime*, 1978 (the Norris Committee Report); Peter Sallmann, 'The Beach Report resurrected: reason for hope or despair?', p. 262, for 'steady as she goes', and p. 267, for retention of the status quo. Sallmann provides an accurate and succinct summary of the events surrounding the Beach Inquiry and his is the only published scholarly analysis of it; *Age*, 19 October 1976, p. 9, for comments and closing quotation.

[44] *Police Association Victoria*, 1976–79, *passim*, for post-Beach activities and disputation; ibid., August 1979, pp. 62-5, for no-confidence resolution including Splatt's motion and specific instances; *Victoria Police Gazette*, 11 August 1977, p. 378, for Executive Instruction no. 94; 22 September 1977, p. 498, for Executive Instruction no. 97; 29 September 1977, p. 507, for temporary deferral of no. 97; 11 February 1982, p. 85, for cancellation of no. 94; Victoria Police CCB file, nos 5-1-1415, 68-8-1, 24-15-21, for lack of support and quotation from Miller.

[45] Toffler, pp. 20-1, for discussion of change and its measurement.

[46] *Police Life*, January–February 1984, p. 3, for opening quote and Chief Commissioner's warning; ibid., May 1982, pp. 8-9, for Community Policing Squads; ibid., June–July 1982, p. 3, and March 1983, p. 5, for Police Community Involvement Programme; ibid., March 1984, pp. 27-30, for Neighbourhood Watch. Details of Neighbourhood Watch at the end of 1984 were obtained from Victoria Police, Neighbourhood Watch Project Team, Police Headquarters, Melbourne.

[47] *Police Life*, August 1983, p. 16, for Safety House; ibid., June–July 1982, p. 3, for Crime Beat; ibid., June–July 1981, p. 3, and August 1981, p. 3, for formation of liaison committees; ibid., November–December 1982, pp. 3 and 16, and March 1983, p. 7, for

Operation Ethos; ibid., May 1982, p. 3, for Blue Light Discos; ibid., August 1983, p. 3, for Operation Olympus; ibid., May 1983, pp. 4-5, for 'did a good job'; ibid., May 1982, p. 3, for Parents Without Partners award; ibid., September 1983, p. 11, for Father of the Year; Gallup Poll details were obtained by the writer direct from the Roy Morgan Research Centre, Melbourne.

[48] *Police Annual Report*, 1984, *passim*, for organizational breakdown of force and relevant statistics; Office of the Victoria Police Statistician, for age statistics.

[49] *Police Annual Report*, 1984, p. ix, for shortfall of 2383; ibid., p. 36, for one-third female applicants; *Police Life*, April 1984, p. 3, for recruiting data including languages and qualifications, and p. 71, for sporting clubs; Police Careers Office, *Appointment Requirements*, Melbourne, Victoria Police, n.d., *passim*, for recruiting criteria, outline of entrance examinations, pay scales, conditions of service and promotion rates; Mimeographed notes, Chief Inspector M. E. W. Stafferton, 'Probationary Constables Extended Training Scheme', n.d., for details of training scheme; Office of the Victoria Police Statistician, for education statistics.

[50] *Police Annual Report*, 1984, pp. 8-9, for police station hours of opening; *Police in Victoria*, p. 33, for last country troop horse.

[51] *Police Annual Report*, 1984, pp. 47, 84-7, for complaints against police; ibid., p. 41, for Freedom of Information requests; ibid., *passim*, for police–citizen contacts.

[52] *Police Annual Report*, 1984, p. 2, for Chief Commissioner's comments on ill-health retirements, and p. 68, for relevant figures; *Victoria Police Association Journal*, September 1984, pp. 11 and 19, for Personal Assistance Programme; ibid., December 1984, pp. 23-9 and 41, for association articles on police stress and ill health; *Police Life*, January–February 1984, pp. 7-8, for Personal Assistance Programme. Victoria Police Surgeon, Dr J. Peter Bush, for additional details and statistics re police road deaths and blood alcohol concentrations.

[53] Based on figures from the 1981 Census there were in Victoria more than 6000 Aborigines and more than 50 000 people born in Asia. The appointment of an Ethnic Liaison Officer, the planned appointment of an Aboriginal Liaison Officer, and the formation of related liaison committees all resulted from recognition that special problems existed between police and members of Aboriginal and ethnic communities. (Police figures drawn from Computer Systems Division print-out of 1 July 1984. Victorian population figures obtained from Australian Bureau of Statistics: Victorian Office, *Census 81 — Characteristics of Persons and Dwellings*.)

[54] *Police Annual Report*, 1984, p. 19, for task forces; *Police Life*, December 1984, pp. 224-5, for National Crime Authority.

[55] News release by the Minister for Police and Emergency Services, C. R. T. Mathews, dated 9 September 1982, and including an eleven-page 'Ministerial Statement', for formation of Committee of Inquiry, terms of reference, details of members and Labor Party policy pledge; *Police Life*, June–July 1983, pp. 4-5, for Committee's activities. At the end of 1984 the Committee had not completed its work.

7 Conclusion

[1] K.S. Inglis, *The Stuart Case*, p. 320.

[2] VPA, for awards and deaths on duty; *Police Life*, August 1983, p. 7, for poem.

Bibliography

This Bibliography is divided into the following sections:

1. *Biographical and Reference Works*
2. *Archives*
3. *Private Papers*
4. *Other Manuscript Sources, Films and Pamphlets*
5. *Interviews*
6. *Newspapers and Periodicals*
7. *Legislation*
8. *Police Manuals and Regulations*
9. *Police Inquiry Reports*
10. *Other Government Reports and Printed Papers*
11. *Books*
12. *Articles in Journals and Chapters in Books*
13. *Theses and Research Reports*

1. *Biographical and Reference Works*

Australian Dictionary of Biography, 8 vols. Melbourne University Press, 1961–1981.

Cyclopedia of Victoria. Melbourne, the Cyclopedia Co., 1903.

Featherstone, Guy. *Victorian History, 1835-1900. A Bibliography of Bibliographies, and Works of Reference*. Melbourne, Red Rooster Press, 1979.

International Police Association. *International Bibliography of Selected Police Literature*. London, 1968.

Mitchell Library. *Dictionary Catalogue of Printed Books*, vol. 27. Boston, G. K. Hall, 1968.

Monie, Joanna. *Victorian History and Politics*. Bundoora, La Trobe University, 1982.

Serle, Percival. *Dictionary of Australian Biography*. Sydney, Angus and Robertson, 1949.

Swanton, Bruce, *et al. Police Source Book*. Canberra, Australian Institute of Criminology, 1983.

Thomson, Kathleen, and Geoffrey Serle. *A Biographical Register of the Victorian Parliament 1859–1900.* Canberra, Australian National University Press, 1972.

In addition, selective use has been made of Commonwealth *Censuses, Government Gazettes, Parliamentary Debates, Year Books,* New South Wales *Government Gazettes,* Victoria *Government Gazettes, Hansard, Parliamentary Debates, Parliamentary Papers, Year Books,* Victoria Police *Annual Reports, Gazettes, Statistical Reviews of Crime.*

2. *Archives*

(i) NEW SOUTH WALES

Archives Office of New South Wales, Sydney.
Colonial Secretary's correspondence relevant to the establishment of police at Port Phillip. Microform material located at reels 95, 96, 2568, 2569. Manuscript material located at 4/2471.

State Library of New South Wales, Mitchell Library, Sydney. Miscellaneous papers relevant to the establishment of police at Port Phillip, especially Arthur Papers 1833–1839 (A2193), and Despatches from the Governor of N.S.W. 1836–1837 (A1267-14).

(ii) VICTORIA

Melbourne Town Hall Archives. Papers relevant to the formation of the Special Constabulary Force, 1923–1924. No index or reference number.

Public Record Office, Laverton. A broad range of material was consulted including Premier's, Chief Secretary's and Chief Commissioner's correspondence, general police papers and Royal Commission reports and transcripts. All this material is cited using the prefix VPRS (Victorian Public Record Series).

Victoria Police Archives. Located at numerous locations within the force and mainly comprising personnel records and related papers. Important files are held by the Central Correspondence Bureau and prefixed CCB.

State Library of Victoria. The general manuscript collection was searched. Items of particular importance are the Order Book for B Division of City Police (La Trobe Collection MS 8718) and the Private Diary of F. C. Standish (La Trobe Collection MS 9502).

3. *Private Papers*

Downie, F. W. Papers held by H. Downie, Greensborough, Victoria.
Nicholson, A. Papers J.N. Nicholson, Box Hill, Victoria.
O'Donnell, D. G. Papers K. Cue, East Ivanhoe, Victoria.

4. *Other Manuscript Sources, Films and Pamphlets*

Barraclough, Linda. MS. papers relating to private research regarding Day, Dwyer and Hooson.
Beginnings: a documentary account of student dissent on the La Trobe University campus, and a stylistic [sic] coverage of the Moratoriums, filmed in Melbourne during June and July 1970. Held by the university.

McCallum, Austin. *The Eureka Flag*. Ballarat, Council of the Ballarat Fine Art Gallery, 1973.

National Trust of Australia (Victoria). Research into Victoria Mounted Police Stables, St Kilda Road, MS. notes, 29 March 1976, ref. no. 3824, prepared by Dr C. Kellaway.

Police Dispute: Case for the Men. Trades Hall Council, Melbourne, 1923.

Police Education Scheme. MS. training notes.

Police Statistician. MS. report to the Chief Commissioner, July 1983, containing major crime index offence clearance rates 1945–83.

Priestley, Susan. MS. letter to writer, 11 October 1983, containing details of early motoring in Victoria.

Royal Commission on the September Moratorium Demonstration (South Australia). MS. typescript of evidence, held by Victoria Police.

Scotland Yard. MS. letter to Chief Commissioner, 16 July 1984, containing Alexander M. Duncan's career details.

Scully, Superintendent Jack. MS. letter to writer, 11 July 1983, containing details about Royal Irish Constabulary history and uniforms.

Stafferton, Chief Inspector M. E. W. MS. mimeographed notes, 'Probationary Constables Extended Training Scheme', n.d.

Victorian Police Mutiny: The Facts. Melbourne, Sands and McDougall, 1923.

5. *Interviews*

Allison, Clifford, Sandringham, 5 April 1984.

Ashby, Jack, telephone interview, 14 September 1984.

Ball, P. N. D., Melbourne, 6 September 1984.

Cairns, Dr J. F., Narre Warren East, 4 November 1984.

Canning, Frederick, Sandringham, 5 April 1984.

Cherry, Bill, telephone interview, 11 September 1984.

Cooper, Harrie Horatio, Glenhuntly, 28 May 1982.

Dillon, Sir John, Melbourne, 19 June 1984.

Downie, Harry, Greensborough, 29 March 1984.

Draper, James Chester, Yan Yean, 6 August 1984.

Frowd, Isaac, Forest Hills, 22 March 1982.

Golding, James Reeve, Altona, 7 June 1982.

Grieve, John, Forest Hills, 22 March 1982.

Hickey, Gerald, Melbourne, 21 November 1984.

Hobley, Fred, telephone interview, 20 July 1984.

Hutchings, Isabella, Essendon, 20 June 1980.

Jackson, Reginald, telephone interview, 8 November 1984.

King, Bill, telephone interview, 7 March 1985.

McErlain, Archibald, Leongatha, 1 June 1982.

MacPhail, Lindsay, Tarraville, 7 May 1980.

McPherson, D. J., Melbourne, 30 November 1984.

Medhurst, James W., Bright, 4 June 1984.

Midgley, Fred, Ascot Vale, 29 April 1980.

Miller, Ian, Melbourne, 20 November 1982.

Miller, S. I., Melbourne, 24 October, 1984.

Nicholson, A. M., telephone interview, 5 May 1980.

Nicholson, J. N., Box, Hill, 9 December 1980.
Newton, George, Dandenong, 16 July 1982.
O'Gorman, Leo James, Pascoe Vale, 16 March 1982.
O'Loughlin, Robert, Melbourne, 16 November 1984.
Parsons, The Rev. Dr Ian, telephone interview, 3 April 1985.
Stewart, R. W., Melbourne, 13 December 1984.
Street, Thomas, Blackburn, 8 August 1980.
Thomson, Robert, Coburg, 3 August 1980.
Vickery, Roy, Geelong West, 19 March 1982.
Woodford, Lionel, Eltham, 1 August 1984.

6. *Newspapers and Periodicals (selective use)*

Age (Melbourne)
Argus (Melbourne)
Australian Medical Journal
Australian Police Journal
Ballarat Star
Benalla Standard
Evening Sun (Melbourne)
Farrago (University of Melbourne)
Maryborough and Dunolly Advertiser
Melbourne Punch
Moratorium News
Ovens and Murray Advertiser
Police Journal (Victoria, title varies: *Police Association Victoria; Victoria Police Journal; Victoria Police Association Journal)*
Police Life (Victoria)
Police Review (England)
Reporter (Australian Institute of Criminology)
Repression (La Trobe University)
Saturday Evening Herald (Melbourne)
Sun (Melbourne)
Truth (Melbourne)

7. *Legislation*

15 Vic., No. 12 (1852), an Act to Restrain the Practice of Gambling and the use of Obscene Language
15 Vic., No. 14 (1852), an Act to Consolidate and Amend the Laws relating to the Licensing of Public-houses, and to Regulate the Sale of Fermented and Spirituous Liquors
15 Vic., No. 15 (1852), an Act to Restrain by Summary Proceeding Unauthorised Mining on Waste Lands of the Crown
16 Vic., No. 22 (1853), an Act for the better prevention of Vagrancy and other offences
An Act for the Regulation of the Police Force 1853

An Act for the Regulation of the Police Force 1854
Police Offences Statute 1865
Police Regulation Statute 1865
Police Regulation Statute 1873
Civil Service Act 1883
Police Offences Act 1890
Police Regulation Act 1890
Police Regulation Act 1902
Lotteries Gaming and Betting Act 1906
Motor Car Act 1909
Police Regulation Act 1915
Constitution Amendment Act 1916
Police Pensions Act 1923
Police Regulation Act 1928
Police Regulation Act 1946
Police Regulation Act 1958

8. *Police Manuals and Regulations*

Barry, John. *Victorian Police Guide*. Sandhurst, J. W. Burrows, 1888.
Crowe, Cornelius. *Crowe's Police Manual*. Fitzroy, Robert Barr, 1896.
O'Callaghan, Thomas. *Victorian Police Code*. Melbourne, Government Printer, 1906.
———. *List of Chief Constables, District Constables, Police Cadets, and Police Officers in Victoria, 1836 to 1907*. Melbourne, Government Printer, 1907.
Paul, William. *Victoria Police Code*. Melbourne, Government Printer, 1969 (1st edn 1924).
Victoria Police Force. *Manual of Police Regulations for the guidance of The Constabulary of Victoria*. Melbourne, Government Printer, 1856.
———. *Regulations for the guidance of the Constabulary of Victoria*. Melbourne, Government Printer, 1877.
———. *Victorian Police Manual*. Melbourne, Government Printer, n.d., (issued under the authority of the Chief Commissioner, T. A. Blamey).
———. *Victoria Police Manual*. Melbourne, Government Printer, 1957.
———. *Job Description Manual*. Melbourne, Government Printer, 1981.
———. *Manual* and *Standing Orders* (2 vols). Melbourne, Government Printer, 1983.

9. *Police Inquiry Reports*

Report of the Committee on Police and Gaols. Sydney, T. Trood, 1839.
Report from the Select Committee on Police. Melbourne, Government Printer, 1852. (Snodgrass)
Report of the Commission appointed to Enquire into the State of the Police (Melbourne Police). Melbourne, Government Printer, 1855. (Chapman)
Report from the Select Committee on The Police Force, together with the Proceedings of the Committee, Minutes of Evidence, and Appendices. Melbourne, Government Printer, 1863.

Progress Report of the Royal Commission of Enquiry into the Circumstances of the Kelly Outbreak, the Present State and Organization of the Police Force, etc. Melbourne, Government Printer, 1881. (Longmore)

Second Progress Report of the Royal Commission of Enquiry into the Circumstances of the Kelly Outbreak, the Present State and Organization of the Police Force, etc. Melbourne, Government Printer, 1881. (Longmore)

Minutes of Evidence taken before [1881] Royal Commission on the Police Force of Victoria, together with Appendices. Melbourne, Pioneer Facsimile Edition, Heinemann, 1968. (Longmore)

Ad Interim Report of the Royal Commission of Enquiry into the Circumstances of the Kelly Outbreak, the Present State and Organization of the Police Force, etc. Melbourne, Government Printer, 1882. (Longmore)

Royal Commission on Police Special Report on the Detective Branch. Melbourne, Government Printer, 1883. (Longmore)

General Report of the Royal Commission on Present State and Organization of the Police Force. Melbourne, Government Printer, 1883. (Longmore)

Royal Commission on Police, The Proceedings, Minutes of Evidence, Appendices, etc. Melbourne, Government Printer, 1883.

Report of the Royal Commission on the Victorian Police Force. Melbourne, Government Printer, 1906. (Cameron)

Report of the Royal Commission on the Victorian Police Force. Melbourne, Government Printer, 1925. (Monash)

Report of the Board of Inquiry appointed to Inquire into Certain Allegations and Complaints made against Certain Members of the Police Force, including the Chief Commissioner of Police. Melbourne, Government Printer, 1933. (Kelley)

Report of the Royal Commission on the Alleged Shooting at and Wounding of John O'Connell Brophy, A Superintendent of Police. Melbourne, Government Printer, 1936. (Macindoe)

Interim Report of Alexander M. Duncan, Esq., Chief Inspector, London Metropolitan Police, on the Police Force of Victoria. Melbourne, Government Printer, 1936.

Final Report of Alexander M. Duncan, Esq., Chief Inspector, London Metropolitan Police, on the Police Force of Victoria. Melbourne, Government Printer, 1937.

Report of the Board of Inquiry into Allegations of Corruption in the Police Force in Connection with Illegal Abortion Practices in the State of Victoria. Melbourne, Government Printer, 1971. (Kaye)

A Report on The Victoria Police Force Following an Inspection by Colonel Sir Eric St Johnston, C.B.E, Q.P.M, H.M. Chief Inspector of Constabulary for England and Wales, 1967-70. Melbourne, Government Printer, 1971.

Report of the Board of Inquiry into Allegations Against Members of the Victoria Police Force. Melbourne, Government Printer, 1976. (Beach)

Reports of the Committee Appointed to Examine and Advise in Relation to the Recommendations Made in Chapter 8 of Volume 1 of the Report of the Board of Inquiry Appointed for the Purpose of Inquiring Into and Reporting Upon Certain Allegations Against Members of the Victoria Police Force. Melbourne, Government Printer, 1979-80. (Norris)

10. *Other Government Reports and Printed Papers*

Report of the Board appointed to enquire into circumstances connected with the late Disturbances at Ballarat. Melbourne, Government Printer, 1854.

Report of the Commission Appointed to Enquire into the Conditions of the Gold Fields of Victoria. Melbourne, Government Printer, 1855.

Report from the Select Committee on Captain MacMahon's Case. Melbourne, Government Printer, 1858.

Papers relating to the Retirement of Captain MacMahon from the Government Service. Melbourne, Government Printer, 1858.

Progress Report of the Commissioners Appointed to Consider the Best Mode of Carrying out the Recommendations of The Defences Commission of 1858. Melbourne, Government Printer, 1859.

Report of The Commissioners appointed to Inquire Into and Report Upon The Civil Service of The Colony. Melbourne, Government Printer, 1859.

Petition to the Legislative Assembly for the Colony of Victoria signed by 440 Inhabitants of Richmond. Melbourne, Government Printer, 1864.

Report of Colonel Anderson, dated 4 July 1870, on The Defences of The Colony. Melbourne, Government Printer, 1871.

Report from the Select Committee upon The Artillery Corps. Melbourne, Government Printer, 1871.

Report of the Royal Commission appointed to enquire into the State of the Public Service and Working of the Civil Service Act. Melbourne, Government Printer, 1873.

Employees in Shops Commission, Second Progress Report. Melbourne, Government Printer, 1883.

Final Report of the Royal Commission on the State Public Service. Melbourne, Government Printer, 1917.

The Report of the Working Party to Review the operation of the Private Agents Act 1966. Melbourne, Government Printer, 1983.

11. *Books*

Abbott, Edith S. *Everybody's Friend The Inspiring Career of Miss Kate Cocks, M.B.E.* Adelaide, Hassell Press, 1939.

Anderson, Hugh. *Larrikin Crook: The Rise and Fall of Squizzy Taylor.* Melbourne, Jacaranda Press, 1971.

Ascoli, David. *The Queen's Peace: The Origins and Development of the Metropolitan Police 1829–1979*. London, Hamish Hamilton, 1979.

Bean, C. E. W. *The Official History of Australia in The War of 1914–1918*, vol. 1, *The Story of Anzac*. St Lucia, University of Queensland Press, 1981 (1st edn 1921).

Berman, Peggy, with Kevin Childs. *Why Isn't She Dead!* Melbourne, Gold Star Publications, 1972.

Blake, Les. *Young Ned*. Belmont, Neptune Press, 1980.

————. *Captain Dana and The Native Police*. Newtown, Neptune Press, 1982.

Bottom, Bob. *The Godfather in Australia*. Sydney, A. H. and A. W. Reed, 1979.

Breathnach, Seamus. *The Irish Police from Earliest Times to the Present Day*. Dublin, Anvil Books, 1974.

Brennan, Niall. *John Wren: Gambler His Life and Times*. Melbourne, Hill of Content, 1972.

Broome, Richard, Tony Dingle, and Susan Priestley. *The Victorians* (3 vols). Melbourne, Fairfax, Syme and Weldon, 1984.

Brown, Max. *Ned Kelly: Australian Son*. Melbourne, Georgian House, 1981 (1st edn 1948).

Buggy, Hugh. *The Real John Wren*. Camberwell, Widescope International, 1977.

Cain, Frank. *The Origins of Political Surveillance in Australia*. Sydney, Angus and Robertson, 1983.

Cairns, J. F. *Silence Kills*. Richmond North, Vietnam Moratorium Committee, 1970.

Carlyon, Norman D. *I Remember Blamey*. South Melbourne, Sun Books, 1981.

Carte, Gene E., and Elaine H. Carte. *Police Reform in the United States. The Era of August Vollmer*. Berkeley, University of California Press, 1975.

Castieau, J. B. *The Reminiscences of Detective-Inspector Christie*. Melbourne, George Robertson, n.d.

Cave, Colin (ed.). *Ned Kelly: Man and Myth*. Melbourne, Cassell, 1980.

Chappell, D., and P. R. Wilson. *The Police and the Public in Australia and New Zealand*. St Lucia, University of Queensland Press, 1969.

Cleary, P. S. *Australia's Debt to Irish Nation Builders*. Sydney, Angus and Robertson, 1933.

Coghlan, T. A. *Labour and Industry in Australia*, vol. 3. Melbourne, Oxford University Press, 1918.

Critchley, T. A. *A History of Police in England and Wales*. London, Constable, 1978.

Curr, Edward M. *Recollections of Squatting in Victoria*. Melbourne University Press, 1965. (1st edition published by George Robertson, 1883).

Currey, C. H. *The Irish at Eureka*. Sydney, Angus and Robertson, 1954.

Curtis, Robert. *History of The Royal Irish Constabulary*. Dublin, Moffat, 1869.

Cuthbert, C. R. M. *Science and the Detection of Crime*. London, Hutchinson, 1958.

Deakin, Alfred. *The Crisis in Victorian Politics 1879–1881*. Melbourne University Press, 1957.

Disher, Garry. *Wretches and Rebels*. Melbourne, Oxford University Press, 1981.

Dower, Alan. *Crime Chemist*. London, John Long, 1965.

Encel, Sol, *et al*. *Women and Society*. London, Malaby Press, 1975.

Findlay, P. T. *Protest Politics and Psychological Warfare*. Melbourne, Hawthorn Press, 1968.

Finn, Edmund. *Chronicles of Early Melbourne*. Melbourne, Ferguson and Mitchell, 1888.

Foxcroft, Edmund J. B. *Australian Native Policy: Its History Especially in Victoria*. Melbourne University Press, 1941.

Glazer, Nathan, and Daniel P. Moynihan. *Beyond The Melting Pot*. Cambridge, M.I.T. Press, 1966.

Goode, John. *Smoke, Smell and Clatter*. Melbourne, Lansdowne Press, 1969.

Hall, Richard. *The Secret State*. Stanmore, Cassell Australia, 1978.

Harding, R. W. *Police Killings in Australia*. Ringwood, Penguin Books, 1970.

Hardy, Frank J. *Power Without Glory*. Melbourne, Realist Printing and Publishing, 1950.

————. *The Hard Way.* Hawthorn, Gold Star Publications, 1971.

Hare, Francis Augustus. *The Last of The Bushrangers.* London, Hurst and Blackett, 1892.

Harris, Stewart. *Political Football—the Springbok Tour of Australia, 1971.* Melbourne, Gold Star Publications, 1972.

Hasluck, Paul. *The Government and The People, 1939–1941.* Canberra, Australian War Memorial, 1952.

Haydon, A. L. *The Trooper Police of Australia.* London, Andrew Melrose, 1911.

Hetherington, John. *Blamey.* Melbourne, F.W. Cheshire, 1954.

————. *Blamey Controversial Soldier.* Canberra, Australian Government Publishing Service, 1973.

Hoban, L. E. *New South Wales Police Force 1862–1962.* Sydney, Government Printer, n.d.

Hobsbawm, E. J. *Primitive Rebels.* Manchester, The University Press, 1959.

————. *Bandits.* New York, Pantheon Books, 1982.

Hogan, J. F. *The Irish in Australia.* London, Ward and Downey, 1888.

Horne, Donald. *Time of Hope: Australia 1966–72.* Sydney, Angus and Robertson, 1980.

Horrall, S. W. *The Pictorial History of the Royal Canadian Mounted Police.* Toronto, McGraw-Hill Ryerson, 1973.

Inglis, K. S. *The Stuart Case.* Melbourne University Press, 1961.

Isaac, J. E., and G. W. Ford (eds). *Australian Labour Relations Readings.* Melbourne, Sun Books, 1966.

Jeffries, Sir Charles. *The Colonial Police.* London, Max Parrish, 1952.

Jones, Pauline (ed.). *Historical Records of Victoria,* vol. 1, *Beginnings of Permanent Government.* Melbourne, Victorian Government Printing Office, 1981.

Kelly, Vince. *Rugged Angel.* Sydney, Angus and Robertson, 1961.

King, Peter (ed.). *Australia's Vietnam.* Sydney, George Allen and Unwin, 1983.

Latch, Brian, and Bill Hitchings. *Mr X: Police Informer.* Melbourne, Dingo Books, 1975.

Lawrence, R. M. *Police Review 1829–1979.* Perth, Government Printer, 1979.

Lewis, Brian. *Sunday at Kooyong Road.* Melbourne, Hutchinson, 1976.

McCoy, Alfred W. *Drug Traffic, Narcotics and Organised Crime in Australia.* Sydney, Harper and Row, 1980.

Mackenzie, Norman. *Women in Australia.* Melbourne, Cheshire, 1962.

McQuilton, John. *The Kelly Outbreak, 1878–1880.* Melbourne University Press, 1979.

Macready, General Sir Nevil. *Annals of an Active Life.* London, Hutchinson and Co., n.d.

Mark, Sir Robert. *In the Office of Constable.* London, Collins, 1978.

Martin, J. P., and G. Wilson. *The Police: A Study in Manpower. The Evolution of The Service in England.* London, Heinemann, 1969.

Martin, R. M. *Whitecollar Unions in Australia.* Melbourne, Monash University, n.d.

Marzorini, John M. *Memoir of The Life and Deeds of the Late Senior Constable Waldron: the Hercules of the Victorian Police Force.* Melbourne, the author, 1899.

Menadue, J. E. *A Centenary History of the Australian Natives Association.* Melbourne, Horticultural Press, 1971.

Meredith, John, and Bill Scott. *Ned Kelly After a Century of Acrimony.* Dee Why West, Lansdowne Press, 1980.

Miller, Wilbur R. *Cops and Bobbies.* Chicago, University of Chicago Press, 1977.

Milte, Kerry L., and Thomas A. Weber. *Police in Australia.* Melbourne, Butterworths, 1977.

Molony, John. *I Am Ned Kelly.* Ringwood, Penguin Books, 1980.

Monash, Sir John. *The Australian Victories in France in 1918.* London, Hutchinson, 1920.

Morgan, John. *The Life and Adventures of William Buckley.* Canberra, Australian National University Press, 1979.

Mukherjee, Satyansku K. *Crime Trends in Twentieth-Century Australia.* North Sydney, George Allen and Unwin, 1981.

Murray, James. *Larrikins.* Melbourne, Lansdowne Press, 1970.

Niederhoffer, Arthur. *Behind The Shield: The Police in Urban Society.* New York, Anchor Books, 1969.

O'Brien, G. M. *The Australian Police Forces.* Melbourne, Oxford University Press, 1960.

O'Sullivan, John. *Mounted Police of Victoria and Tasmania.* Adelaide, Rigby, 1980.

Paynting, H. H. (ed.). *The James Flood Book of Early Motoring.* Melbourne, A. E. Keating, 1968.

Pulling, Christopher. *Mr Punch and the Police.* London, Butterworths, 1964.

Queensland Police Force. *A Centenary History of the Queensland Police Force 1864–1963.* Queensland Police, 1964.

Radzinowicz, Leon. *A History of English Criminal Law and its Administration from 1750,* vol. 2, *The Enforcement of the Law.* London, Stevens and Sons Limited, 1956.

Read, C. Rudston. *What I Heard, Saw and Did at the Australia Goldfields.* London, Routledge, 1853.

Rees, A. S. (ed.). *Policing and Private Security.* Canberra, Australian Institute of Criminology, 1983.

Reiner, Robert. *The Blue-Coated Worker.* Cambridge University Press, 1978.

Reith, Charles. *A New Study of Police History.* London, Oliver and Boyd, 1956.

Reynolds, Gerald W., and Anthony Judge. *The Night the Police went on Strike.* London, Weidenfeld and Nicolson, 1968.

Russell, Francis. *A City in Terror: 1919 The Boston Police Strike.* New York, Viking Press, 1975.

Sadleir, John. *Recollections of a Victorian Police Officer.* Melbourne, George Robertson, 1913.

St Johnston, Eric. *One Policeman's Story.* London, Barry Rose, 1978.

Scott, Ernest. *Australia during the War.* Sydney, Angus and Robertson, 1936 (vol. 11 of *The Official History of Australia in the War of 1914–1918*).

Serle, Geoffrey. *The Golden Age.* Melbourne University Press, 1963.

Spence, William Guthrie. *Australia's Awakening.* Melbourne, The Worker Trustees, 1909.

Stead, Philip (ed.). *Pioneers in Policing.* Maidenhead, McGraw-Hill, 1977.

Toffler, Alvin. *Future Shock.* New York, Bantam Books, 1970.

Turner, Henry Gyles. *Our Own Little Rebellion.* Melbourne, Whitcombe and Tombs, n.d.

Turner, J. W. Cecil (ed.). *Kenny's Outlines of Criminal Law*. Cambridge University Press, 1966.

Vazenry, G. R. *Military Forces of Victoria 1854–1967*. Melbourne, the author, 1967.

Victoria Police Force. *Police in Victoria 1836–1980*. Melbourne, Government Printer, 1980.

Wainer, Bertram. *It Isn't Nice*. Sydney, Alpha Books, 1972.

Walls, H. J. *Forensic Science*. London, Sweet and Maxwell, 1968.

Wannan, Bill (ed.). *The Wearing of the Green*. Melbourne, Lansdowne Press, 1965.

Ward, Paul, and Greg Woods. *Law and Order in Australia*. Sydney, Angus and Robertson, 1972.

Ward, Russel. *The Australian Legend*. Melbourne, Oxford University Press, 1981 (1st edn 1958).

Wilson, Paul R., and John S. Western. *The Policeman's Position Today and Tomorrow*. St Lucia, University of Queensland Press, 1972.

12. *Articles in Journals and Chapters in Books*

Blake, L. J. 'Past Presidents of the Society'. *Victorian Historical Magazine*, February–May 1969, pp. 10-15.

Bridges, Barry. 'The Native Police Corps, Port Phillip District and Victoria, 1837–53'. *Journal of the Royal Australian Historical Society*, vol. 57, part 2 (June 1971), pp. 113-42.

Cohen, Bernard. 'Leadership Styles of Commanders in the New York City Police Department'. *Journal of Police Science and Administration*, vol. 8, no. 2 (1980), pp. 125-38.

Coughlan, Neil. 'The Coming of The Irish to Victoria'. *Historical Studies*, vol. 12, no. 45 (October 1965), pp. 68-86.

Dow, Hume. 'Eureka and the Creative Writer'. *Historical Studies Eureka Supplement*, Melbourne University Press, 1965, pp. 87-102.

Ferdinand, Theodore N. 'Politics, The Police and Arresting Policies in Salem, Massachusetts since the Civil War'. *Social Problems*, vol. 19, no. 14 (Spring 1972), pp. 572-88.

Fitzpatrick, David. 'Irish Emigration in the Later Nineteenth Century'. *Irish Historical Studies*, vol. 22, no. 86 (September 1980), pp. 126-43.

Ford, F. T. West. 'The Vital Statistics of the Police Force of the Colony of Victoria for the last ten years'. *Australian Medical Journal*, vol. 2 (July 1866), pp. 193-6.

Frances, Raelene, *et al*. 'What Rough Beast?' *Journal of Australian Studies*, no. 15 (November 1984), pp. 72-9.

Gammage, Allen Z., and Stanley L. Sachs. 'Development of Public Employee/Police Unions', in Richard M. Ayres and Thomas L. Wheelen (eds). *Collective Bargaining in The Public Sector*, Maryland, International Association of Chiefs of Police, 1977, pp. 71-92.

Gillison, Douglas. *A Reporter Looks at his Trade*. A. N. Smith Memorial Lecture in Journalism, University of Melbourne, 6 October 1964.

Hamel-Green, Michael E. 'The Resisters: A history of the anti-conscription movement 1964-1972', in Peter King (ed.). *Australia's Vietnam*. Sydney, George Allen and Unwin, 1983, pp. 100-29.

Horrall, S. W. 'Sir John A. MacDonald and the Mounted Police Force for the Northwest Territories'. *Canadian Historical Review*, vol. 53, no. 2 (June 1972), pp. 179-200.

MacDonagh, Oliver. 'The Irish in Victoria, 1851-91: A Demographic Essay'. *Historical Studies* (Papers read before the Irish Conference of Historians), Dublin, Gill and MacMillan, 1971, pp. 67-92.

McNicoll, David. 'Blamey: controversial but born leader'. *Bulletin*. 17 January 1984, pp. 24-6.

Mericka, Peter J. 'Keeping a Good Man Down'. *Victoria Police Association Journal*, April 1985, pp. 37-9.

Meyer, John C. Jr. 'Police Strikes: A Model to Study Underlying Factors'. *Australia and New Zealand Journal of Criminology*, September-December 1975, pp. 191-208.

Moore, Andrew. 'Guns Across The Yarra', in Sydney Labour History Group, *What Rough Beast?* Sydney, George Allen and Unwin, 1982, pp. 220-33.

Morgan, Patrick, and Warren Osmond. 'The state of student protest'. *Current Affairs Bulletin*, vol. 46, no. 8 (September 1970), pp. 114-28.

Morrison, W. R. 'The North-West Mounted Police and the Klondike Gold Rush'. *Journal of Contemporary History*, vol. 9, no. 2 (1974), pp. 93-105.

Morrissey, Doug. 'Ned Kelly's World'. *R.H.S.V. Journal*, vol. 55, no. 2 (June 1984), pp. 29-34.

O'Callaghan, Thomas. 'Scraps of Early Melbourne History, 1835-1839'. *Victorian Historical Magazine*, vol. 3, no. 4 (June 1914), pp. 145-67.

————. 'Police in Port Phillip and Victoria, 1836-1913'. *Victorian Historical Magazine*, vol. 12, no. 4 (June 1928), pp. 181-203.

O'Donnell, N. M. 'The Australian Career of Henry Fysche Gisborne'. *Victorian Historical Magazine*, vol. 5, no. 3 (March 1917), pp. 112-36.

Packer, D. R. G. 'Victorian Population Data, 1851-61: A Preliminary Analysis'. *Historical Studies Australia and New Zealand*, vol. 5, no. 20 (May 1953), pp. 307-23.

Perry, Warren. 'The Police Strike in Melbourne'. *Victorian Historical Magazine*, vol. 43, no. 3 (August 1972), pp. 896-935.

Sadleir, J. 'The Early Days of the Victorian Police Force'. *Victorian Historical Magazine*, vol. 1, no. 3 (September 1911), pp. 73-9.

Sallmann, Peter. 'The Beach Report resurrected: reason for hope or despair?', in John Basten, et al. (eds). *The Criminal Injustice System*, Clayton, Legal Service Bulletin Co-op. Ltd, 1982, pp. 249-71.

Sanderson, W. A. 'Mr John Waugh's Reminiscences of Early Melbourne'. *Victorian Historical Magazine*, vol. 15, no. 1 (December 1933), pp. 1-18.

Scott, Ernest. 'Captain Lonsdale and the Foundation of Melbourne'. *Victorian Historical Magazine*, vol. 4, no. 3 (March 1915), pp. 97-116.

Sellwood, A. V. *Police Strike—1919*. London, W. H. Allen, 1978.

Smith, Robert H. 'Private Police Forces'. *Police Association, Victoria*, vol. 47, no. 15 (May 1977), pp. 21-5.

Spero, Sterling D. 'The Boston Police Strike', in Richard M. Ayres and Thomas L. Wheelen (eds). *Collective Bargaining in the Public Sector*, Maryland, International Association of Chiefs of Police, 1977, pp. 380-400.

Storer, B. 'Symbol of Authority: Head-dress badge'. *Police Life*, March–April 1975, p. 5.

Swanton, Bruce. 'Origins and Development of Police Unions in Australia'. *Australia and New Zealand Journal of Criminology*, December 1976, pp. 207-19.

Turner, Ian. 'Prisoners in Petticoats: A Shocking History of Female Emancipation in Australia', in Julie Rigg (ed.). *In Her Own Right*, Melbourne, Thomas Nelson, 1969, pp. 3-23.

Walker, R. B. 'Bushranging in Fact and Legend'. *Historical Studies*, vol. 11, no. 42 (April 1964), pp. 206-21.

Walker, Robin. 'The New South Wales Police Force, 1862-1900'. *Journal of Australian Studies*, no. 15 (November 1984), pp. 25-38.

Walshe, R. D. 'The Significance of Eureka in Australian History'. *Historical Studies Eureka Supplement*, Melbourne University Press, 1965, pp. 103-27.

Westcott, G. I. 'The Police Force, 1907-1944'. *Police Journal*, vol. 14, no. 14 (February 1946), pp. 1551-3.

Wilson, James Q. 'Generational and Ethnic Differences Among Career Police Officers'. *American Journal of Sociology*, vol. LXIX (1964), pp. 522-8.

York, Barry. 'Police, Students and Dissent: Melbourne, 1966-1972', *Journal of Australian Studies*, no. 14 (May 1984), pp. 58-77.

————. 'Sources of Student Dissent: La Trobe University, 1967-72', *Vestes*, vol. 27, 1984 no. 1, pp. 21-31.

13. *Theses and Research Reports*

Bayley, Robert. *Optimizing Investigative Resources*. Melbourne, Victoria Police, 1983.

Brown, Gavin P., et al. *Police Patrol in Victoria*. Melbourne, Victoria Police, 1980.

Coish, Gregory. Victorian Attitudes to the Strike in the Victoria Police Force in 1923. B.A. (Hons) thesis, La Trobe University, 1971.

Haldane, R. K. Victoria Police Strike—1923. B.A. (Hons) thesis, La Trobe University, 1981.

Idzikowski, Hilary. Internal Colonialism and the Emergence of the Irish Police. Master of Philosophy thesis, University of Edinburgh, 1977.

Jackman, A. K. Development of Police Administration in Tasmania 1804-1960. Diploma of Public Administration thesis, University of Tasmania, 1966.

McCahon, J. The Victorian Police Strike. B.A. (Hons) thesis, University of Melbourne, 1962.

McVeigh, C. M., and V. E. Werner. 'The comparative situations of policemen and policewomen in the Victoria Police Force in the context of career prospects and maintenance of efficiency of the force'. Unpublished paper prepared for Sixth Senior Executive Police Officers' Course, Australian Police College, 1984.

Morrissey, Doug. 'Pioneer community life, land selection and the Kelly outbreak'. Unpublished paper presented at History Postgraduate Seminar, La Trobe University, 9 June 1983.

————. 'Selection in the Kelly Country: Success or failure?' Unpublished paper presented at History Postgraduate Seminar, La Trobe University, 11 October 1984.

O'Meara, A. J. The Establishment and Development of the Role of Women Police in Victoria. M.A. thesis, La Trobe University, 1977.

Western Australia Police Department [author Andrew Gill?], '*Some Aspects of the Western Australia Police Force 1887–1905*', Perth, Public Relations Branch, n.d.

Withers, Glenn. 'Police Manpower Adequacy in Victoria'. Unpublished research paper prepared at the Research School of Social Sciences, Australian National University, 1982.

Index

Compiled by Elmar Zalums